D0498261

Breaking Stephan

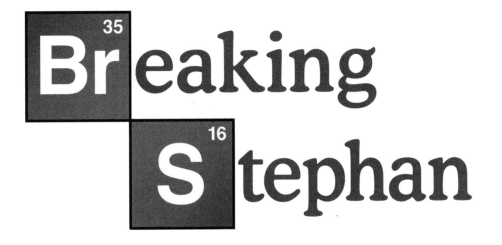

Other *Pearls Before Swine* Collections

Rat's Wars
Unsportsmanlike Conduct
Because Sometimes You Just Gotta Draw a Cover with Your Left Hand
Larry in Wonderland
When Pigs Fly
50,000,000 Pearls Fans Can't Be Wrong
The Saturday Evening Pearls
Macho Macho Animals
The Sopratos
Da Brudderhood of Zeeba Zeeba Eata
The Ratvolution Will Not Be Televised
Nighthogs
This Little Piggy Stayed Home
BLTs Taste So Darn Good

Treasuries

Pearls Falls Fast
Pearls Freaks the #%# Out*
Pearls Blows Up
Pearls Sells Out
The Crass Menagerie
Lions and Tigers and Crocs, Oh My!
Sgt. Piggy's Lonely Hearts Club Comic

Gift Books

Friends Should Know When They're Not Wanted
Da Crockydile Book o' Frendsheep

AMP! Comics for Kids

The Croc Ate My Homework
Beginning Pearls

Breaking Stephan

A *Pearls Before Swine* Collection

By Stephan Pastis

Andrews McMeel
Publishing

Kansas City • Sydney • London

Introduction

I have total anonymity when I write in cafes.

No one knows who I am. Or the comic strip I draw.

But occasionally, the person sitting next to me will be reading the newspaper comics page, and I can tell that they're staring in the general vicinity of my strip. I always dream they'll laugh, or better yet, spontaneously turn to me and tell me how much they like *Pearls Before Swine*. In which case I could proclaim, "Hey, you're not gonna believe this. But I draw that strip!"

But I've never seen them laugh.

And they've never turned to me.

And I've never interacted with any of them.

Until recently.

I was sitting next to an old man who was smiling as he read the comics page. I couldn't tell which strip he was reading. And I wasn't about to ask.

But a younger man who had just entered the cafe and apparently knew the older man stopped at the older man's table.

"You reading *Pearls*?" asked the younger guy.

"Yup," said the older guy.

"That's about the only one I still read in there," said the younger man, pointing at the newspaper.

I was floored.

I had waited years for someone in a cafe to laugh or say something nice about my strip, and now there was not just one person saying something nice, *but two*.

And I wasn't about to let the moment pass.

"*I do that one!*" I practically shouted.

I quickly realized that my declaration was vague. So I kept going.

"I'm the guy who draws it. And writes it. I'm the creator. I'm the guy."

They both laughed. Not in a good way. But in the way you reserve for your Aunt Melba when she claims to have met Superman.

So I thought fast. "Here," I blurted out, "I'll show you."

I grabbed the sketchpad I had been using and held it open in front of them. "See?" I asked. "This is a strip I just wrote."

But the page I was showing them contained only words. Scribbling, really. Meaningless and indecipherable to anyone but me.

And it proved nothing.

And from the men's faces, I could see I was descending from the role of intruding stranger to that of deluded sociopath.

"Okay, okay, wait," I said, flipping quickly through my sketch pad. "I'm sure I drew Rat on one of these pages."

"Aha! Here," I said, holding out the first page I could find with Rat on it. But as I did so, I immediately realized I had a problem.

It looked nothing like Rat.

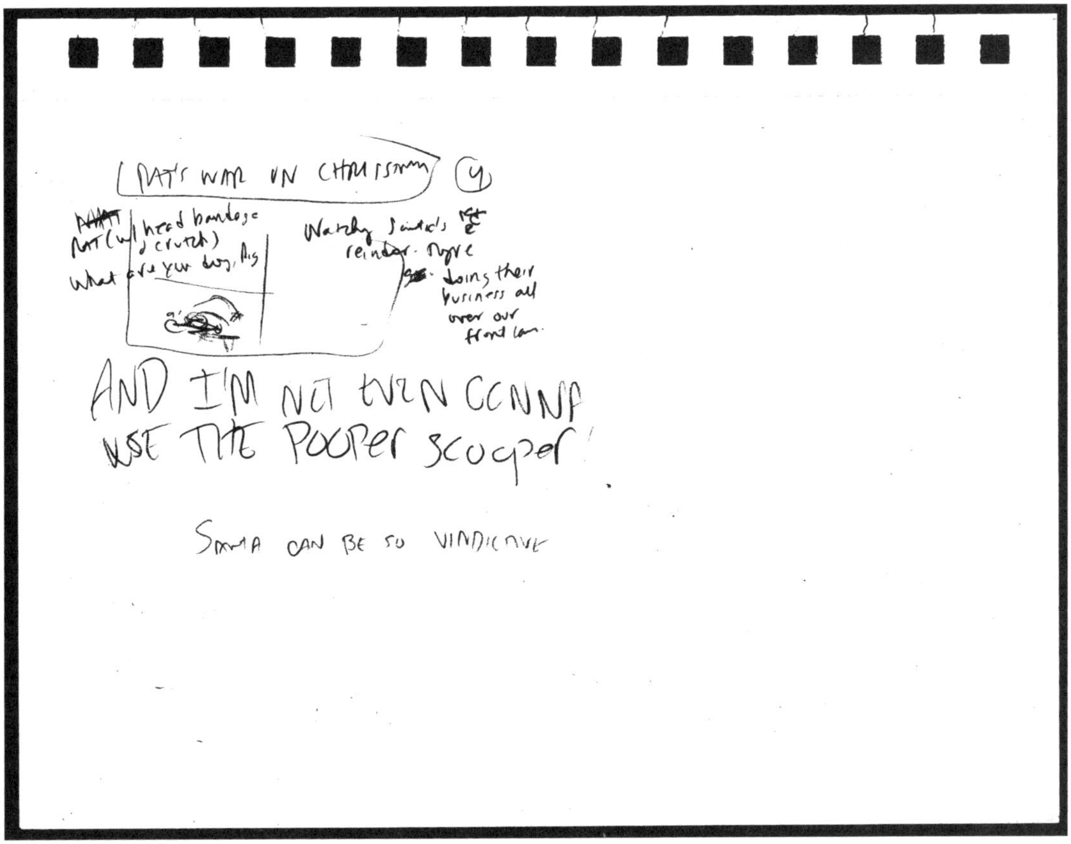
RAT'S WAR ON CHRISTMAS
AND I'M NOT EVEN GONNA USE THE POOPER SCOOPER
SANTA CAN BE SO VINDICTIVE

(The page from my sketchpad.)

The page contained my notes from a strip where Rat was wearing a head bandage. So he had no ears.

Plus, there was a random scribble right over his face. So he had no eyes.

Plus, he was really small.

Sure, I could have kept looking for another drawing in my sketchpad. Or better yet, drawn them a better one.

But it was too late.

Because when I looked up, the two men were just staring at me.

It was not quite the look of fright. But it was close.

I had only one option remaining.

Flee.

"Well, I better get going." I muttered, grabbing my jacket and pencil. "It was nice meeting you."

One of them nodded faintly. The other remained motionless.

Not even *I* still believed I was Stephan Pastis.

So I left.

A defeated loon.

Dreaming of anonymity.

Stephan Pastis
November, 2014

Dedication

To the two men in the cafe. I swear, it was me.

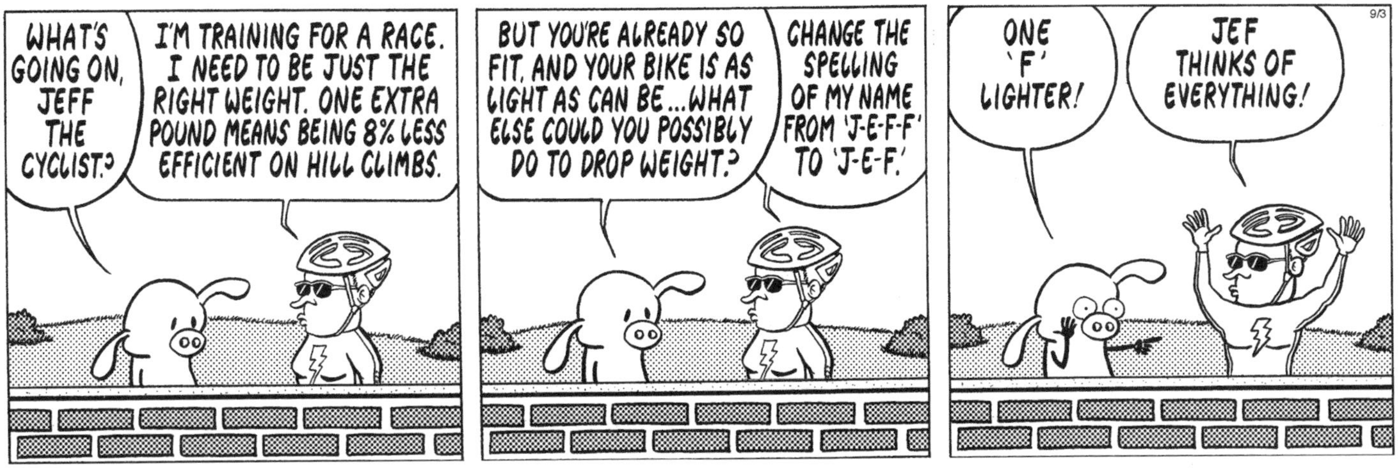
WHAT'S GOING ON, JEFF THE CYCLIST?
I'M TRAINING FOR A RACE. I NEED TO BE JUST THE RIGHT WEIGHT. ONE EXTRA POUND MEANS BEING 8% LESS EFFICIENT ON HILL CLIMBS.
BUT YOU'RE ALREADY SO FIT, AND YOUR BIKE IS AS LIGHT AS CAN BE... WHAT ELSE COULD YOU POSSIBLY DO TO DROP WEIGHT?
CHANGE THE SPELLING OF MY NAME FROM 'J-E-F-F' TO 'J-E-F.'
ONE 'F' LIGHTER!
JEF THINKS OF EVERYTHING!
9/3

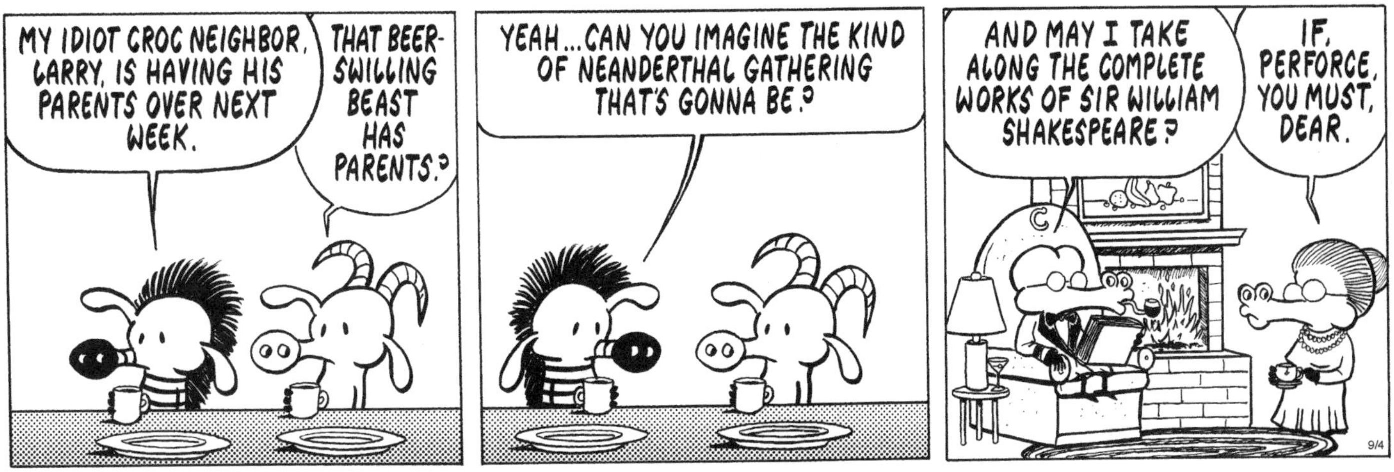
MY IDIOT CROC NEIGHBOR, LARRY, IS HAVING HIS PARENTS OVER NEXT WEEK.
THAT BEER-SWILLING BEAST HAS PARENTS?
YEAH... CAN YOU IMAGINE THE KIND OF NEANDERTHAL GATHERING THAT'S GONNA BE?
C
AND MAY I TAKE ALONG THE COMPLETE WORKS OF SIR WILLIAM SHAKESPEARE?
IF, PERFORCE, YOU MUST, DEAR.
9/4

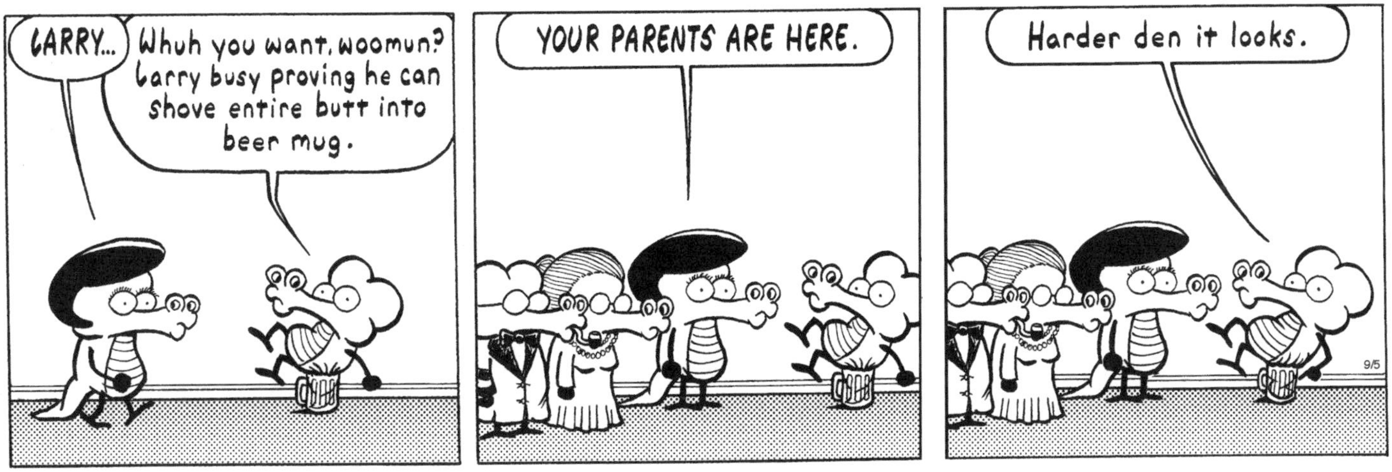
LARRY...
Whuh you want, woomun? Larry busy proving he can shove entire butt into beer mug.
YOUR PARENTS ARE HERE.
Harder den it looks.
9/5

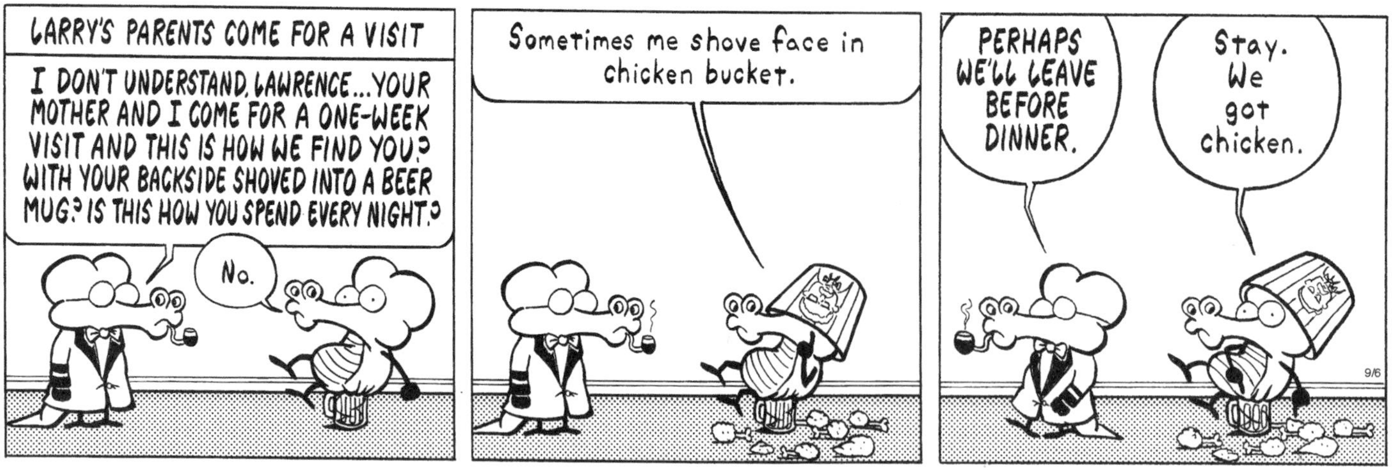
LARRY'S PARENTS COME FOR A VISIT
I DON'T UNDERSTAND, LAWRENCE...YOUR MOTHER AND I COME FOR A ONE-WEEK VISIT AND THIS IS HOW WE FIND YOU? WITH YOUR BACKSIDE SHOVED INTO A BEER MUG? IS THIS HOW YOU SPEND EVERY NIGHT?
No.
Sometimes me shove face in chicken bucket.
PERHAPS WE'LL LEAVE BEFORE DINNER.
Stay. We got chicken.
9/6

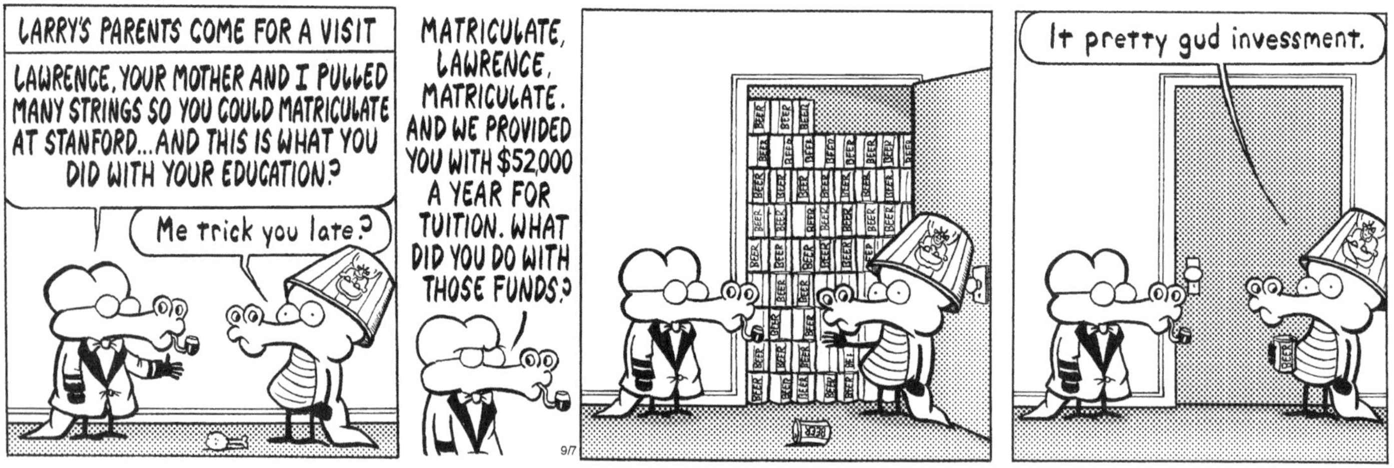
LARRY'S PARENTS COME FOR A VISIT
LAWRENCE, YOUR MOTHER AND I PULLED MANY STRINGS SO YOU COULD MATRICULATE AT STANFORD...AND THIS IS WHAT YOU DID WITH YOUR EDUCATION?
Me trick you late?
MATRICULATE, LAWRENCE, MATRICULATE. AND WE PROVIDED YOU WITH $52,000 A YEAR FOR TUITION. WHAT DID YOU DO WITH THOSE FUNDS?
9/7
It pretty gud invessment.

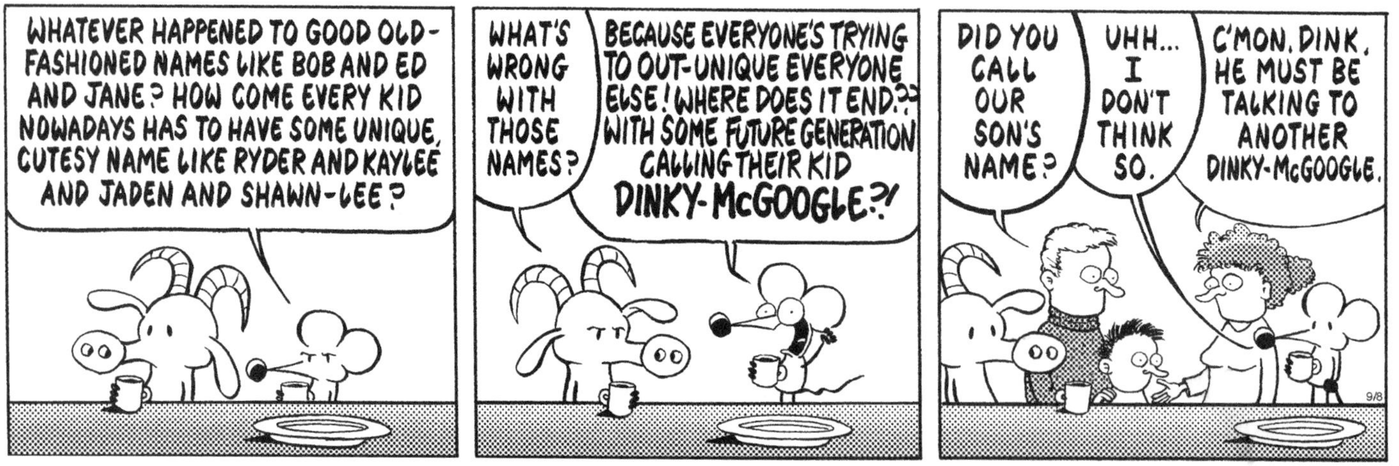
WHATEVER HAPPENED TO GOOD OLD-FASHIONED NAMES LIKE BOB AND ED AND JANE? HOW COME EVERY KID NOWADAYS HAS TO HAVE SOME UNIQUE, CUTESY NAME LIKE RYDER AND KAYLEE AND JADEN AND SHAWN-LEE?
WHAT'S WRONG WITH THOSE NAMES?
BECAUSE EVERYONE'S TRYING TO OUT-UNIQUE EVERYONE ELSE! WHERE DOES IT END?? WITH SOME FUTURE GENERATION CALLING THEIR KID DINKY-McGOOGLE?!
DID YOU CALL OUR SON'S NAME?
UHH... I DON'T THINK SO.
C'MON, DINK. HE MUST BE TALKING TO ANOTHER DINKY-McGOOGLE.
9/8

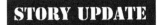

STORY UPDATE Larry's sophisticated parents are making their first visit to Larry's home. They are disappointed.

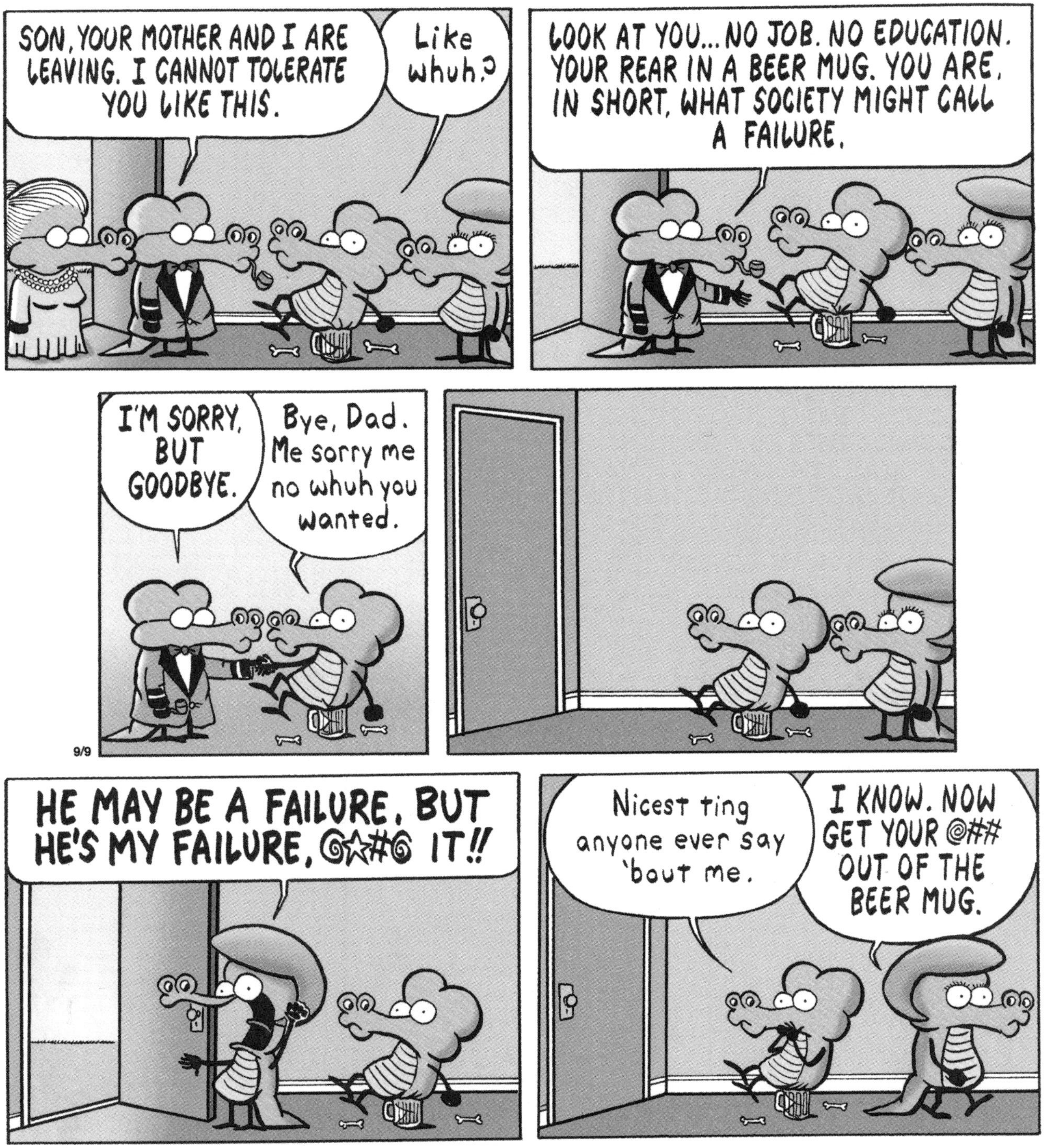
SON, YOUR MOTHER AND I ARE LEAVING. I CANNOT TOLERATE YOU LIKE THIS.
Like whuh?
LOOK AT YOU... NO JOB. NO EDUCATION. YOUR REAR IN A BEER MUG. YOU ARE, IN SHORT, WHAT SOCIETY MIGHT CALL A FAILURE.
I'M SORRY, BUT GOODBYE.
Bye, Dad. Me sorry me no whuh you wanted.
9/9
HE MAY BE A FAILURE, BUT HE'S MY FAILURE, G☆#G IT!!
Nicest ting anyone ever say 'bout me.
I KNOW. NOW GET YOUR @## OUT OF THE BEER MUG.

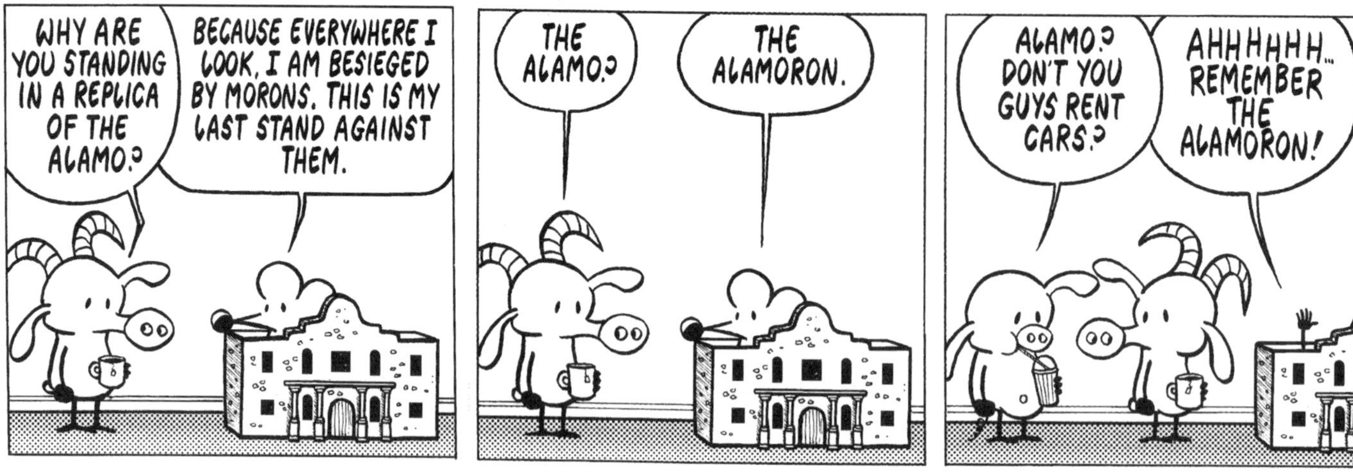
WHY ARE YOU STANDING IN A REPLICA OF THE ALAMO?
BECAUSE EVERYWHERE I LOOK, I AM BESIEGED BY MORONS. THIS IS MY LAST STAND AGAINST THEM.
THE ALAMO?
THE ALAMORON.
9/10
ALAMO? DON'T YOU GUYS RENT CARS?
AHHHHHH... REMEMBER THE ALAMORON!

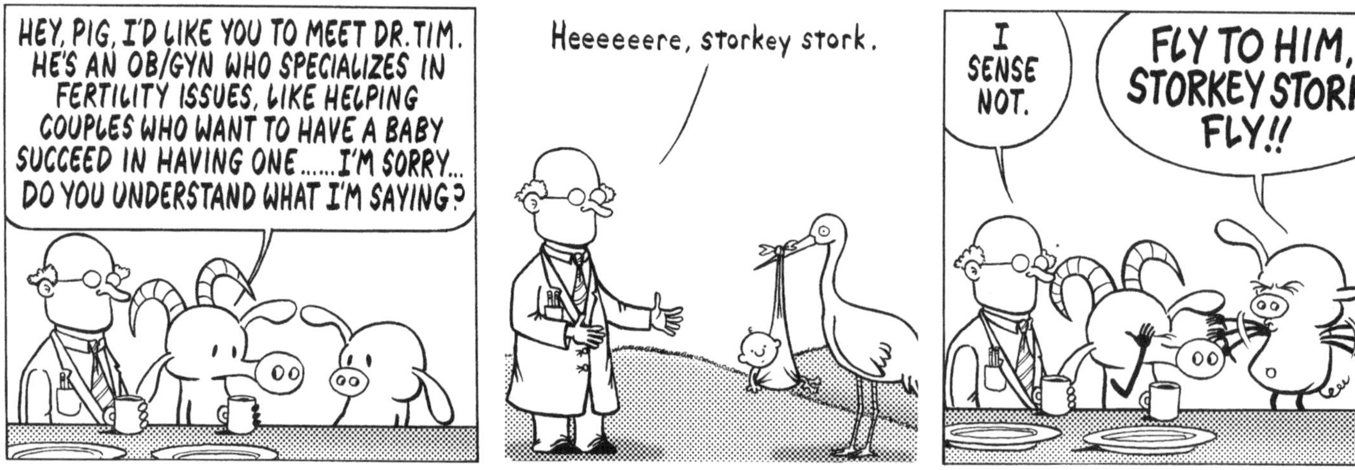
HEY, PIG, I'D LIKE YOU TO MEET DR. TIM. HE'S AN OB/GYN WHO SPECIALIZES IN FERTILITY ISSUES, LIKE HELPING COUPLES WHO WANT TO HAVE A BABY SUCCEED IN HAVING ONE......I'M SORRY... DO YOU UNDERSTAND WHAT I'M SAYING?
Heeeeeere, storkey stork.
I SENSE NOT.
FLY TO HIM, STORKEY STORK, FLY!!
9/11

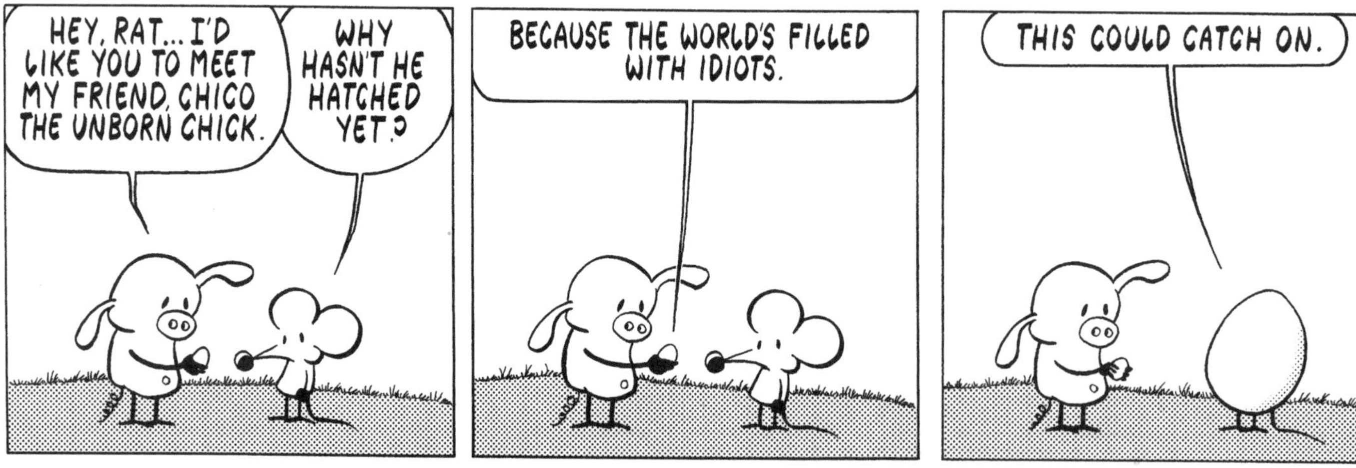
HEY, RAT... I'D LIKE YOU TO MEET MY FRIEND, CHICO THE UNBORN CHICK.
WHY HASN'T HE HATCHED YET?
BECAUSE THE WORLD'S FILLED WITH IDIOTS.
9/12
THIS COULD CATCH ON.

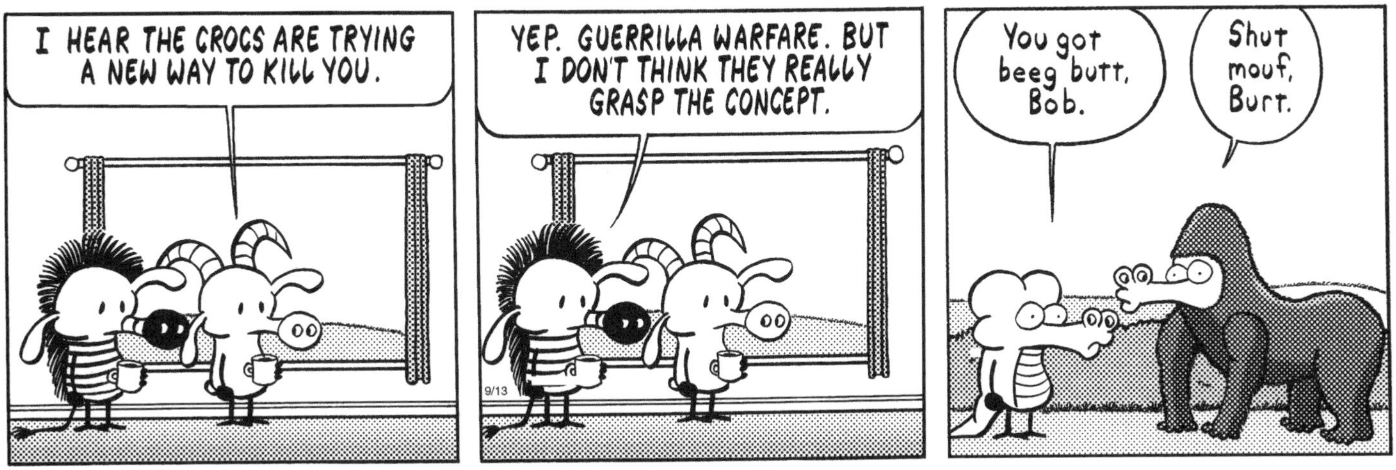
I HEAR THE CROCS ARE TRYING A NEW WAY TO KILL YOU.
YEP. GUERRILLA WARFARE. BUT I DON'T THINK THEY REALLY GRASP THE CONCEPT.
You got beeg butt, Bob.
Shut mouf, Burt.
9/13

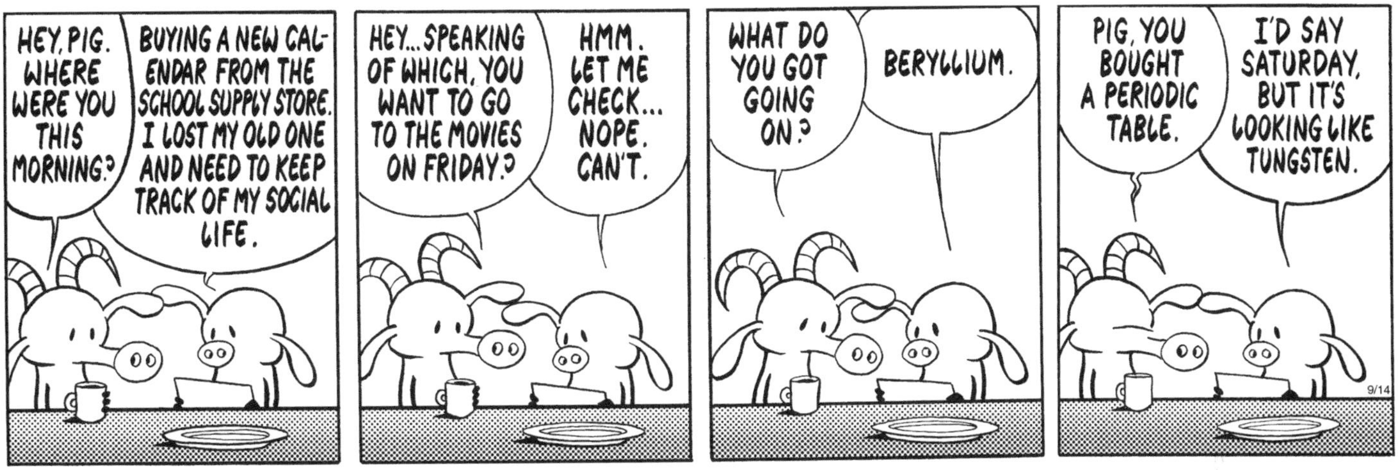
HEY, PIG. WHERE WERE YOU THIS MORNING?
BUYING A NEW CALENDAR FROM THE SCHOOL SUPPLY STORE. I LOST MY OLD ONE AND NEED TO KEEP TRACK OF MY SOCIAL LIFE.
HEY...SPEAKING OF WHICH, YOU WANT TO GO TO THE MOVIES ON FRIDAY?
HMM. LET ME CHECK... NOPE. CAN'T.
WHAT DO YOU GOT GOING ON?
BERYLLIUM.
PIG, YOU BOUGHT A PERIODIC TABLE.
I'D SAY SATURDAY, BUT IT'S LOOKING LIKE TUNGSTEN.
9/14

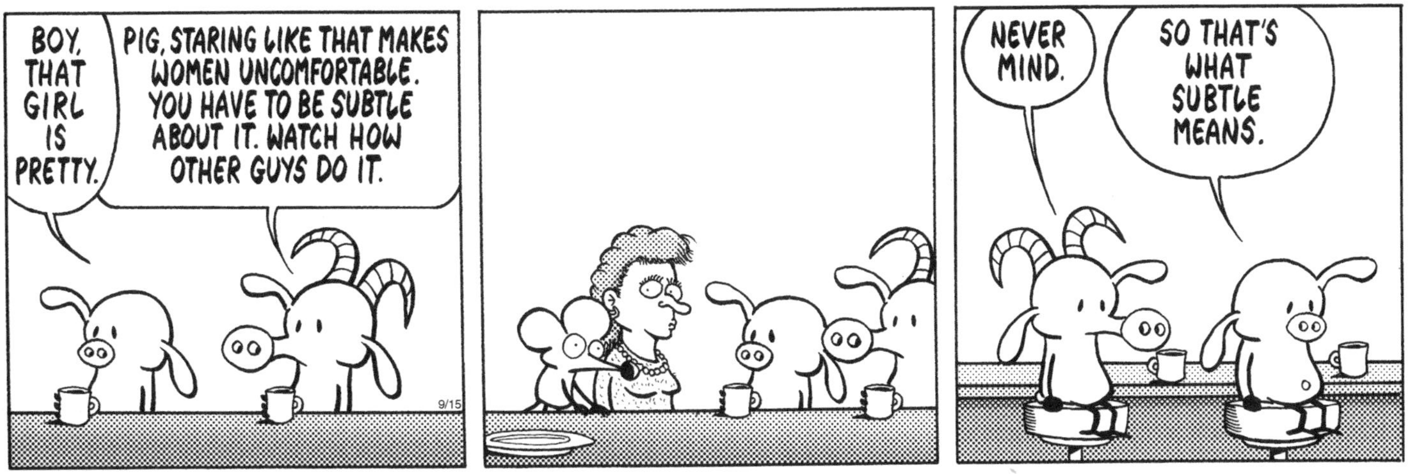
BOY, THAT GIRL IS PRETTY.
PIG, STARING LIKE THAT MAKES WOMEN UNCOMFORTABLE. YOU HAVE TO BE SUBTLE ABOUT IT. WATCH HOW OTHER GUYS DO IT.
9/15
NEVER MIND.
SO THAT'S WHAT SUBTLE MEANS.

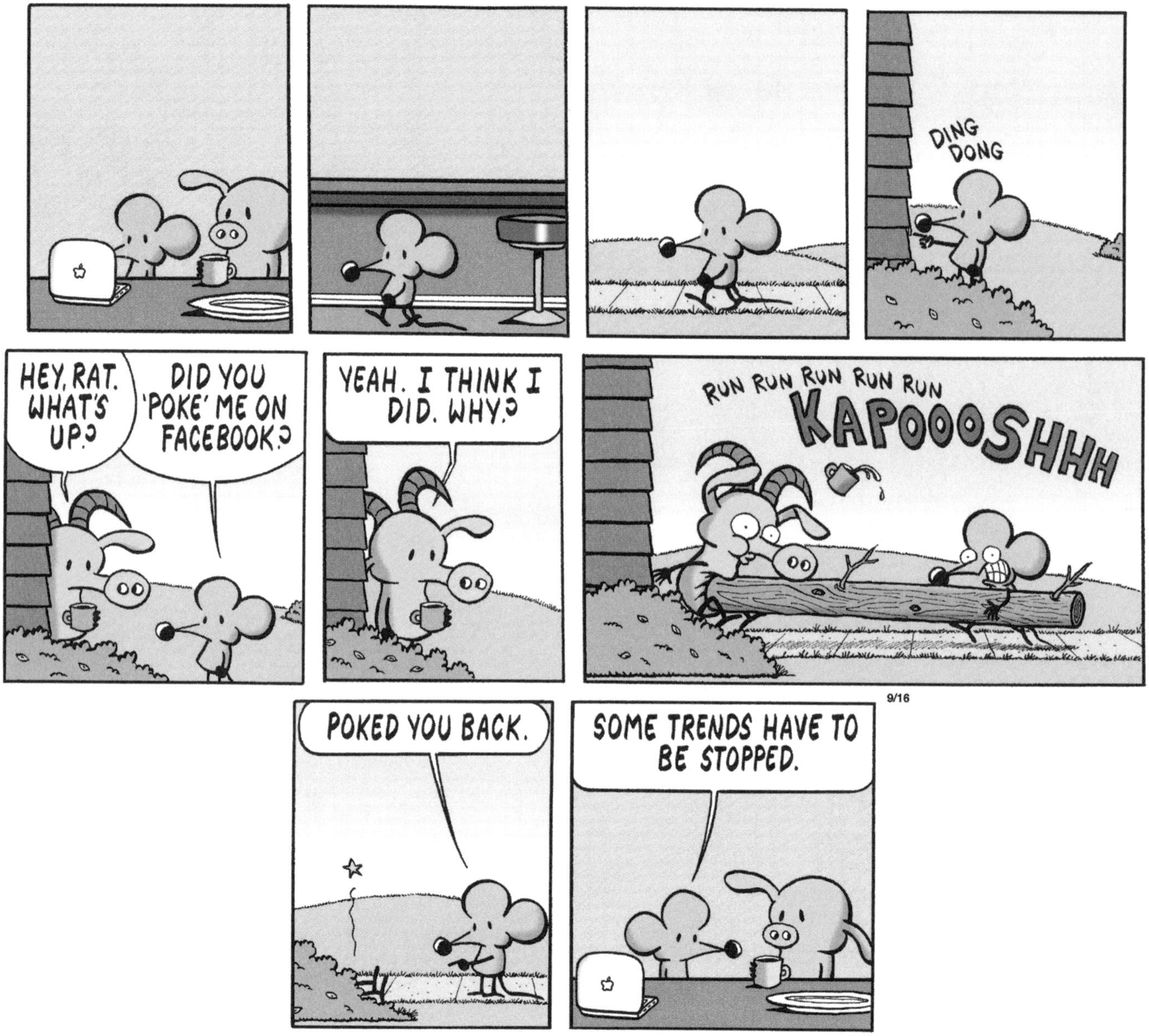
DING DONG
HEY, RAT. WHAT'S UP?
DID YOU 'POKE' ME ON FACEBOOK?
YEAH. I THINK I DID. WHY?
RUN RUN RUN RUN RUN
KAPOOOSHHH
9/16
POKED YOU BACK.
SOME TRENDS HAVE TO BE STOPPED.

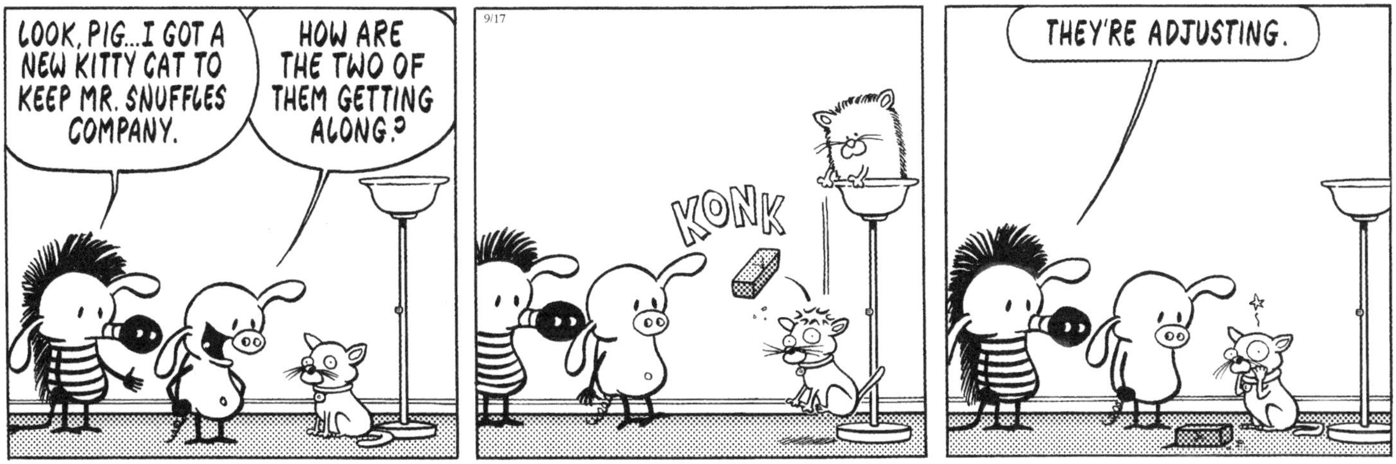
LOOK, PIG... I GOT A NEW KITTY CAT TO KEEP MR. SNUFFLES COMPANY.
HOW ARE THE TWO OF THEM GETTING ALONG?
9/17
KONK
THEY'RE ADJUSTING.

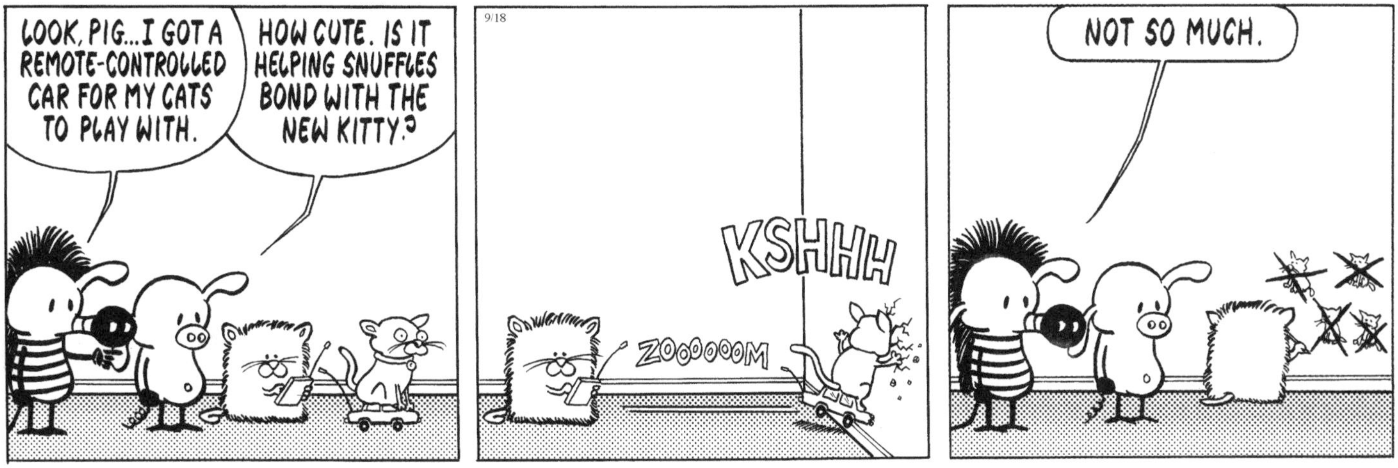
LOOK, PIG... I GOT A REMOTE-CONTROLLED CAR FOR MY CATS TO PLAY WITH.
HOW CUTE. IS IT HELPING SNUFFLES BOND WITH THE NEW KITTY?
9/18
KSHHH
ZOOOOOOM
NOT SO MUCH.

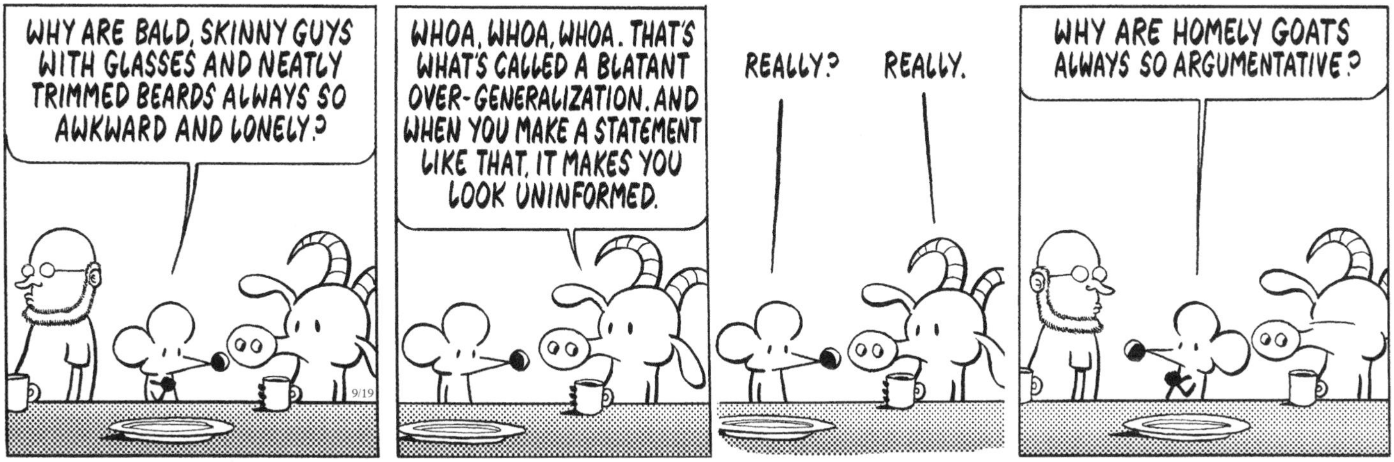
WHY ARE BALD, SKINNY GUYS WITH GLASSES AND NEATLY TRIMMED BEARDS ALWAYS SO AWKWARD AND LONELY?
9/19
WHOA, WHOA, WHOA. THAT'S WHAT'S CALLED A BLATANT OVER-GENERALIZATION. AND WHEN YOU MAKE A STATEMENT LIKE THAT, IT MAKES YOU LOOK UNINFORMED.
REALLY?
REALLY.
WHY ARE HOMELY GOATS ALWAYS SO ARGUMENTATIVE?

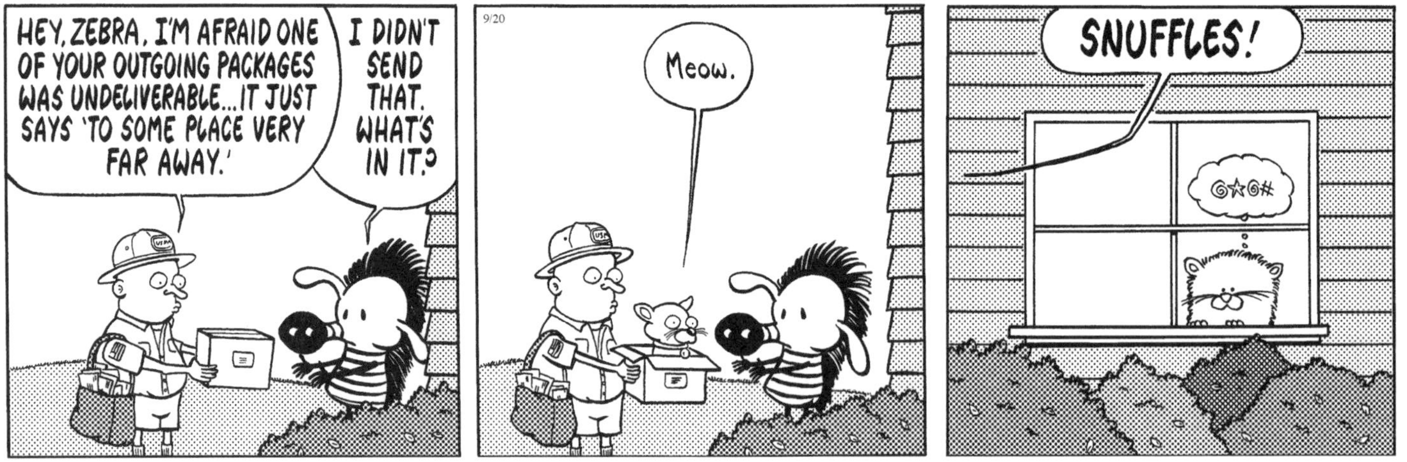
HEY, ZEBRA, I'M AFRAID ONE OF YOUR OUTGOING PACKAGES WAS UNDELIVERABLE... IT JUST SAYS 'TO SOME PLACE VERY FAR AWAY.'
I DIDN'T SEND THAT. WHAT'S IN IT?
9/20
Meow.
SNUFFLES!

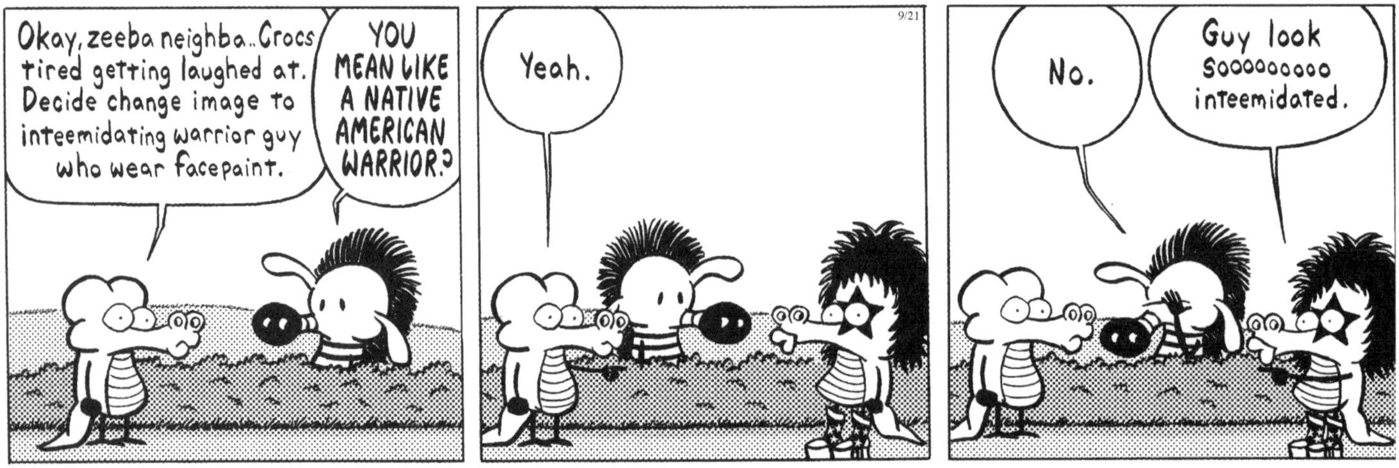
Okay, zeeba neighba.. Crocs tired getting laughed at. Decide change image to inteemidating warrior guy who wear facepaint.
YOU MEAN LIKE A NATIVE AMERICAN WARRIOR?
9/21
Yeah.
No.
Guy look sooooooooo inteemidated.

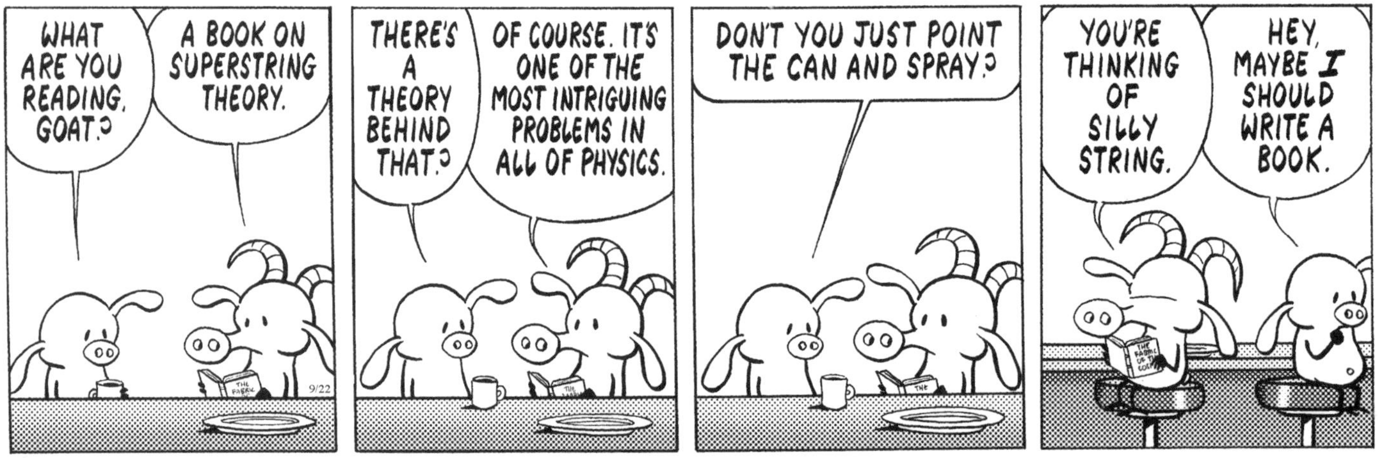
WHAT ARE YOU READING, GOAT?
A BOOK ON SUPERSTRING THEORY.
9/22
THERE'S A THEORY BEHIND THAT?
OF COURSE. IT'S ONE OF THE MOST INTRIGUING PROBLEMS IN ALL OF PHYSICS.
DON'T YOU JUST POINT THE CAN AND SPRAY?
YOU'RE THINKING OF SILLY STRING.
HEY, MAYBE I SHOULD WRITE A BOOK.

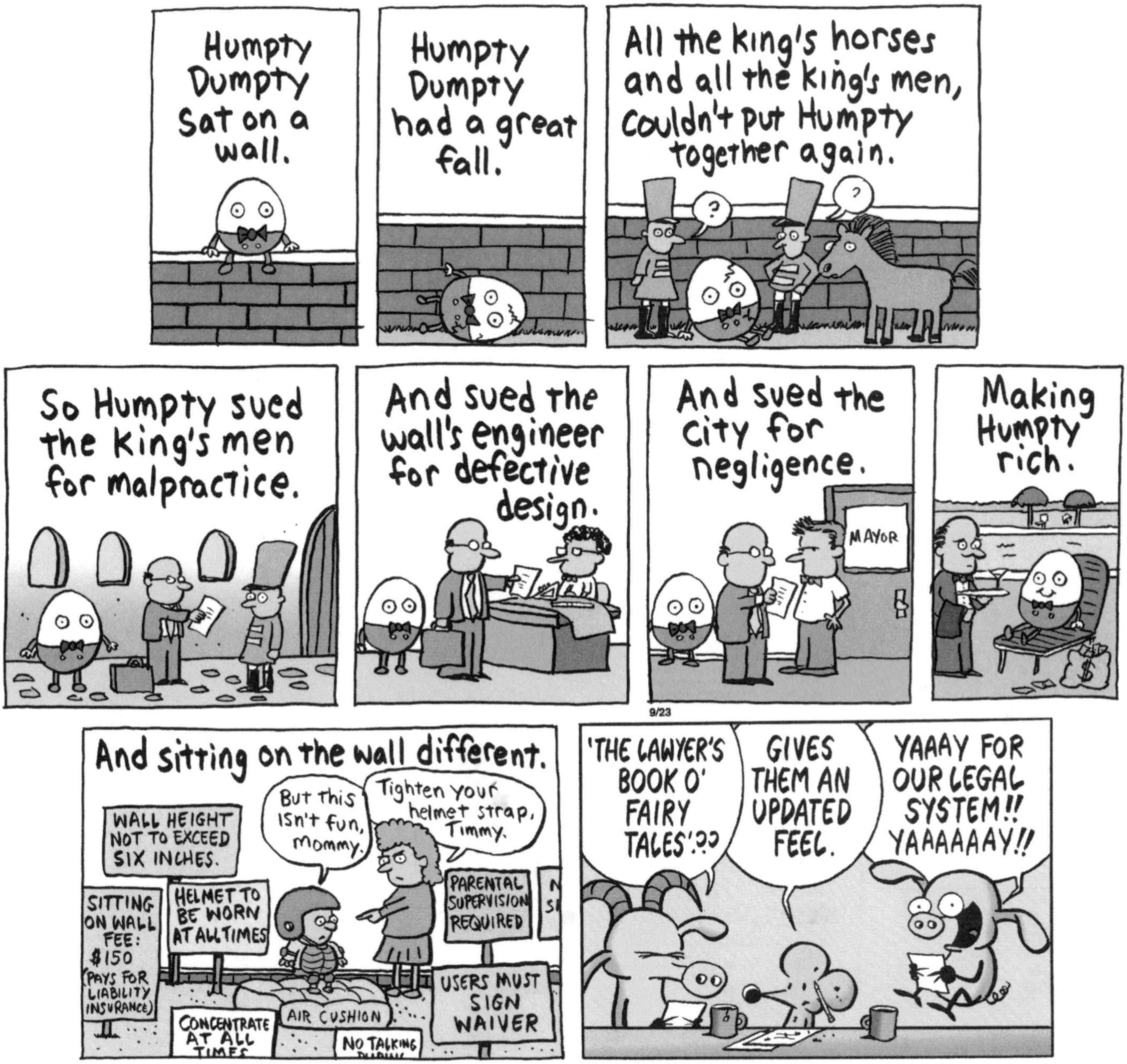
Humpty Dumpty sat on a wall.
Humpty Dumpty had a great fall.
All the king's horses and all the king's men, couldn't put Humpty together again.
?
?
So Humpty sued the King's men for malpractice.
And sued the wall's engineer for defective design.
And sued the city for negligence.
MAYOR
Making Humpty rich.
9/23
And sitting on the wall different.
WALL HEIGHT NOT TO EXCEED SIX INCHES.
But this isn't fun, mommy.
Tighten your helmet strap, Timmy.
SITTING ON WALL FEE: $150 (PAYS FOR LIABILITY INSURANCE)
HELMET TO BE WORN AT ALL TIMES
PARENTAL SUPERVISION REQUIRED
AIR CUSHION
USERS MUST SIGN WAIVER
CONCENTRATE AT ALL TIMES
NO TALKING
'THE LAWYER'S BOOK O' FAIRY TALES'??
GIVES THEM AN UPDATED FEEL.
YAAAY FOR OUR LEGAL SYSTEM!! YAAAAAAY!!

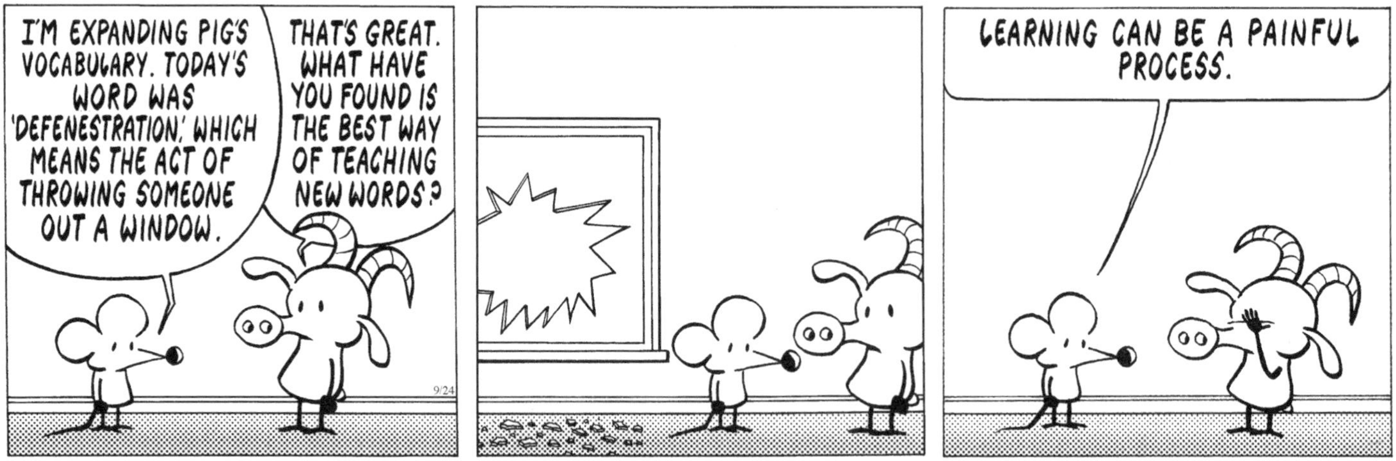
I'M EXPANDING PIG'S VOCABULARY. TODAY'S WORD WAS 'DEFENESTRATION,' WHICH MEANS THE ACT OF THROWING SOMEONE OUT A WINDOW.
THAT'S GREAT. WHAT HAVE YOU FOUND IS THE BEST WAY OF TEACHING NEW WORDS?
9/24
LEARNING CAN BE A PAINFUL PROCESS.

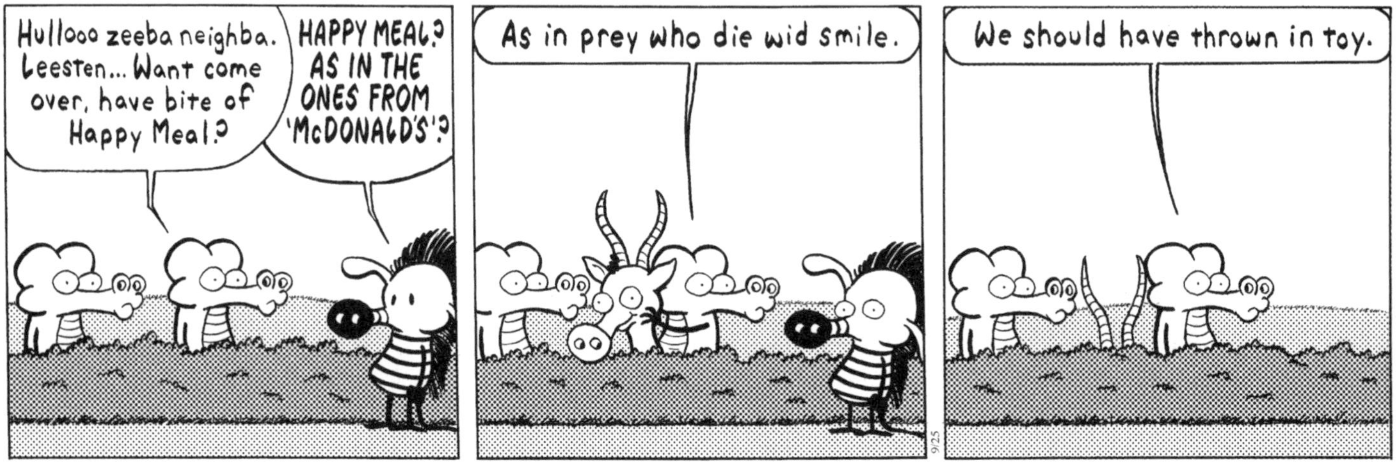
Hullooo zeeba neighba. Leesten... Want come over, have bite of Happy Meal?
HAPPY MEAL? AS IN THE ONES FROM 'McDONALD'S'?
As in prey who die wid smile.
9/25
We should have thrown in toy.

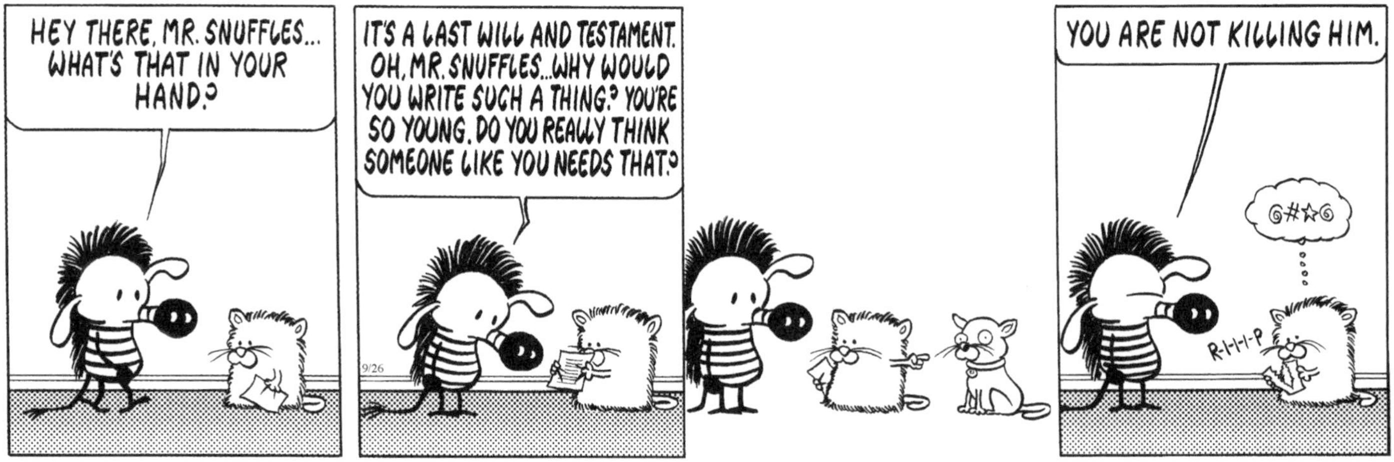
HEY THERE, MR. SNUFFLES... WHAT'S THAT IN YOUR HAND?
9/26
IT'S A LAST WILL AND TESTAMENT. OH, MR. SNUFFLES...WHY WOULD YOU WRITE SUCH A THING? YOU'RE SO YOUNG. DO YOU REALLY THINK SOMEONE LIKE YOU NEEDS THAT?
YOU ARE NOT KILLING HIM.
R-I-I-I-P

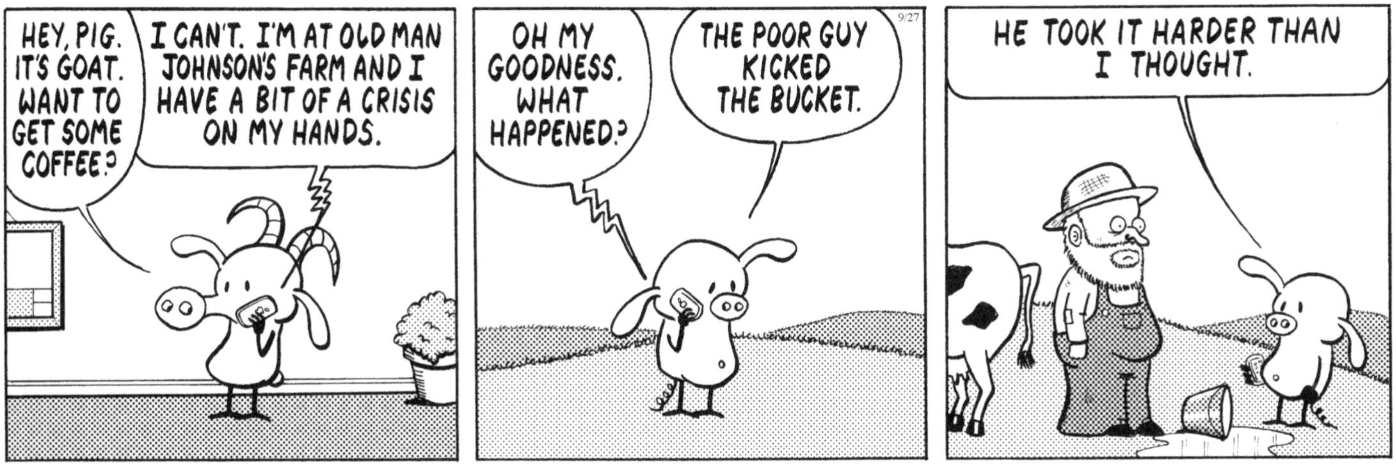
HEY, PIG. IT'S GOAT. WANT TO GET SOME COFFEE?
I CAN'T. I'M AT OLD MAN JOHNSON'S FARM AND I HAVE A BIT OF A CRISIS ON MY HANDS.
OH MY GOODNESS. WHAT HAPPENED?
THE POOR GUY KICKED THE BUCKET.
9/27
HE TOOK IT HARDER THAN I THOUGHT.

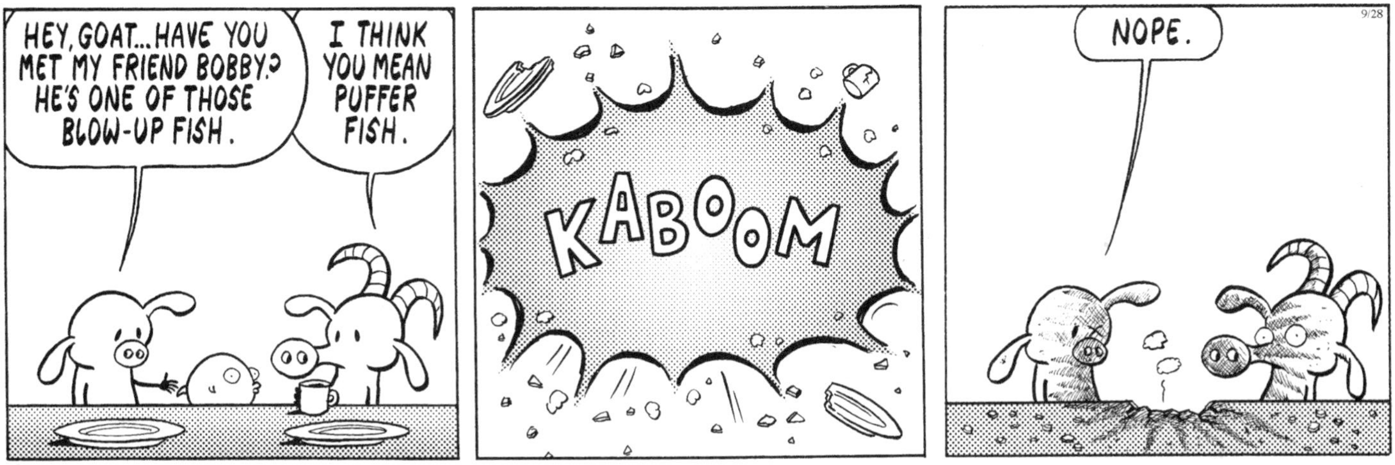
HEY, GOAT...HAVE YOU MET MY FRIEND BOBBY? HE'S ONE OF THOSE BLOW-UP FISH.
I THINK YOU MEAN PUFFER FISH.
KABOOM
NOPE.
9/28

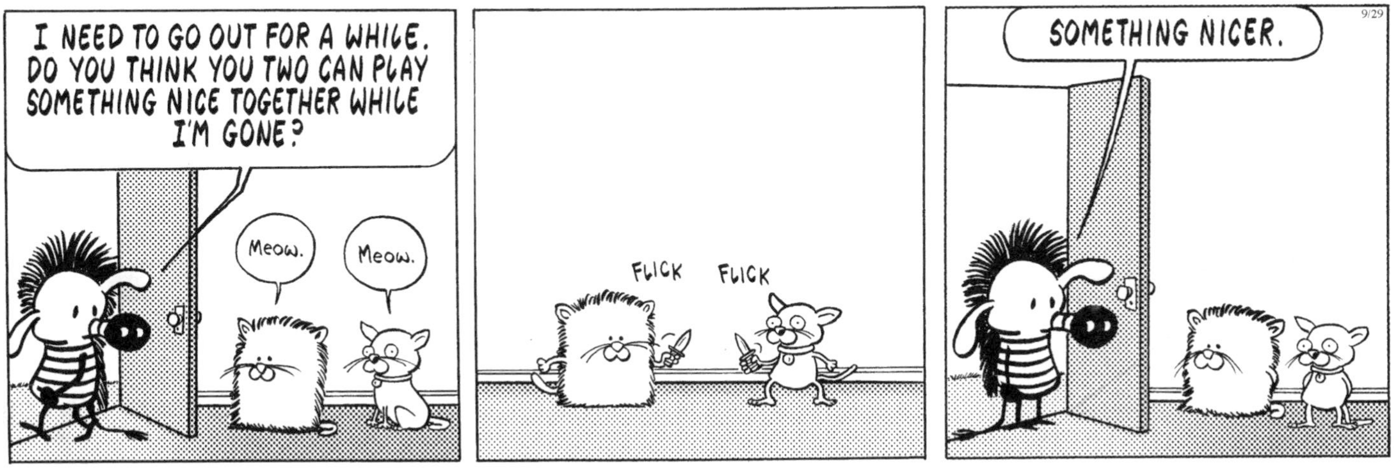
I NEED TO GO OUT FOR A WHILE. DO YOU THINK YOU TWO CAN PLAY SOMETHING NICE TOGETHER WHILE I'M GONE?
Meow.
Meow.
FLICK
FLICK
SOMETHING NICER.
9/29

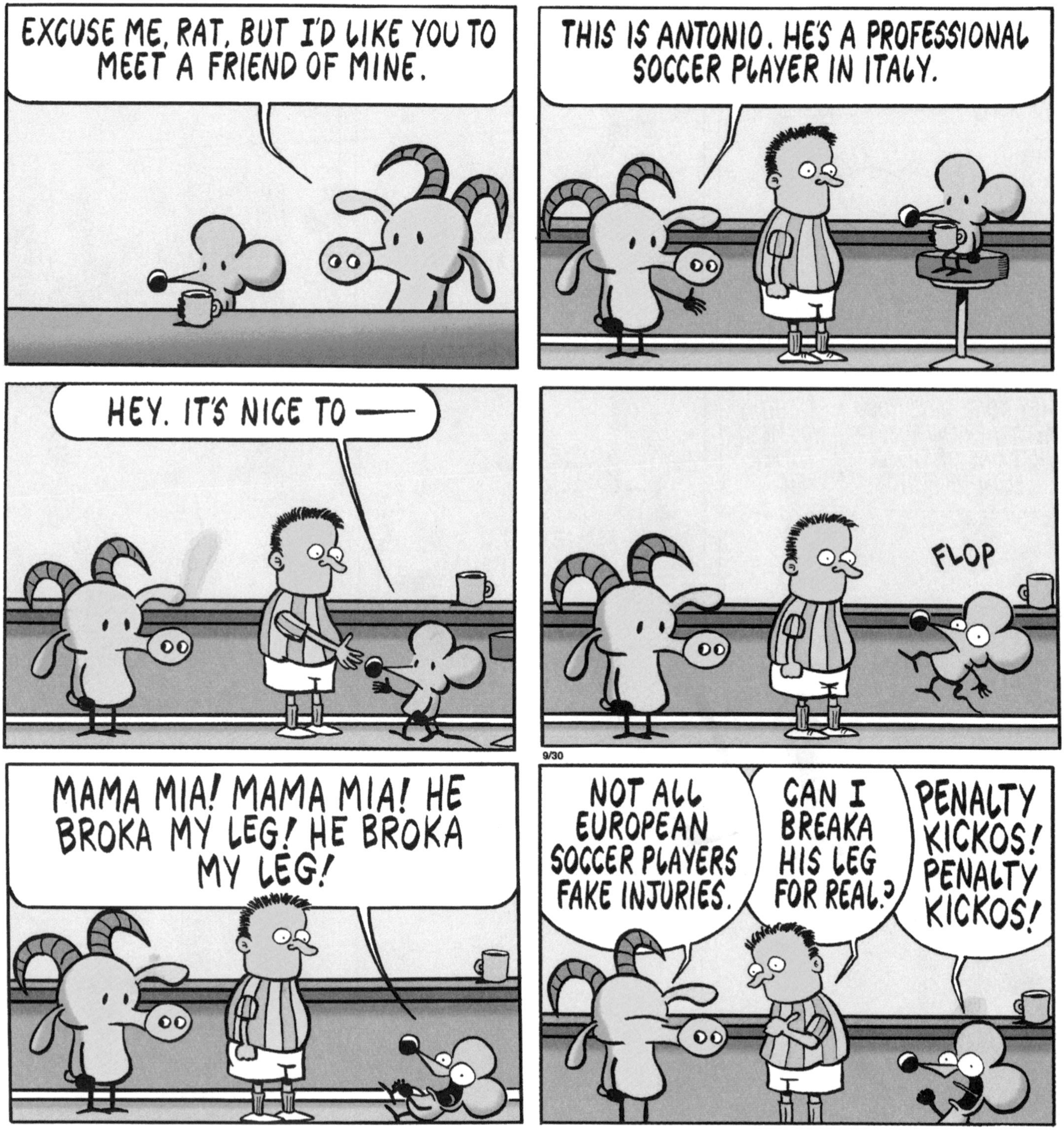
EXCUSE ME, RAT, BUT I'D LIKE YOU TO MEET A FRIEND OF MINE.
THIS IS ANTONIO. HE'S A PROFESSIONAL SOCCER PLAYER IN ITALY.
HEY. IT'S NICE TO —
FLOP
9/30
MAMA MIA! MAMA MIA! HE BROKA MY LEG! HE BROKA MY LEG!
NOT ALL EUROPEAN SOCCER PLAYERS FAKE INJURIES.
CAN I BREAKA HIS LEG FOR REAL?
PENALTY KICKOS! PENALTY KICKOS!

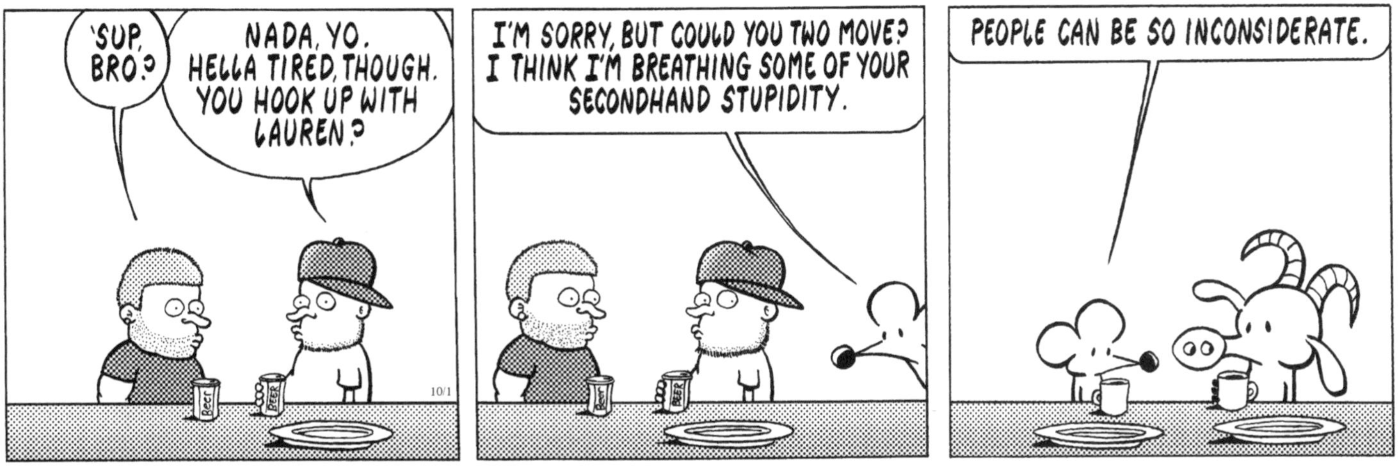

'SUP, BRO?
NADA, YO. HELLA TIRED, THOUGH. YOU HOOK UP WITH LAUREN?
10/1
I'M SORRY, BUT COULD YOU TWO MOVE? I THINK I'M BREATHING SOME OF YOUR SECONDHAND STUPIDITY.
PEOPLE CAN BE SO INCONSIDERATE.

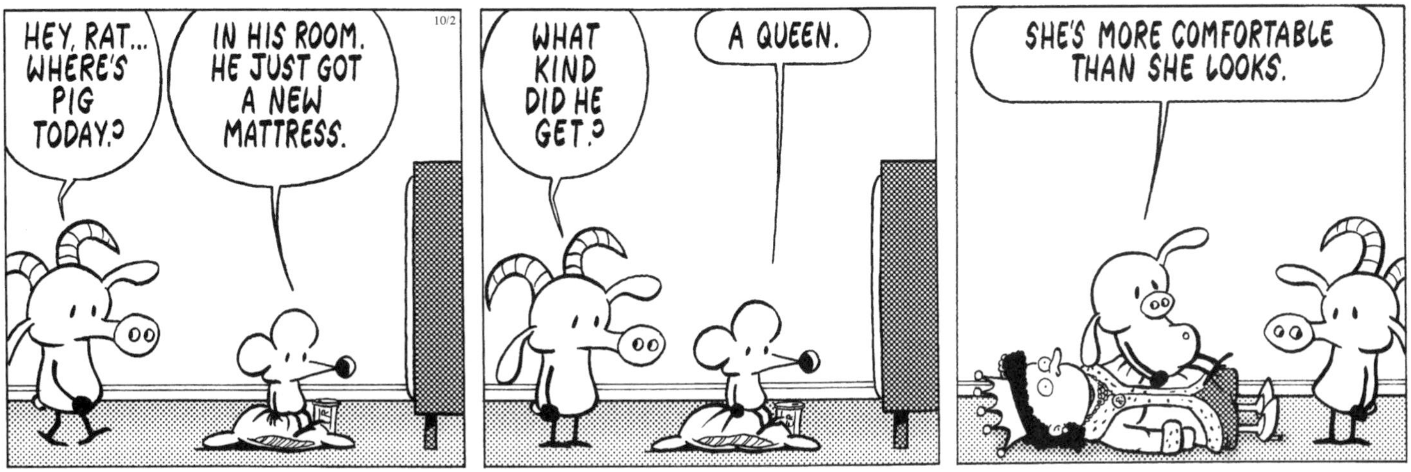

HEY, RAT... WHERE'S PIG TODAY?
IN HIS ROOM. HE JUST GOT A NEW MATTRESS.
10/2
WHAT KIND DID HE GET?
A QUEEN.
SHE'S MORE COMFORTABLE THAN SHE LOOKS.

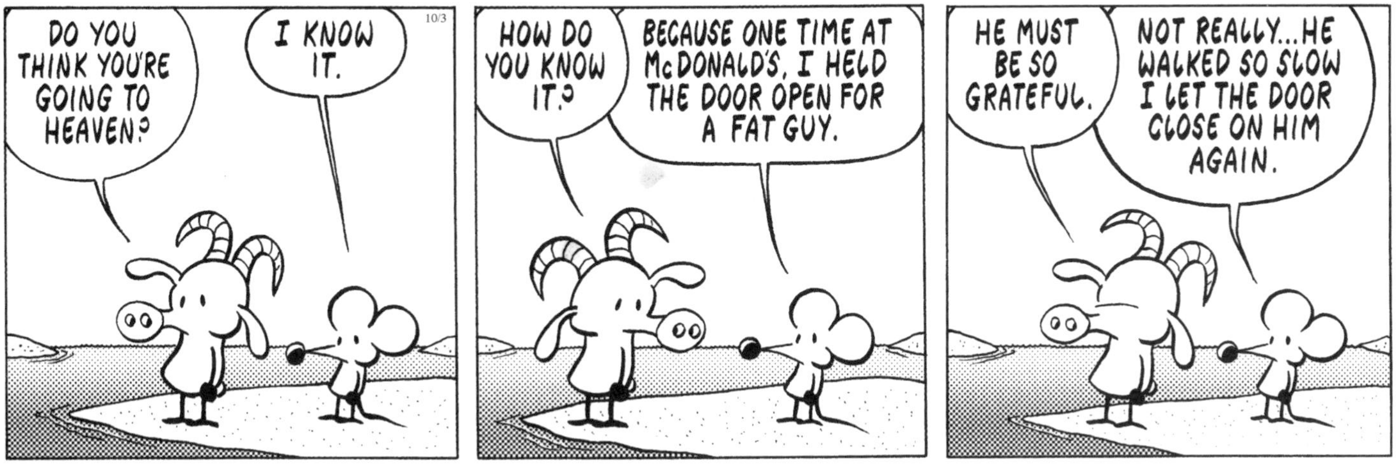

DO YOU THINK YOU'RE GOING TO HEAVEN?
I KNOW IT.
10/3
HOW DO YOU KNOW IT?
BECAUSE ONE TIME AT McDONALD'S, I HELD THE DOOR OPEN FOR A FAT GUY.
HE MUST BE SO GRATEFUL.
NOT REALLY...HE WALKED SO SLOW I LET THE DOOR CLOSE ON HIM AGAIN.

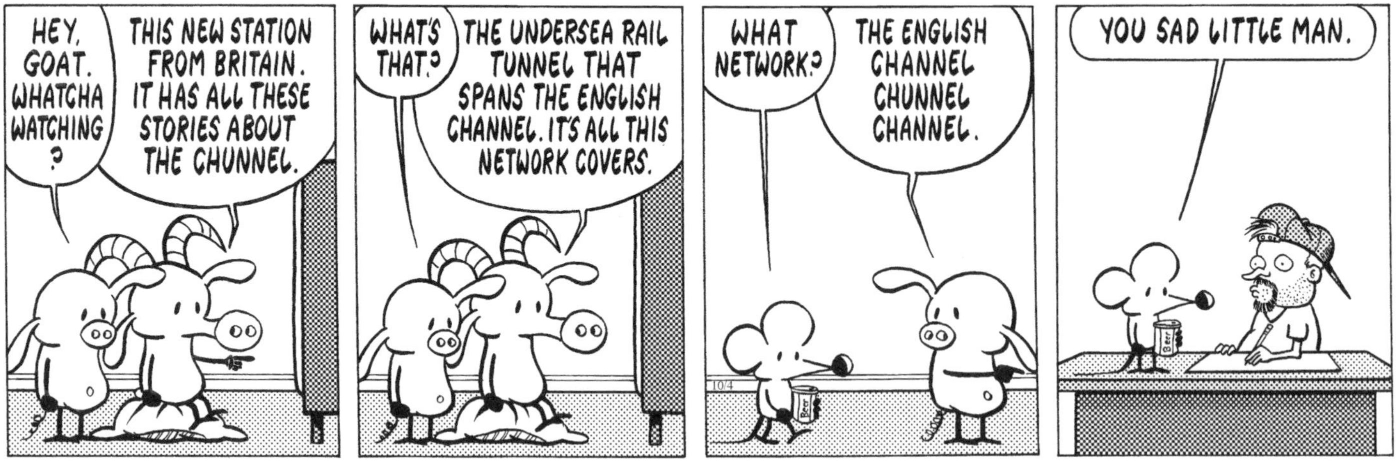
HEY, GOAT. WHATCHA WATCHING?
THIS NEW STATION FROM BRITAIN. IT HAS ALL THESE STORIES ABOUT THE CHUNNEL.
WHAT'S THAT?
THE UNDERSEA RAIL TUNNEL THAT SPANS THE ENGLISH CHANNEL. IT'S ALL THIS NETWORK COVERS.
WHAT NETWORK?
THE ENGLISH CHANNEL CHUNNEL CHANNEL.
10/4
YOU SAD LITTLE MAN.

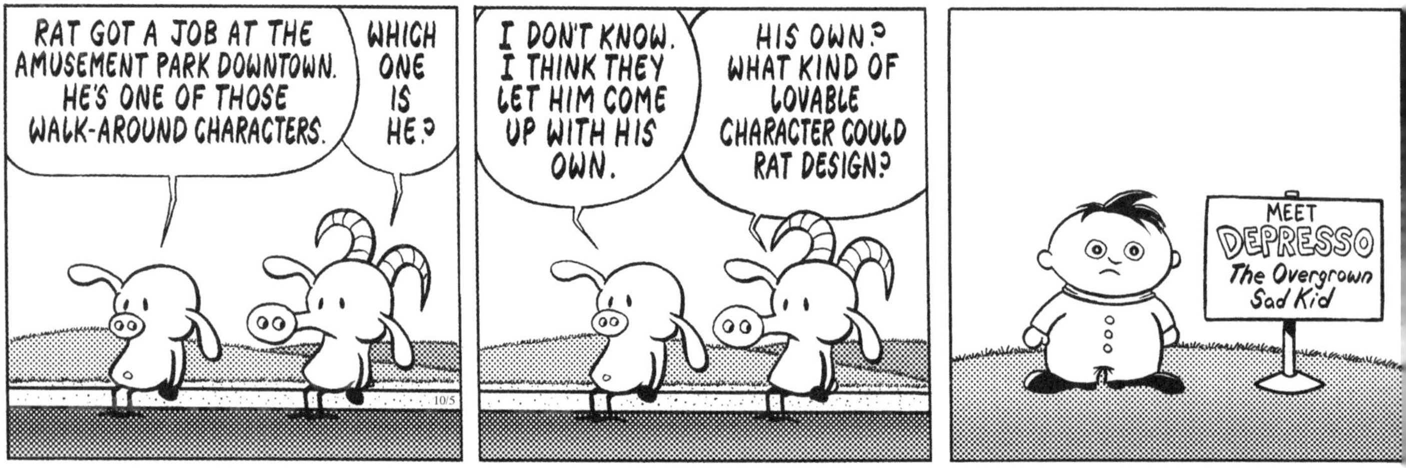
RAT GOT A JOB AT THE AMUSEMENT PARK DOWNTOWN. HE'S ONE OF THOSE WALK-AROUND CHARACTERS.
WHICH ONE IS HE?
10/5
I DON'T KNOW. I THINK THEY LET HIM COME UP WITH HIS OWN.
HIS OWN? WHAT KIND OF LOVABLE CHARACTER COULD RAT DESIGN?
MEET
DEPRESSO
The Overgrown Sad Kid

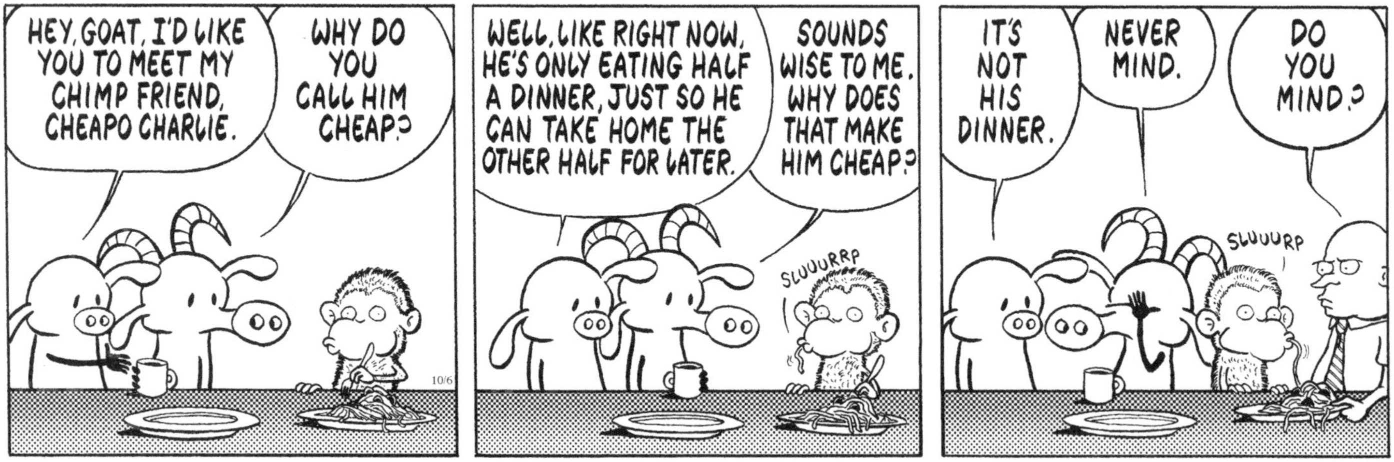
HEY, GOAT, I'D LIKE YOU TO MEET MY CHIMP FRIEND, CHEAPO CHARLIE.
WHY DO YOU CALL HIM CHEAP?
10/6
WELL, LIKE RIGHT NOW, HE'S ONLY EATING HALF A DINNER, JUST SO HE CAN TAKE HOME THE OTHER HALF FOR LATER.
SOUNDS WISE TO ME. WHY DOES THAT MAKE HIM CHEAP?
SLUUURRP
IT'S NOT HIS DINNER.
NEVER MIND.
SLUUURP
DO YOU MIND?

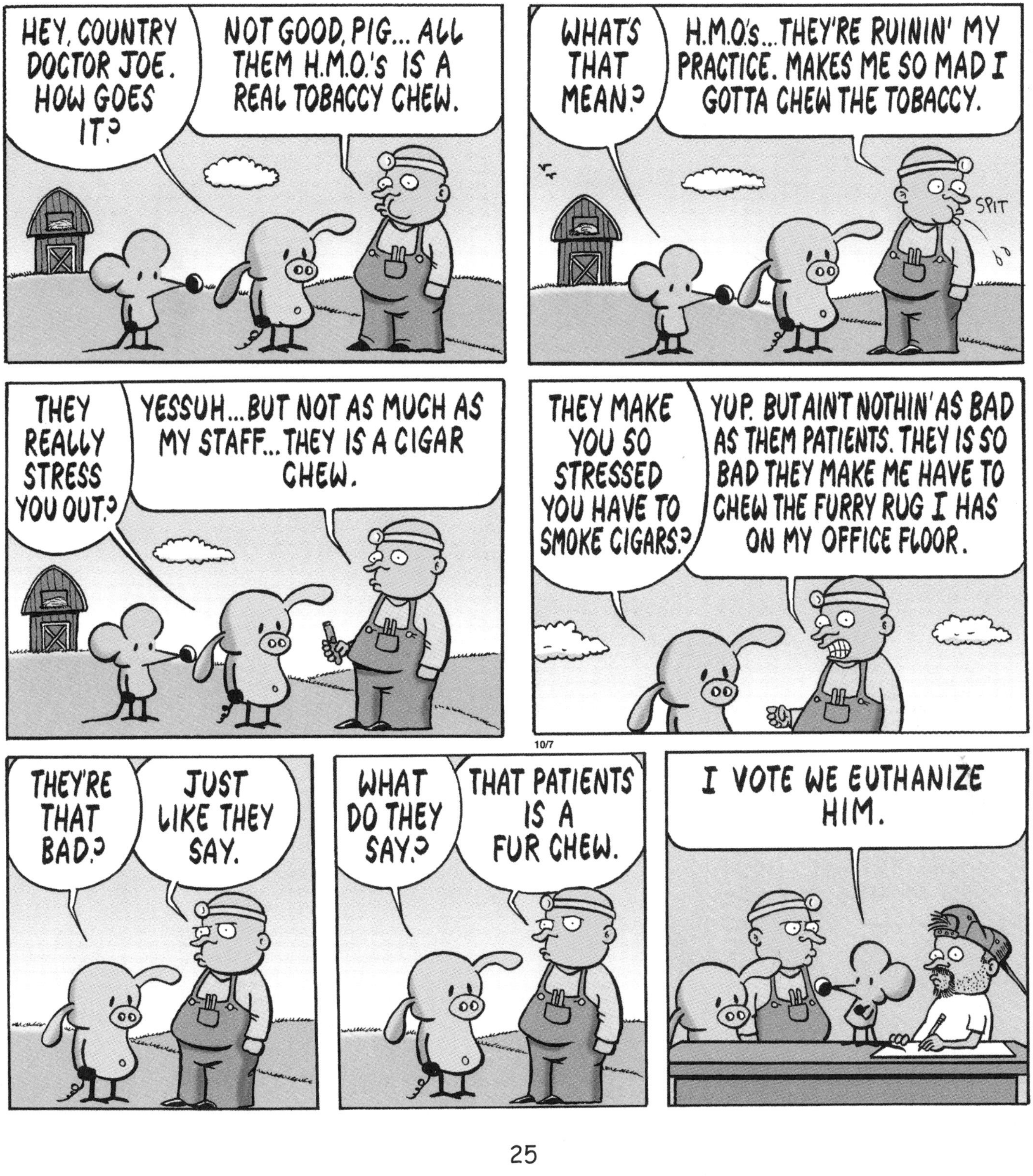
HEY, COUNTRY DOCTOR JOE. HOW GOES IT?
NOT GOOD, PIG... ALL THEM H.M.O.'s IS A REAL TOBACCY CHEW.
WHAT'S THAT MEAN?
H.M.O.'s... THEY'RE RUININ' MY PRACTICE. MAKES ME SO MAD I GOTTA CHEW THE TOBACCY.
SPIT
THEY REALLY STRESS YOU OUT?
YESSUH... BUT NOT AS MUCH AS MY STAFF... THEY IS A CIGAR CHEW.
THEY MAKE YOU SO STRESSED YOU HAVE TO SMOKE CIGARS?
YUP. BUT AIN'T NOTHIN' AS BAD AS THEM PATIENTS. THEY IS SO BAD THEY MAKE ME HAVE TO CHEW THE FURRY RUG I HAS ON MY OFFICE FLOOR.
10/7
THEY'RE THAT BAD?
JUST LIKE THEY SAY.
WHAT DO THEY SAY?
THAT PATIENTS IS A FUR CHEW.
I VOTE WE EUTHANIZE HIM.

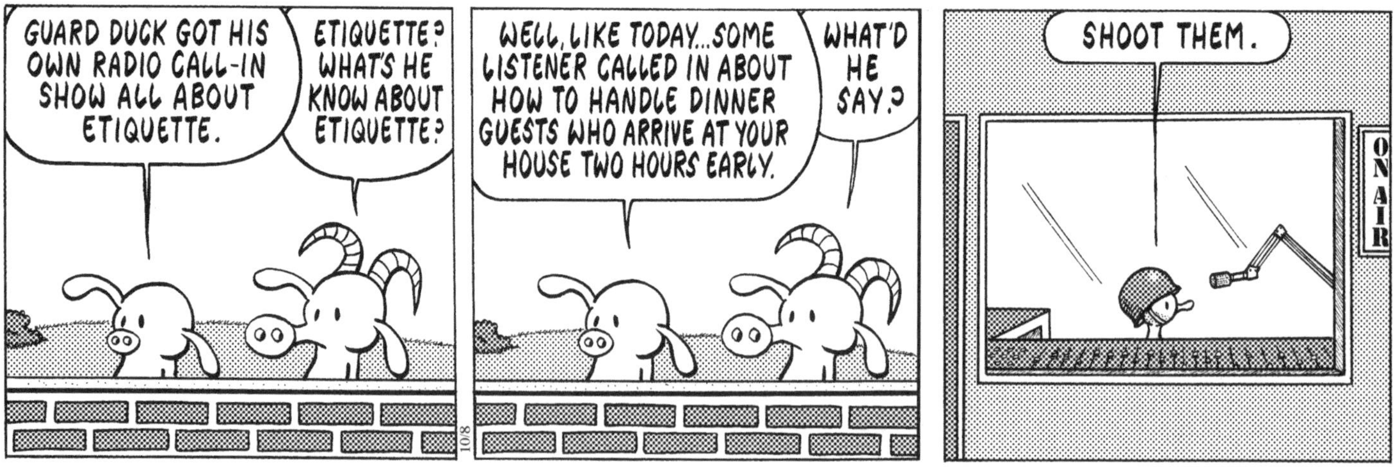
GUARD DUCK GOT HIS OWN RADIO CALL-IN SHOW ALL ABOUT ETIQUETTE.
ETIQUETTE? WHAT'S HE KNOW ABOUT ETIQUETTE?
WELL, LIKE TODAY...SOME LISTENER CALLED IN ABOUT HOW TO HANDLE DINNER GUESTS WHO ARRIVE AT YOUR HOUSE TWO HOURS EARLY.
WHAT'D HE SAY?
SHOOT THEM.
ON AIR
10/8

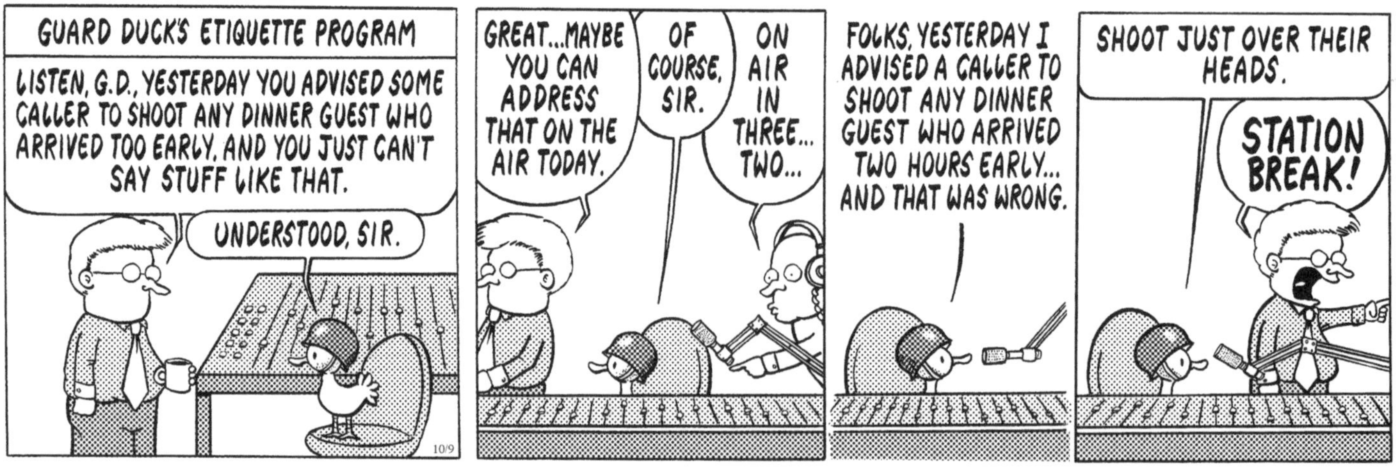
GUARD DUCK'S ETIQUETTE PROGRAM
LISTEN, G.D., YESTERDAY YOU ADVISED SOME CALLER TO SHOOT ANY DINNER GUEST WHO ARRIVED TOO EARLY, AND YOU JUST CAN'T SAY STUFF LIKE THAT.
UNDERSTOOD, SIR.
GREAT...MAYBE YOU CAN ADDRESS THAT ON THE AIR TODAY.
OF COURSE, SIR.
ON AIR IN THREE... TWO...
FOLKS, YESTERDAY I ADVISED A CALLER TO SHOOT ANY DINNER GUEST WHO ARRIVED TWO HOURS EARLY... AND THAT WAS WRONG.
SHOOT JUST OVER THEIR HEADS.
STATION BREAK!
10/9

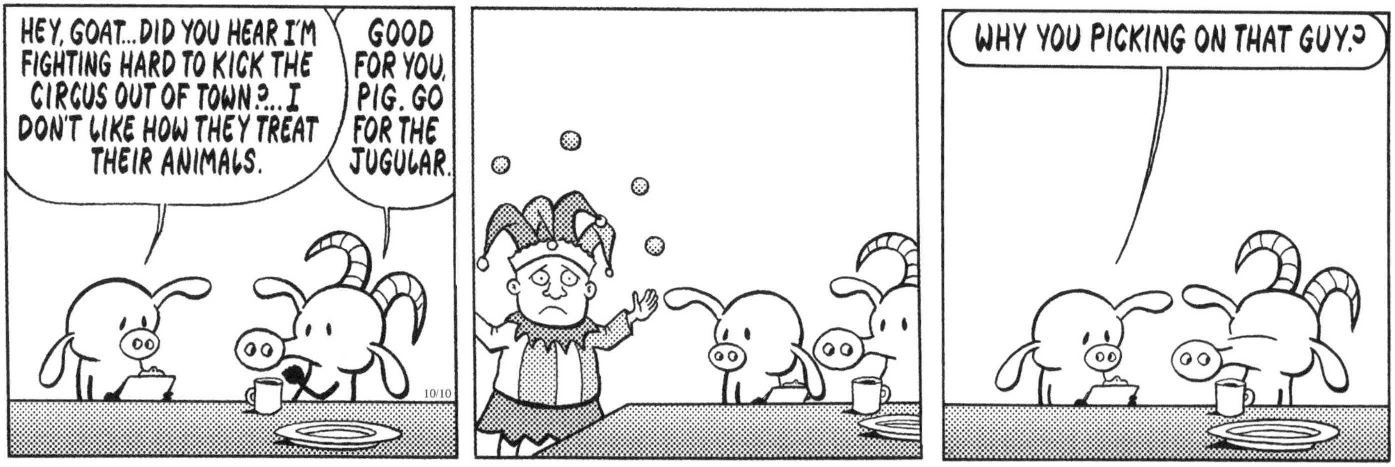
HEY, GOAT...DID YOU HEAR I'M FIGHTING HARD TO KICK THE CIRCUS OUT OF TOWN?...I DON'T LIKE HOW THEY TREAT THEIR ANIMALS.
GOOD FOR YOU, PIG. GO FOR THE JUGULAR.
WHY YOU PICKING ON THAT GUY?
10/10

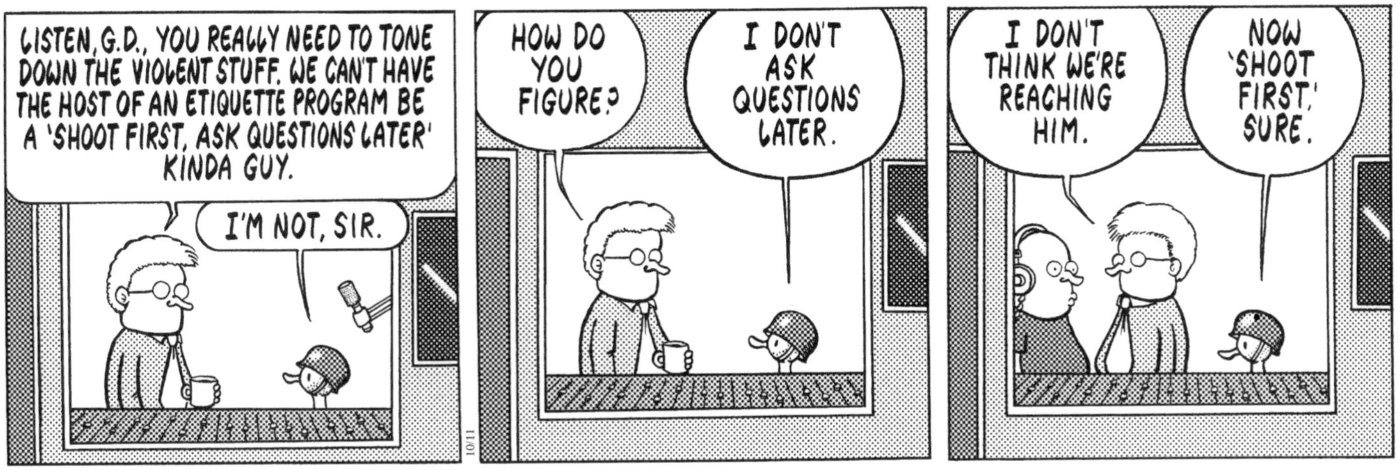
LISTEN, G.D., YOU REALLY NEED TO TONE DOWN THE VIOLENT STUFF. WE CAN'T HAVE THE HOST OF AN ETIQUETTE PROGRAM BE A 'SHOOT FIRST, ASK QUESTIONS LATER' KINDA GUY.
I'M NOT, SIR.
10/11
HOW DO YOU FIGURE?
I DON'T ASK QUESTIONS LATER.
I DON'T THINK WE'RE REACHING HIM.
NOW 'SHOOT FIRST,' SURE.

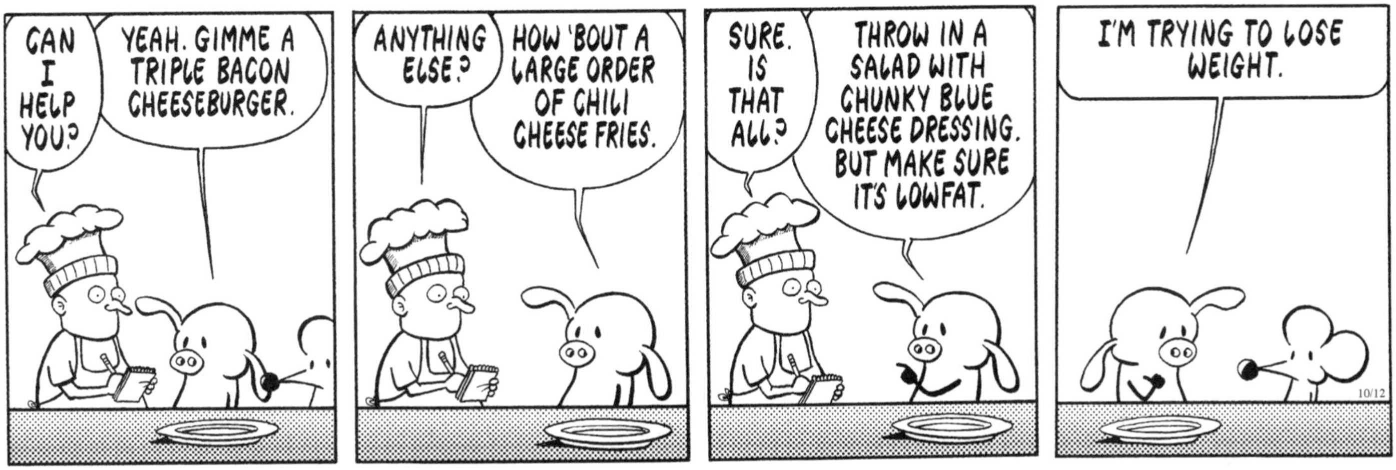
CAN I HELP YOU?
YEAH. GIMME A TRIPLE BACON CHEESEBURGER.
ANYTHING ELSE?
HOW 'BOUT A LARGE ORDER OF CHILI CHEESE FRIES.
SURE. IS THAT ALL?
THROW IN A SALAD WITH CHUNKY BLUE CHEESE DRESSING. BUT MAKE SURE IT'S LOWFAT.
I'M TRYING TO LOSE WEIGHT.
10/12

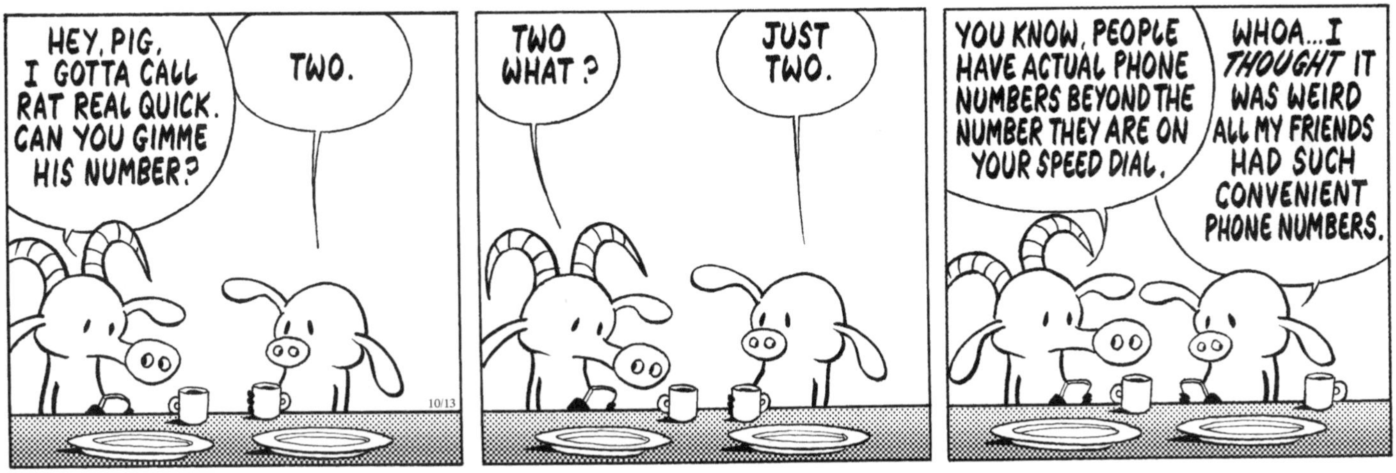
HEY, PIG, I GOTTA CALL RAT REAL QUICK. CAN YOU GIMME HIS NUMBER?
TWO.
10/13
TWO WHAT?
JUST TWO.
YOU KNOW, PEOPLE HAVE ACTUAL PHONE NUMBERS BEYOND THE NUMBER THEY ARE ON YOUR SPEED DIAL.
WHOA...I *THOUGHT* IT WAS WEIRD ALL MY FRIENDS HAD SUCH CONVENIENT PHONE NUMBERS.

STORY UPDATE:

Guard Duck has gotten a job giving etiquette advice on the radio. He has occasionally clashed with station management.

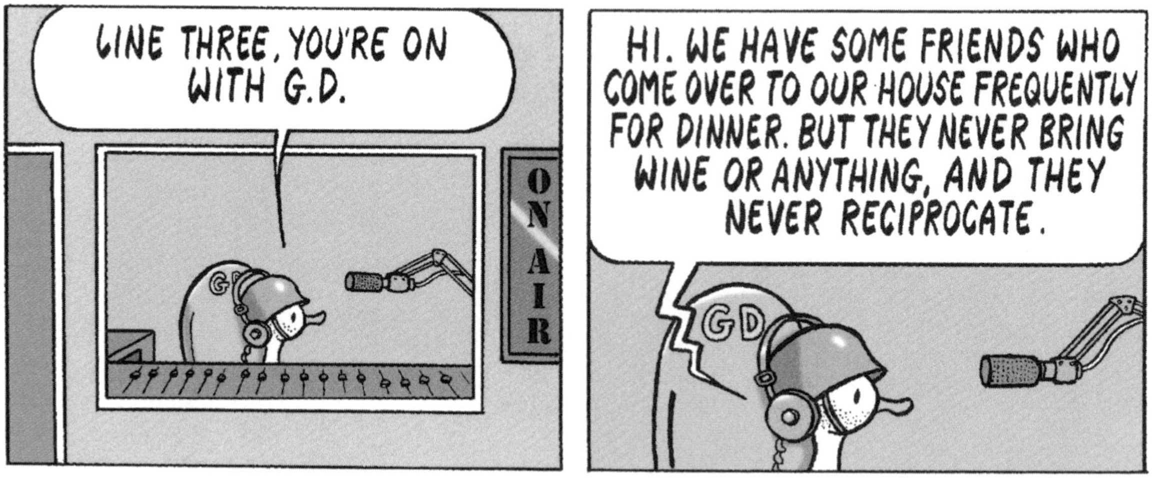
LINE THREE, YOU'RE ON WITH G.D.
ON AIR
HI. WE HAVE SOME FRIENDS WHO COME OVER TO OUR HOUSE FREQUENTLY FOR DINNER. BUT THEY NEVER BRING WINE OR ANYTHING, AND THEY NEVER RECIPROCATE.
GD

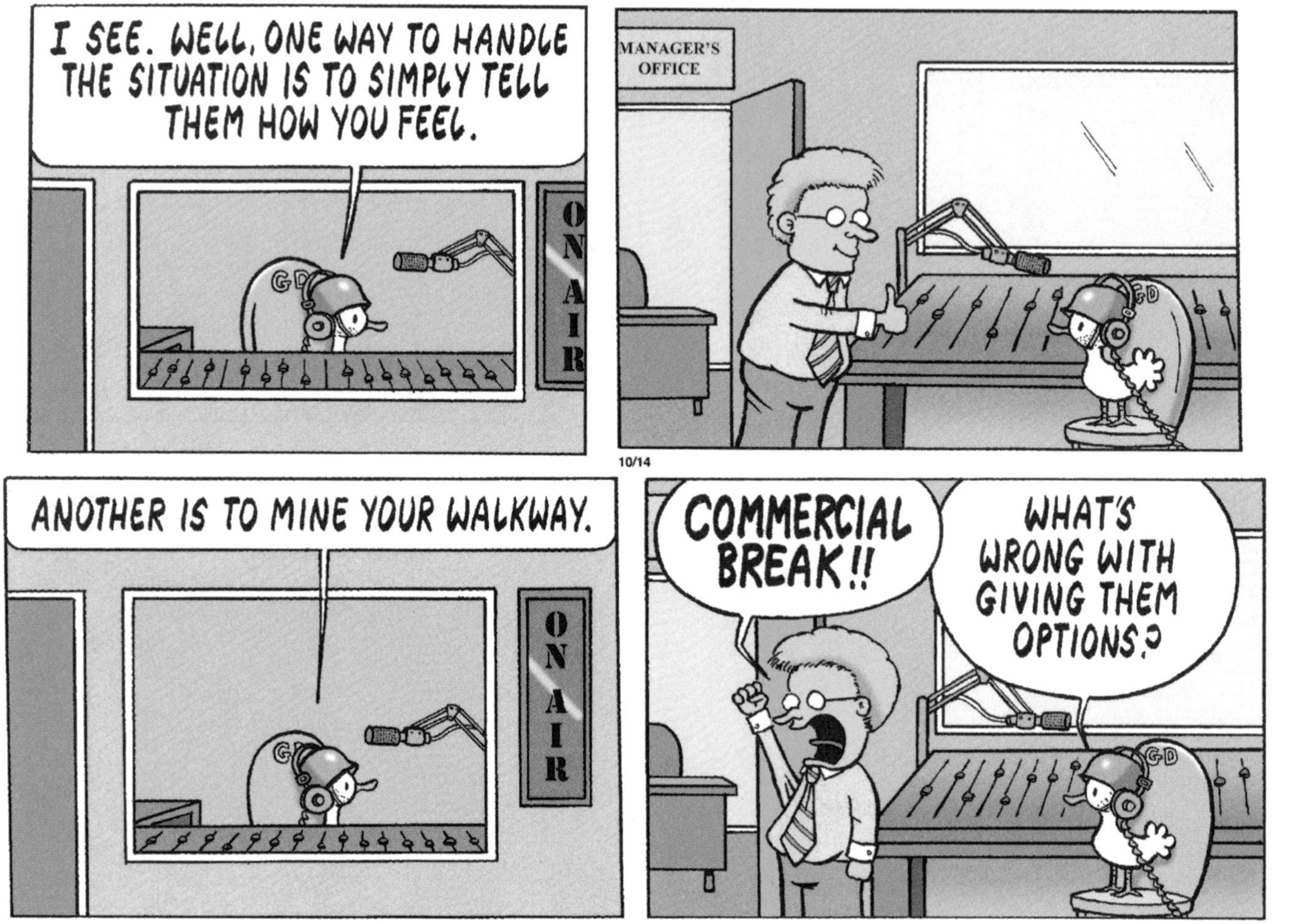
I SEE. WELL, ONE WAY TO HANDLE THE SITUATION IS TO SIMPLY TELL THEM HOW YOU FEEL.
ON AIR
MANAGER'S OFFICE
10/14
ANOTHER IS TO MINE YOUR WALKWAY.
ON AIR
COMMERCIAL BREAK!!
WHAT'S WRONG WITH GIVING THEM OPTIONS?

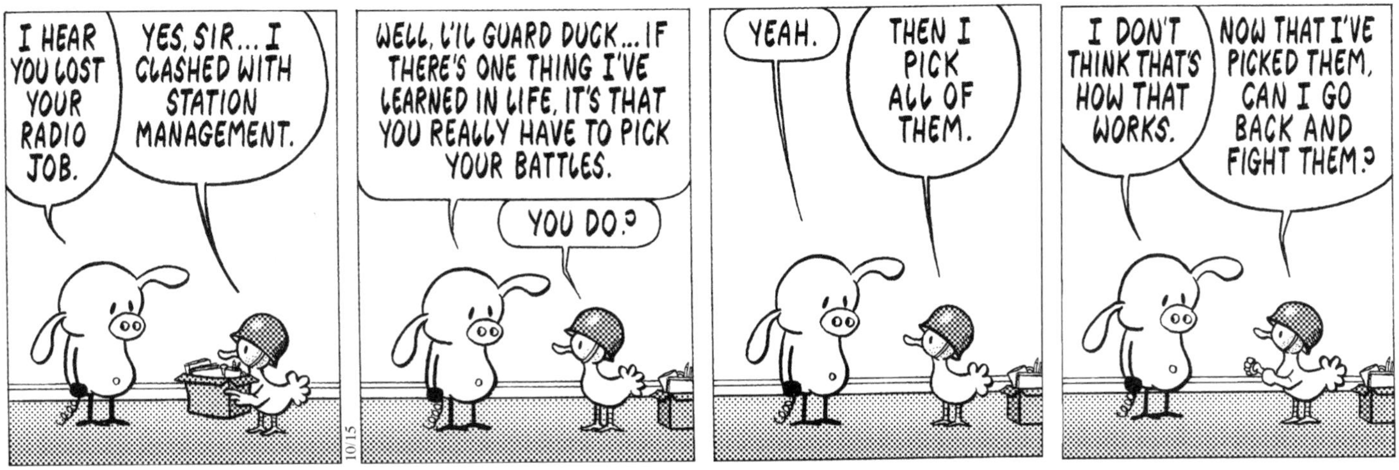
I HEAR YOU LOST YOUR RADIO JOB.
YES, SIR... I CLASHED WITH STATION MANAGEMENT.
10/15
WELL, L'IL GUARD DUCK... IF THERE'S ONE THING I'VE LEARNED IN LIFE, IT'S THAT YOU REALLY HAVE TO PICK YOUR BATTLES.
YOU DO?
YEAH.
THEN I PICK ALL OF THEM.
I DON'T THINK THAT'S HOW THAT WORKS.
NOW THAT I'VE PICKED THEM, CAN I GO BACK AND FIGHT THEM?

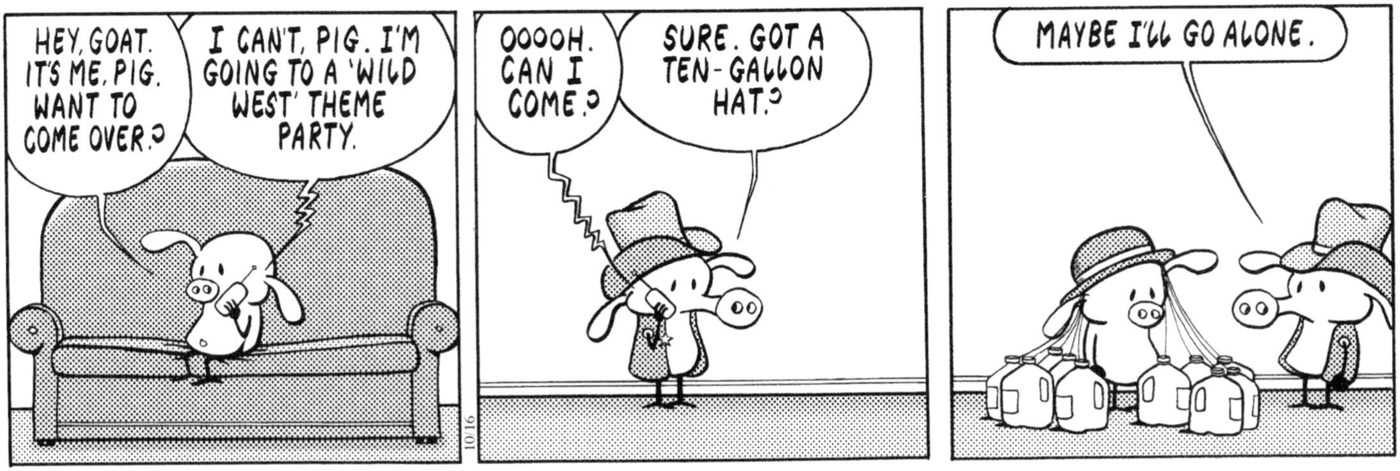
HEY, GOAT. IT'S ME, PIG. WANT TO COME OVER?
I CAN'T, PIG. I'M GOING TO A 'WILD WEST' THEME PARTY.
10/16
OOOOH. CAN I COME?
SURE. GOT A TEN-GALLON HAT?
MAYBE I'LL GO ALONE.

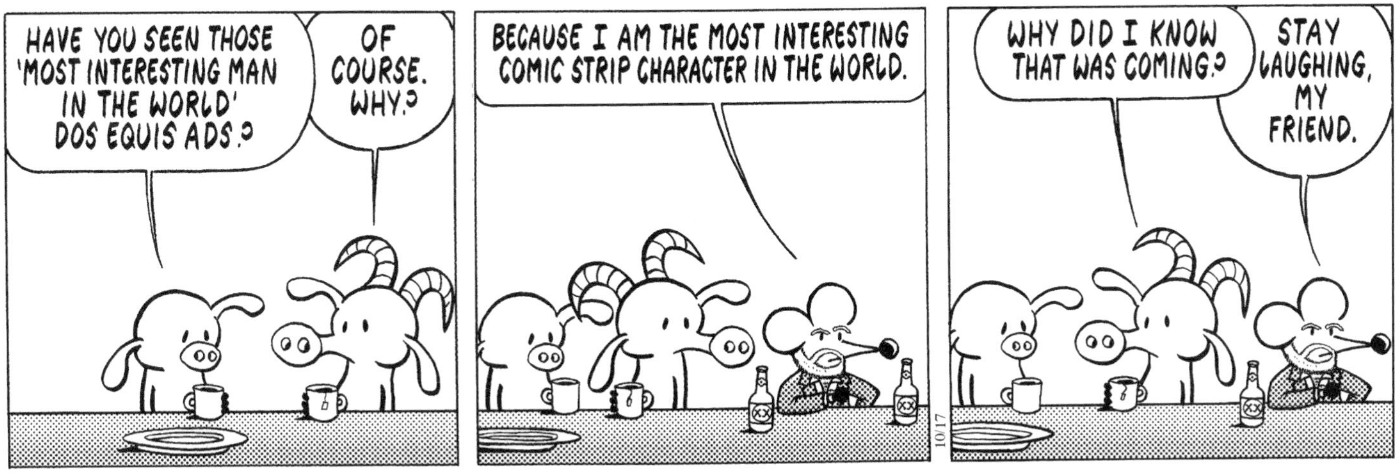
HAVE YOU SEEN THOSE 'MOST INTERESTING MAN IN THE WORLD' DOS EQUIS ADS?
OF COURSE. WHY?
BECAUSE I AM THE MOST INTERESTING COMIC STRIP CHARACTER IN THE WORLD.
10/17
WHY DID I KNOW THAT WAS COMING?
STAY LAUGHING, MY FRIEND.

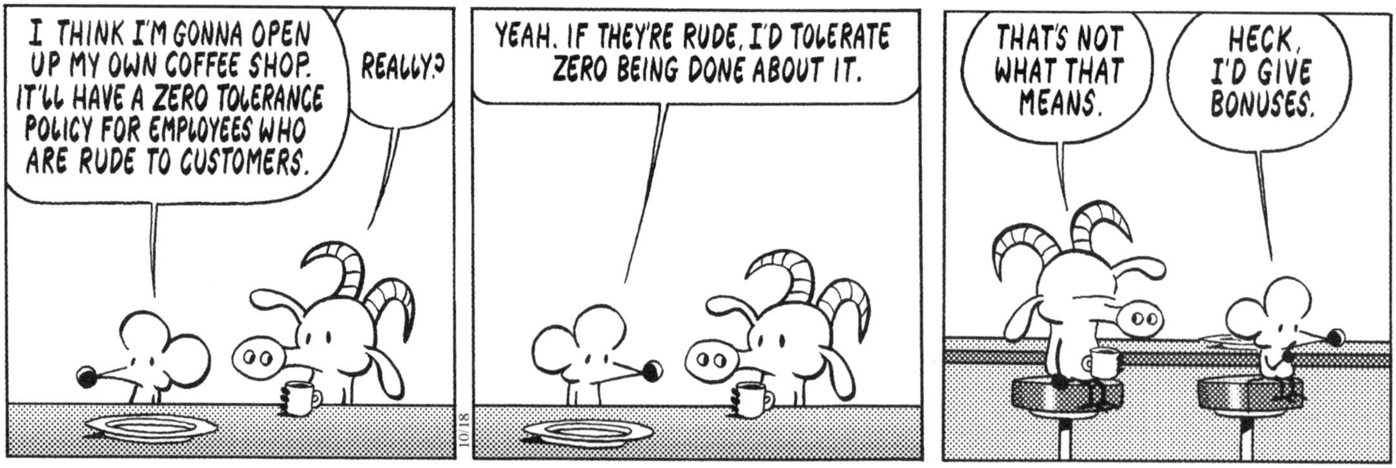
I THINK I'M GONNA OPEN UP MY OWN COFFEE SHOP. IT'LL HAVE A ZERO TOLERANCE POLICY FOR EMPLOYEES WHO ARE RUDE TO CUSTOMERS.
REALLY?
10/18
YEAH. IF THEY'RE RUDE, I'D TOLERATE ZERO BEING DONE ABOUT IT.
THAT'S NOT WHAT THAT MEANS.
HECK, I'D GIVE BONUSES.

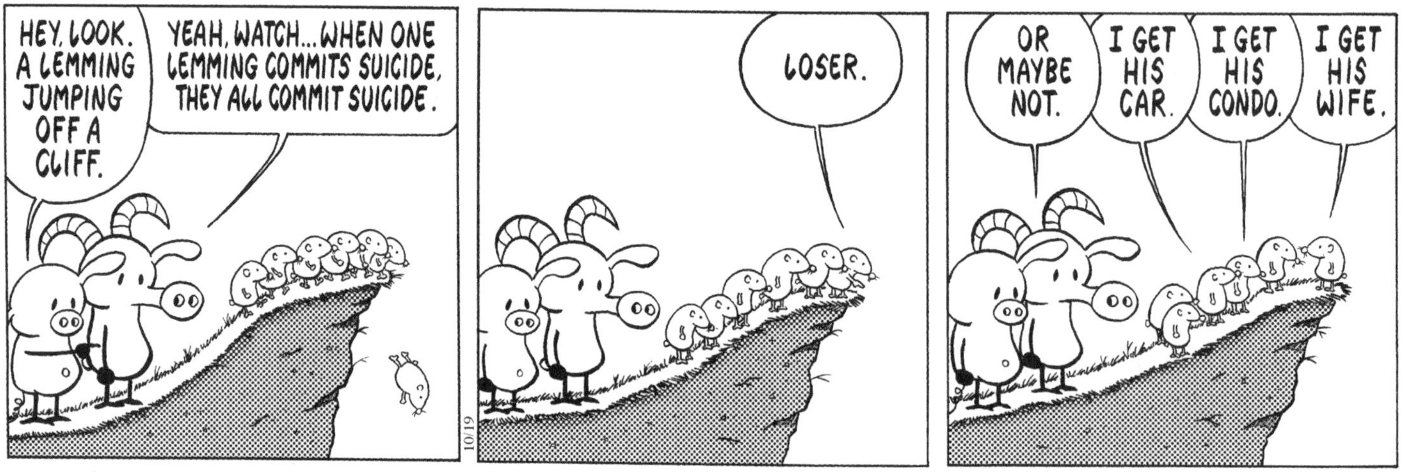
HEY, LOOK. A LEMMING JUMPING OFF A CLIFF.
YEAH, WATCH... WHEN ONE LEMMING COMMITS SUICIDE, THEY ALL COMMIT SUICIDE.
10/19
LOSER.
OR MAYBE NOT.
I GET HIS CAR.
I GET HIS CONDO.
I GET HIS WIFE.

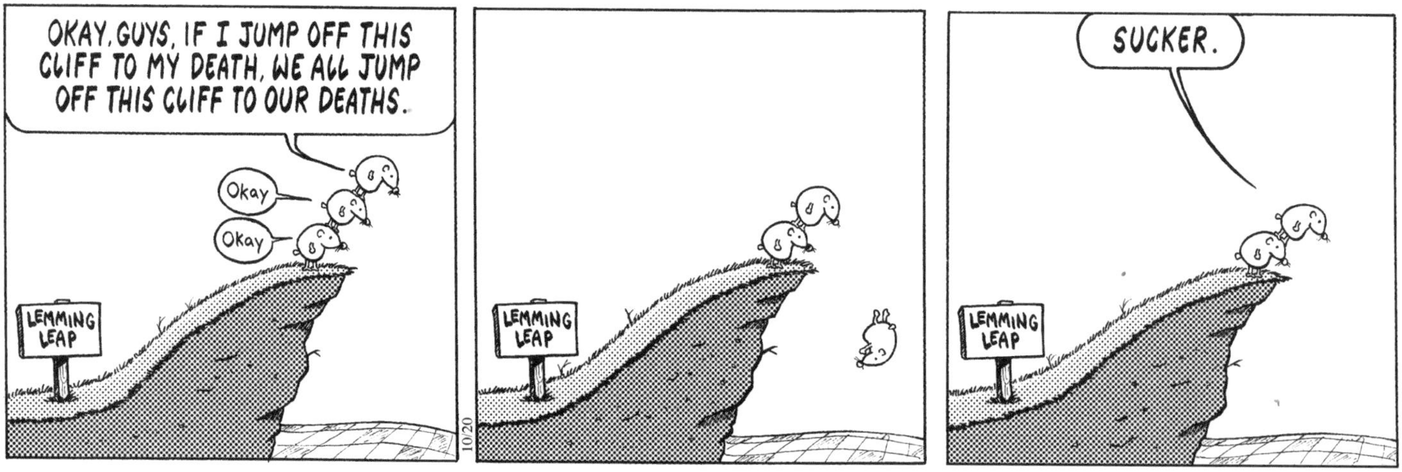
OKAY, GUYS, IF I JUMP OFF THIS CLIFF TO MY DEATH, WE ALL JUMP OFF THIS CLIFF TO OUR DEATHS.
Okay
Okay
LEMMING LEAP
10/20
LEMMING LEAP
SUCKER.
LEMMING LEAP

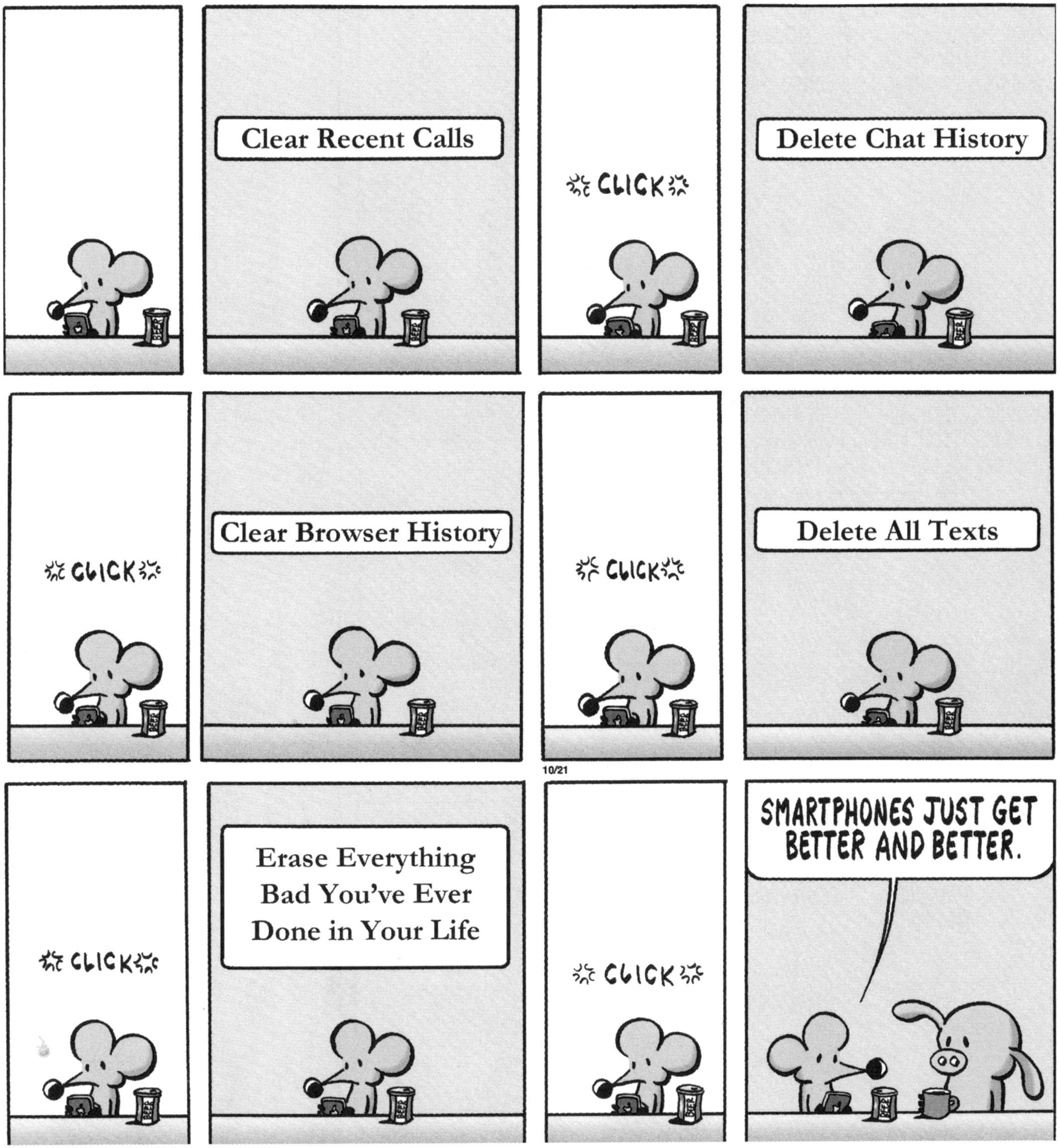
Clear Recent Calls
CLICK
Delete Chat History
CLICK
Clear Browser History
CLICK
Delete All Texts
10/21
CLICK
Erase Everything Bad You've Ever Done in Your Life
CLICK
SMARTPHONES JUST GET BETTER AND BETTER.

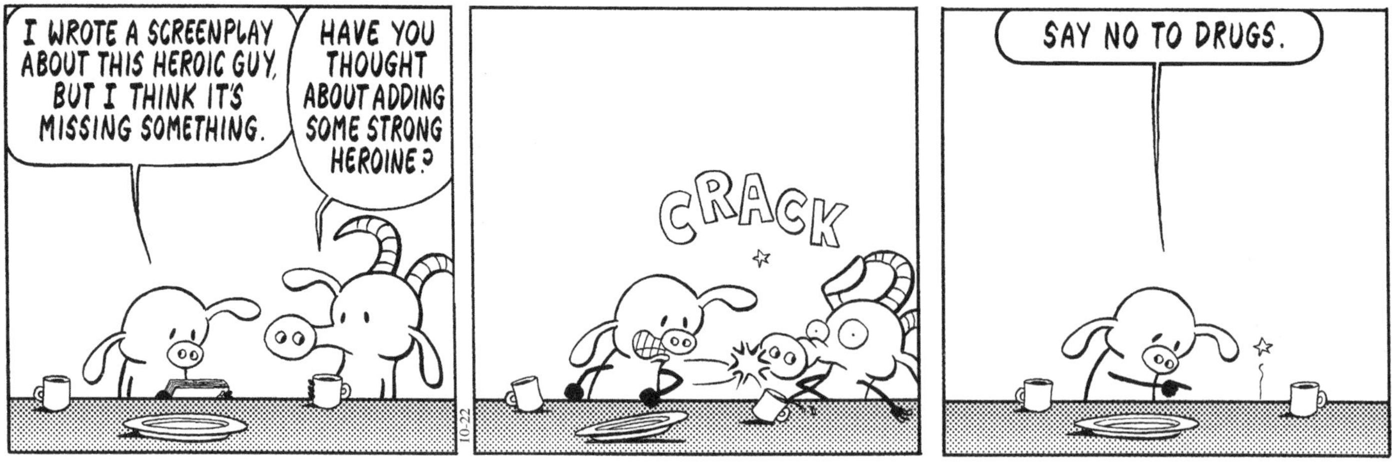
I WROTE A SCREENPLAY ABOUT THIS HEROIC GUY, BUT I THINK IT'S MISSING SOMETHING.
HAVE YOU THOUGHT ABOUT ADDING SOME STRONG HEROINE?
CRACK
SAY NO TO DRUGS.
10-22

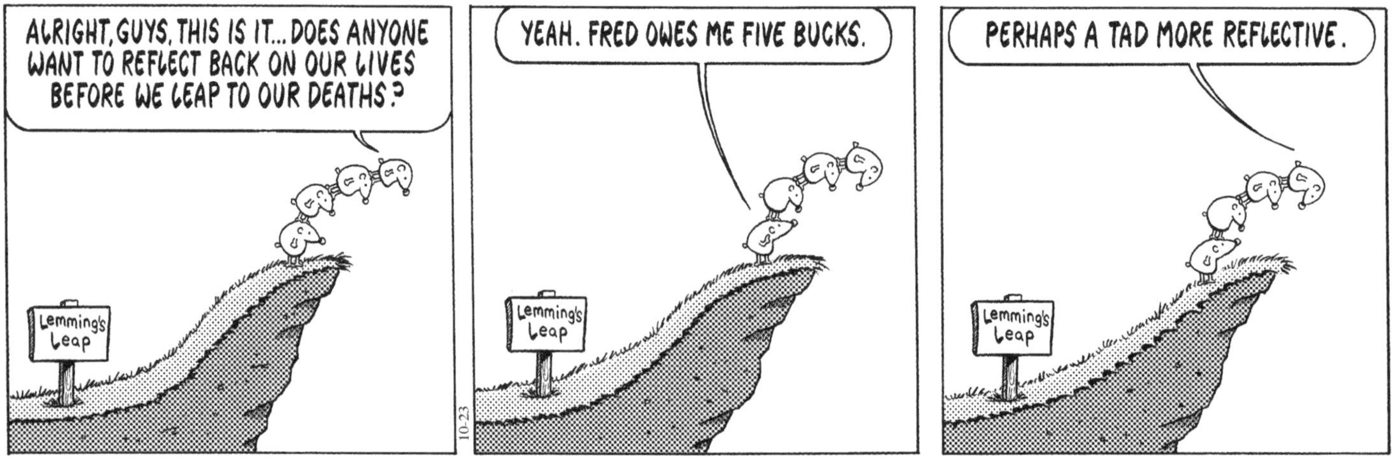
ALRIGHT, GUYS, THIS IS IT... DOES ANYONE WANT TO REFLECT BACK ON OUR LIVES BEFORE WE LEAP TO OUR DEATHS?
Lemming's Leap
YEAH. FRED OWES ME FIVE BUCKS.
PERHAPS A TAD MORE REFLECTIVE.
10-23

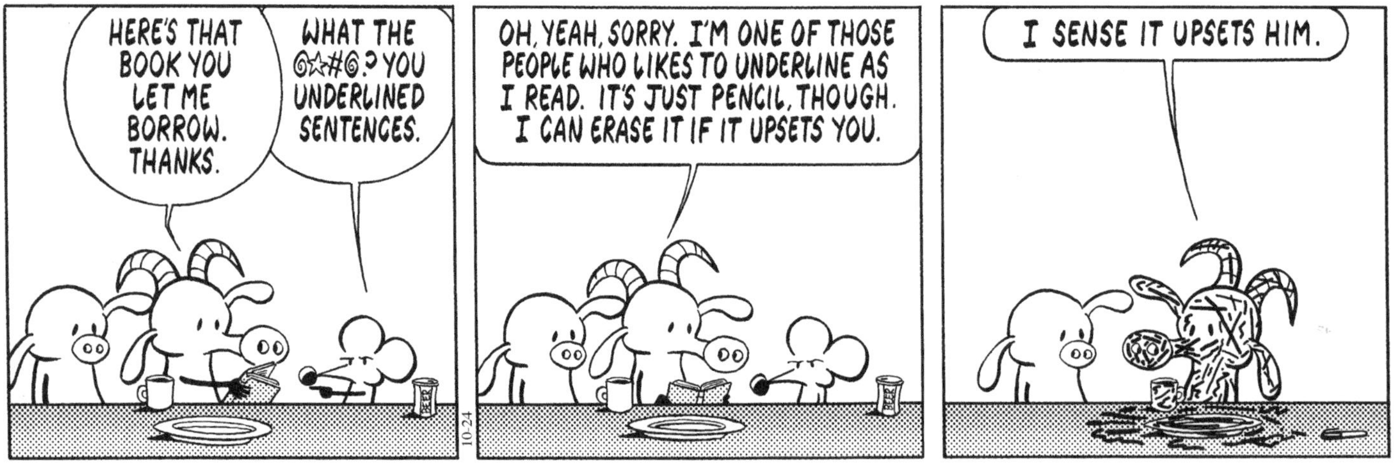
HERE'S THAT BOOK YOU LET ME BORROW. THANKS.
WHAT THE @☆#@? YOU UNDERLINED SENTENCES.
BEER
OH, YEAH, SORRY. I'M ONE OF THOSE PEOPLE WHO LIKES TO UNDERLINE AS I READ. IT'S JUST PENCIL, THOUGH. I CAN ERASE IT IF IT UPSETS YOU.
I SENSE IT UPSETS HIM.
10-24

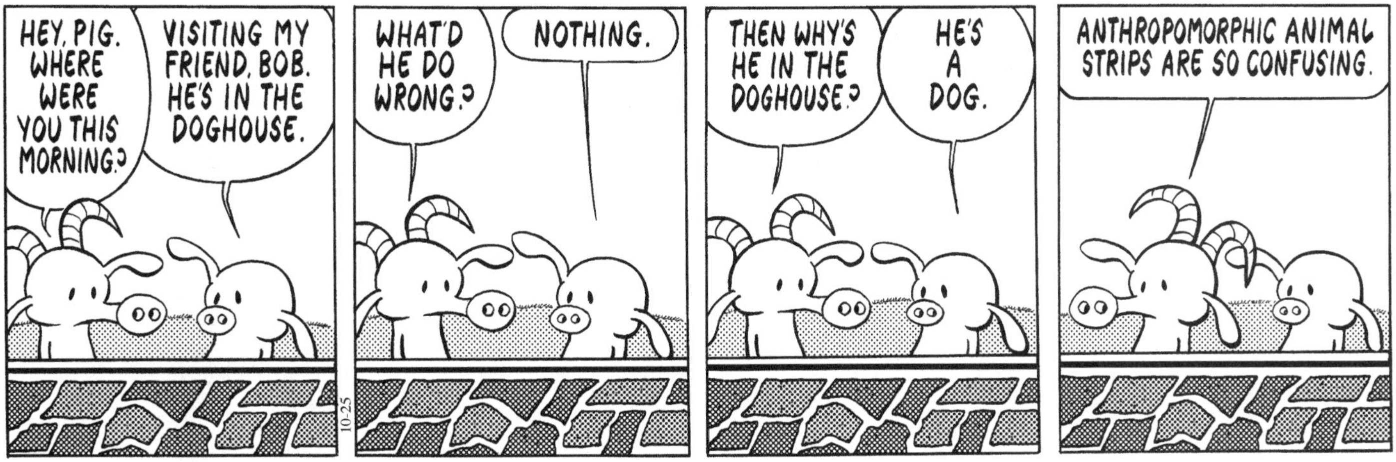
HEY, PIG. WHERE WERE YOU THIS MORNING?
VISITING MY FRIEND, BOB. HE'S IN THE DOGHOUSE.
WHAT'D HE DO WRONG?
NOTHING.
THEN WHY'S HE IN THE DOGHOUSE?
HE'S A DOG.
ANTHROPOMORPHIC ANIMAL STRIPS ARE SO CONFUSING.

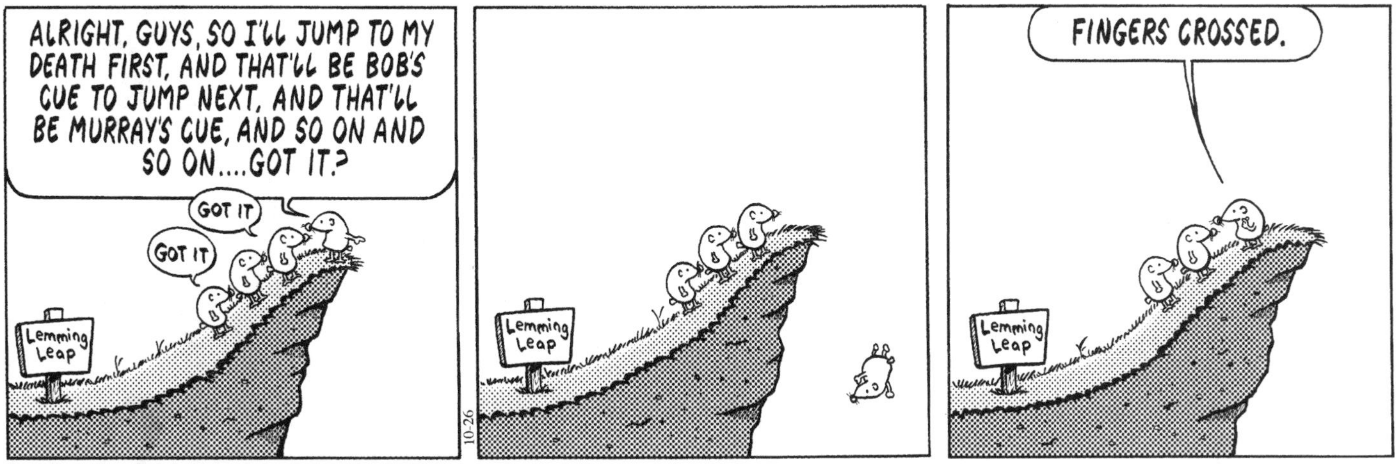
ALRIGHT, GUYS, SO I'LL JUMP TO MY DEATH FIRST, AND THAT'LL BE BOB'S CUE TO JUMP NEXT, AND THAT'LL BE MURRAY'S CUE, AND SO ON AND SO ON....GOT IT?
GOT IT
GOT IT
Lemming Leap
Lemming Leap
Lemming Leap
FINGERS CROSSED.

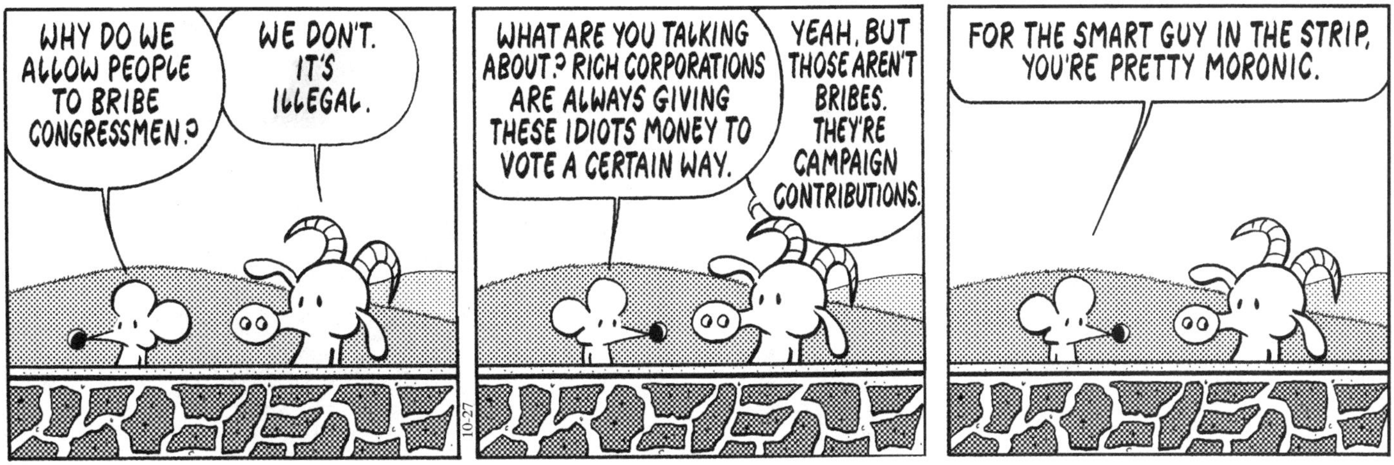
WHY DO WE ALLOW PEOPLE TO BRIBE CONGRESSMEN?
WE DON'T. IT'S ILLEGAL.
WHAT ARE YOU TALKING ABOUT? RICH CORPORATIONS ARE ALWAYS GIVING THESE IDIOTS MONEY TO VOTE A CERTAIN WAY.
YEAH, BUT THOSE AREN'T BRIBES. THEY'RE CAMPAIGN CONTRIBUTIONS.
FOR THE SMART GUY IN THE STRIP, YOU'RE PRETTY MORONIC.

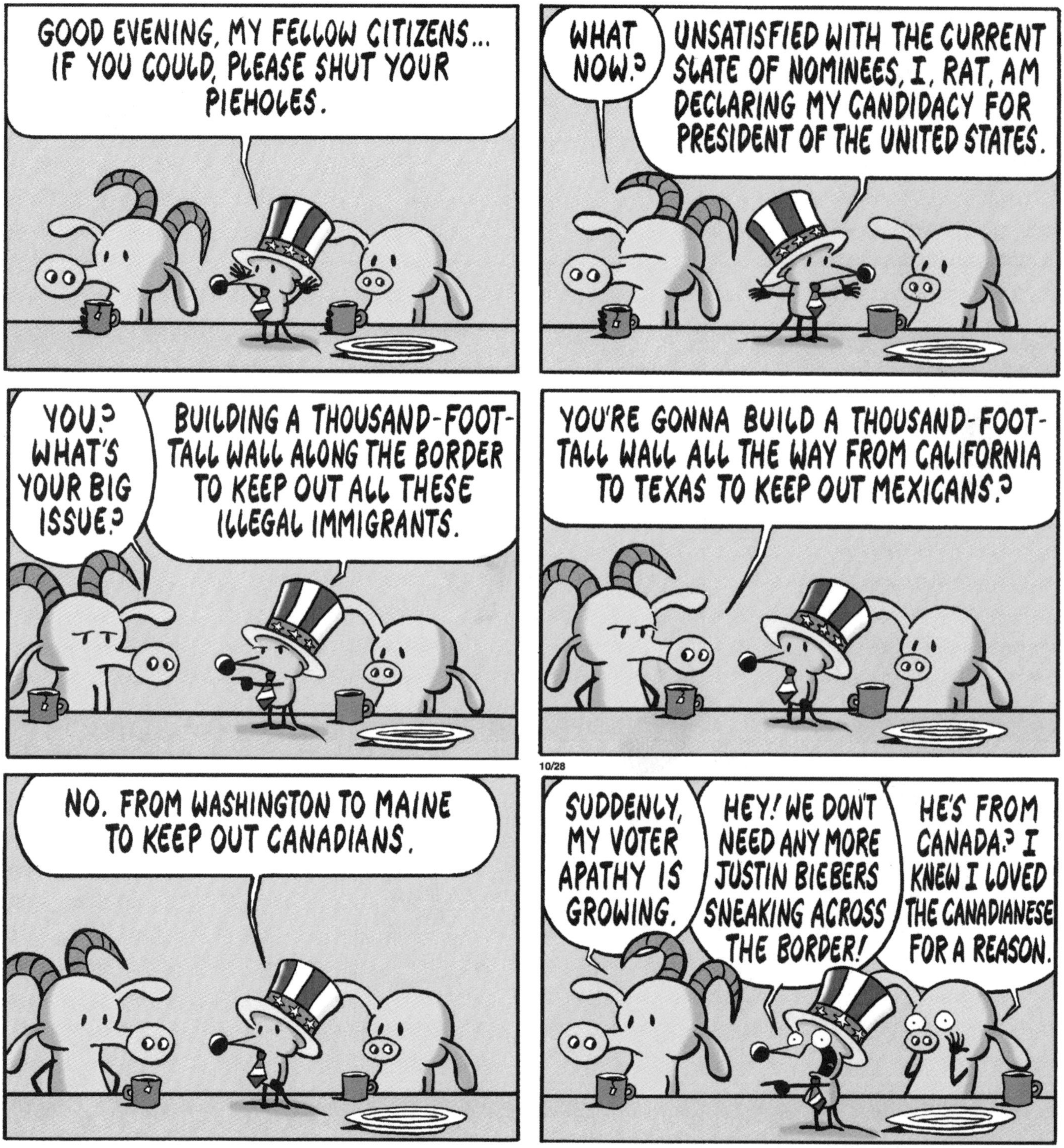
GOOD EVENING, MY FELLOW CITIZENS... IF YOU COULD, PLEASE SHUT YOUR PIEHOLES.
WHAT NOW?
UNSATISFIED WITH THE CURRENT SLATE OF NOMINEES, I, RAT, AM DECLARING MY CANDIDACY FOR PRESIDENT OF THE UNITED STATES.
YOU? WHAT'S YOUR BIG ISSUE?
BUILDING A THOUSAND-FOOT-TALL WALL ALONG THE BORDER TO KEEP OUT ALL THESE ILLEGAL IMMIGRANTS.
YOU'RE GONNA BUILD A THOUSAND-FOOT-TALL WALL ALL THE WAY FROM CALIFORNIA TO TEXAS TO KEEP OUT MEXICANS?
10/28
NO. FROM WASHINGTON TO MAINE TO KEEP OUT CANADIANS.
SUDDENLY, MY VOTER APATHY IS GROWING.
HEY! WE DON'T NEED ANY MORE JUSTIN BIEBERS SNEAKING ACROSS THE BORDER!
HE'S FROM CANADA? I KNEW I LOVED THE CANADIANESE FOR A REASON.

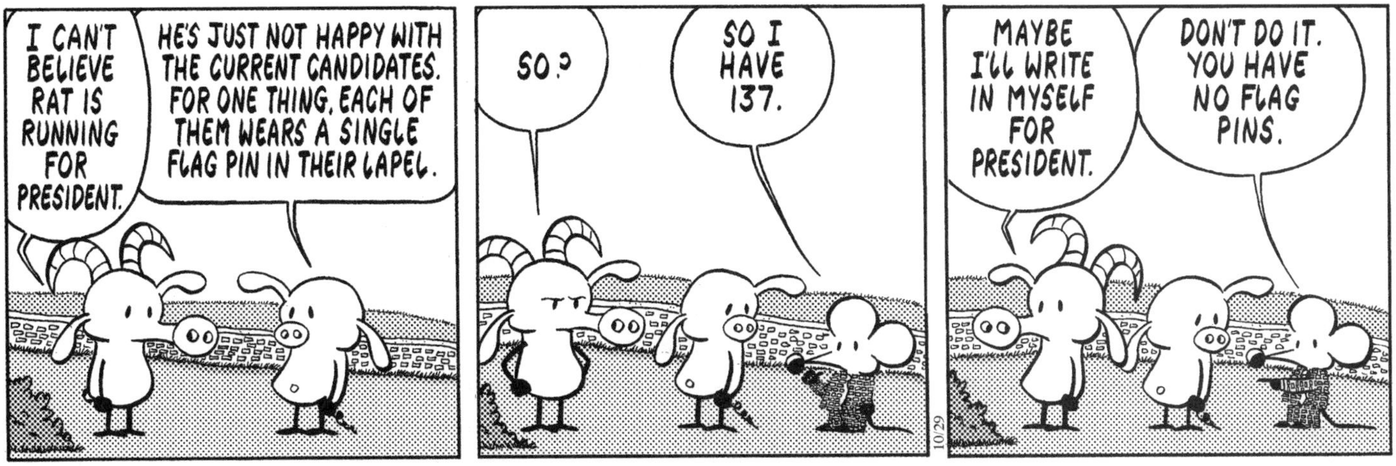
I CAN'T BELIEVE RAT IS RUNNING FOR PRESIDENT.
HE'S JUST NOT HAPPY WITH THE CURRENT CANDIDATES. FOR ONE THING, EACH OF THEM WEARS A SINGLE FLAG PIN IN THEIR LAPEL.
SO?
SO I HAVE 137.
MAYBE I'LL WRITE IN MYSELF FOR PRESIDENT.
DON'T DO IT. YOU HAVE NO FLAG PINS.
10/29

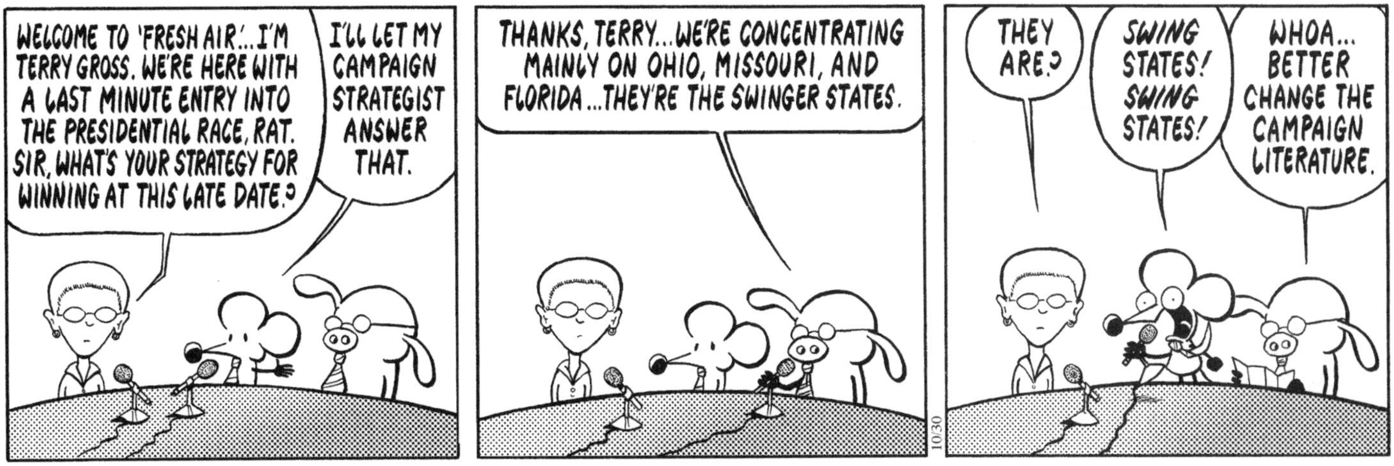
WELCOME TO 'FRESH AIR'...I'M TERRY GROSS. WE'RE HERE WITH A LAST MINUTE ENTRY INTO THE PRESIDENTIAL RACE, RAT. SIR, WHAT'S YOUR STRATEGY FOR WINNING AT THIS LATE DATE?
I'LL LET MY CAMPAIGN STRATEGIST ANSWER THAT.
THANKS, TERRY...WE'RE CONCENTRATING MAINLY ON OHIO, MISSOURI, AND FLORIDA...THEY'RE THE SWINGER STATES.
THEY ARE?
SWING STATES! SWING STATES!
WHOA... BETTER CHANGE THE CAMPAIGN LITERATURE.
10/30

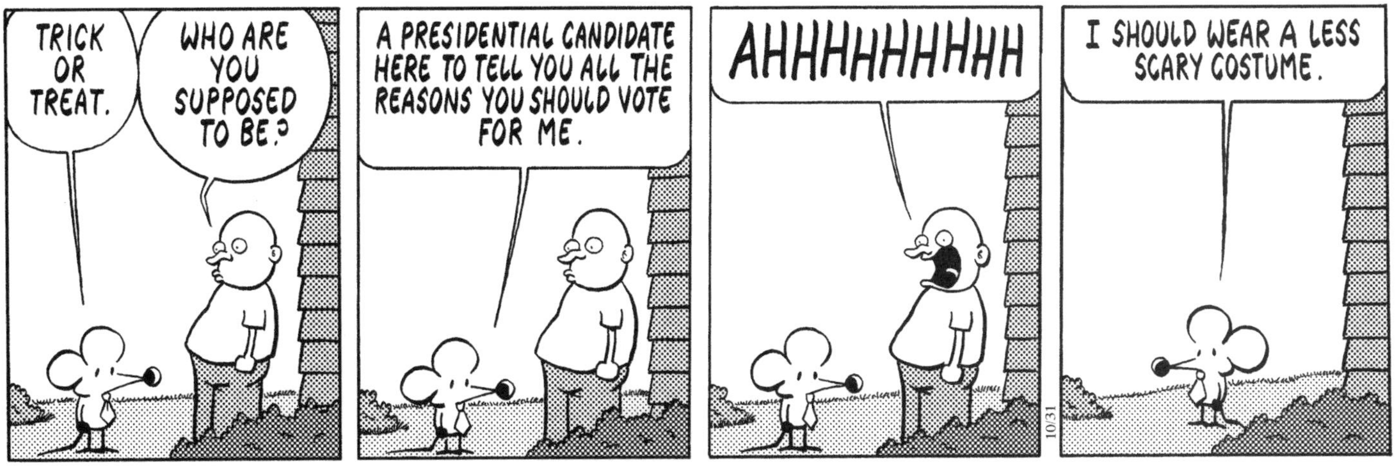
TRICK OR TREAT.
WHO ARE YOU SUPPOSED TO BE?
A PRESIDENTIAL CANDIDATE HERE TO TELL YOU ALL THE REASONS YOU SHOULD VOTE FOR ME.
AHHHHHHHHH
I SHOULD WEAR A LESS SCARY COSTUME.
10/31

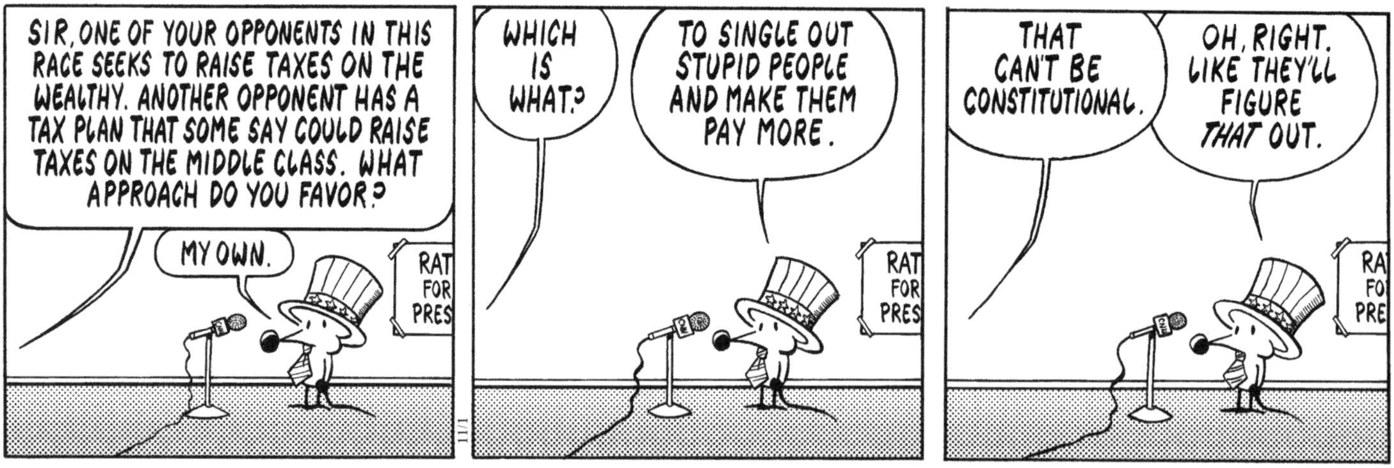
SIR, ONE OF YOUR OPPONENTS IN THIS RACE SEEKS TO RAISE TAXES ON THE WEALTHY. ANOTHER OPPONENT HAS A TAX PLAN THAT SOME SAY COULD RAISE TAXES ON THE MIDDLE CLASS. WHAT APPROACH DO YOU FAVOR?
MY OWN.
WHICH IS WHAT?
TO SINGLE OUT STUPID PEOPLE AND MAKE THEM PAY MORE.
THAT CAN'T BE CONSTITUTIONAL.
OH, RIGHT. LIKE THEY'LL FIGURE *THAT* OUT.
11/1

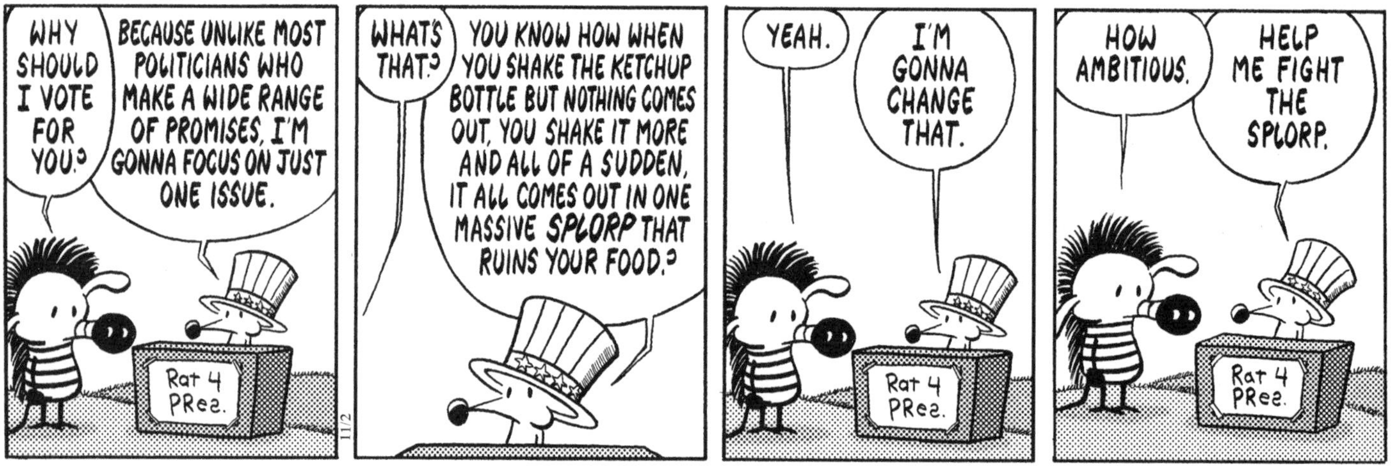
WHY SHOULD I VOTE FOR YOU?
BECAUSE UNLIKE MOST POLITICIANS WHO MAKE A WIDE RANGE OF PROMISES, I'M GONNA FOCUS ON JUST ONE ISSUE.
Rat 4 PRez.
WHAT'S THAT?
YOU KNOW HOW WHEN YOU SHAKE THE KETCHUP BOTTLE BUT NOTHING COMES OUT, YOU SHAKE IT MORE AND ALL OF A SUDDEN, IT ALL COMES OUT IN ONE MASSIVE *SPLORP* THAT RUINS YOUR FOOD?
YEAH.
I'M GONNA CHANGE THAT.
HOW AMBITIOUS.
HELP ME FIGHT THE SPLORP.
11/2

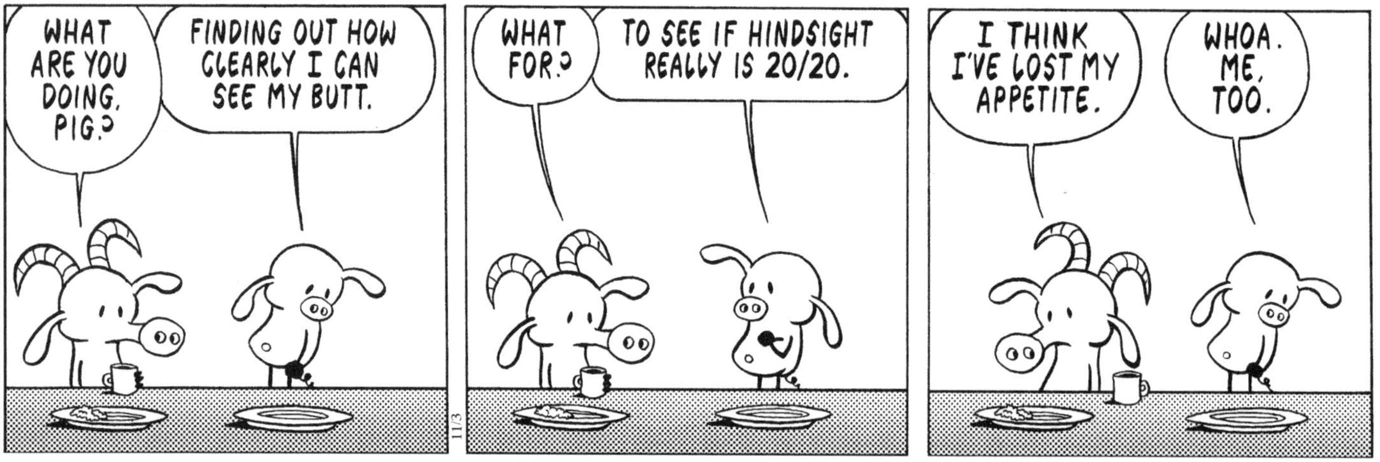
WHAT ARE YOU DOING, PIG?
FINDING OUT HOW CLEARLY I CAN SEE MY BUTT.
WHAT FOR?
TO SEE IF HINDSIGHT REALLY IS 20/20.
I THINK I'VE LOST MY APPETITE.
WHOA. ME, TOO.
11/3

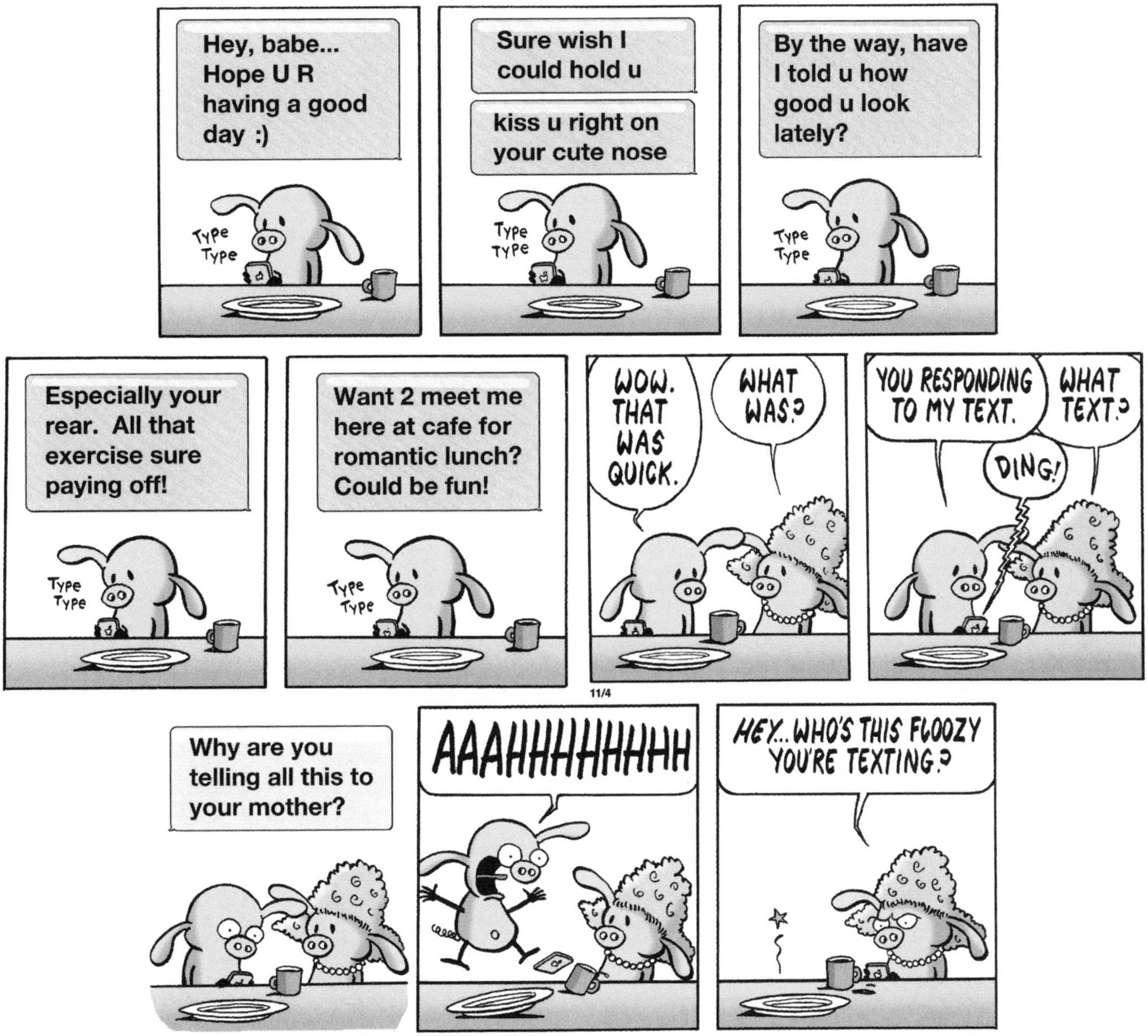
Hey, babe...
Hope U R
having a good
day :)
Type
Type
Sure wish I
could hold u
kiss u right on
your cute nose
Type
Type
By the way, have
I told u how
good u look
lately?
Type
Type
Especially your
rear. All that
exercise sure
paying off!
Type
Type
Want 2 meet me
here at cafe for
romantic lunch?
Could be fun!
Type
Type
WOW. THAT WAS QUICK.
WHAT WAS?
YOU RESPONDING TO MY TEXT.
WHAT TEXT?
DING!
11/4
Why are you
telling all this to
your mother?
AAAHHHHHHHH
HEY...WHO'S THIS FLOOZY YOU'RE TEXTING?

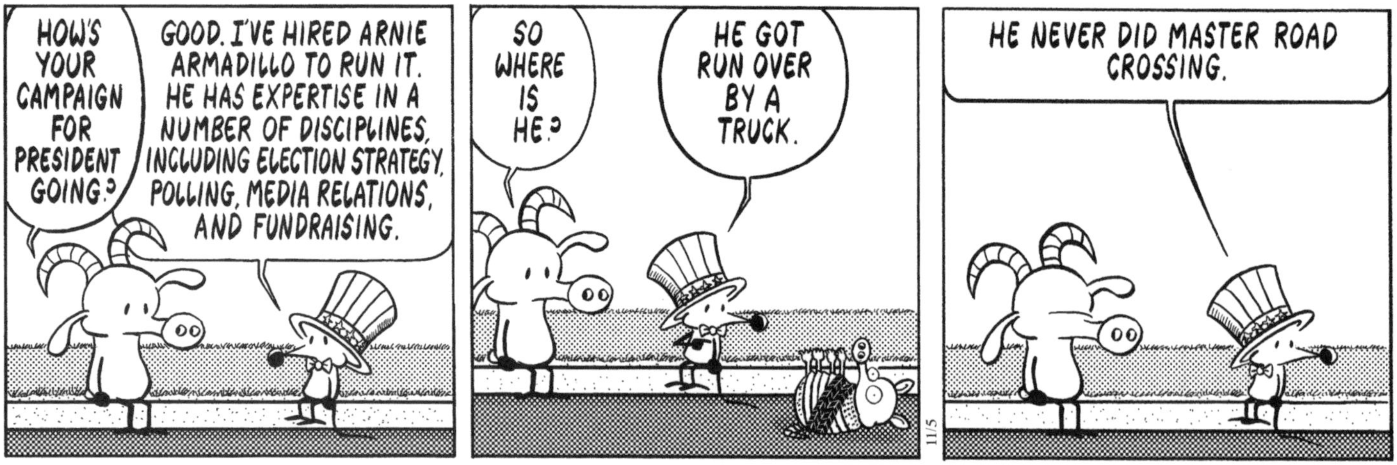
HOW'S YOUR CAMPAIGN FOR PRESIDENT GOING?
GOOD. I'VE HIRED ARNIE ARMADILLO TO RUN IT. HE HAS EXPERTISE IN A NUMBER OF DISCIPLINES, INCLUDING ELECTION STRATEGY, POLLING, MEDIA RELATIONS, AND FUNDRAISING.
SO WHERE IS HE?
HE GOT RUN OVER BY A TRUCK.
HE NEVER DID MASTER ROAD CROSSING.
11/5

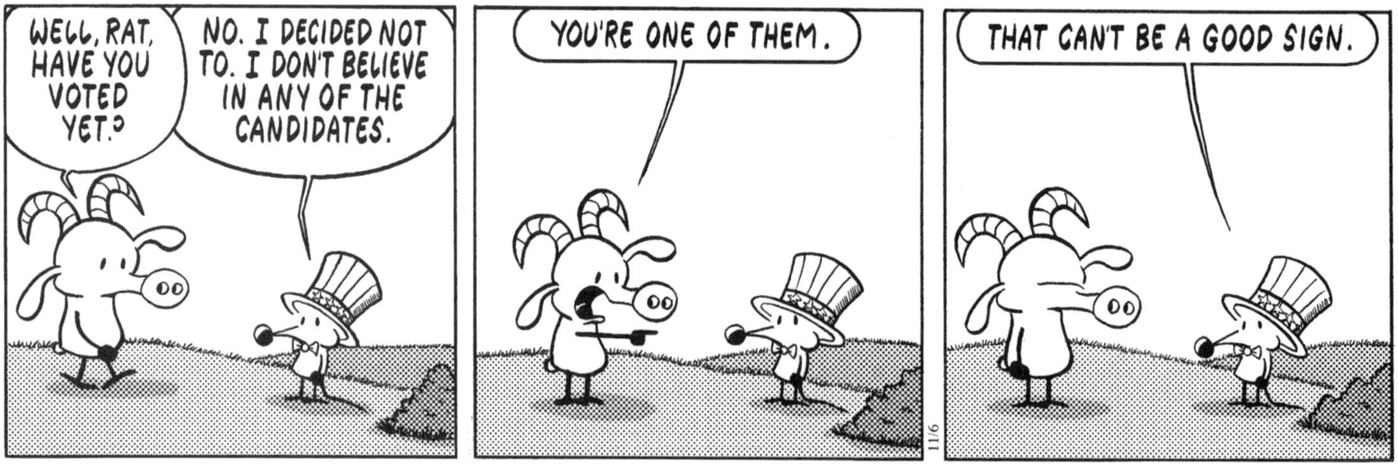
WELL, RAT, HAVE YOU VOTED YET?
NO. I DECIDED NOT TO. I DON'T BELIEVE IN ANY OF THE CANDIDATES.
YOU'RE ONE OF THEM.
THAT CAN'T BE A GOOD SIGN.
11/6

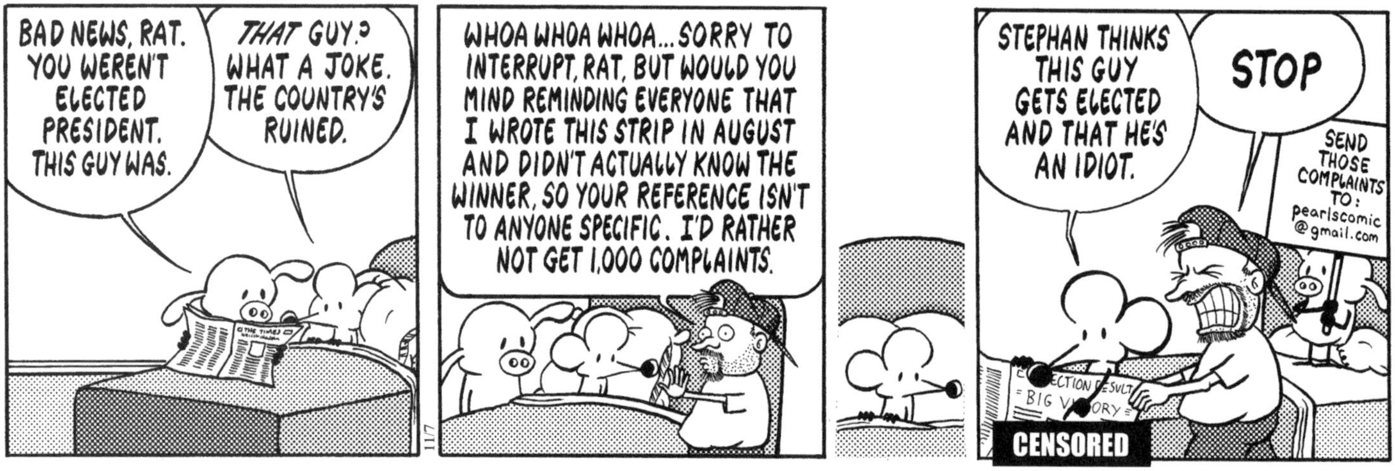
BAD NEWS, RAT. YOU WEREN'T ELECTED PRESIDENT. THIS GUY WAS.
THAT GUY? WHAT A JOKE. THE COUNTRY'S RUINED.
11/7
WHOA WHOA WHOA... SORRY TO INTERRUPT, RAT, BUT WOULD YOU MIND REMINDING EVERYONE THAT I WROTE THIS STRIP IN AUGUST AND DIDN'T ACTUALLY KNOW THE WINNER, SO YOUR REFERENCE ISN'T TO ANYONE SPECIFIC. I'D RATHER NOT GET 1,000 COMPLAINTS.
STEPHAN THINKS THIS GUY GETS ELECTED AND THAT HE'S AN IDIOT.
STOP
SEND THOSE COMPLAINTS TO: pearlscomic@gmail.com
CENSORED

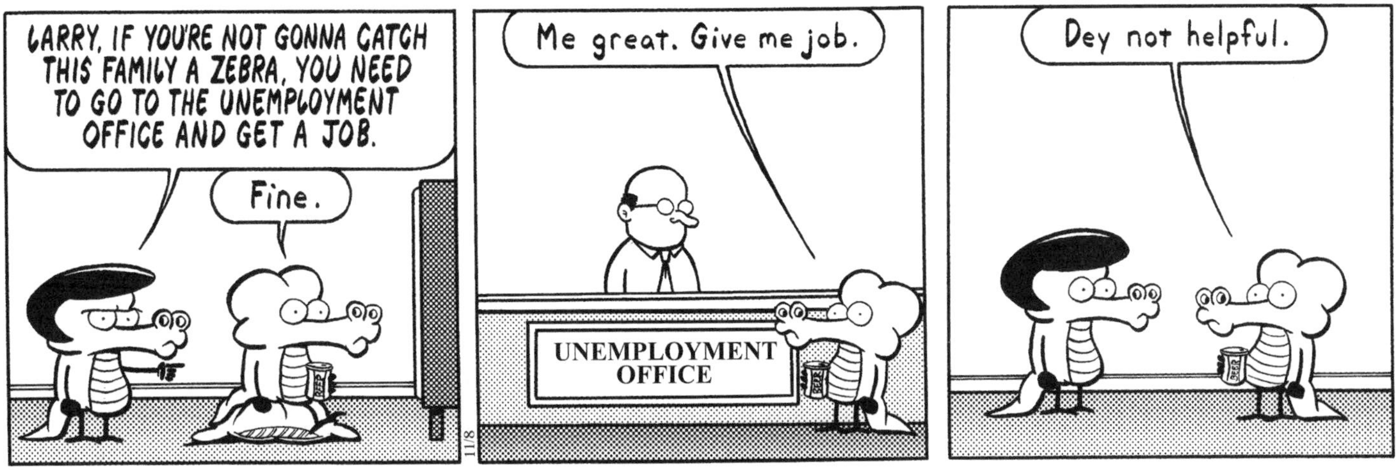
LARRY, IF YOU'RE NOT GONNA CATCH THIS FAMILY A ZEBRA, YOU NEED TO GO TO THE UNEMPLOYMENT OFFICE AND GET A JOB.
Fine.
11/8
Me great. Give me job.
UNEMPLOYMENT OFFICE
Dey not helpful.

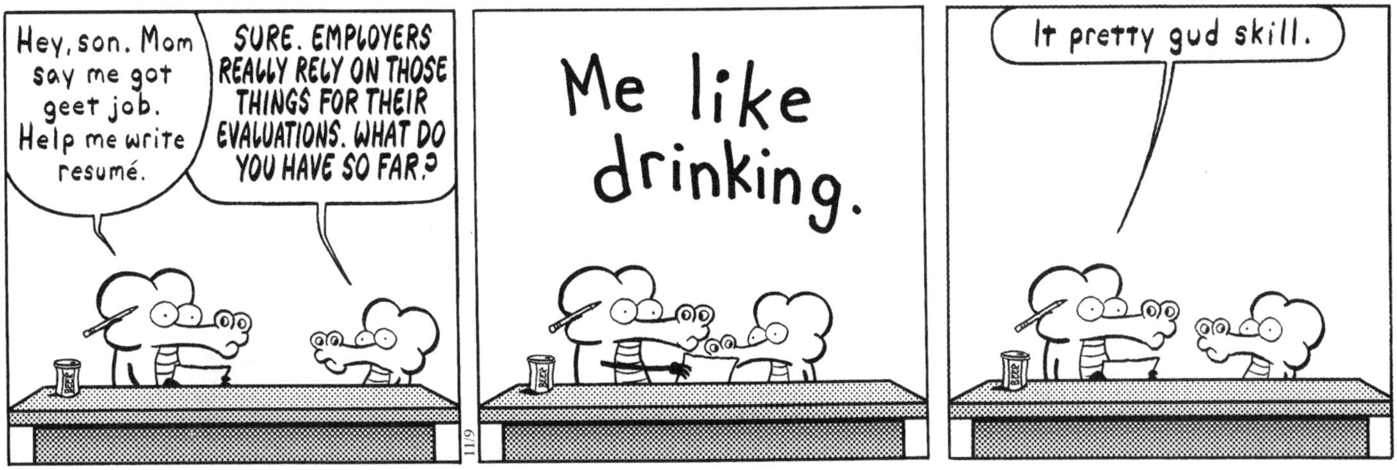
Hey, son. Mom say me got geet job. Help me write resumé.
SURE. EMPLOYERS REALLY RELY ON THOSE THINGS FOR THEIR EVALUATIONS. WHAT DO YOU HAVE SO FAR?
11/9
Me like drinking.
It pretty gud skill.

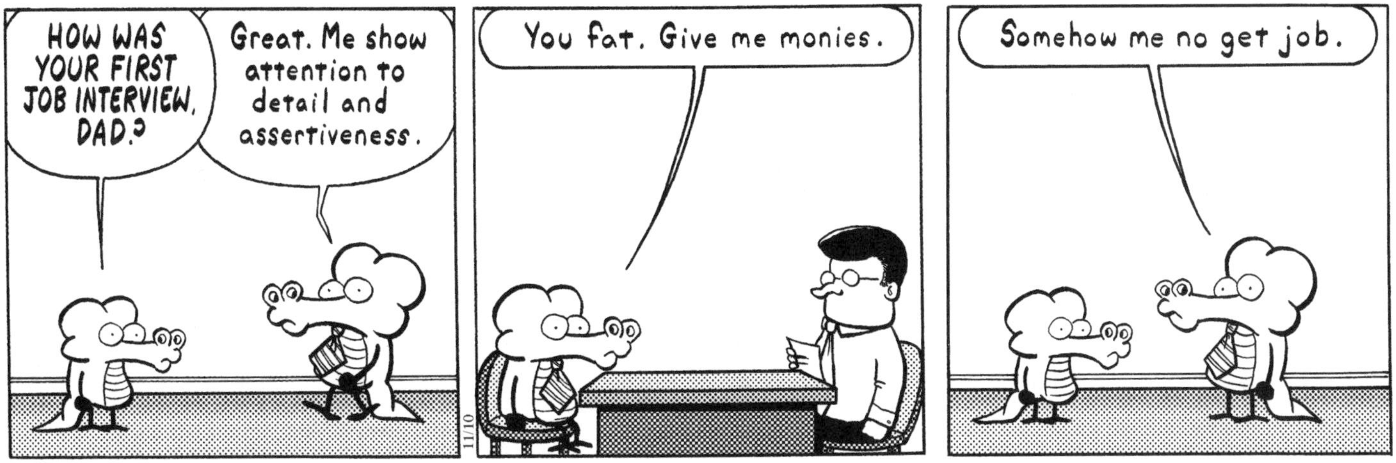
HOW WAS YOUR FIRST JOB INTERVIEW, DAD?
Great. Me show attention to detail and assertiveness.
11/10
You fat. Give me monies.
Somehow me no get job.

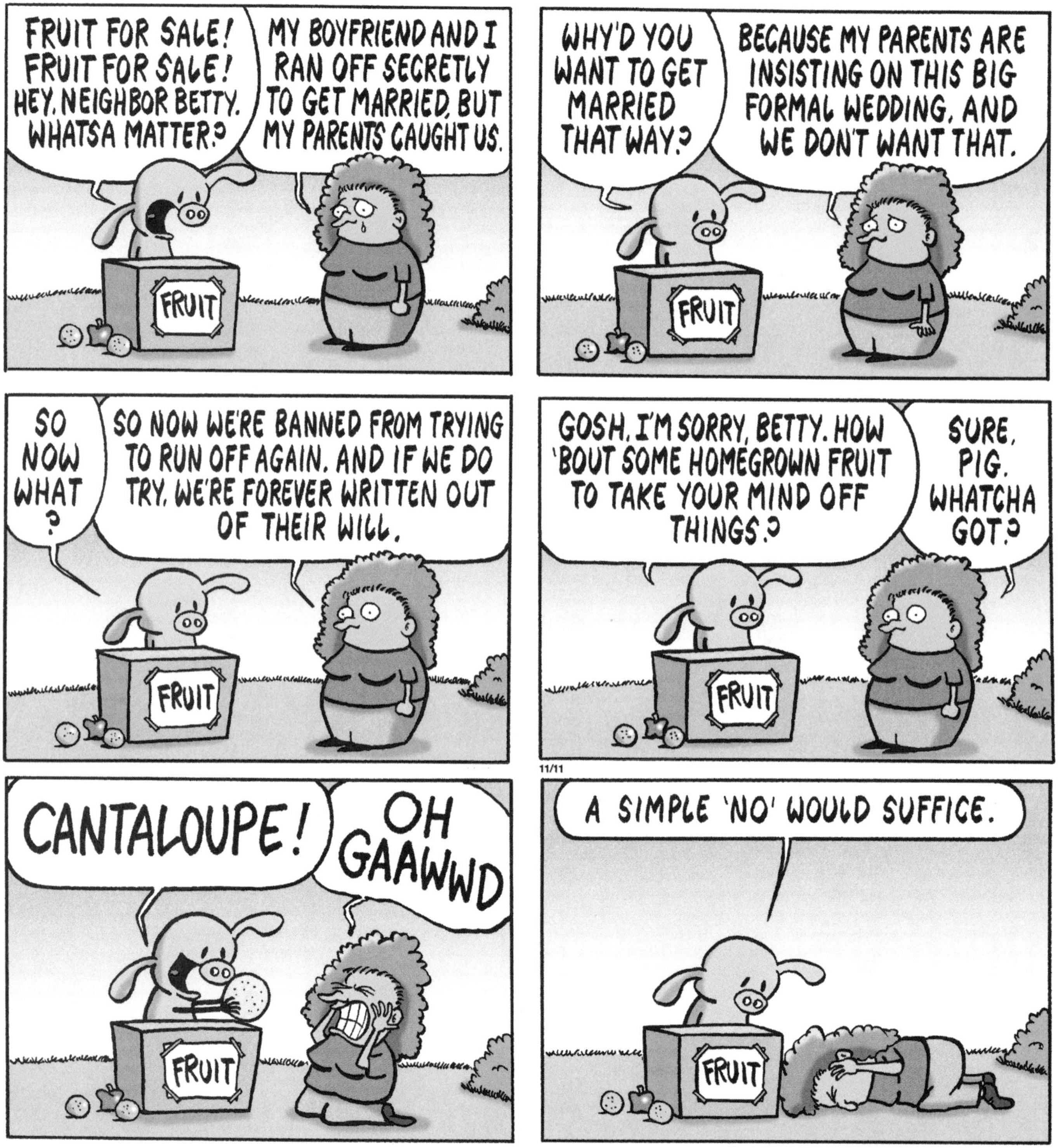
FRUIT FOR SALE! FRUIT FOR SALE! HEY, NEIGHBOR BETTY. WHATSA MATTER?
MY BOYFRIEND AND I RAN OFF SECRETLY TO GET MARRIED, BUT MY PARENTS CAUGHT US.
FRUIT
WHY'D YOU WANT TO GET MARRIED THAT WAY?
BECAUSE MY PARENTS ARE INSISTING ON THIS BIG FORMAL WEDDING, AND WE DON'T WANT THAT.
FRUIT
SO NOW WHAT?
SO NOW WE'RE BANNED FROM TRYING TO RUN OFF AGAIN, AND IF WE DO TRY, WE'RE FOREVER WRITTEN OUT OF THEIR WILL.
FRUIT
GOSH, I'M SORRY, BETTY. HOW 'BOUT SOME HOMEGROWN FRUIT TO TAKE YOUR MIND OFF THINGS?
SURE, PIG. WHATCHA GOT?
FRUIT
11/11
CANTALOUPE!
OH GAAWWD
FRUIT
A SIMPLE 'NO' WOULD SUFFICE.
FRUIT

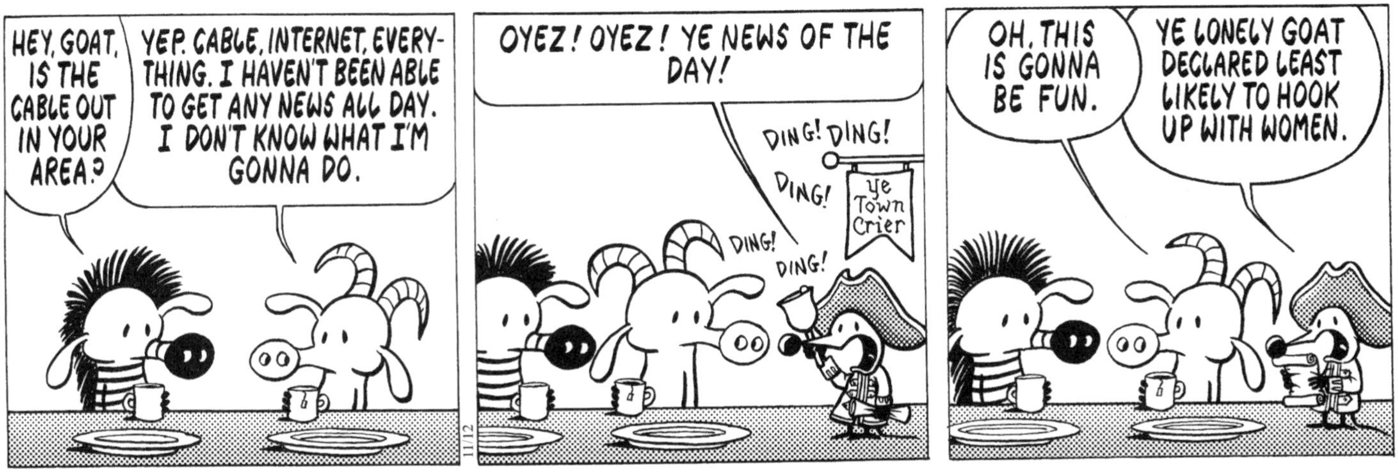
HEY, GOAT, IS THE CABLE OUT IN YOUR AREA?
YEP. CABLE, INTERNET, EVERYTHING. I HAVEN'T BEEN ABLE TO GET ANY NEWS ALL DAY. I DON'T KNOW WHAT I'M GONNA DO.
11/12
OYEZ! OYEZ! YE NEWS OF THE DAY!
DING! DING! DING! DING! DING!
ye Town Crier
OH, THIS IS GONNA BE FUN.
YE LONELY GOAT DECLARED LEAST LIKELY TO HOOK UP WITH WOMEN.

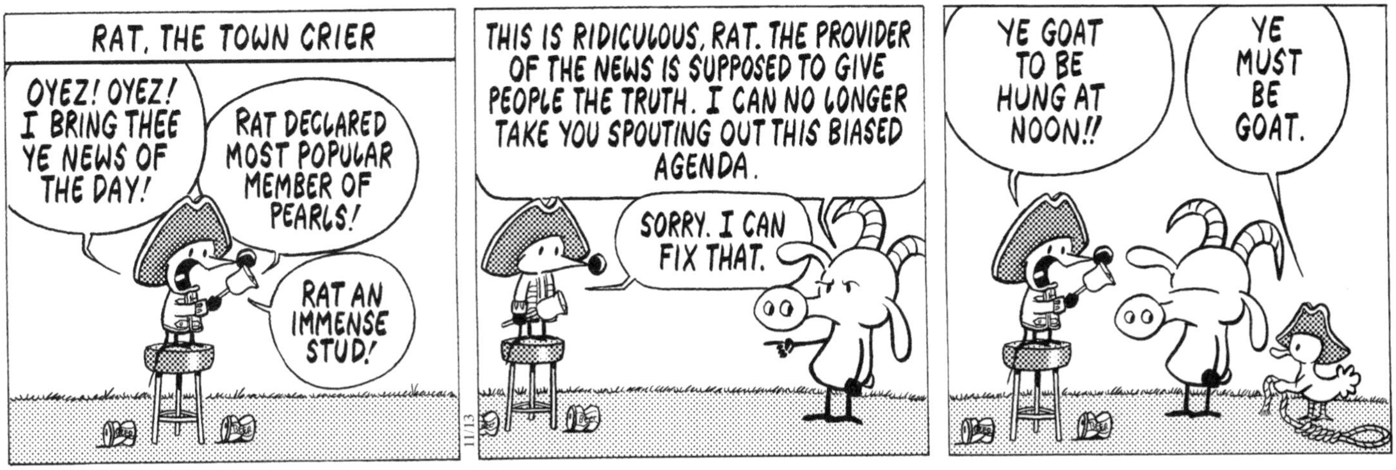
RAT, THE TOWN CRIER
OYEZ! OYEZ! I BRING THEE YE NEWS OF THE DAY!
RAT DECLARED MOST POPULAR MEMBER OF PEARLS!
RAT AN IMMENSE STUD!
11/13
THIS IS RIDICULOUS, RAT. THE PROVIDER OF THE NEWS IS SUPPOSED TO GIVE PEOPLE THE TRUTH. I CAN NO LONGER TAKE YOU SPOUTING OUT THIS BIASED AGENDA.
SORRY. I CAN FIX THAT.
YE GOAT TO BE HUNG AT NOON!!
YE MUST BE GOAT.

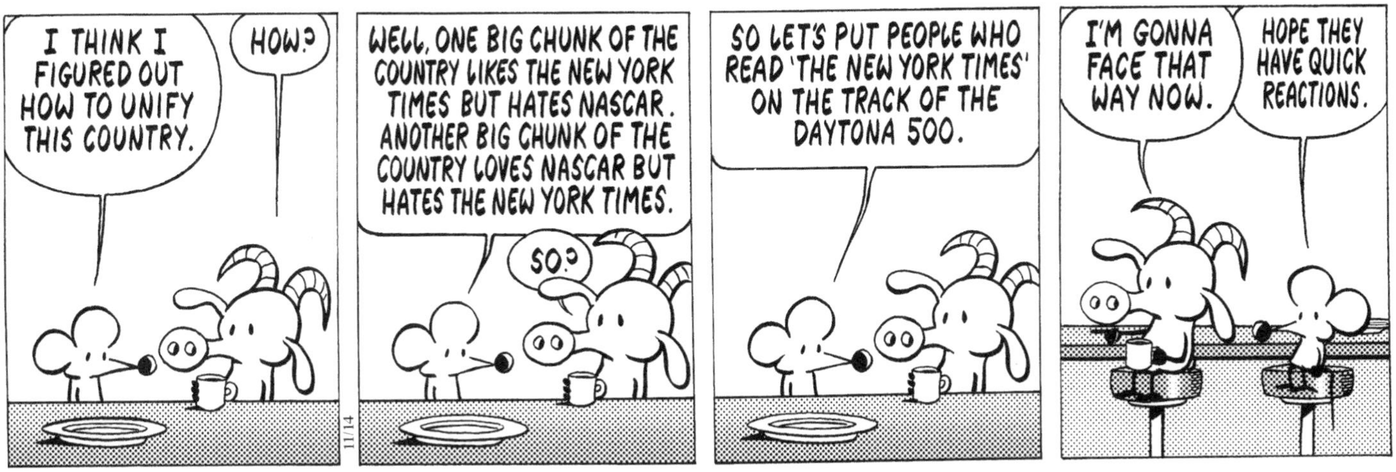
I THINK I FIGURED OUT HOW TO UNIFY THIS COUNTRY.
HOW?
11/14
WELL, ONE BIG CHUNK OF THE COUNTRY LIKES THE NEW YORK TIMES BUT HATES NASCAR. ANOTHER BIG CHUNK OF THE COUNTRY LOVES NASCAR BUT HATES THE NEW YORK TIMES.
SO?
SO LET'S PUT PEOPLE WHO READ 'THE NEW YORK TIMES' ON THE TRACK OF THE DAYTONA 500.
I'M GONNA FACE THAT WAY NOW.
HOPE THEY HAVE QUICK REACTIONS.

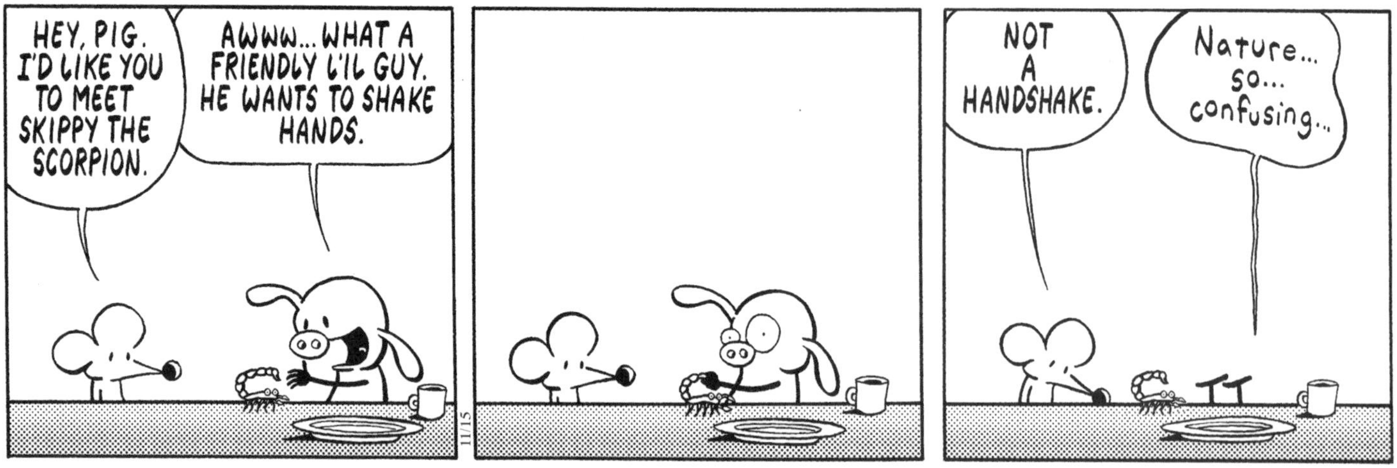
HEY, PIG. I'D LIKE YOU TO MEET SKIPPY THE SCORPION.
AWWW... WHAT A FRIENDLY L'IL GUY. HE WANTS TO SHAKE HANDS.
11/15
NOT A HANDSHAKE.
Nature... so... confusing...

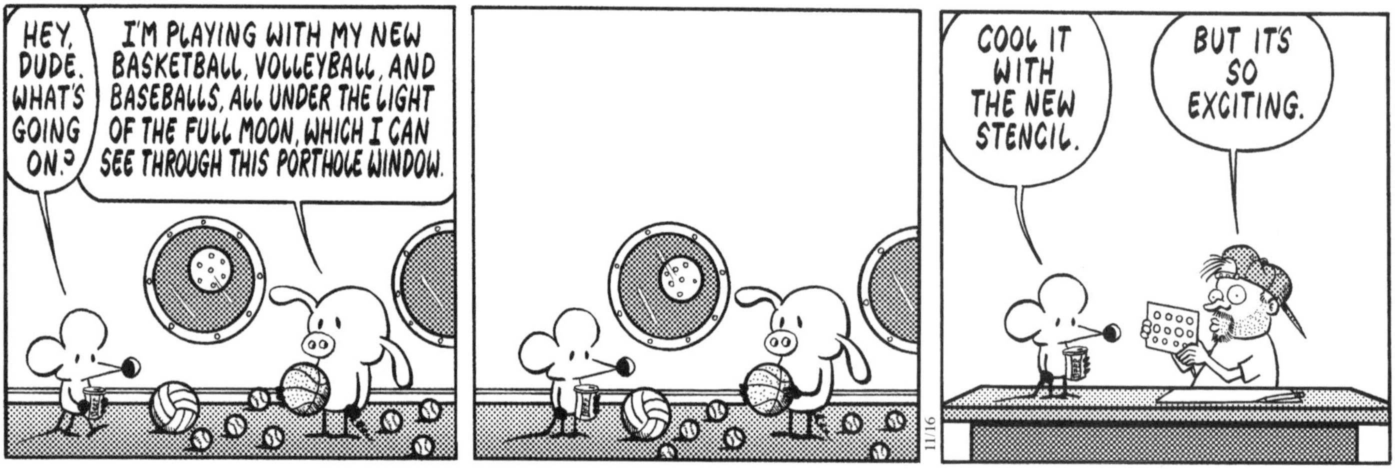
HEY, DUDE. WHAT'S GOING ON.?
I'M PLAYING WITH MY NEW BASKETBALL, VOLLEYBALL, AND BASEBALLS, ALL UNDER THE LIGHT OF THE FULL MOON, WHICH I CAN SEE THROUGH THIS PORTHOLE WINDOW.
11/16
COOL IT WITH THE NEW STENCIL.
BUT IT'S SO EXCITING.

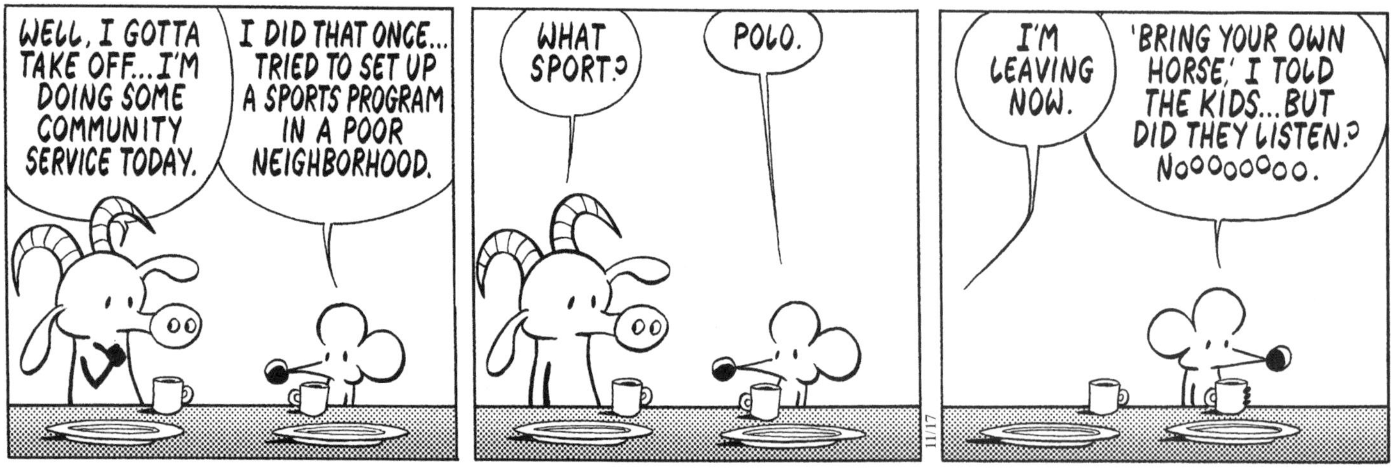
WELL, I GOTTA TAKE OFF... I'M DOING SOME COMMUNITY SERVICE TODAY.
I DID THAT ONCE... TRIED TO SET UP A SPORTS PROGRAM IN A POOR NEIGHBORHOOD.
WHAT SPORT.?
POLO.
11/17
I'M LEAVING NOW.
'BRING YOUR OWN HORSE,' I TOLD THE KIDS... BUT DID THEY LISTEN.? Nooooooo.

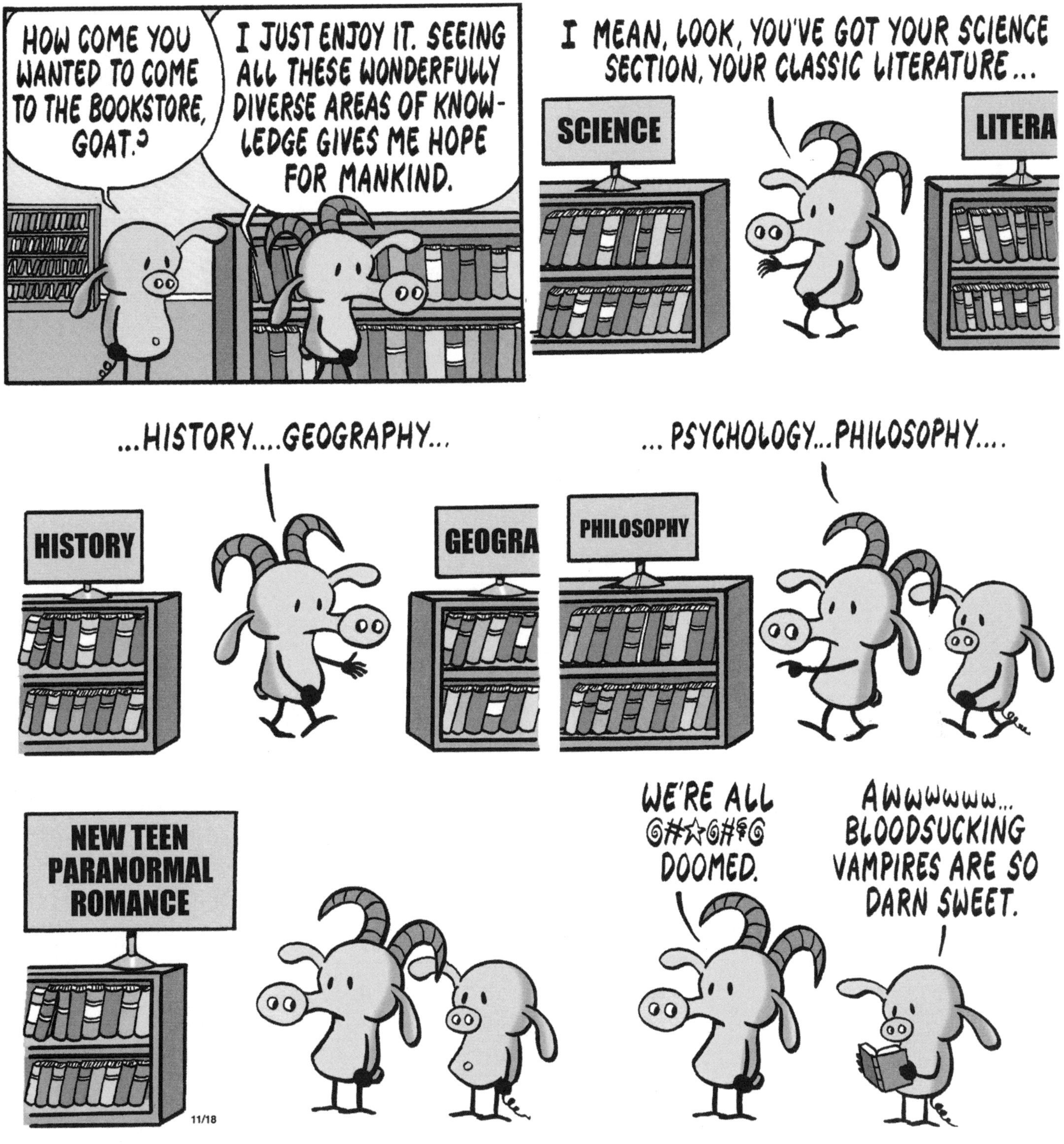
HOW COME YOU WANTED TO COME TO THE BOOKSTORE, GOAT?
I JUST ENJOY IT. SEEING ALL THESE WONDERFULLY DIVERSE AREAS OF KNOWLEDGE GIVES ME HOPE FOR MANKIND.
I MEAN, LOOK, YOU'VE GOT YOUR SCIENCE SECTION, YOUR CLASSIC LITERATURE...
SCIENCE
LITERA
...HISTORY....GEOGRAPHY...
HISTORY
GEOGRA
...PSYCHOLOGY...PHILOSOPHY....
PHILOSOPHY
NEW TEEN PARANORMAL ROMANCE
11/18
WE'RE ALL @#☆@#$@ DOOMED.
AWWWWWW... BLOODSUCKING VAMPIRES ARE SO DARN SWEET.

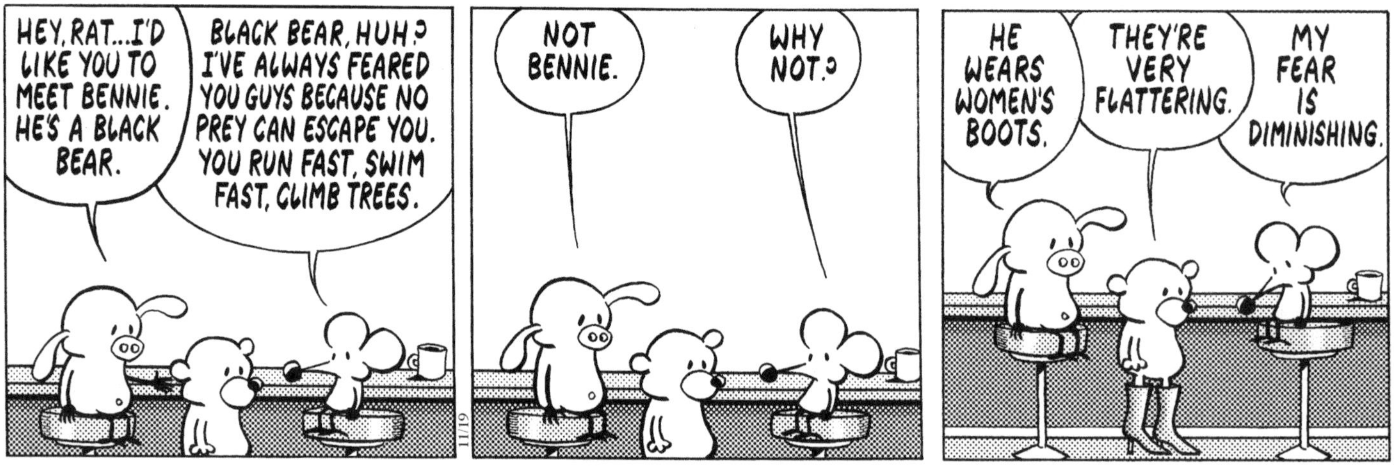
HEY, RAT...I'D LIKE YOU TO MEET BENNIE. HE'S A BLACK BEAR.
BLACK BEAR, HUH? I'VE ALWAYS FEARED YOU GUYS BECAUSE NO PREY CAN ESCAPE YOU. YOU RUN FAST, SWIM FAST, CLIMB TREES.
11/19
NOT BENNIE.
WHY NOT?
HE WEARS WOMEN'S BOOTS.
THEY'RE VERY FLATTERING.
MY FEAR IS DIMINISHING.

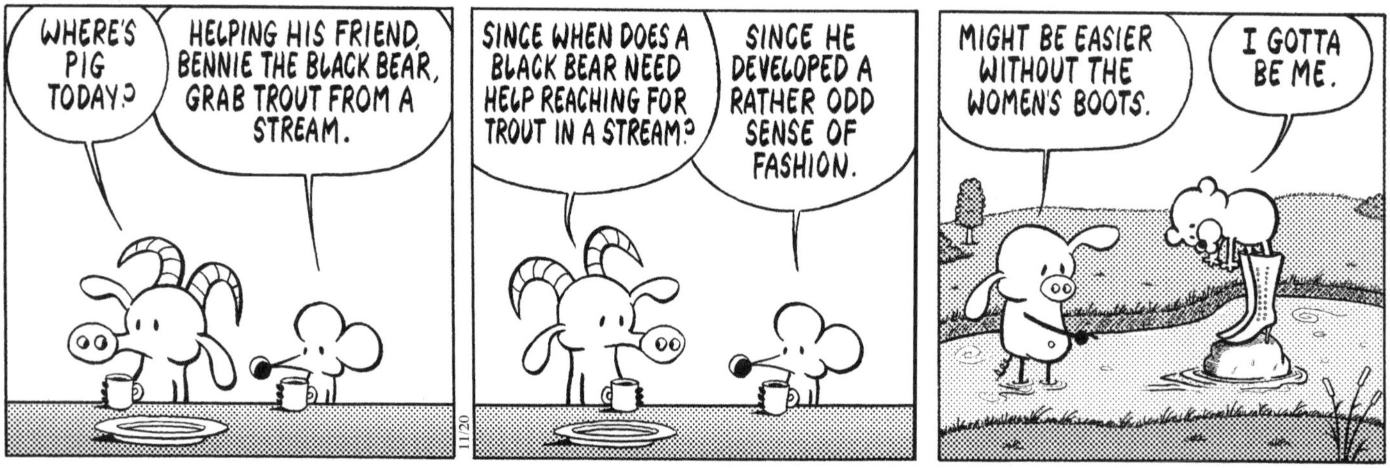
WHERE'S PIG TODAY?
HELPING HIS FRIEND, BENNIE THE BLACK BEAR, GRAB TROUT FROM A STREAM.
11/20
SINCE WHEN DOES A BLACK BEAR NEED HELP REACHING FOR TROUT IN A STREAM?
SINCE HE DEVELOPED A RATHER ODD SENSE OF FASHION.
MIGHT BE EASIER WITHOUT THE WOMEN'S BOOTS.
I GOTTA BE ME.

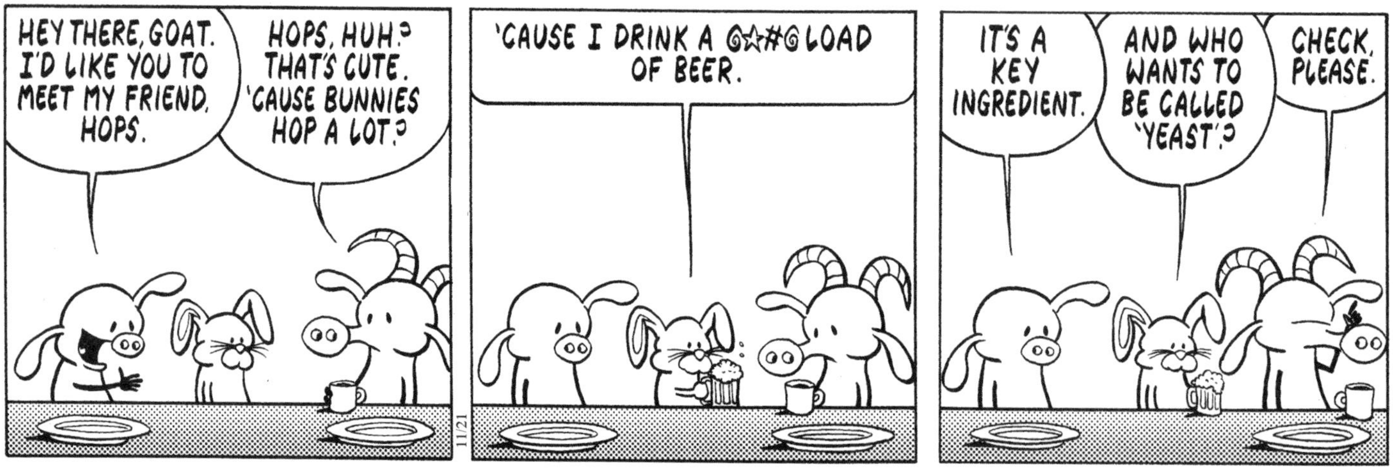
HEY THERE, GOAT. I'D LIKE YOU TO MEET MY FRIEND, HOPS.
HOPS, HUH? THAT'S CUTE. 'CAUSE BUNNIES HOP A LOT?
11/21
'CAUSE I DRINK A @☆#@ LOAD OF BEER.
IT'S A KEY INGREDIENT.
AND WHO WANTS TO BE CALLED 'YEAST'?
CHECK, PLEASE.

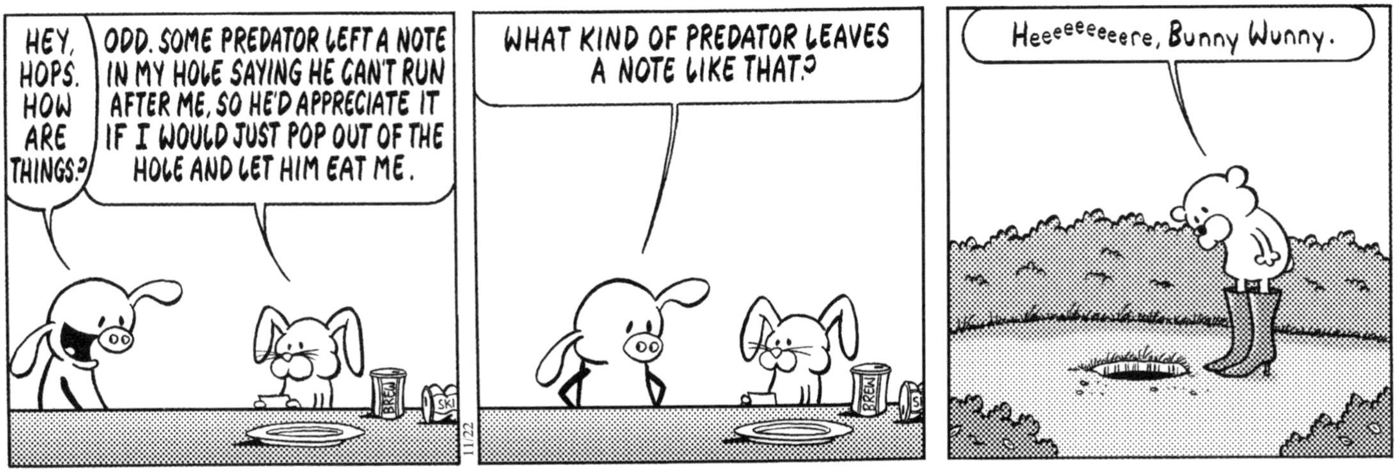
HEY, HOPS. HOW ARE THINGS?
ODD. SOME PREDATOR LEFT A NOTE IN MY HOLE SAYING HE CAN'T RUN AFTER ME, SO HE'D APPRECIATE IT IF I WOULD JUST POP OUT OF THE HOLE AND LET HIM EAT ME.
BREW
SKI
11/22
WHAT KIND OF PREDATOR LEAVES A NOTE LIKE THAT?
Heeeeeeeeeere, Bunny Wunny.

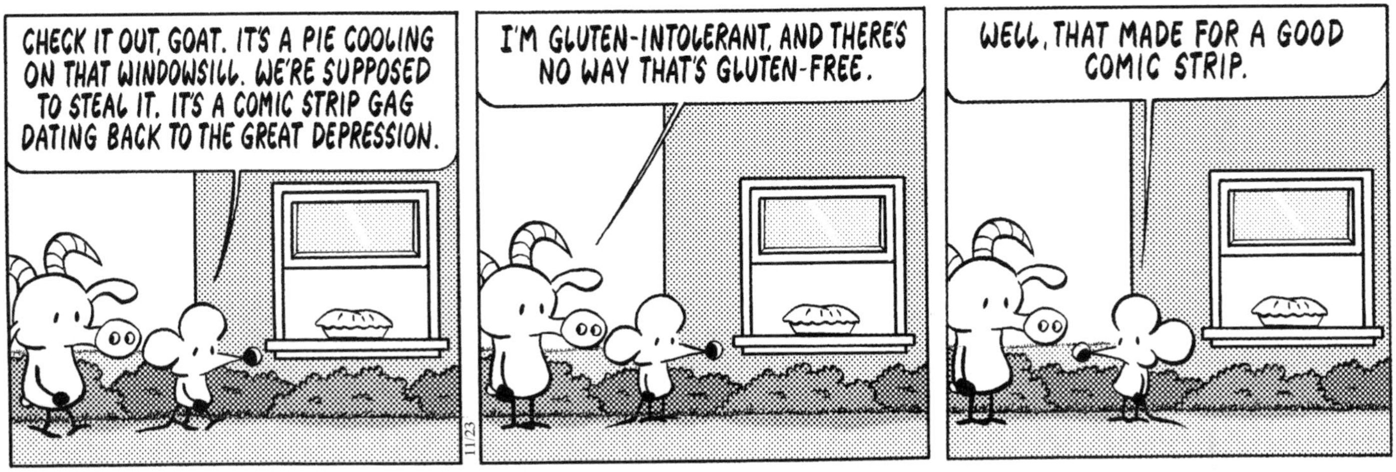
CHECK IT OUT, GOAT. IT'S A PIE COOLING ON THAT WINDOWSILL. WE'RE SUPPOSED TO STEAL IT. IT'S A COMIC STRIP GAG DATING BACK TO THE GREAT DEPRESSION.
11/23
I'M GLUTEN-INTOLERANT, AND THERE'S NO WAY THAT'S GLUTEN-FREE.
WELL, THAT MADE FOR A GOOD COMIC STRIP.

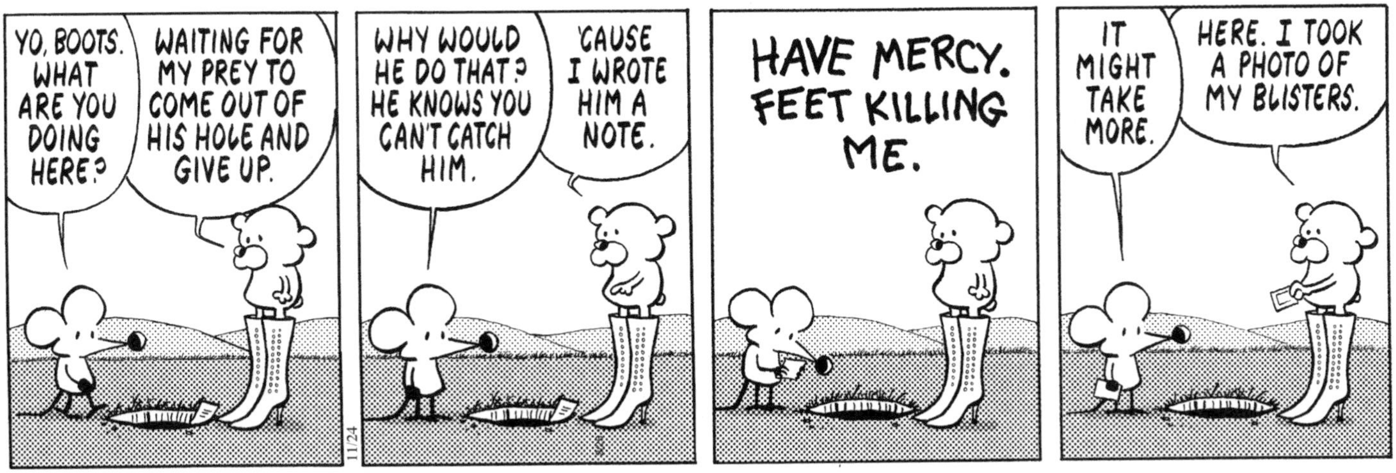
YO, BOOTS. WHAT ARE YOU DOING HERE?
WAITING FOR MY PREY TO COME OUT OF HIS HOLE AND GIVE UP.
11/24
WHY WOULD HE DO THAT? HE KNOWS YOU CAN'T CATCH HIM.
'CAUSE I WROTE HIM A NOTE.
HAVE MERCY. FEET KILLING ME.
IT MIGHT TAKE MORE.
HERE. I TOOK A PHOTO OF MY BLISTERS.

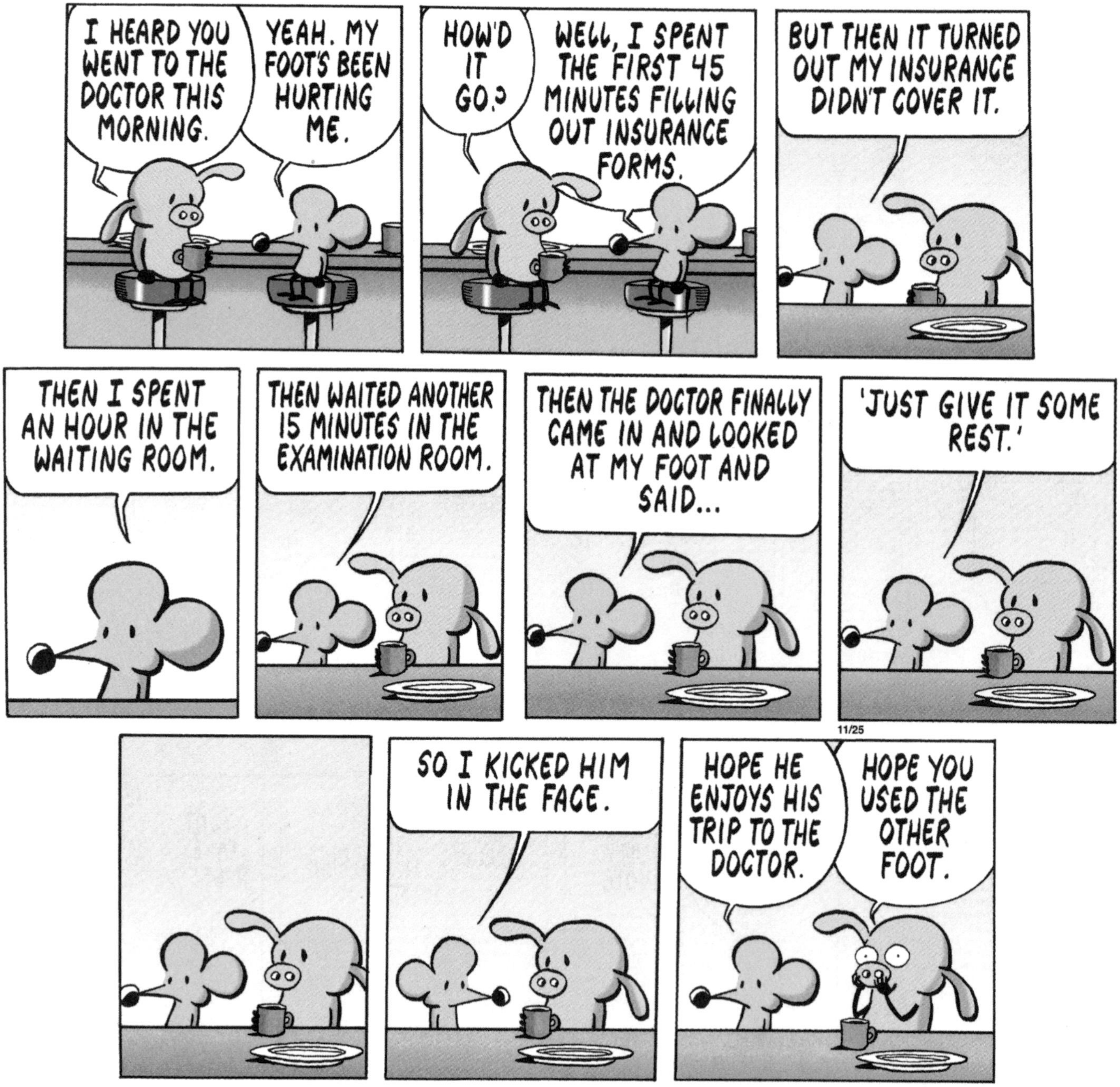
I HEARD YOU WENT TO THE DOCTOR THIS MORNING.
YEAH. MY FOOT'S BEEN HURTING ME.
HOW'D IT GO?
WELL, I SPENT THE FIRST 45 MINUTES FILLING OUT INSURANCE FORMS.
BUT THEN IT TURNED OUT MY INSURANCE DIDN'T COVER IT.
THEN I SPENT AN HOUR IN THE WAITING ROOM.
THEN WAITED ANOTHER 15 MINUTES IN THE EXAMINATION ROOM.
THEN THE DOCTOR FINALLY CAME IN AND LOOKED AT MY FOOT AND SAID...
'JUST GIVE IT SOME REST.'
11/25
SO I KICKED HIM IN THE FACE.
HOPE HE ENJOYS HIS TRIP TO THE DOCTOR.
HOPE YOU USED THE OTHER FOOT.

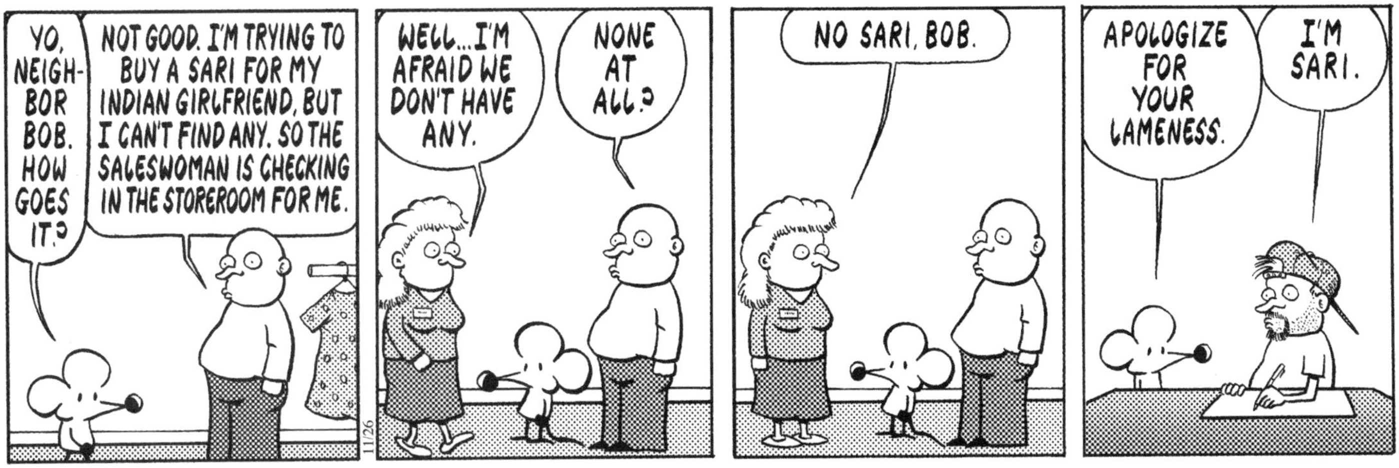
YO, NEIGHBOR BOB. HOW GOES IT?
NOT GOOD. I'M TRYING TO BUY A SARI FOR MY INDIAN GIRLFRIEND, BUT I CAN'T FIND ANY. SO THE SALESWOMAN IS CHECKING IN THE STOREROOM FOR ME.
11/26
WELL...I'M AFRAID WE DON'T HAVE ANY.
NONE AT ALL?
NO SARI, BOB.
APOLOGIZE FOR YOUR LAMENESS.
I'M SARI.

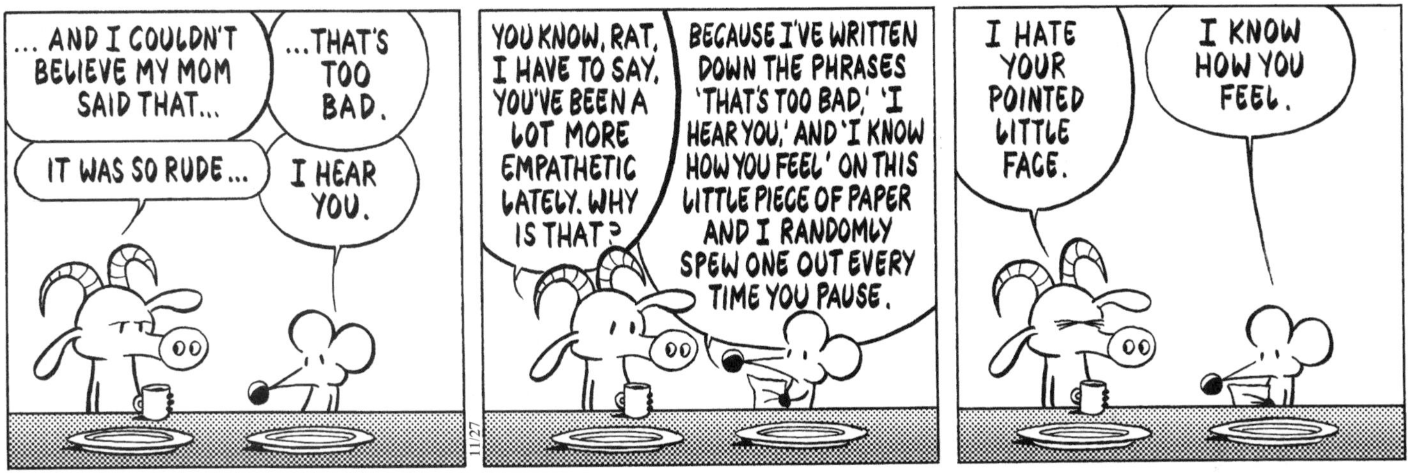
... AND I COULDN'T BELIEVE MY MOM SAID THAT...
...THAT'S TOO BAD.
IT WAS SO RUDE...
I HEAR YOU.
11/27
YOU KNOW, RAT, I HAVE TO SAY, YOU'VE BEEN A LOT MORE EMPATHETIC LATELY. WHY IS THAT?
BECAUSE I'VE WRITTEN DOWN THE PHRASES 'THAT'S TOO BAD,' 'I HEAR YOU,' AND 'I KNOW HOW YOU FEEL' ON THIS LITTLE PIECE OF PAPER AND I RANDOMLY SPEW ONE OUT EVERY TIME YOU PAUSE.
I HATE YOUR POINTED LITTLE FACE.
I KNOW HOW YOU FEEL.

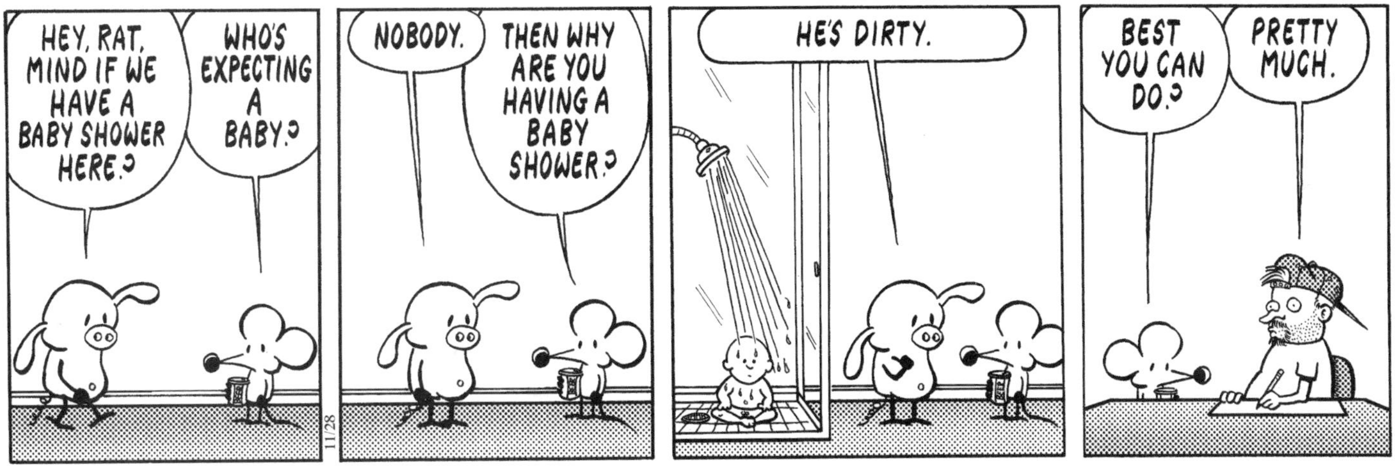
HEY, RAT, MIND IF WE HAVE A BABY SHOWER HERE?
WHO'S EXPECTING A BABY?
11/28
NOBODY.
THEN WHY ARE YOU HAVING A BABY SHOWER?
HE'S DIRTY.
BEST YOU CAN DO?
PRETTY MUCH.

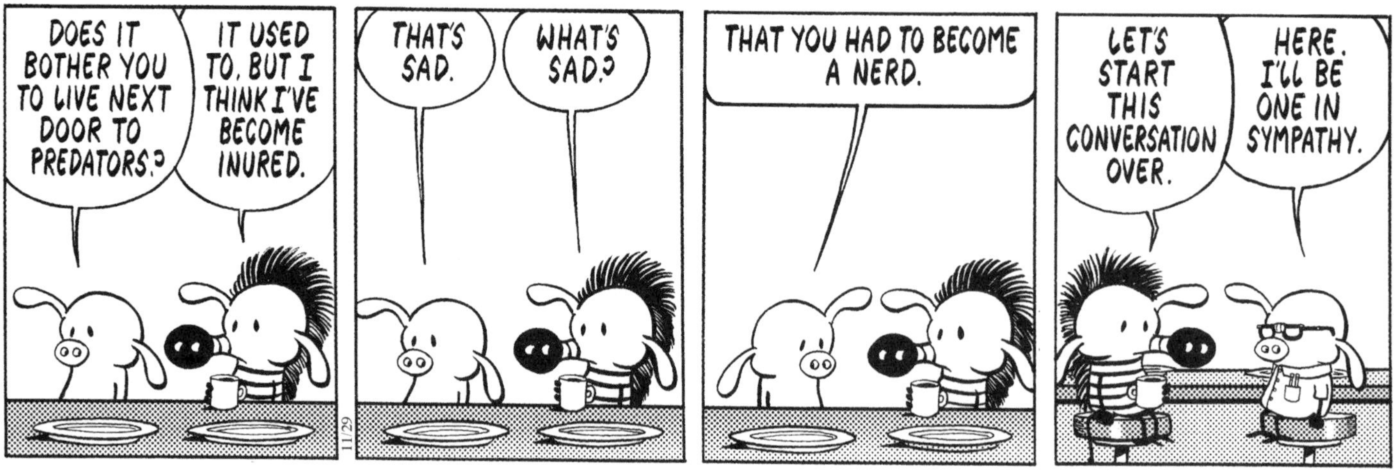
DOES IT BOTHER YOU TO LIVE NEXT DOOR TO PREDATORS?
IT USED TO, BUT I THINK I'VE BECOME INURED.
11/29
THAT'S SAD.
WHAT'S SAD?
THAT YOU HAD TO BECOME A NERD.
LET'S START THIS CONVERSATION OVER.
HERE. I'LL BE ONE IN SYMPATHY.

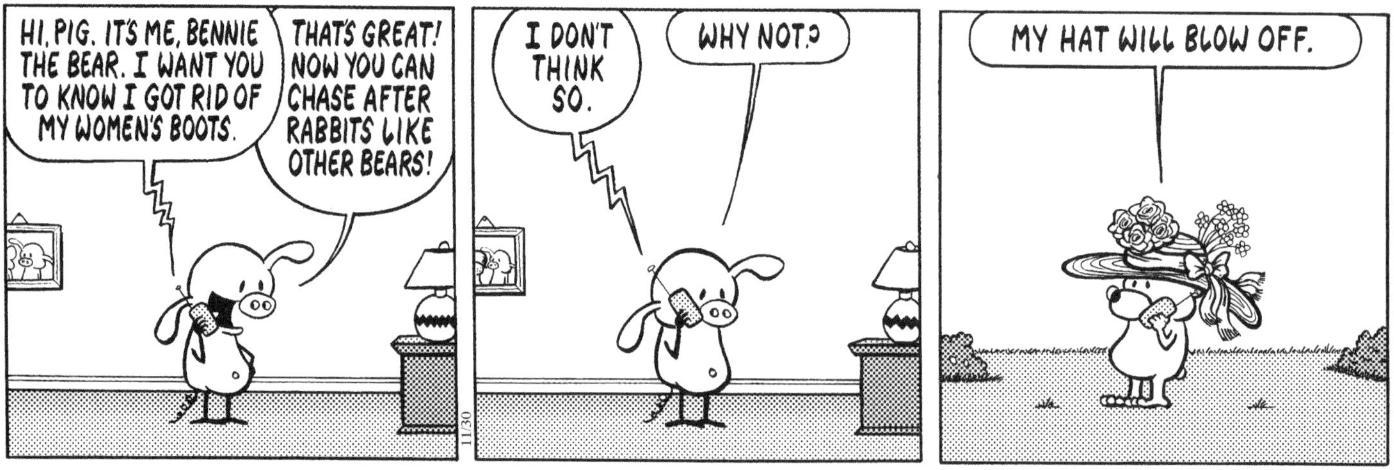
HI, PIG. IT'S ME, BENNIE THE BEAR. I WANT YOU TO KNOW I GOT RID OF MY WOMEN'S BOOTS.
THAT'S GREAT! NOW YOU CAN CHASE AFTER RABBITS LIKE OTHER BEARS!
11/30
I DON'T THINK SO.
WHY NOT?
MY HAT WILL BLOW OFF.

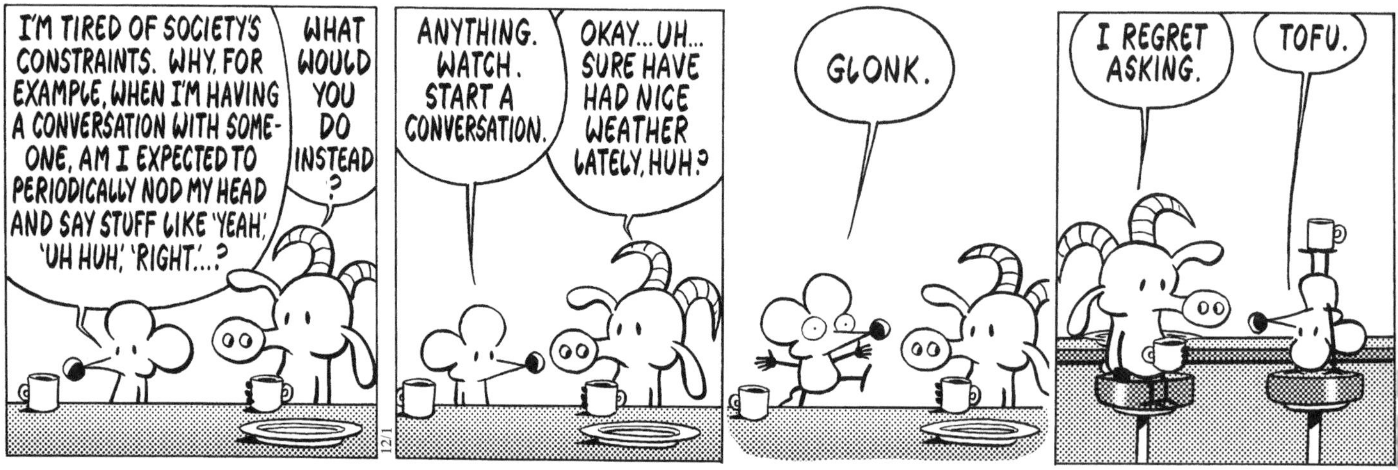
I'M TIRED OF SOCIETY'S CONSTRAINTS. WHY, FOR EXAMPLE, WHEN I'M HAVING A CONVERSATION WITH SOME-ONE, AM I EXPECTED TO PERIODICALLY NOD MY HEAD AND SAY STUFF LIKE 'YEAH,' 'UH HUH,' 'RIGHT'...?
WHAT WOULD YOU DO INSTEAD?
12/1
ANYTHING. WATCH. START A CONVERSATION.
OKAY...UH... SURE HAVE HAD NICE WEATHER LATELY, HUH?
GLONK.
I REGRET ASKING.
TOFU.

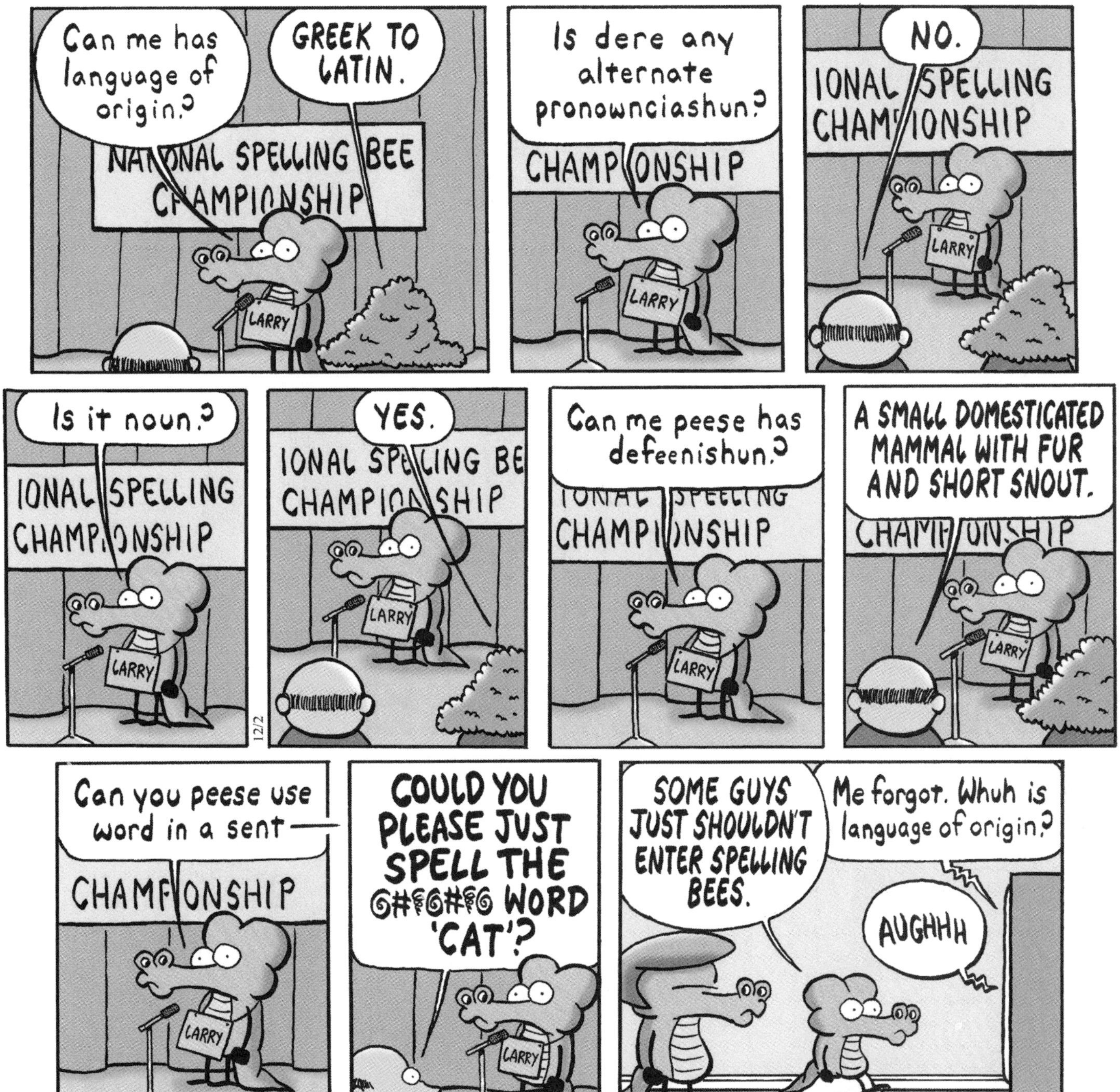

Can me has language of origin?
GREEK TO LATIN.
Is dere any alternate pronowncaishun?
NO.
Is it noun?
YES.
Can me peese has defeenishun?
A SMALL DOMESTICATED MAMMAL WITH FUR AND SHORT SNOUT.
Can you peese use word in a sent—
COULD YOU PLEASE JUST SPELL THE @#%@#%@ WORD 'CAT'?
SOME GUYS JUST SHOULDN'T ENTER SPELLING BEES.
Me forgot. Whuh is language of origin?
AUGHHH

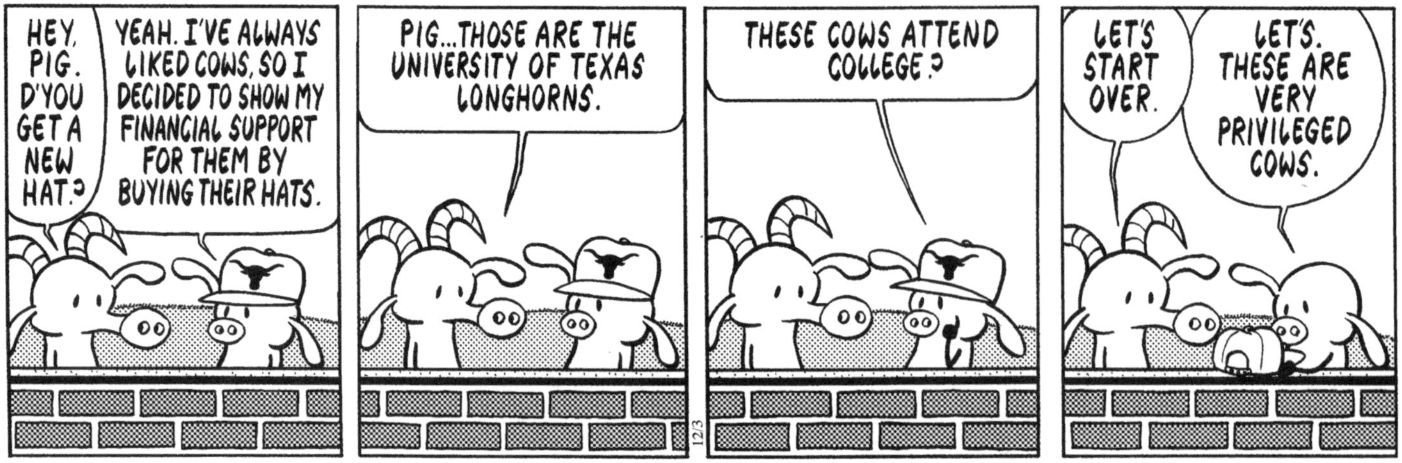
HEY, PIG. D'YOU GET A NEW HAT?
YEAH. I'VE ALWAYS LIKED COWS, SO I DECIDED TO SHOW MY FINANCIAL SUPPORT FOR THEM BY BUYING THEIR HATS.
PIG...THOSE ARE THE UNIVERSITY OF TEXAS LONGHORNS.
12/3
THESE COWS ATTEND COLLEGE?
LET'S START OVER.
LET'S. THESE ARE VERY PRIVILEGED COWS.

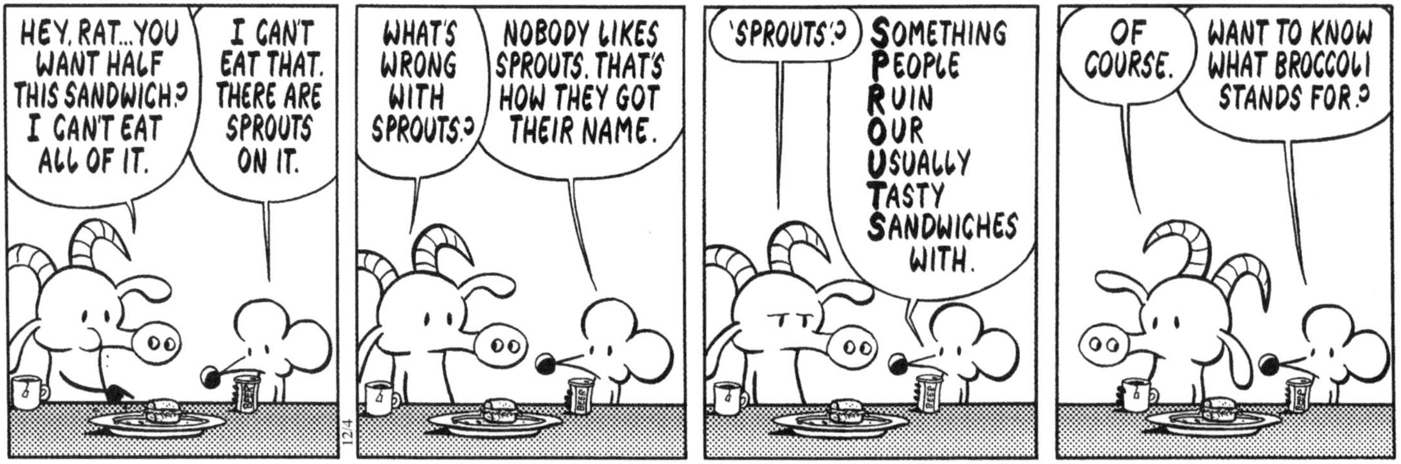
HEY, RAT...YOU WANT HALF THIS SANDWICH? I CAN'T EAT ALL OF IT.
I CAN'T EAT THAT. THERE ARE SPROUTS ON IT.
12/4
WHAT'S WRONG WITH SPROUTS?
NOBODY LIKES SPROUTS. THAT'S HOW THEY GOT THEIR NAME.
'SPROUTS'?
SOMETHING PEOPLE RUIN OUR USUALLY TASTY SANDWICHES WITH.
OF COURSE.
WANT TO KNOW WHAT BROCCOLI STANDS FOR?

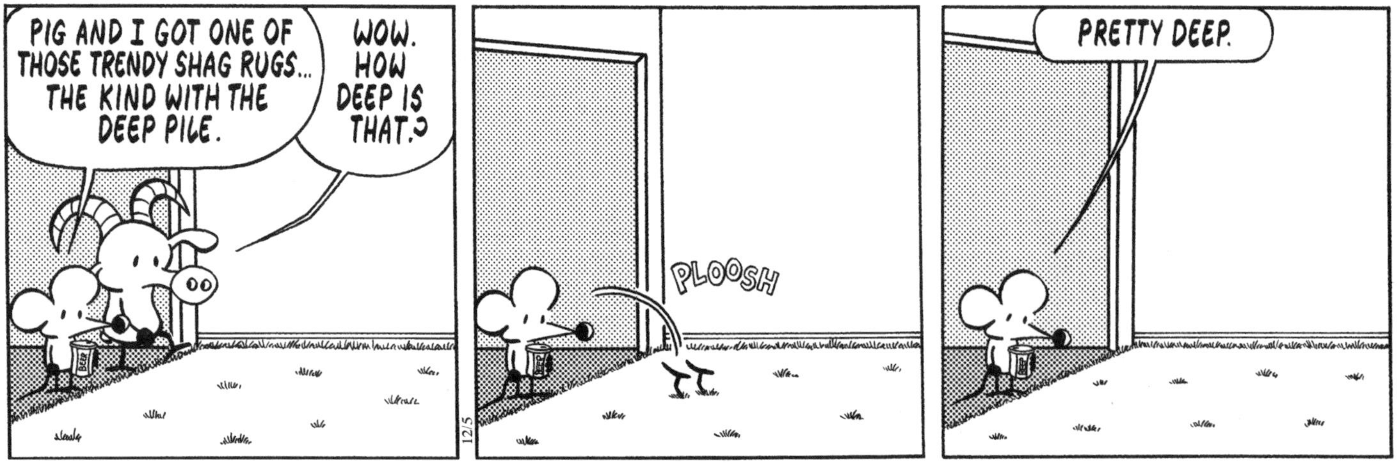
PIG AND I GOT ONE OF THOSE TRENDY SHAG RUGS... THE KIND WITH THE DEEP PILE.
WOW. HOW DEEP IS THAT?
12/5
PLOOSH
PRETTY DEEP.

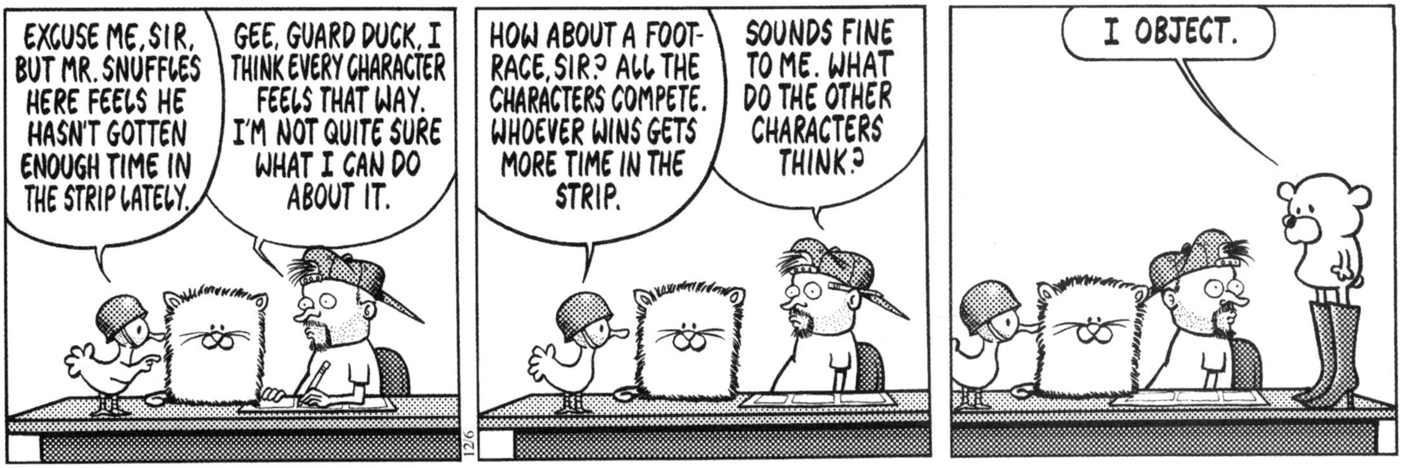
EXCUSE ME, SIR, BUT MR. SNUFFLES HERE FEELS HE HASN'T GOTTEN ENOUGH TIME IN THE STRIP LATELY.
GEE, GUARD DUCK, I THINK EVERY CHARACTER FEELS THAT WAY. I'M NOT QUITE SURE WHAT I CAN DO ABOUT IT.
12/6
HOW ABOUT A FOOT-RACE, SIR? ALL THE CHARACTERS COMPETE. WHOEVER WINS GETS MORE TIME IN THE STRIP.
SOUNDS FINE TO ME. WHAT DO THE OTHER CHARACTERS THINK?
I OBJECT.

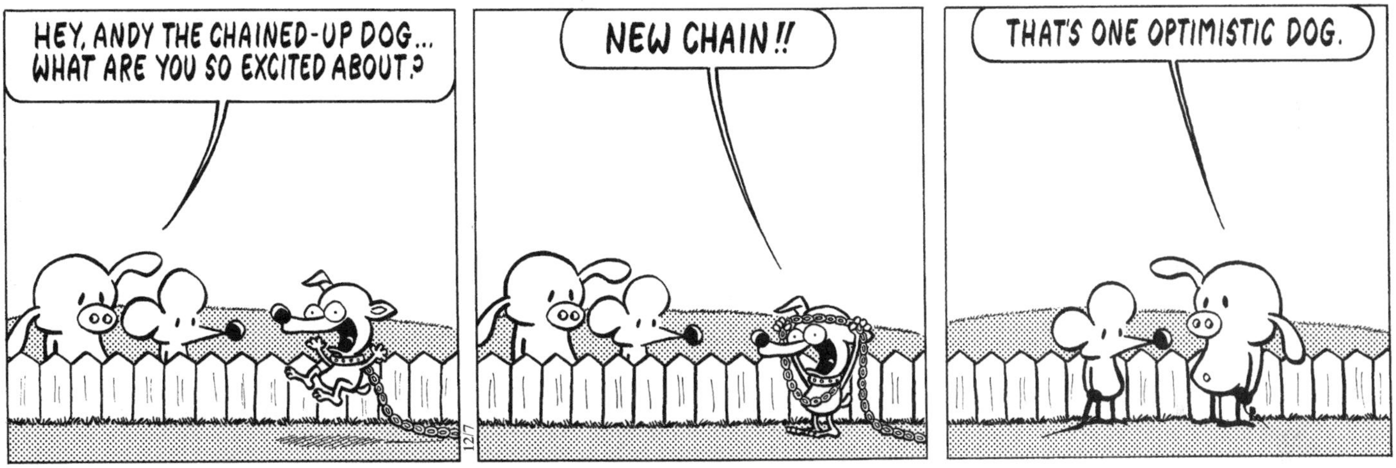
HEY, ANDY THE CHAINED-UP DOG... WHAT ARE YOU SO EXCITED ABOUT?
12/7
NEW CHAIN!!
THAT'S ONE OPTIMISTIC DOG.

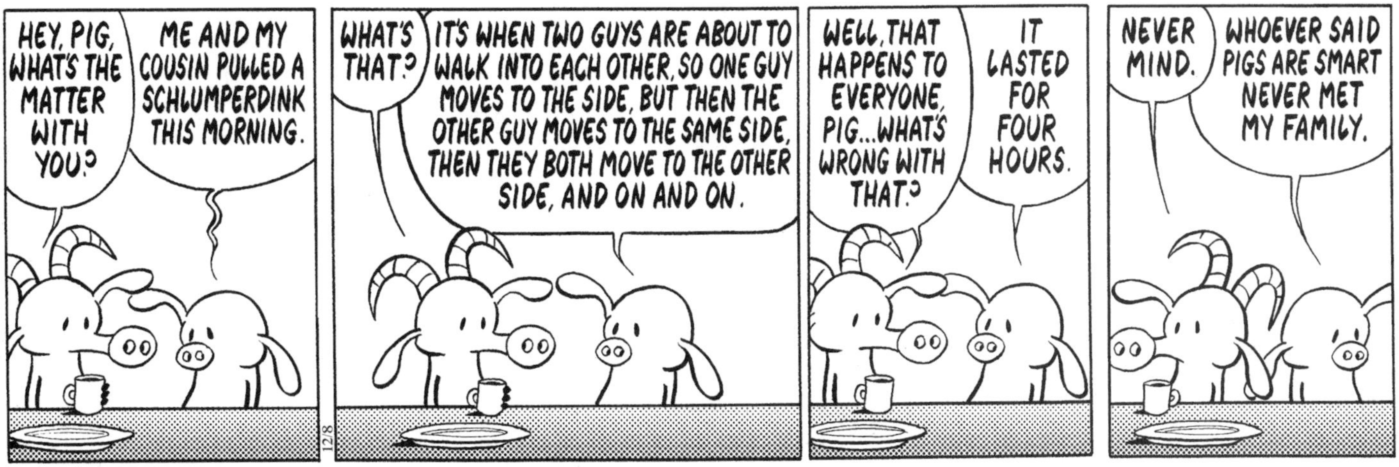
HEY, PIG, WHAT'S THE MATTER WITH YOU?
ME AND MY COUSIN PULLED A SCHLUMPERDINK THIS MORNING.
12/8
WHAT'S THAT?
IT'S WHEN TWO GUYS ARE ABOUT TO WALK INTO EACH OTHER, SO ONE GUY MOVES TO THE SIDE, BUT THEN THE OTHER GUY MOVES TO THE SAME SIDE, THEN THEY BOTH MOVE TO THE OTHER SIDE, AND ON AND ON.
WELL, THAT HAPPENS TO EVERYONE, PIG... WHAT'S WRONG WITH THAT?
IT LASTED FOR FOUR HOURS.
NEVER MIND.
WHOEVER SAID PIGS ARE SMART NEVER MET MY FAMILY.

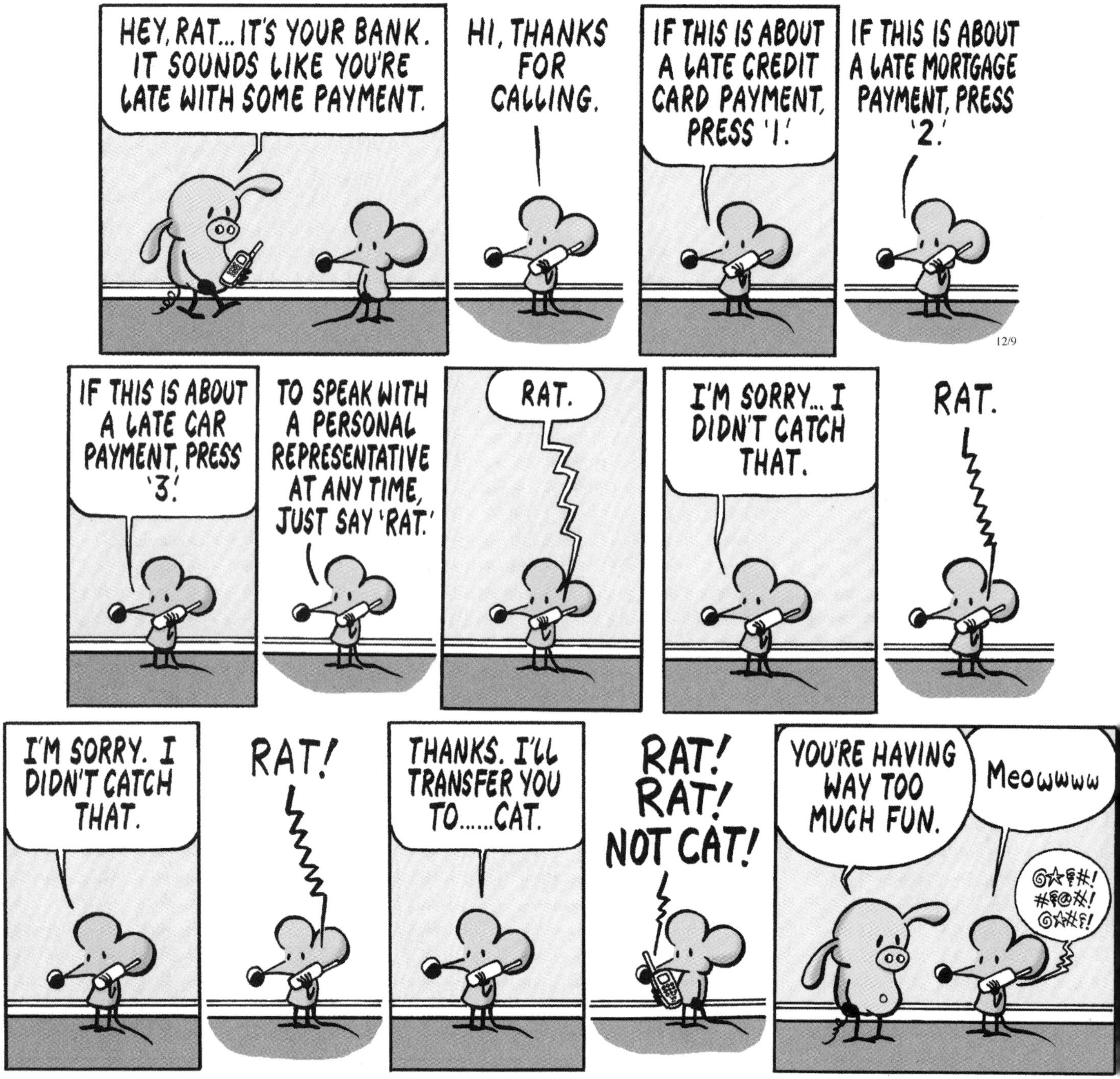
HEY, RAT... IT'S YOUR BANK. IT SOUNDS LIKE YOU'RE LATE WITH SOME PAYMENT.
HI, THANKS FOR CALLING.
IF THIS IS ABOUT A LATE CREDIT CARD PAYMENT, PRESS '1.'
IF THIS IS ABOUT A LATE MORTGAGE PAYMENT, PRESS '2.'
12/9
IF THIS IS ABOUT A LATE CAR PAYMENT, PRESS '3.'
TO SPEAK WITH A PERSONAL REPRESENTATIVE AT ANY TIME, JUST SAY 'RAT.'
RAT.
I'M SORRY... I DIDN'T CATCH THAT.
RAT.
I'M SORRY. I DIDN'T CATCH THAT.
RAT!
THANKS. I'LL TRANSFER YOU TO......CAT.
RAT! RAT! NOT CAT!
YOU'RE HAVING WAY TOO MUCH FUN.
Meowwww

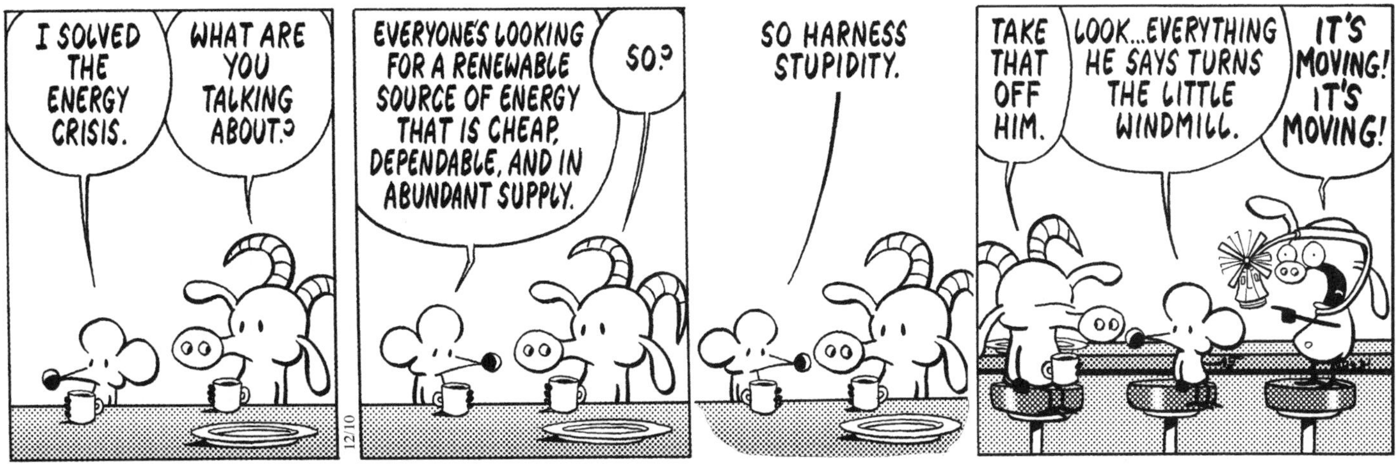
I SOLVED THE ENERGY CRISIS.
WHAT ARE YOU TALKING ABOUT?
12/10
EVERYONE'S LOOKING FOR A RENEWABLE SOURCE OF ENERGY THAT IS CHEAP, DEPENDABLE, AND IN ABUNDANT SUPPLY.
SO?
SO HARNESS STUPIDITY.
TAKE THAT OFF HIM.
LOOK...EVERYTHING HE SAYS TURNS THE LITTLE WINDMILL.
IT'S MOVING! IT'S MOVING!

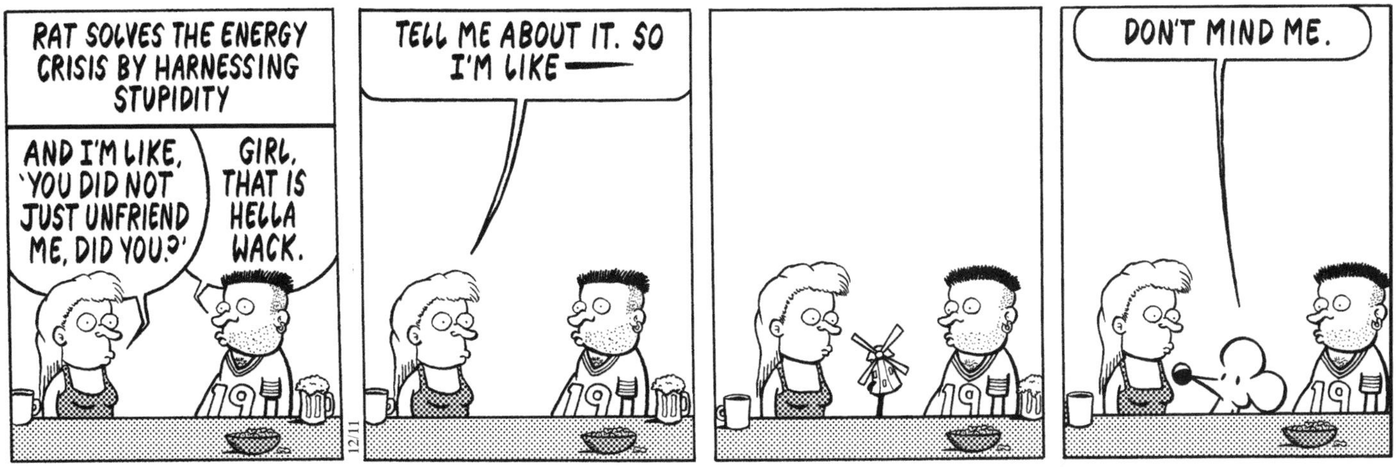
RAT SOLVES THE ENERGY CRISIS BY HARNESSING STUPIDITY
AND I'M LIKE, 'YOU DID NOT JUST UNFRIEND ME, DID YOU?'
GIRL, THAT IS HELLA WACK.
12/11
TELL ME ABOUT IT. SO I'M LIKE—
DON'T MIND ME.

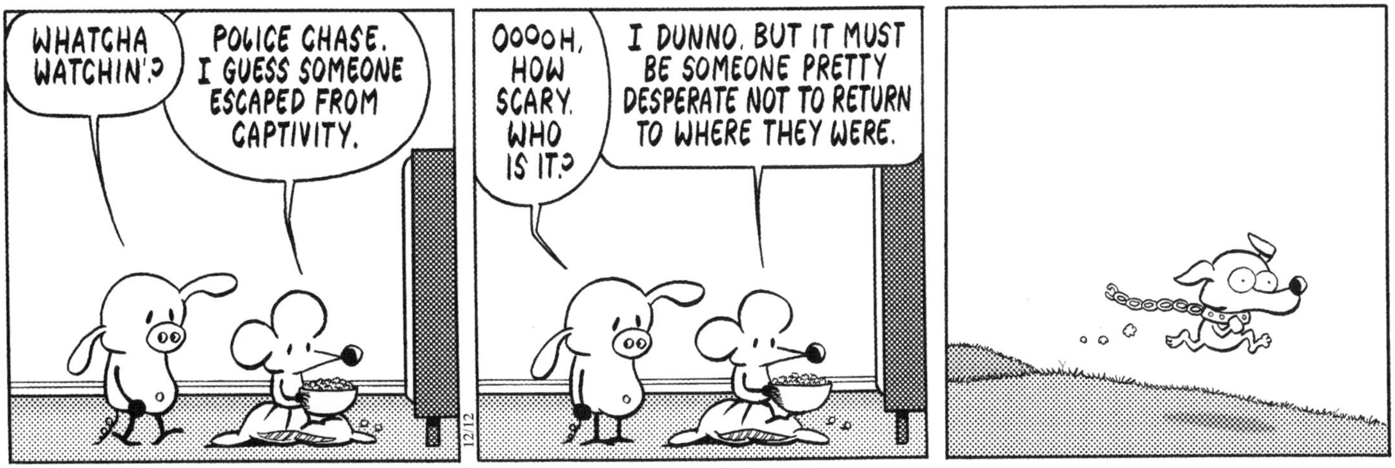
WHATCHA WATCHIN'?
POLICE CHASE. I GUESS SOMEONE ESCAPED FROM CAPTIVITY.
12/12
OOOOH, HOW SCARY. WHO IS IT?
I DUNNO. BUT IT MUST BE SOMEONE PRETTY DESPERATE NOT TO RETURN TO WHERE THEY WERE.

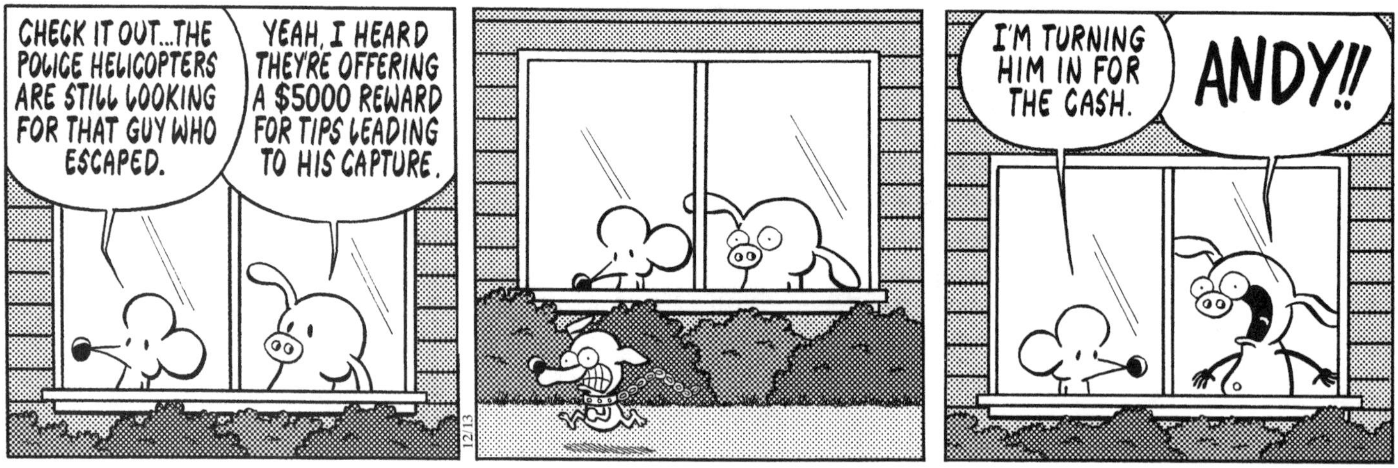
CHECK IT OUT...THE POLICE HELICOPTERS ARE STILL LOOKING FOR THAT GUY WHO ESCAPED.
YEAH, I HEARD THEY'RE OFFERING A $5000 REWARD FOR TIPS LEADING TO HIS CAPTURE.
12/13
I'M TURNING HIM IN FOR THE CASH.
ANDY!!

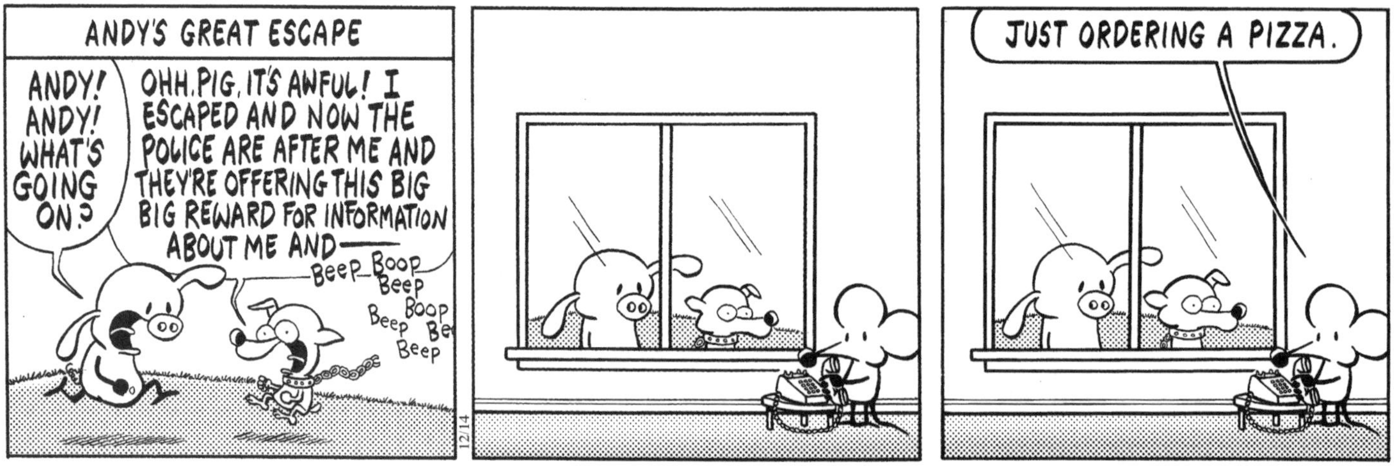
ANDY'S GREAT ESCAPE
ANDY! ANDY! WHAT'S GOING ON?
OHH, PIG, IT'S AWFUL! I ESCAPED AND NOW THE POLICE ARE AFTER ME AND THEY'RE OFFERING THIS BIG BIG REWARD FOR INFORMATION ABOUT ME AND——
Beep Boop Beep Beep Boop Be Beep
12/14
JUST ORDERING A PIZZA.

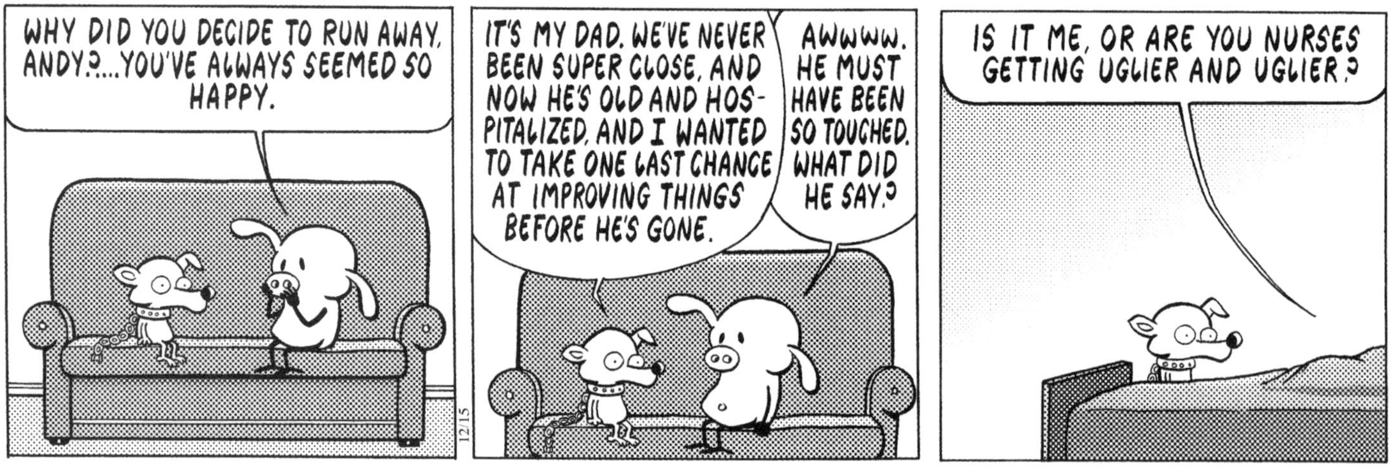
WHY DID YOU DECIDE TO RUN AWAY, ANDY?...YOU'VE ALWAYS SEEMED SO HAPPY.
12/15
IT'S MY DAD. WE'VE NEVER BEEN SUPER CLOSE, AND NOW HE'S OLD AND HOSPITALIZED, AND I WANTED TO TAKE ONE LAST CHANCE AT IMPROVING THINGS BEFORE HE'S GONE.
AWWWW. HE MUST HAVE BEEN SO TOUCHED. WHAT DID HE SAY?
IS IT ME, OR ARE YOU NURSES GETTING UGLIER AND UGLIER?

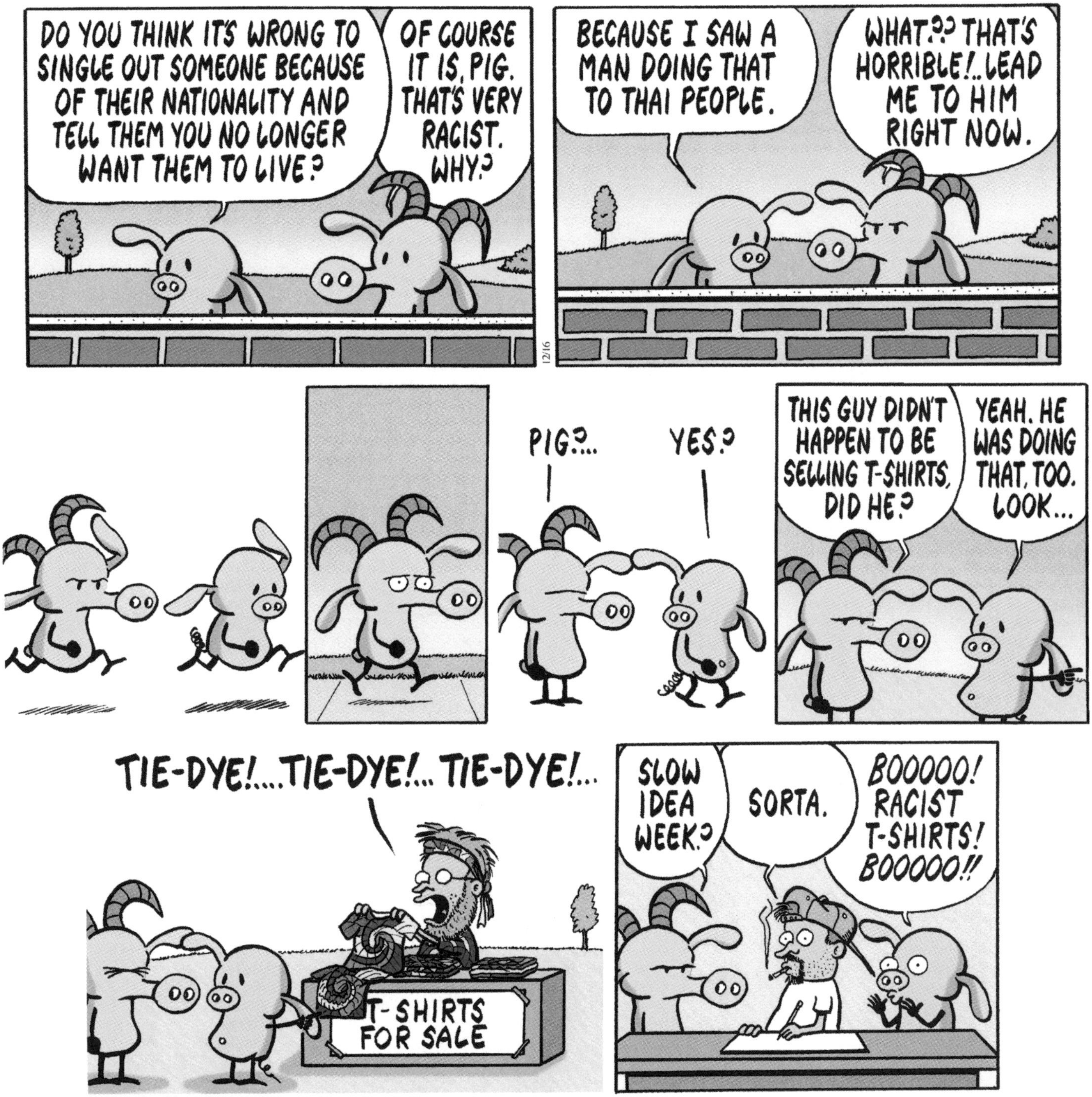
DO YOU THINK IT'S WRONG TO SINGLE OUT SOMEONE BECAUSE OF THEIR NATIONALITY AND TELL THEM YOU NO LONGER WANT THEM TO LIVE?
OF COURSE IT IS, PIG. THAT'S VERY RACIST. WHY?
BECAUSE I SAW A MAN DOING THAT TO THAI PEOPLE.
WHAT?? THAT'S HORRIBLE!..LEAD ME TO HIM RIGHT NOW.
12/16
PIG?...
YES?
THIS GUY DIDN'T HAPPEN TO BE SELLING T-SHIRTS, DID HE?
YEAH. HE WAS DOING THAT, TOO. LOOK...
TIE-DYE!....TIE-DYE!... TIE-DYE!...
T-SHIRTS FOR SALE
SLOW IDEA WEEK?
SORTA.
BOOOOO! RACIST T-SHIRTS! BOOOOO!!

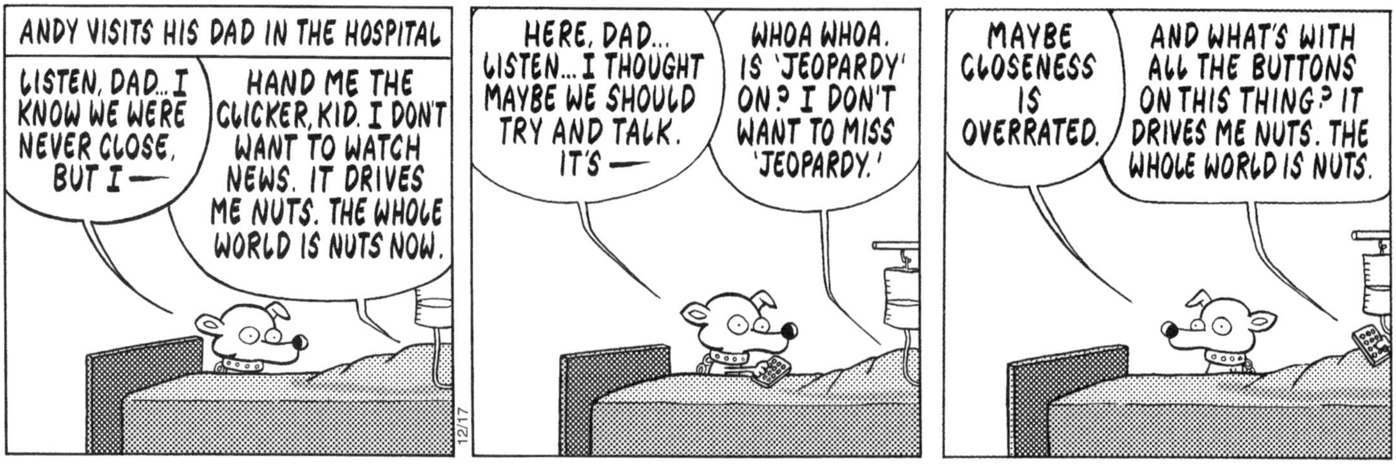
ANDY VISITS HIS DAD IN THE HOSPITAL
LISTEN, DAD... I KNOW WE WERE NEVER CLOSE, BUT I—
HAND ME THE CLICKER, KID. I DON'T WANT TO WATCH NEWS. IT DRIVES ME NUTS. THE WHOLE WORLD IS NUTS NOW.
12/17
HERE, DAD... LISTEN... I THOUGHT MAYBE WE SHOULD TRY AND TALK. IT'S —
WHOA WHOA. IS 'JEOPARDY' ON? I DON'T WANT TO MISS 'JEOPARDY.'
MAYBE CLOSENESS IS OVERRATED.
AND WHAT'S WITH ALL THE BUTTONS ON THIS THING? IT DRIVES ME NUTS. THE WHOLE WORLD IS NUTS.

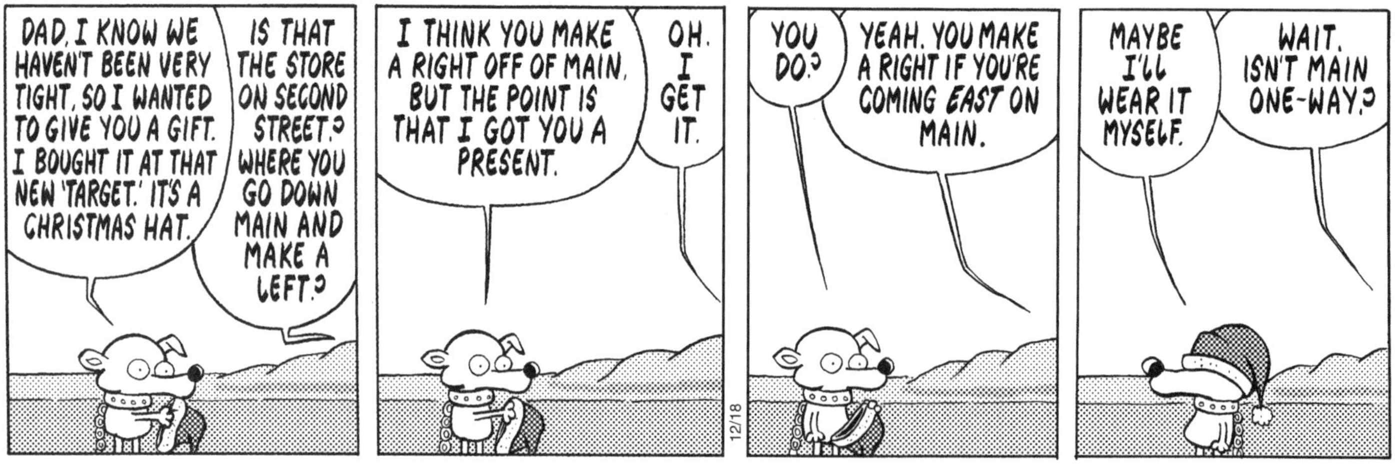
DAD, I KNOW WE HAVEN'T BEEN VERY TIGHT, SO I WANTED TO GIVE YOU A GIFT. I BOUGHT IT AT THAT NEW 'TARGET.' IT'S A CHRISTMAS HAT.
IS THAT THE STORE ON SECOND STREET? WHERE YOU GO DOWN MAIN AND MAKE A LEFT?
I THINK YOU MAKE A RIGHT OFF OF MAIN, BUT THE POINT IS THAT I GOT YOU A PRESENT.
OH. I GET IT.
12/18
YOU DO?
YEAH. YOU MAKE A RIGHT IF YOU'RE COMING EAST ON MAIN.
MAYBE I'LL WEAR IT MYSELF.
WAIT. ISN'T MAIN ONE-WAY?

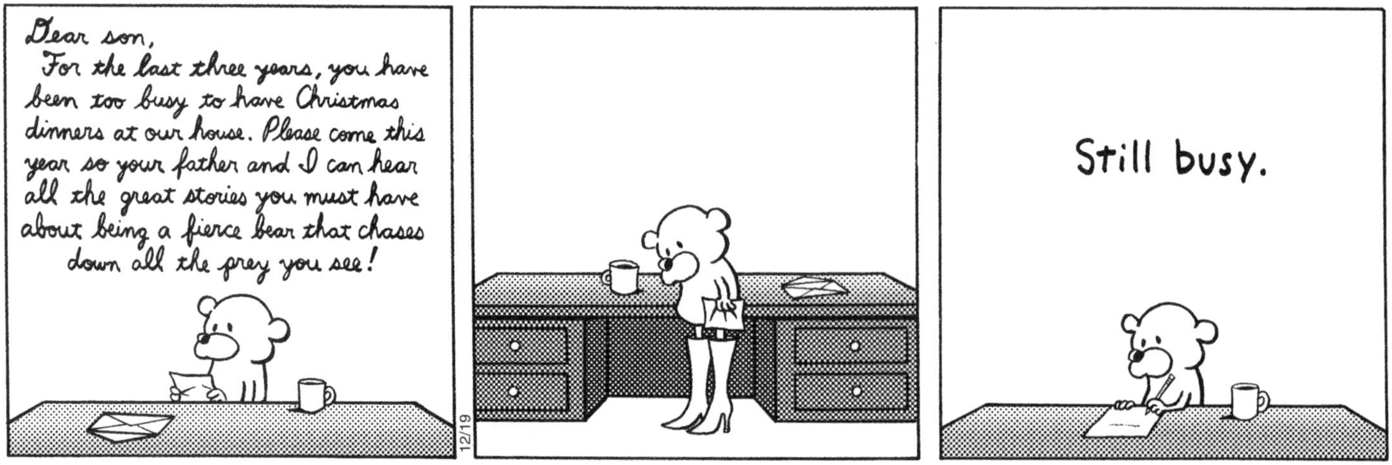
Dear son,
For the last three years, you have been too busy to have Christmas dinners at our house. Please come this year so your father and I can hear all the great stories you must have about being a fierce bear that chases down all the prey you see!
12/19
Still busy.

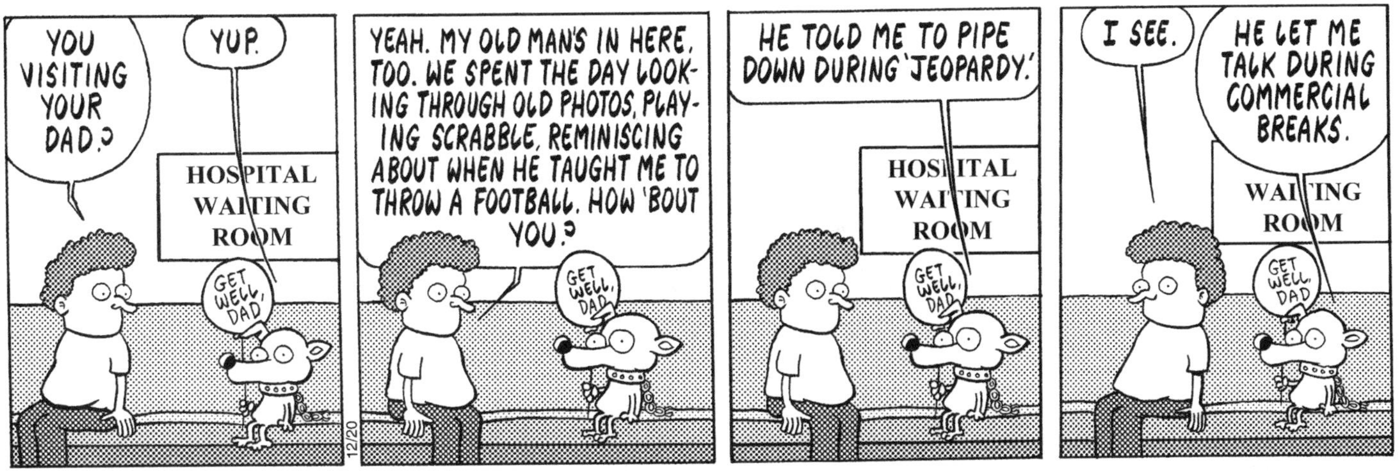
YOU VISITING YOUR DAD?
YUP.
HOSPITAL WAITING ROOM
GET WELL, DAD
12/20
YEAH. MY OLD MAN'S IN HERE, TOO. WE SPENT THE DAY LOOKING THROUGH OLD PHOTOS, PLAYING SCRABBLE, REMINISCING ABOUT WHEN HE TAUGHT ME TO THROW A FOOTBALL. HOW 'BOUT YOU?
GET WELL, DAD
HE TOLD ME TO PIPE DOWN DURING 'JEOPARDY.'
HOSPITAL WAITING ROOM
GET WELL, DAD
I SEE.
HE LET ME TALK DURING COMMERCIAL BREAKS.
WAITING ROOM
GET WELL, DAD

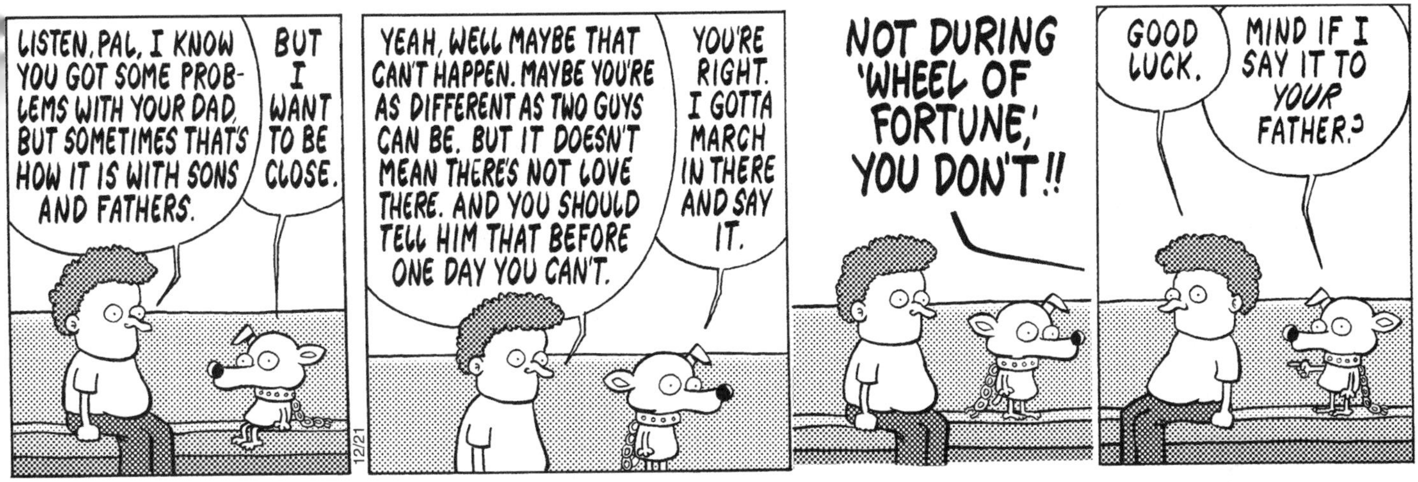
LISTEN, PAL, I KNOW YOU GOT SOME PROBLEMS WITH YOUR DAD, BUT SOMETIMES THAT'S HOW IT IS WITH SONS AND FATHERS.
BUT I WANT TO BE CLOSE.
12/21
YEAH, WELL MAYBE THAT CAN'T HAPPEN. MAYBE YOU'RE AS DIFFERENT AS TWO GUYS CAN BE. BUT IT DOESN'T MEAN THERE'S NOT LOVE THERE. AND YOU SHOULD TELL HIM THAT BEFORE ONE DAY YOU CAN'T.
YOU'RE RIGHT. I GOTTA MARCH IN THERE AND SAY IT.
NOT DURING 'WHEEL OF FORTUNE,' YOU DON'T!!
GOOD LUCK.
MIND IF I SAY IT TO *YOUR* FATHER?

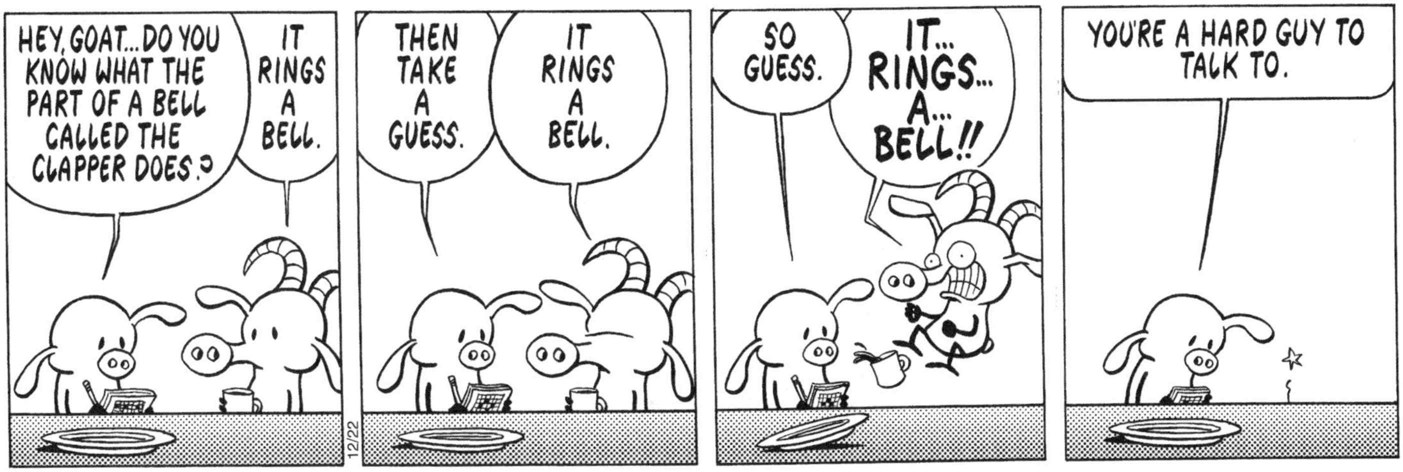
HEY, GOAT...DO YOU KNOW WHAT THE PART OF A BELL CALLED THE CLAPPER DOES?
IT RINGS A BELL.
12/22
THEN TAKE A GUESS.
IT RINGS A BELL.
SO GUESS.
IT... RINGS... A... BELL!!
YOU'RE A HARD GUY TO TALK TO.

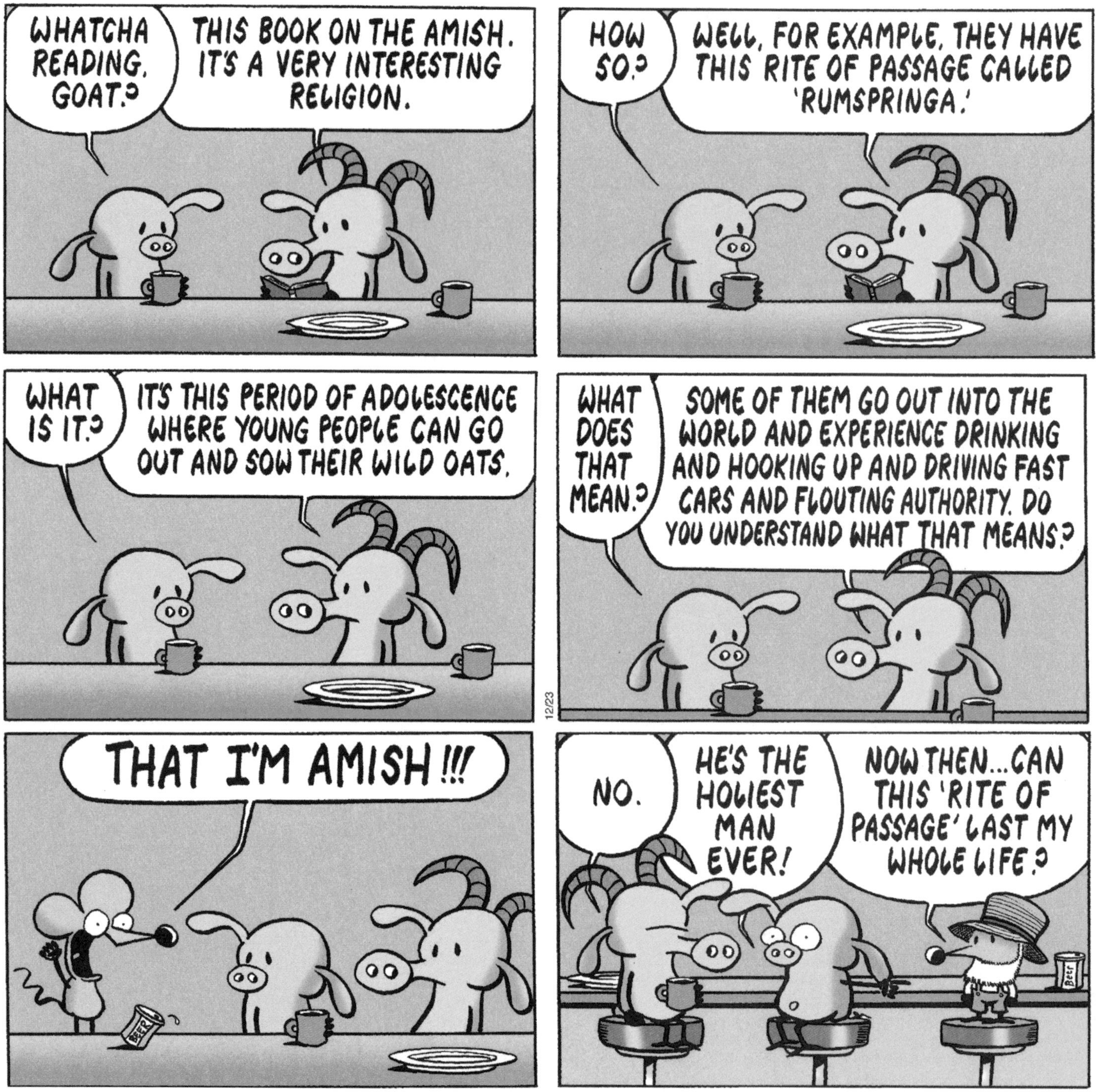
WHATCHA READING, GOAT?
THIS BOOK ON THE AMISH. IT'S A VERY INTERESTING RELIGION.
HOW SO?
WELL, FOR EXAMPLE, THEY HAVE THIS RITE OF PASSAGE CALLED 'RUMSPRINGA.'
WHAT IS IT?
IT'S THIS PERIOD OF ADOLESCENCE WHERE YOUNG PEOPLE CAN GO OUT AND SOW THEIR WILD OATS.
WHAT DOES THAT MEAN?
SOME OF THEM GO OUT INTO THE WORLD AND EXPERIENCE DRINKING AND HOOKING UP AND DRIVING FAST CARS AND FLOUTING AUTHORITY. DO YOU UNDERSTAND WHAT THAT MEANS?
12/23
THAT I'M AMISH !!!
BEER
NO.
HE'S THE HOLIEST MAN EVER!
NOW THEN...CAN THIS 'RITE OF PASSAGE' LAST MY WHOLE LIFE?
BEER

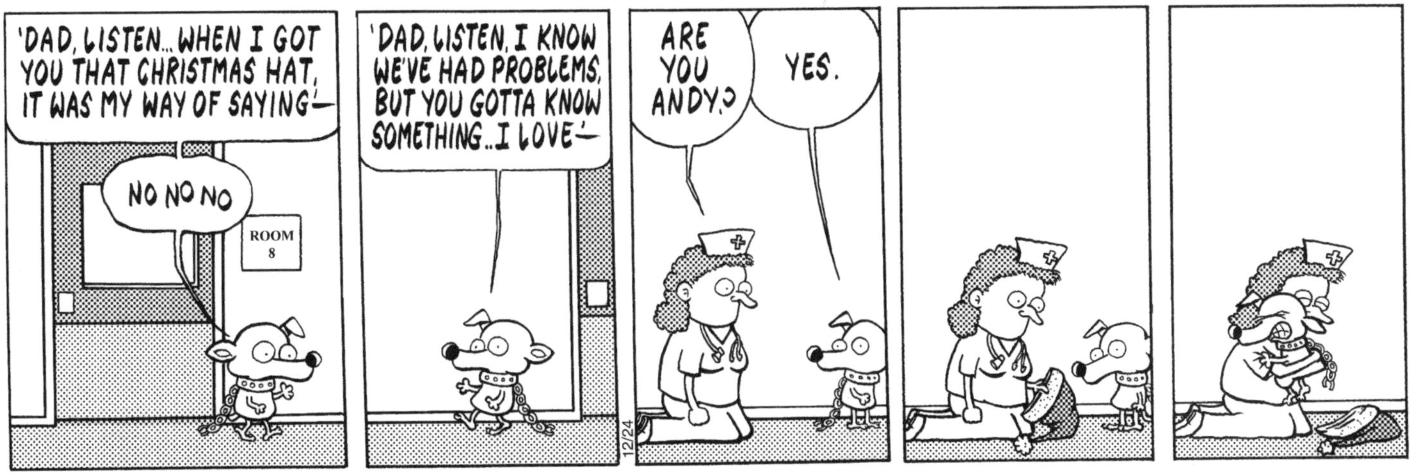
'DAD, LISTEN... WHEN I GOT YOU THAT CHRISTMAS HAT, IT WAS MY WAY OF SAYING'—
NO NO NO
ROOM 8
'DAD, LISTEN, I KNOW WE'VE HAD PROBLEMS, BUT YOU GOTTA KNOW SOMETHING.. I LOVE'—
12/24
ARE YOU ANDY?
YES.

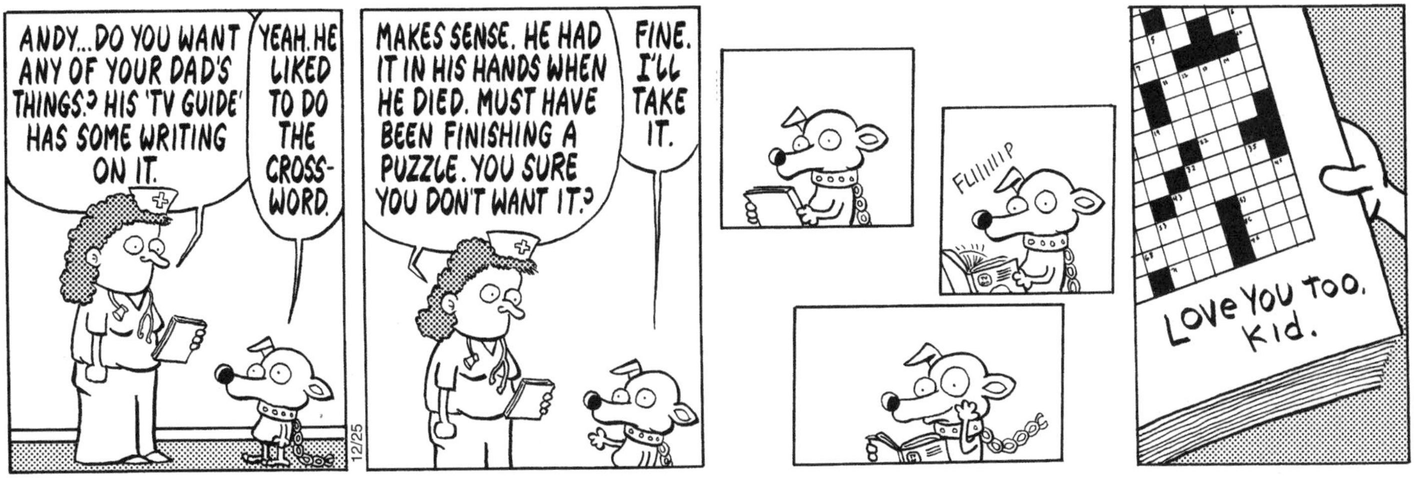
ANDY...DO YOU WANT ANY OF YOUR DAD'S THINGS? HIS 'TV GUIDE' HAS SOME WRITING ON IT.
YEAH. HE LIKED TO DO THE CROSS-WORD.
12/25
MAKES SENSE. HE HAD IT IN HIS HANDS WHEN HE DIED. MUST HAVE BEEN FINISHING A PUZZLE. YOU SURE YOU DON'T WANT IT?
FINE. I'LL TAKE IT.
FLIIIIIP
Love You Too, Kid.

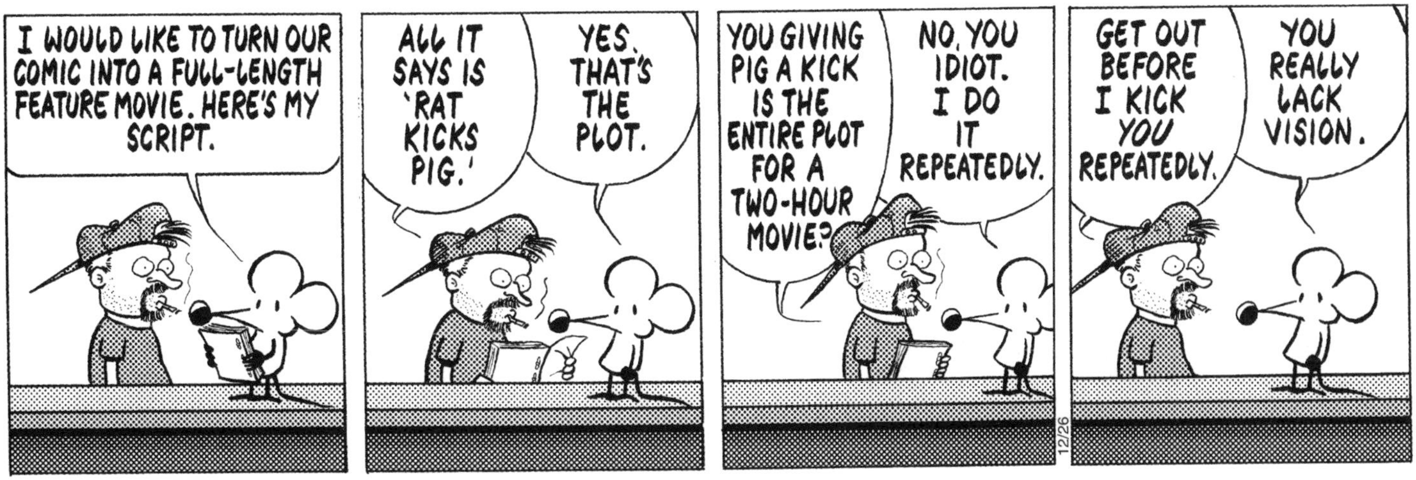
I WOULD LIKE TO TURN OUR COMIC INTO A FULL-LENGTH FEATURE MOVIE. HERE'S MY SCRIPT.
ALL IT SAYS IS 'RAT KICKS PIG.'
YES. THAT'S THE PLOT.
YOU GIVING PIG A KICK IS THE ENTIRE PLOT FOR A TWO-HOUR MOVIE?
NO, YOU IDIOT. I DO IT REPEATEDLY.
12/26
GET OUT BEFORE I KICK YOU REPEATEDLY.
YOU REALLY LACK VISION.

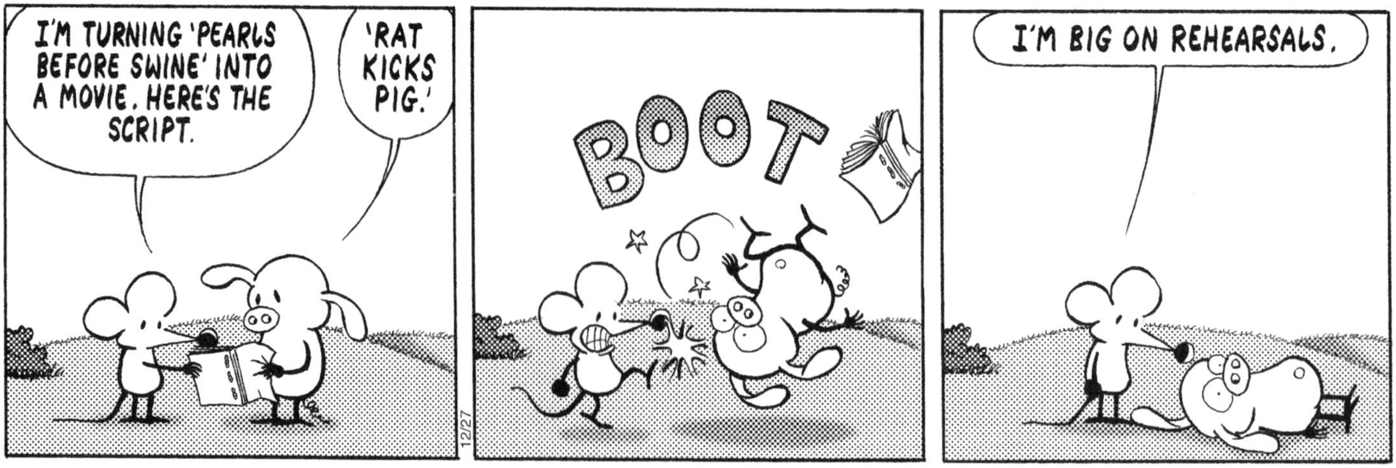
I'M TURNING 'PEARLS BEFORE SWINE' INTO A MOVIE. HERE'S THE SCRIPT.
'RAT KICKS PIG.'
BOOT
12/27
I'M BIG ON REHEARSALS.

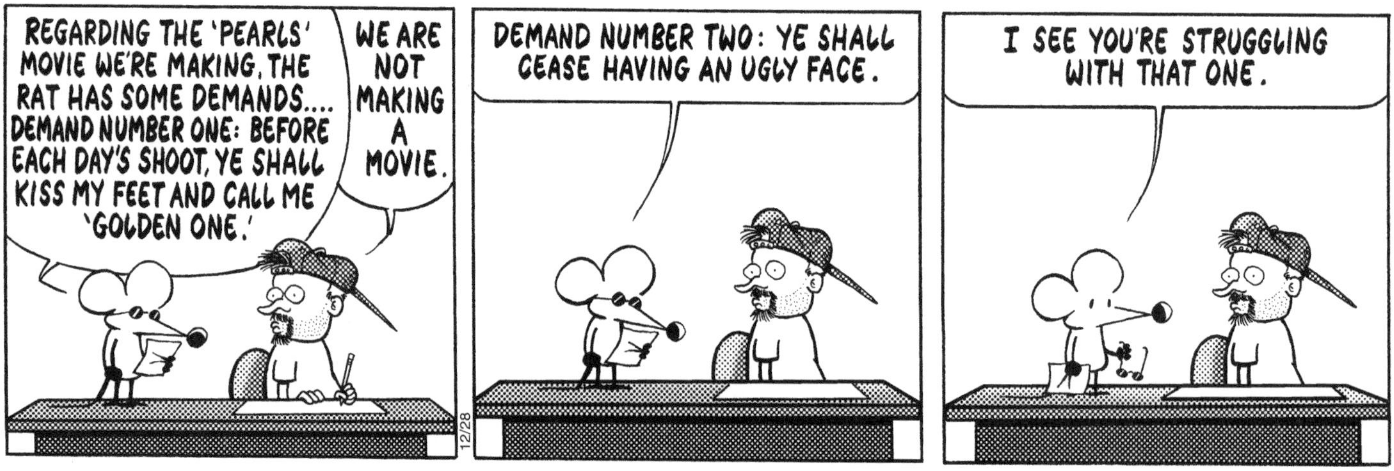
REGARDING THE 'PEARLS' MOVIE WE'RE MAKING, THE RAT HAS SOME DEMANDS.... DEMAND NUMBER ONE: BEFORE EACH DAY'S SHOOT, YE SHALL KISS MY FEET AND CALL ME 'GOLDEN ONE.'
WE ARE NOT MAKING A MOVIE.
12/28
DEMAND NUMBER TWO: YE SHALL CEASE HAVING AN UGLY FACE.
I SEE YOU'RE STRUGGLING WITH THAT ONE.

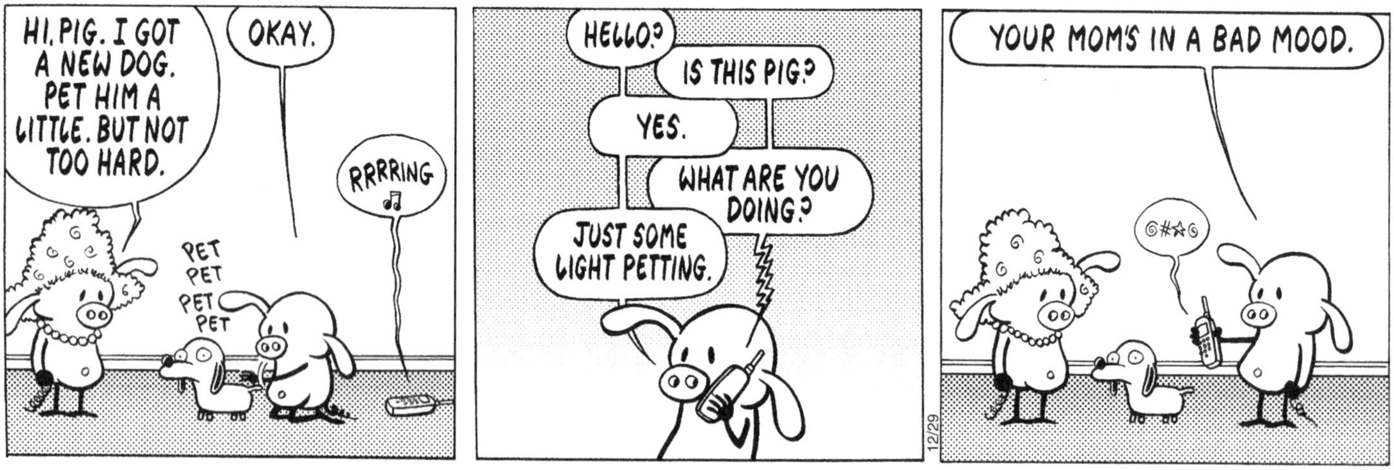
HI, PIG. I GOT A NEW DOG. PET HIM A LITTLE. BUT NOT TOO HARD.
OKAY.
PET PET PET PET
RRRRING
HELLO?
IS THIS PIG?
YES.
WHAT ARE YOU DOING?
JUST SOME LIGHT PETTING.
12/29
YOUR MOM'S IN A BAD MOOD.

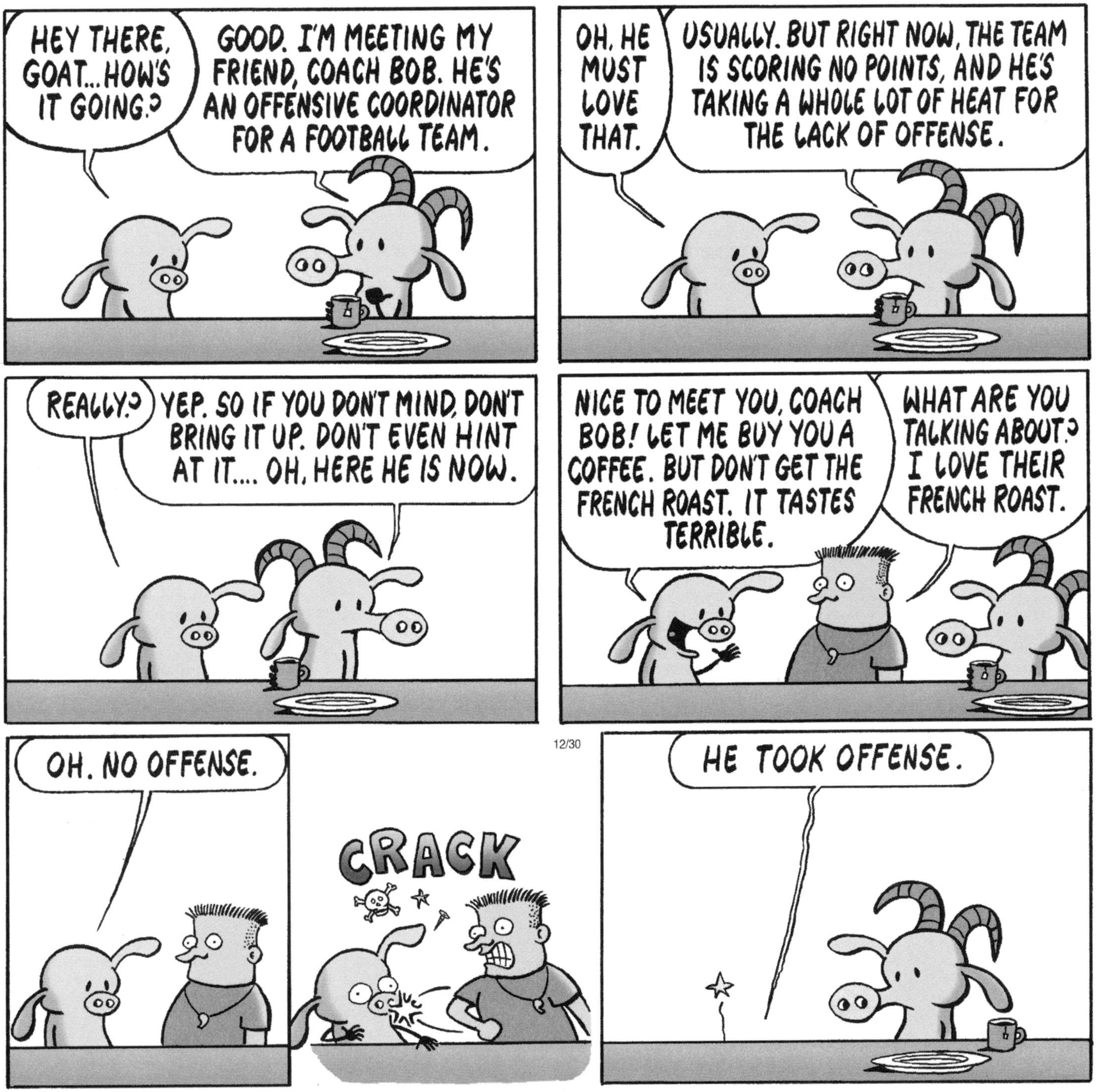

HEY THERE, GOAT...HOW'S IT GOING?
GOOD. I'M MEETING MY FRIEND, COACH BOB. HE'S AN OFFENSIVE COORDINATOR FOR A FOOTBALL TEAM.
OH, HE MUST LOVE THAT.
USUALLY. BUT RIGHT NOW, THE TEAM IS SCORING NO POINTS, AND HE'S TAKING A WHOLE LOT OF HEAT FOR THE LACK OF OFFENSE.
REALLY?
YEP. SO IF YOU DON'T MIND, DON'T BRING IT UP. DON'T EVEN HINT AT IT.... OH, HERE HE IS NOW.
NICE TO MEET YOU, COACH BOB! LET ME BUY YOU A COFFEE. BUT DON'T GET THE FRENCH ROAST. IT TASTES TERRIBLE.
WHAT ARE YOU TALKING ABOUT? I LOVE THEIR FRENCH ROAST.
OH. NO OFFENSE.
12/30
CRACK
HE TOOK OFFENSE.

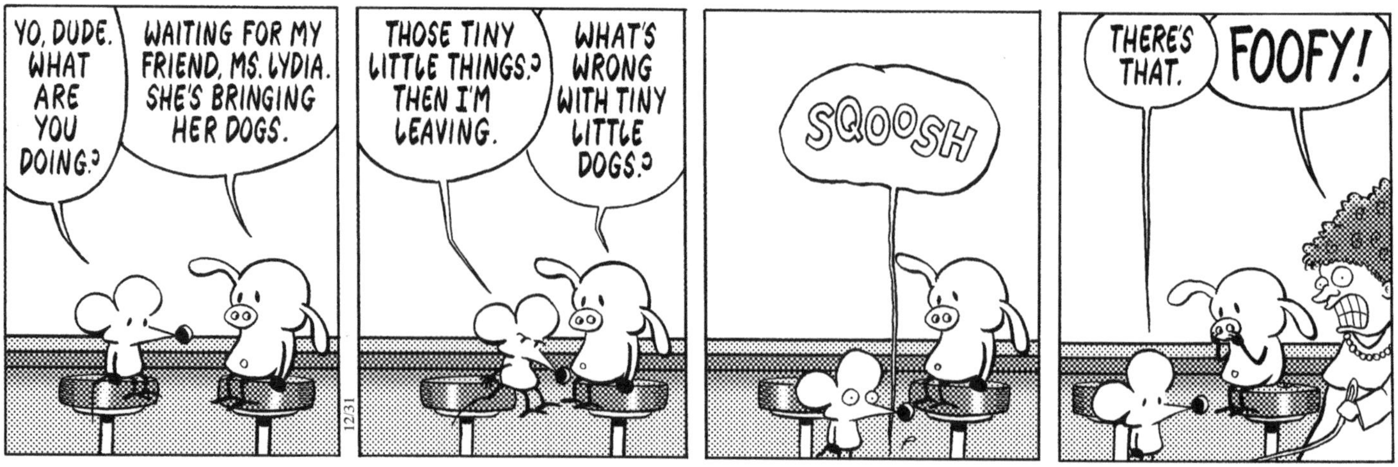
YO, DUDE. WHAT ARE YOU DOING?
WAITING FOR MY FRIEND, MS. LYDIA. SHE'S BRINGING HER DOGS.
12/31
THOSE TINY LITTLE THINGS? THEN I'M LEAVING.
WHAT'S WRONG WITH TINY LITTLE DOGS?
SQOOSH
THERE'S THAT.
FOOFY!

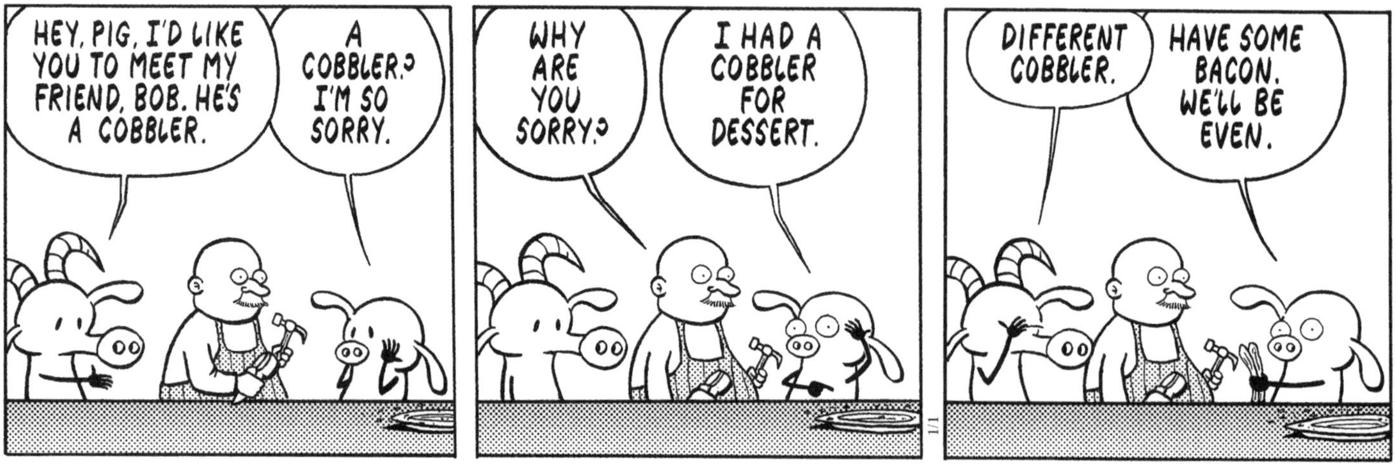
HEY, PIG, I'D LIKE YOU TO MEET MY FRIEND, BOB. HE'S A COBBLER.
A COBBLER? I'M SO SORRY.
WHY ARE YOU SORRY?
I HAD A COBBLER FOR DESSERT.
1/1
DIFFERENT COBBLER.
HAVE SOME BACON. WE'LL BE EVEN.

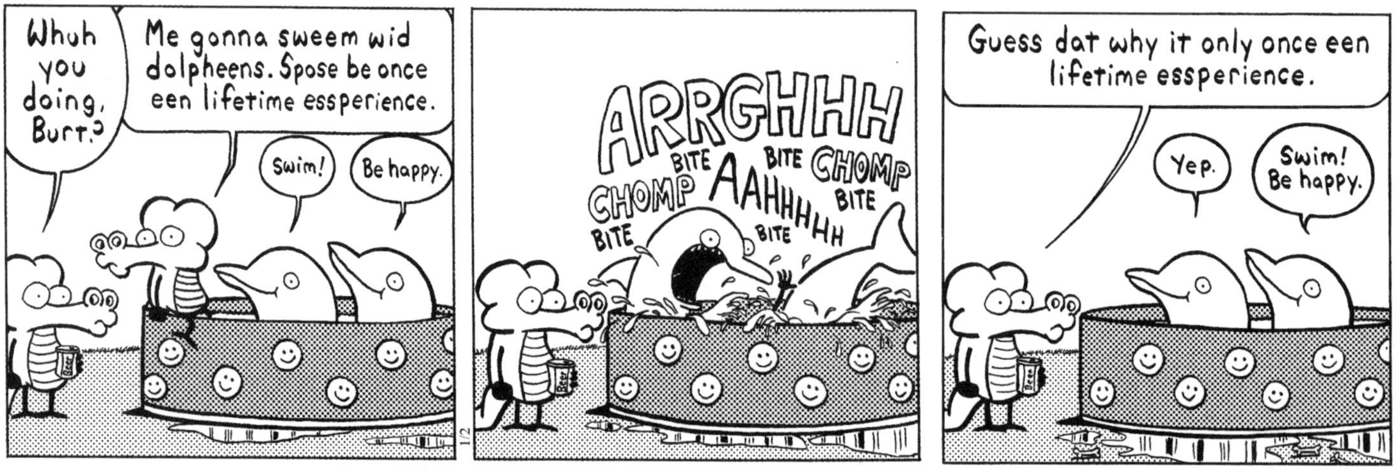
Whuh you doing, Burt?
Me gonna sweem wid dolpheens. Spose be once een lifetime essperience.
Swim!
Be happy.
1/2
ARRGHHH
BITE
BITE
CHOMP
AAHHHHHH
CHOMP
BITE
BITE
BITE
Guess dat why it only once een lifetime essperience.
Yep.
Swim! Be happy.

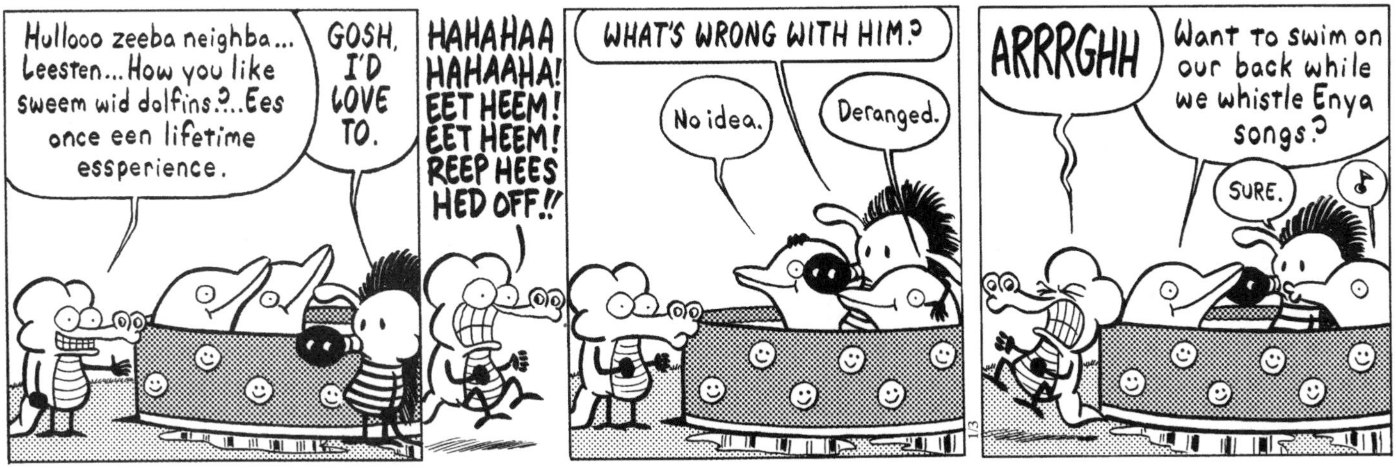
Hullooo zeeba neighba... Leesten... How you like sweem wid dolfins?...Ees once een lifetime essperience.
GOSH, I'D LOVE TO.
HAHAHAA HAHAAHA! EET HEEM! EET HEEM! REEP HEES HED OFF!!
WHAT'S WRONG WITH HIM?
No idea.
Deranged.
ARRRGHH
Want to swim on our back while we whistle Enya songs?
SURE.

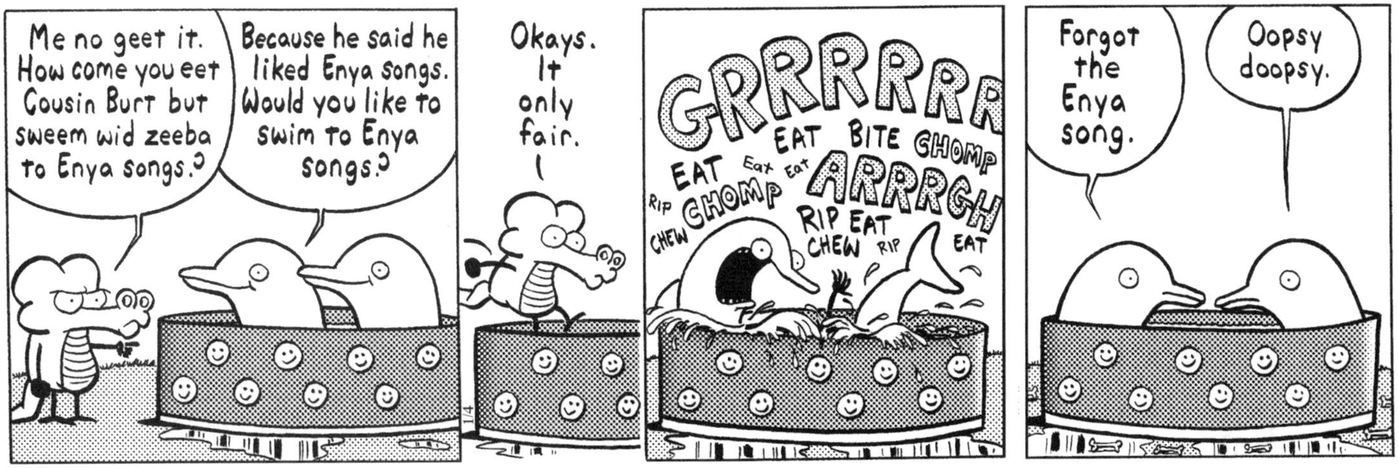
Me no geet it. How come you eet Cousin Burt but sweem wid zeeba to Enya songs?
Because he said he liked Enya songs. Would you like to swim to Enya songs?
Okays. It only fair.
GRRRRRRR
EAT BITE GHOMP
EAT Eat Eat ARRRGH
RIP GHOMP
CHEW
RIP EAT
CHEW RIP
EAT
Forgot the Enya song.
Oopsy doopsy.

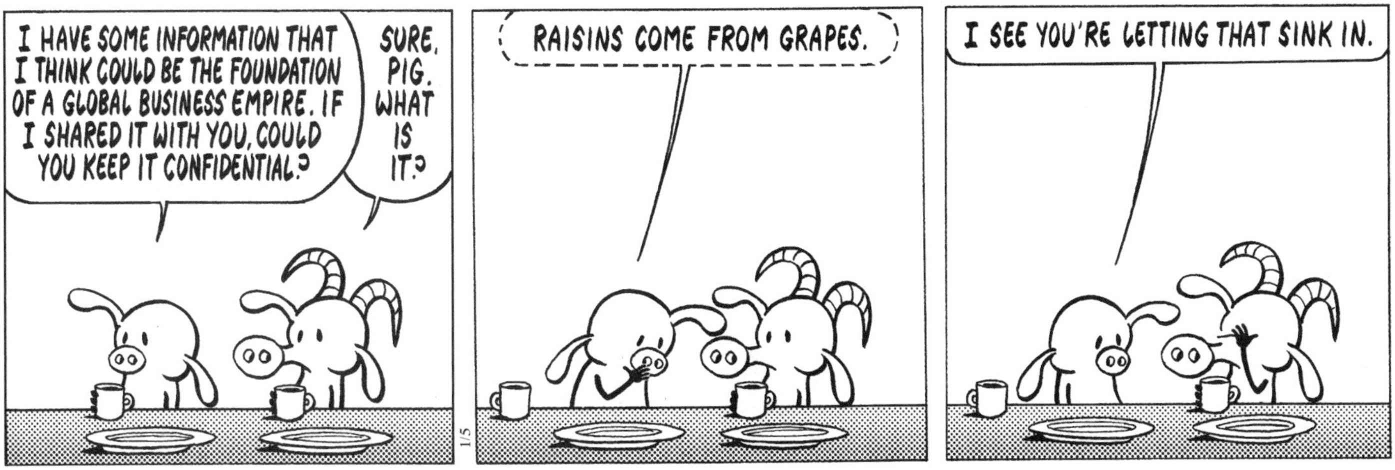
I HAVE SOME INFORMATION THAT I THINK COULD BE THE FOUNDATION OF A GLOBAL BUSINESS EMPIRE. IF I SHARED IT WITH YOU, COULD YOU KEEP IT CONFIDENTIAL?
SURE, PIG. WHAT IS IT?
RAISINS COME FROM GRAPES.
I SEE YOU'RE LETTING THAT SINK IN.

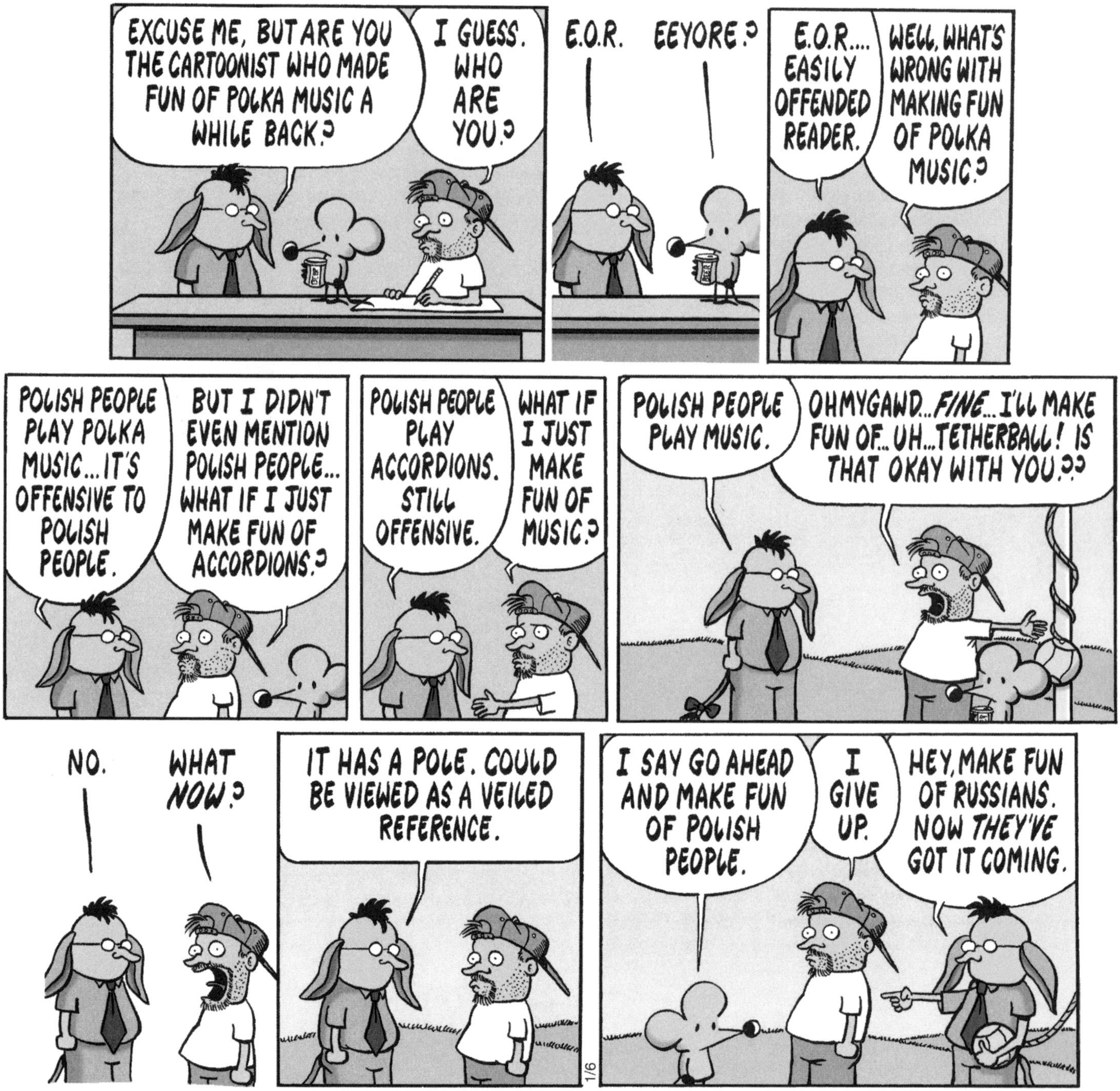
EXCUSE ME, BUT ARE YOU THE CARTOONIST WHO MADE FUN OF POLKA MUSIC A WHILE BACK?
I GUESS. WHO ARE YOU?
E.O.R.
EEYORE?
E.O.R.... EASILY OFFENDED READER.
WELL, WHAT'S WRONG WITH MAKING FUN OF POLKA MUSIC?
POLISH PEOPLE PLAY POLKA MUSIC... IT'S OFFENSIVE TO POLISH PEOPLE.
BUT I DIDN'T EVEN MENTION POLISH PEOPLE... WHAT IF I JUST MAKE FUN OF ACCORDIONS?
POLISH PEOPLE PLAY ACCORDIONS. STILL OFFENSIVE.
WHAT IF I JUST MAKE FUN OF MUSIC?
POLISH PEOPLE PLAY MUSIC.
OHMYGAWD... *FINE*... I'LL MAKE FUN OF... UH... TETHERBALL! IS THAT OKAY WITH YOU??
NO.
WHAT *NOW*?
IT HAS A POLE. COULD BE VIEWED AS A VEILED REFERENCE.
I SAY GO AHEAD AND MAKE FUN OF POLISH PEOPLE.
I GIVE UP.
HEY, MAKE FUN OF RUSSIANS. NOW *THEY'VE* GOT IT COMING.
1/6

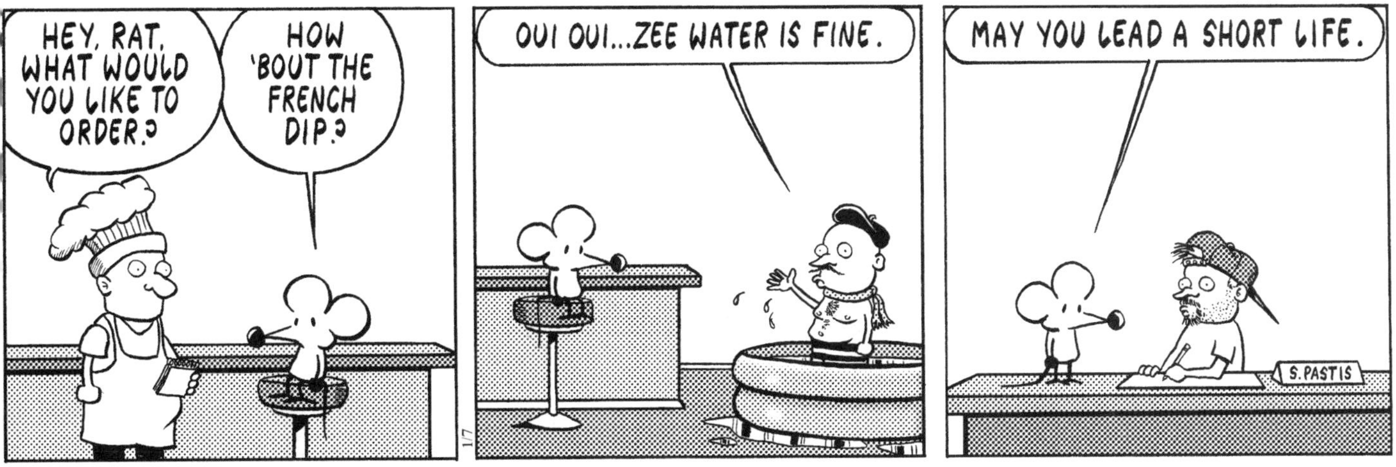
HEY, RAT, WHAT WOULD YOU LIKE TO ORDER?
HOW 'BOUT THE FRENCH DIP?
1/7
OUI OUI...ZEE WATER IS FINE.
MAY YOU LEAD A SHORT LIFE.
S. PASTIS

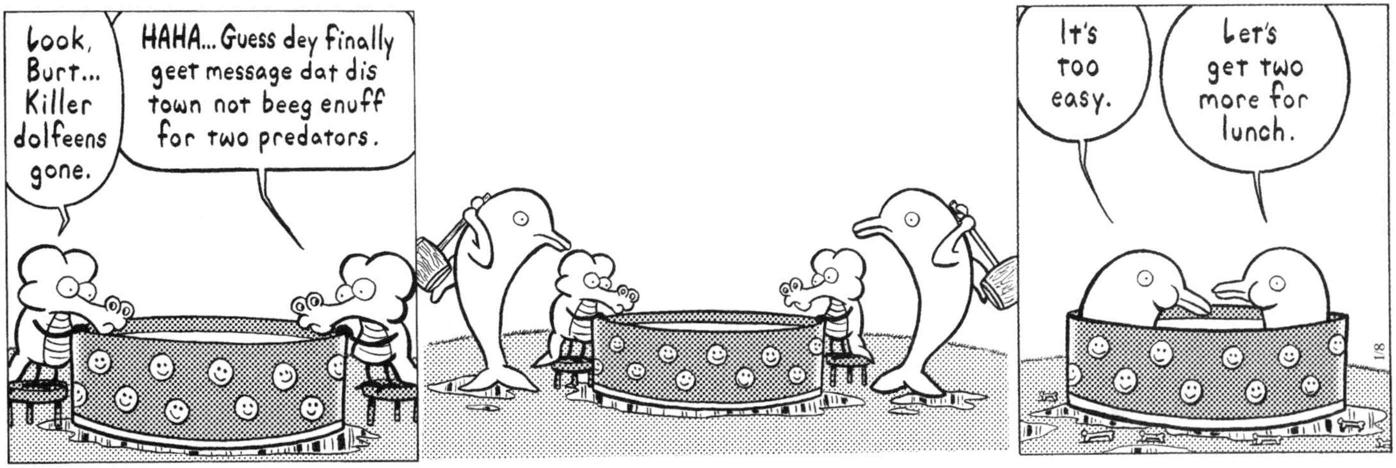
Look, Burt... Killer dolfeens gone.
HAHA... Guess dey finally geet message dat dis town not beeg enuff for two predators.
It's too easy.
Let's get two more for lunch.
1/8

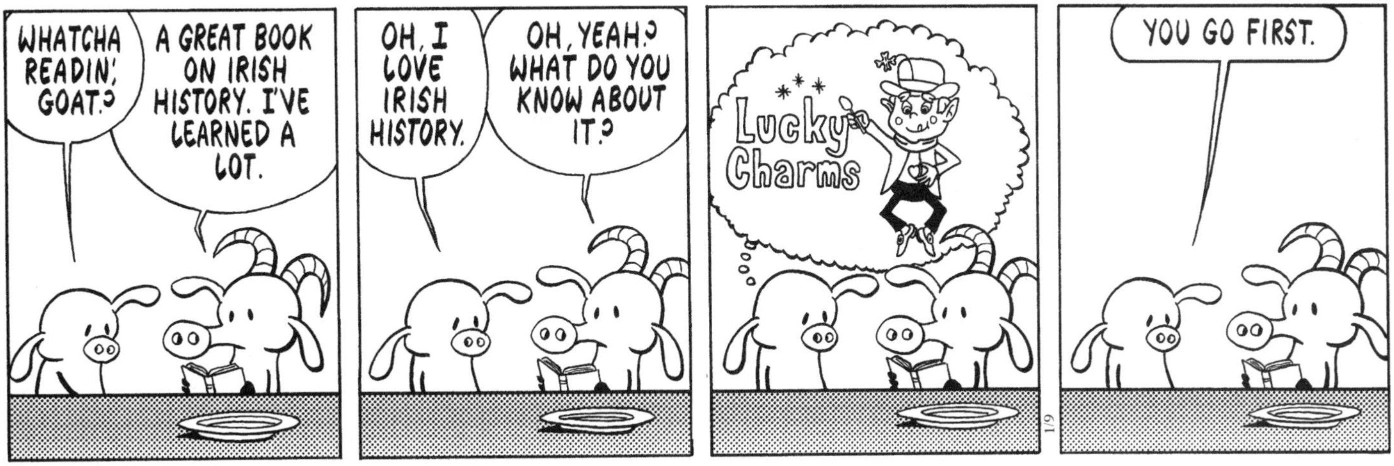
WHATCHA READIN', GOAT?
A GREAT BOOK ON IRISH HISTORY. I'VE LEARNED A LOT.
OH, I LOVE IRISH HISTORY.
OH, YEAH? WHAT DO YOU KNOW ABOUT IT?
1/9
Lucky Charms
YOU GO FIRST.

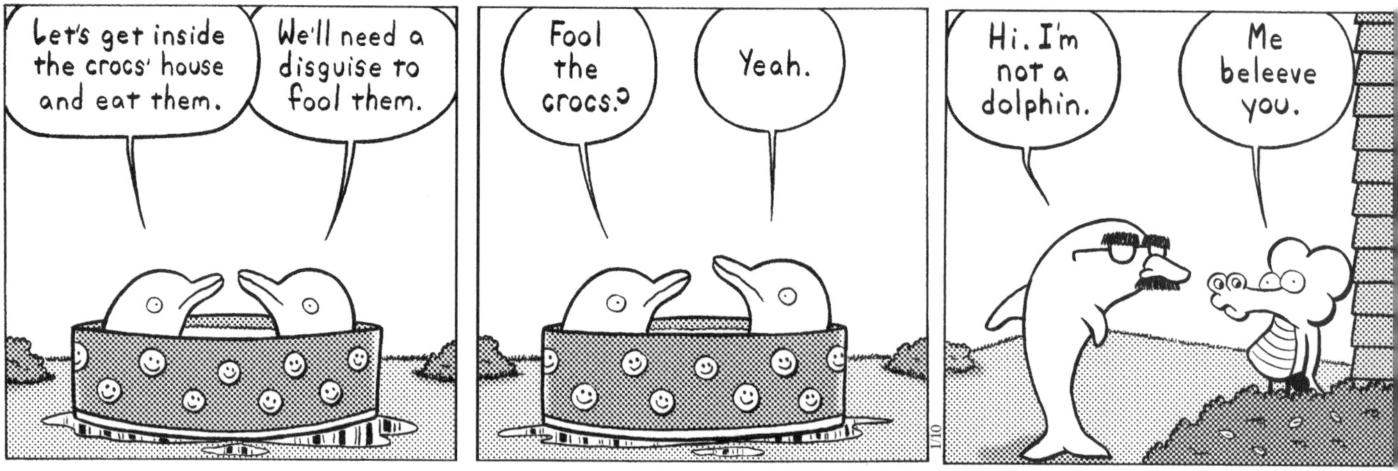
Let's get inside the crocs' house and eat them.
We'll need a disguise to fool them.
Fool the crocs?
Yeah.
1/10
Hi. I'm not a dolphin.
Me beleeve you.

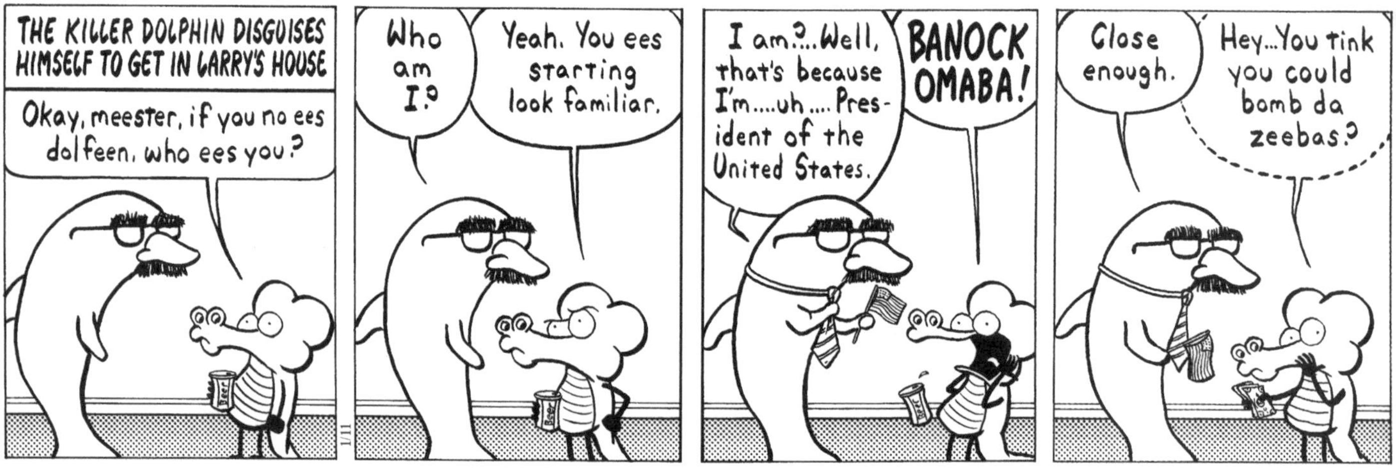
THE KILLER DOLPHIN DISGUISES HIMSELF TO GET IN LARRY'S HOUSE
Okay, meester, if you no ees dolfeen, who ees you?
1/11
Who am I?
Yeah. You ees starting look familiar.
I am?...Well, that's because I'm....uh.... President of the United States.
BANOCK OMABA!
Close enough.
Hey...You tink you could bomb da zeebas?

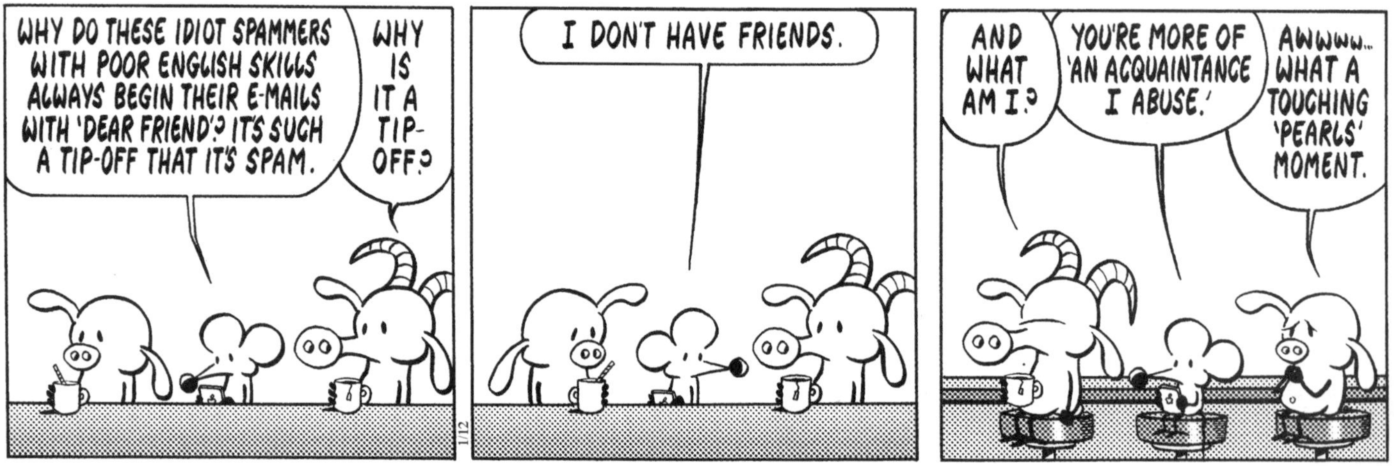
WHY DO THESE IDIOT SPAMMERS WITH POOR ENGLISH SKILLS ALWAYS BEGIN THEIR E-MAILS WITH 'DEAR FRIEND'? IT'S SUCH A TIP-OFF THAT IT'S SPAM.
WHY IS IT A TIP-OFF?
1/12
I DON'T HAVE FRIENDS.
AND WHAT AM I?
YOU'RE MORE OF 'AN ACQUAINTANCE I ABUSE.'
AWWWW... WHAT A TOUCHING 'PEARLS' MOMENT.

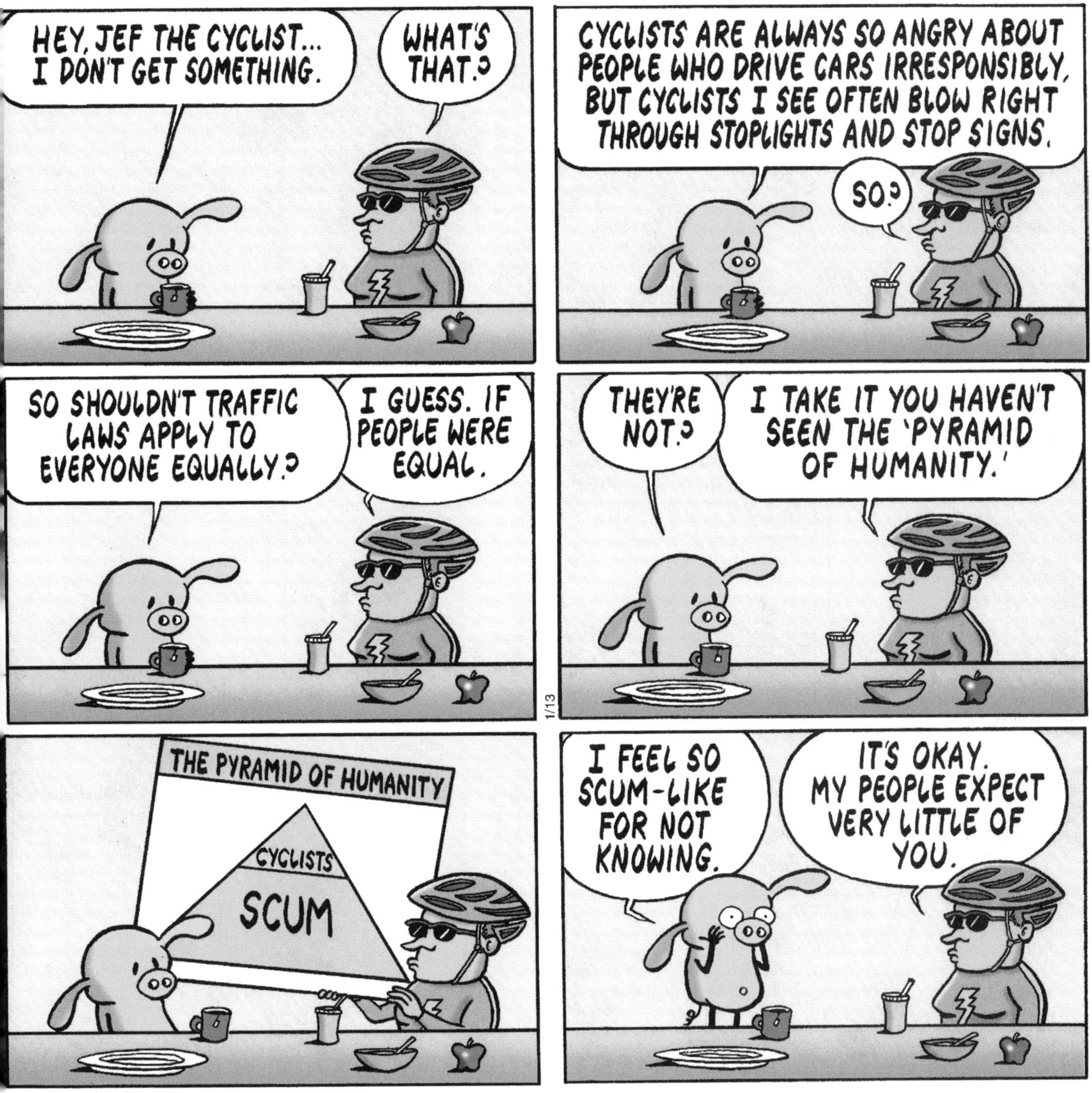
HEY, JEF THE CYCLIST... I DON'T GET SOMETHING.
WHAT'S THAT?
CYCLISTS ARE ALWAYS SO ANGRY ABOUT PEOPLE WHO DRIVE CARS IRRESPONSIBLY, BUT CYCLISTS I SEE OFTEN BLOW RIGHT THROUGH STOPLIGHTS AND STOP SIGNS.
SO?
SO SHOULDN'T TRAFFIC LAWS APPLY TO EVERYONE EQUALLY?
I GUESS. IF PEOPLE WERE EQUAL.
THEY'RE NOT?
I TAKE IT YOU HAVEN'T SEEN THE 'PYRAMID OF HUMANITY.'
1/13
THE PYRAMID OF HUMANITY
CYCLISTS
SCUM
I FEEL SO SCUM-LIKE FOR NOT KNOWING.
IT'S OKAY. MY PEOPLE EXPECT VERY LITTLE OF YOU.

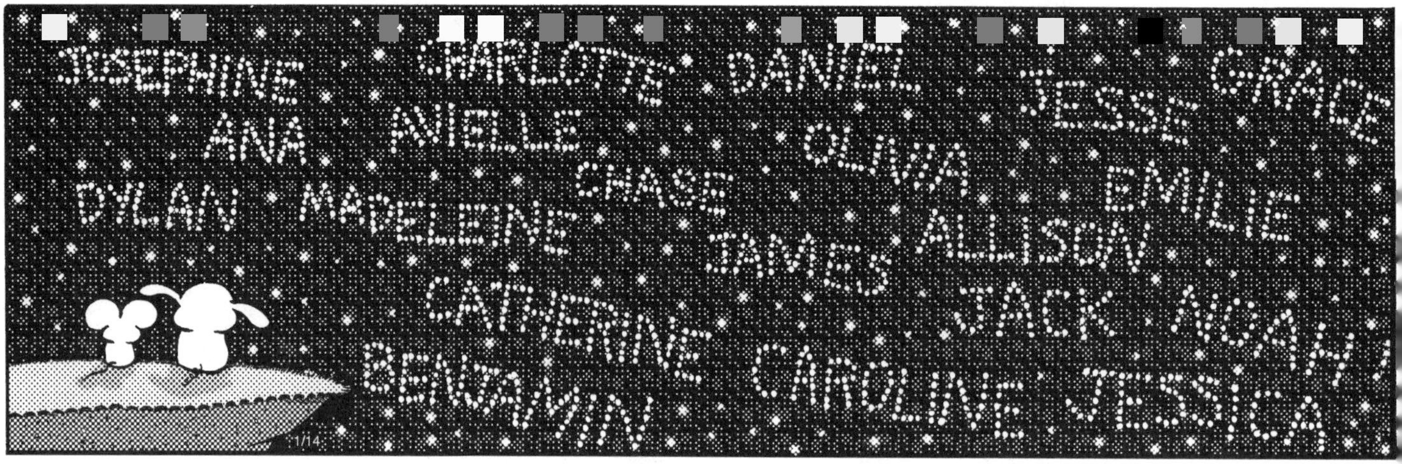
JOSEPHINE
CHARLOTTE
DANIEL
JESSE
GRACE
ANA
ANIELLE
OLIVA
DYLAN
MADELEINE
CHASE
EMILIE
ALLISON
JAMES
CATHERINE
JACK
NOAH
BENJAMIN
CAROLINE
JESSICA

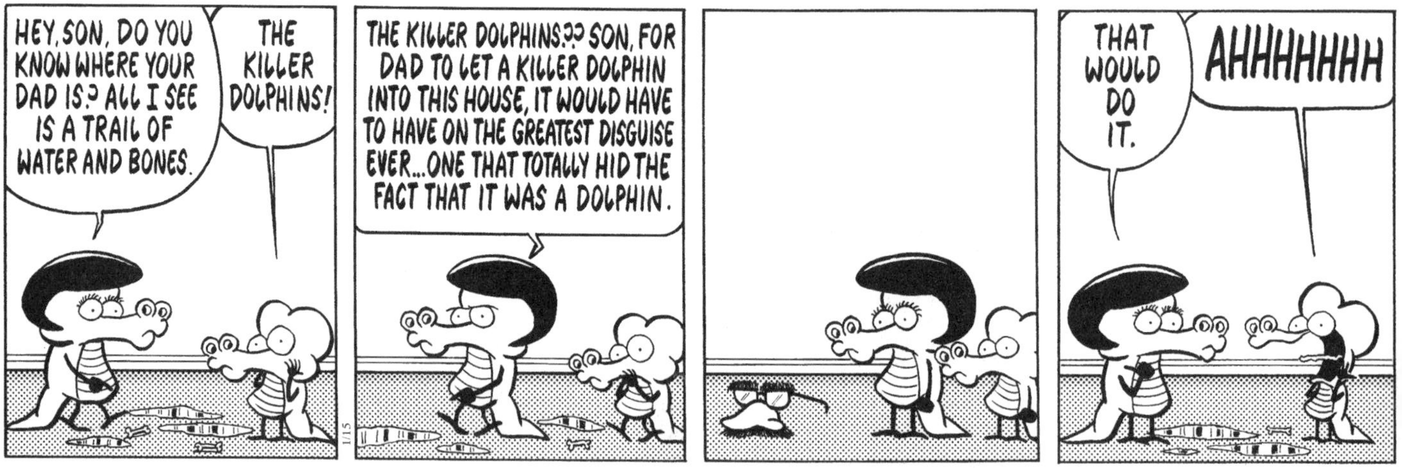
HEY, SON, DO YOU KNOW WHERE YOUR DAD IS? ALL I SEE IS A TRAIL OF WATER AND BONES.
THE KILLER DOLPHINS!
THE KILLER DOLPHINS?? SON, FOR DAD TO LET A KILLER DOLPHIN INTO THIS HOUSE, IT WOULD HAVE TO HAVE ON THE GREATEST DISGUISE EVER...ONE THAT TOTALLY HID THE FACT THAT IT WAS A DOLPHIN.
THAT WOULD DO IT.
AHHHHHHH

STORY UPDATE

Larry allowed a killer dolphin into his house. He now appears to be dead.

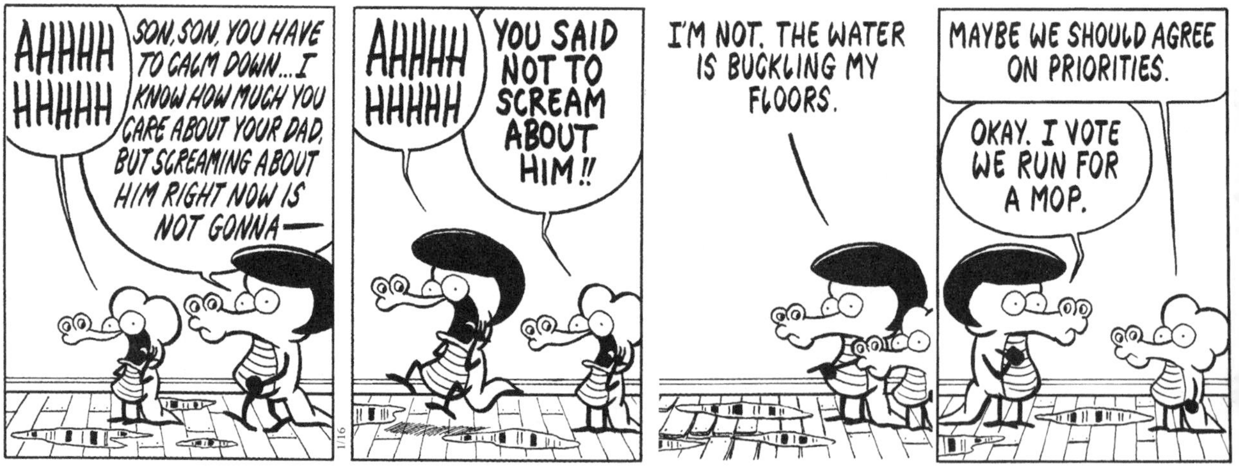
AHHHH HHHHH
SON, SON, YOU HAVE TO CALM DOWN... I KNOW HOW MUCH YOU CARE ABOUT YOUR DAD, BUT SCREAMING ABOUT HIM RIGHT NOW IS NOT GONNA—
AHHHH HHHHH
YOU SAID NOT TO SCREAM ABOUT HIM!!
I'M NOT. THE WATER IS BUCKLING MY FLOORS.
MAYBE WE SHOULD AGREE ON PRIORITIES.
OKAY. I VOTE WE RUN FOR A MOP.

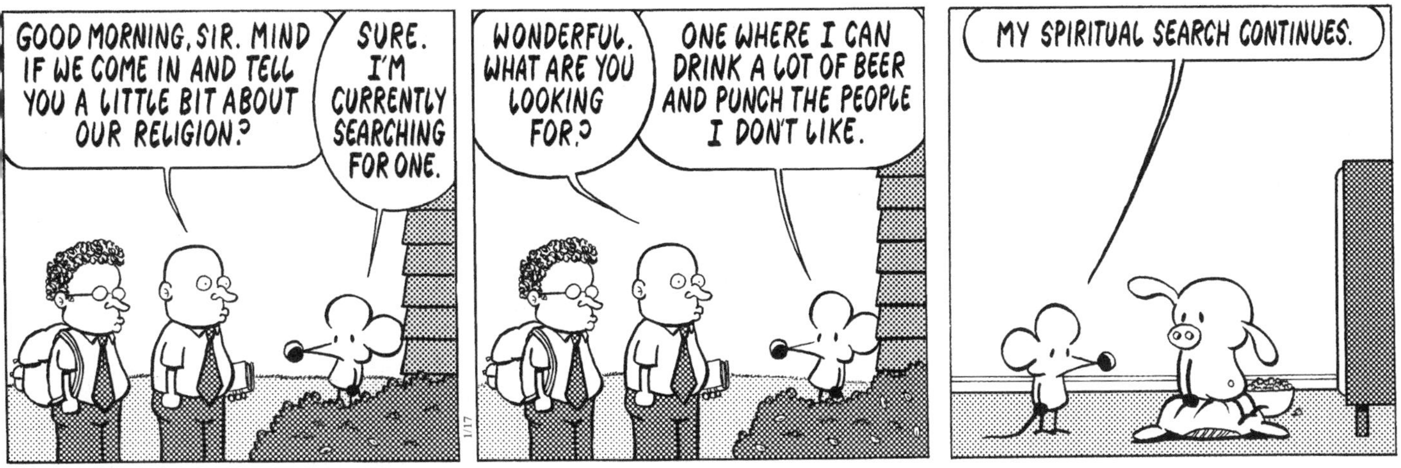
GOOD MORNING, SIR. MIND IF WE COME IN AND TELL YOU A LITTLE BIT ABOUT OUR RELIGION?
SURE. I'M CURRENTLY SEARCHING FOR ONE.
WONDERFUL. WHAT ARE YOU LOOKING FOR?
ONE WHERE I CAN DRINK A LOT OF BEER AND PUNCH THE PEOPLE I DON'T LIKE.
MY SPIRITUAL SEARCH CONTINUES.
1/17

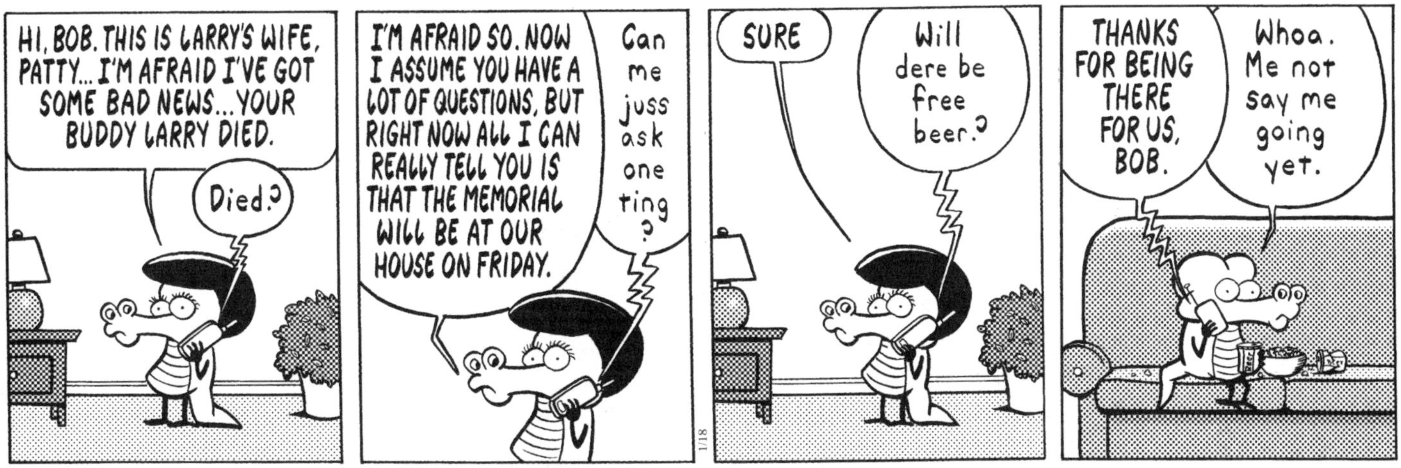
HI, BOB. THIS IS LARRY'S WIFE, PATTY... I'M AFRAID I'VE GOT SOME BAD NEWS... YOUR BUDDY LARRY DIED.
Died?
I'M AFRAID SO. NOW I ASSUME YOU HAVE A LOT OF QUESTIONS, BUT RIGHT NOW ALL I CAN REALLY TELL YOU IS THAT THE MEMORIAL WILL BE AT OUR HOUSE ON FRIDAY.
Can me juss ask one ting?
SURE
Will dere be free beer?
THANKS FOR BEING THERE FOR US, BOB.
Whoa. Me not say me going yet.
1/18

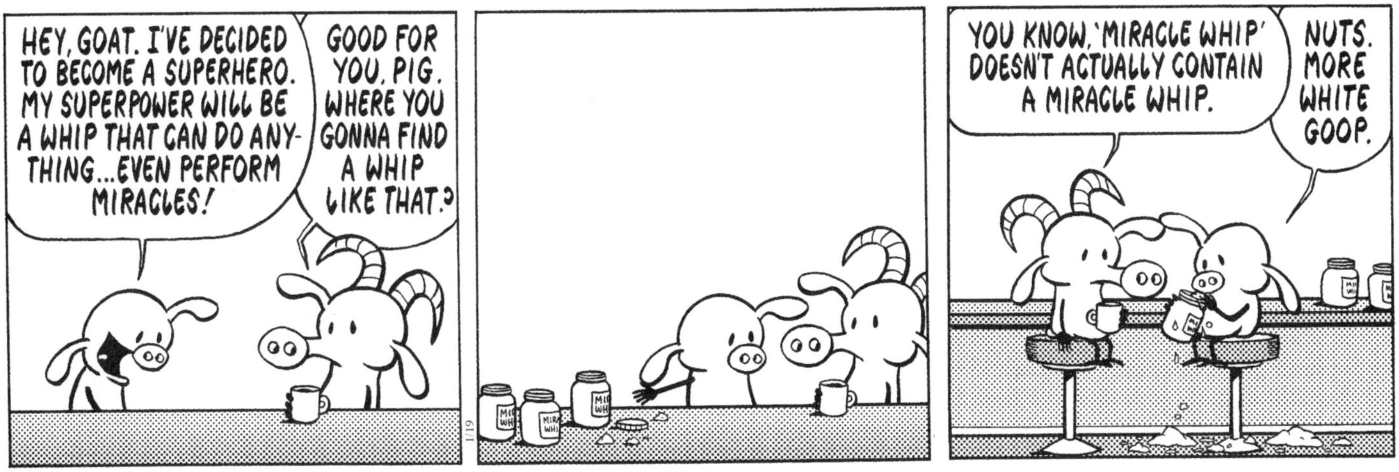
HEY, GOAT. I'VE DECIDED TO BECOME A SUPERHERO. MY SUPERPOWER WILL BE A WHIP THAT CAN DO ANYTHING... EVEN PERFORM MIRACLES!
GOOD FOR YOU, PIG. WHERE YOU GONNA FIND A WHIP LIKE THAT?
YOU KNOW, 'MIRACLE WHIP' DOESN'T ACTUALLY CONTAIN A MIRACLE WHIP.
NUTS. MORE WHITE GOOP.
1/19

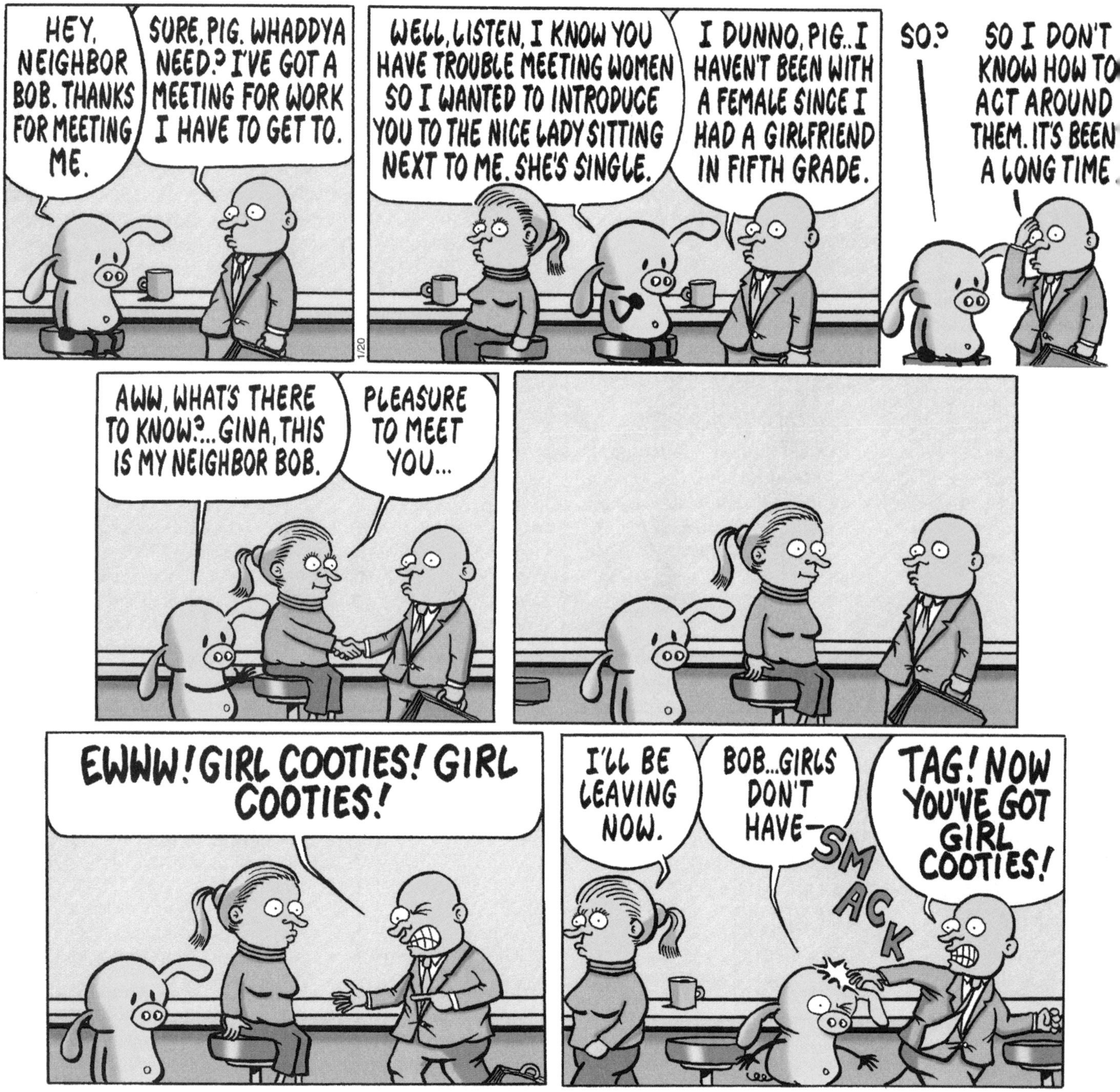
HEY, NEIGHBOR BOB. THANKS FOR MEETING ME.
SURE, PIG. WHADDYA NEED? I'VE GOT A MEETING FOR WORK I HAVE TO GET TO.
1/20
WELL, LISTEN, I KNOW YOU HAVE TROUBLE MEETING WOMEN SO I WANTED TO INTRODUCE YOU TO THE NICE LADY SITTING NEXT TO ME. SHE'S SINGLE.
I DUNNO, PIG.. I HAVEN'T BEEN WITH A FEMALE SINCE I HAD A GIRLFRIEND IN FIFTH GRADE.
SO?
SO I DON'T KNOW HOW TO ACT AROUND THEM. IT'S BEEN A LONG TIME.
AWW, WHAT'S THERE TO KNOW?... GINA, THIS IS MY NEIGHBOR BOB.
PLEASURE TO MEET YOU...
EWWW! GIRL COOTIES! GIRL COOTIES!
I'LL BE LEAVING NOW.
BOB...GIRLS DON'T HAVE—
SMACK
TAG! NOW YOU'VE GOT GIRL COOTIES!

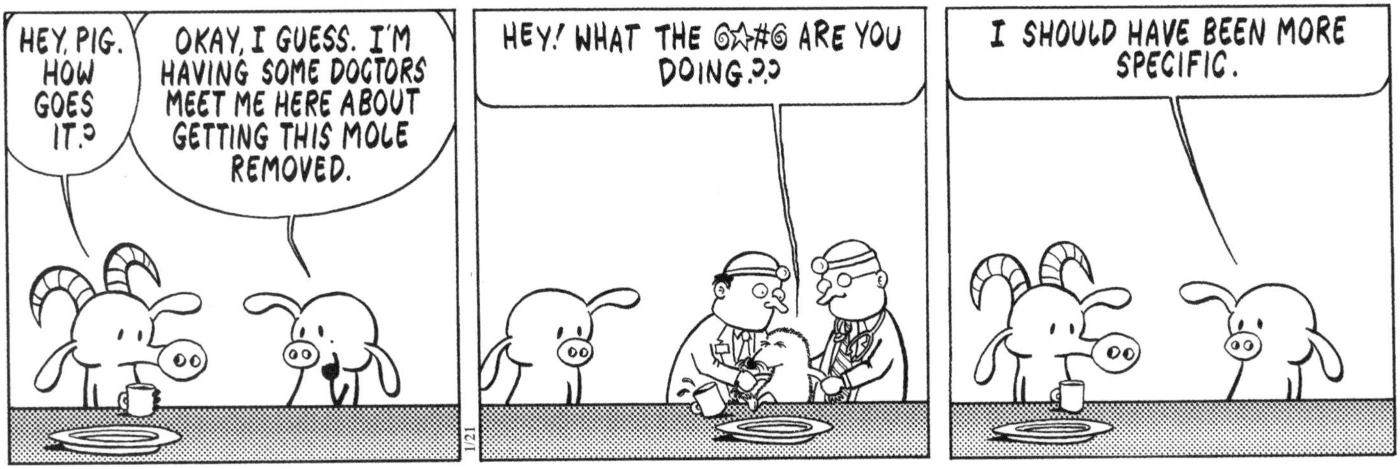
HEY, PIG. HOW GOES IT?
OKAY, I GUESS. I'M HAVING SOME DOCTORS MEET ME HERE ABOUT GETTING THIS MOLE REMOVED.
1/21
HEY! WHAT THE @☆#@ ARE YOU DOING?!?
I SHOULD HAVE BEEN MORE SPECIFIC.

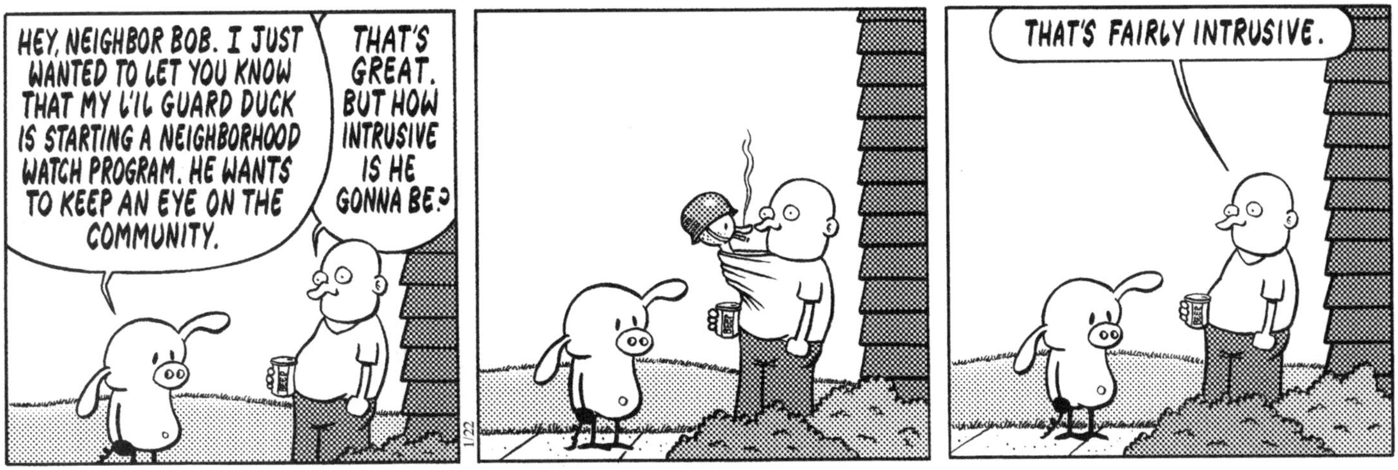
HEY, NEIGHBOR BOB. I JUST WANTED TO LET YOU KNOW THAT MY L'IL GUARD DUCK IS STARTING A NEIGHBORHOOD WATCH PROGRAM. HE WANTS TO KEEP AN EYE ON THE COMMUNITY.
THAT'S GREAT. BUT HOW INTRUSIVE IS HE GONNA BE?
1/22
THAT'S FAIRLY INTRUSIVE.

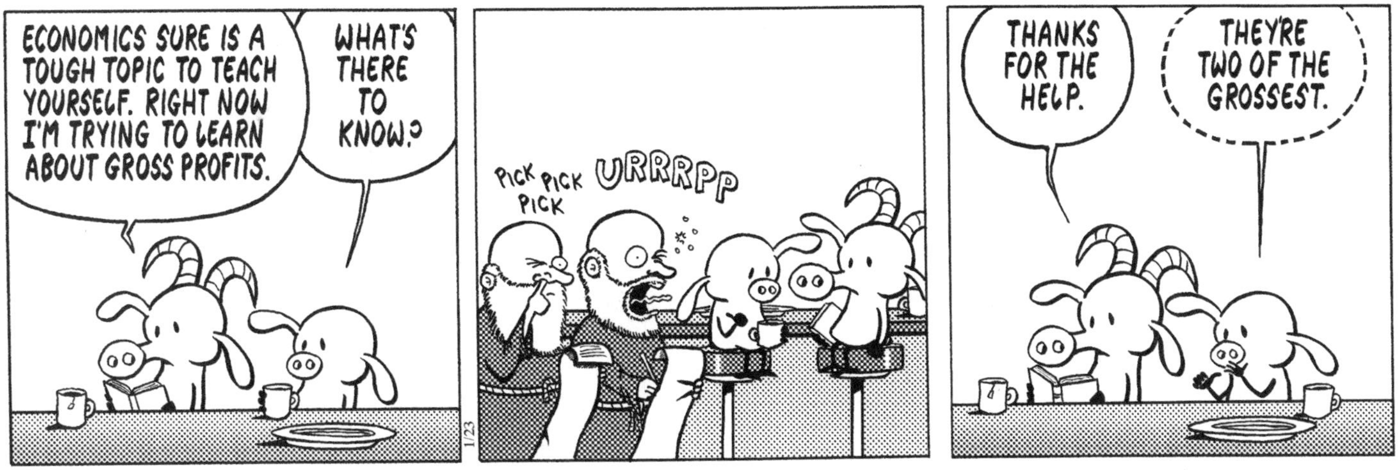
ECONOMICS SURE IS A TOUGH TOPIC TO TEACH YOURSELF. RIGHT NOW I'M TRYING TO LEARN ABOUT GROSS PROFITS.
WHAT'S THERE TO KNOW?
1/23
PICK PICK PICK
URRRPP
THANKS FOR THE HELP.
THEY'RE TWO OF THE GROSSEST.

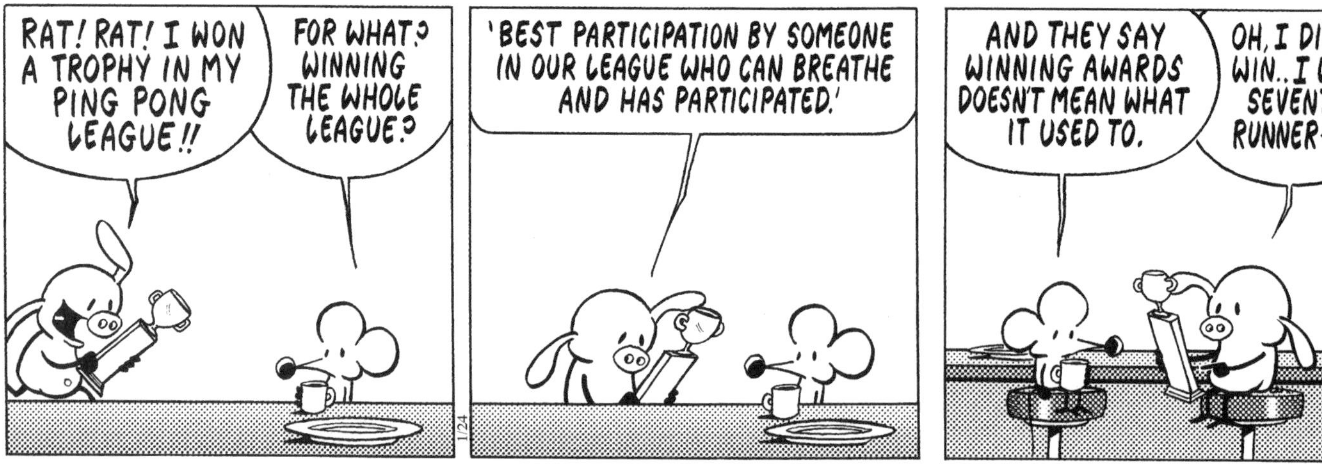
RAT! RAT! I WON A TROPHY IN MY PING PONG LEAGUE!!
FOR WHAT? WINNING THE WHOLE LEAGUE?
'BEST PARTICIPATION BY SOMEONE IN OUR LEAGUE WHO CAN BREATHE AND HAS PARTICIPATED.'
AND THEY SAY WINNING AWARDS DOESN'T MEAN WHAT IT USED TO.
OH, I DIDN'T WIN.. I WAS SEVENTH RUNNER-UP.
1/24

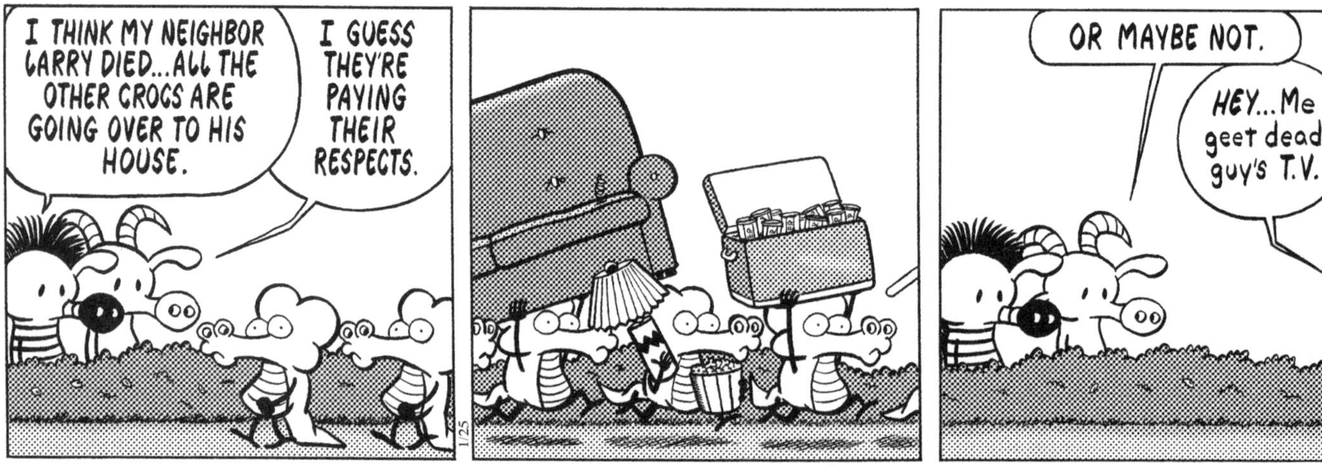
I THINK MY NEIGHBOR LARRY DIED...ALL THE OTHER CROCS ARE GOING OVER TO HIS HOUSE.
I GUESS THEY'RE PAYING THEIR RESPECTS.
OR MAYBE NOT.
HEY... Me geet dead guy's T.V.
1/25

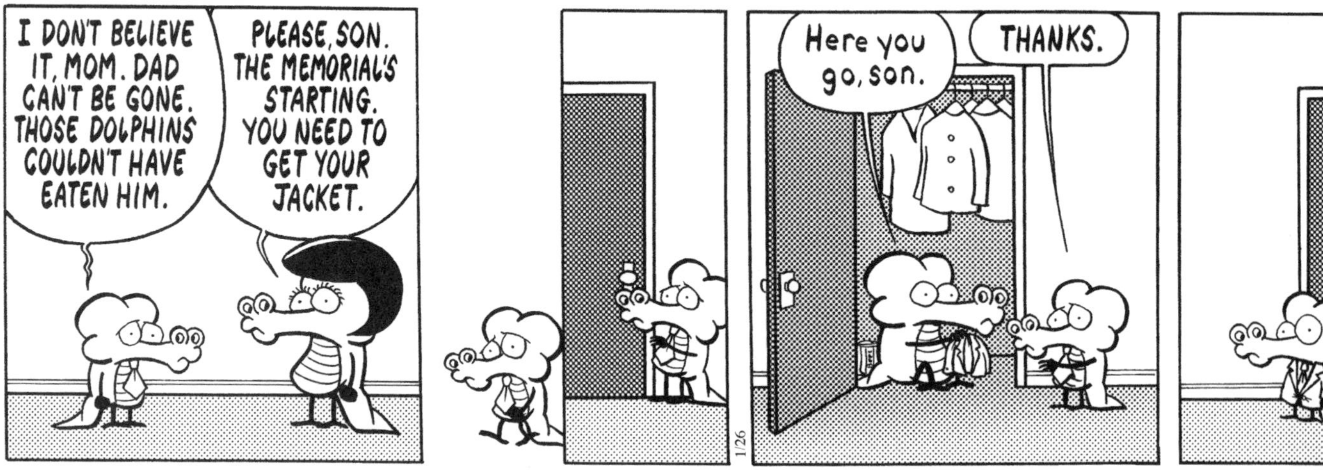
I DON'T BELIEVE IT, MOM. DAD CAN'T BE GONE. THOSE DOLPHINS COULDN'T HAVE EATEN HIM.
PLEASE, SON. THE MEMORIAL'S STARTING. YOU NEED TO GET YOUR JACKET.
Here you go, son.
THANKS.
1/26

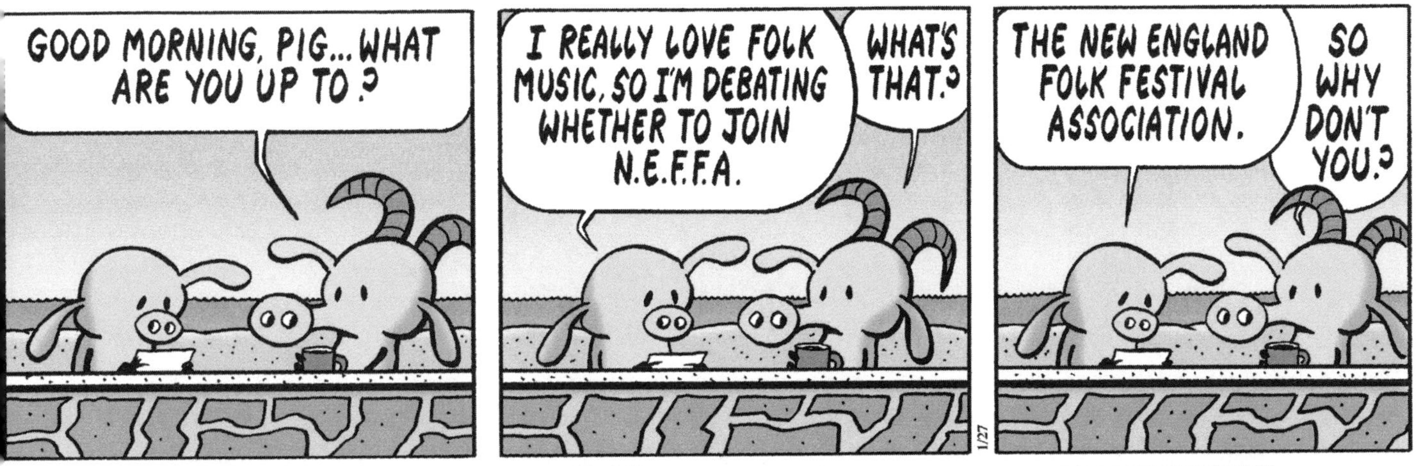
GOOD MORNING, PIG... WHAT ARE YOU UP TO?
I REALLY LOVE FOLK MUSIC, SO I'M DEBATING WHETHER TO JOIN N.E.F.F.A.
WHAT'S THAT?
THE NEW ENGLAND FOLK FESTIVAL ASSOCIATION.
SO WHY DON'T YOU?
1/27

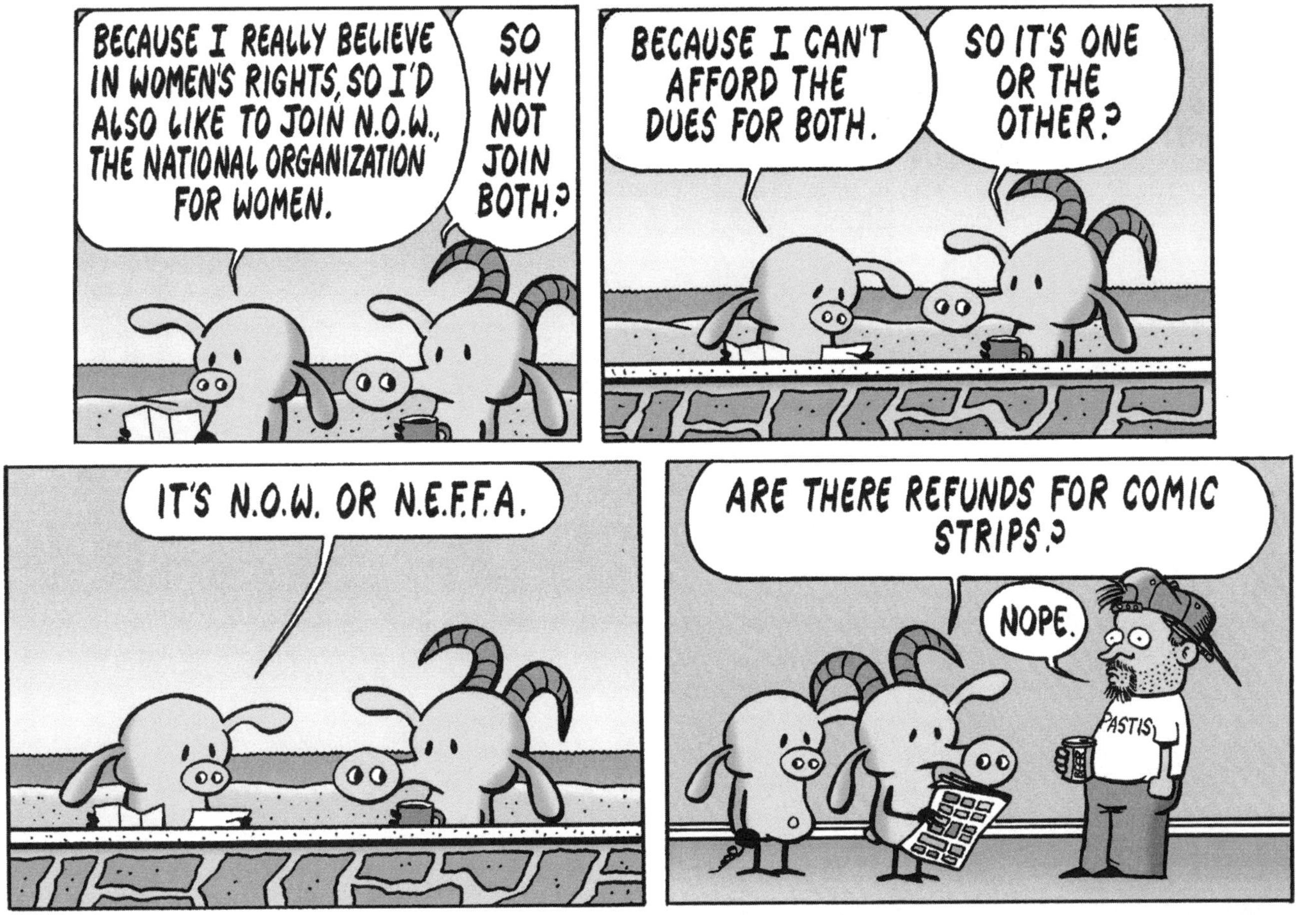
BECAUSE I REALLY BELIEVE IN WOMEN'S RIGHTS, SO I'D ALSO LIKE TO JOIN N.O.W., THE NATIONAL ORGANIZATION FOR WOMEN.
SO WHY NOT JOIN BOTH?
BECAUSE I CAN'T AFFORD THE DUES FOR BOTH.
SO IT'S ONE OR THE OTHER?
IT'S N.O.W. OR N.E.F.F.A.
ARE THERE REFUNDS FOR COMIC STRIPS?
NOPE.
PASTIS

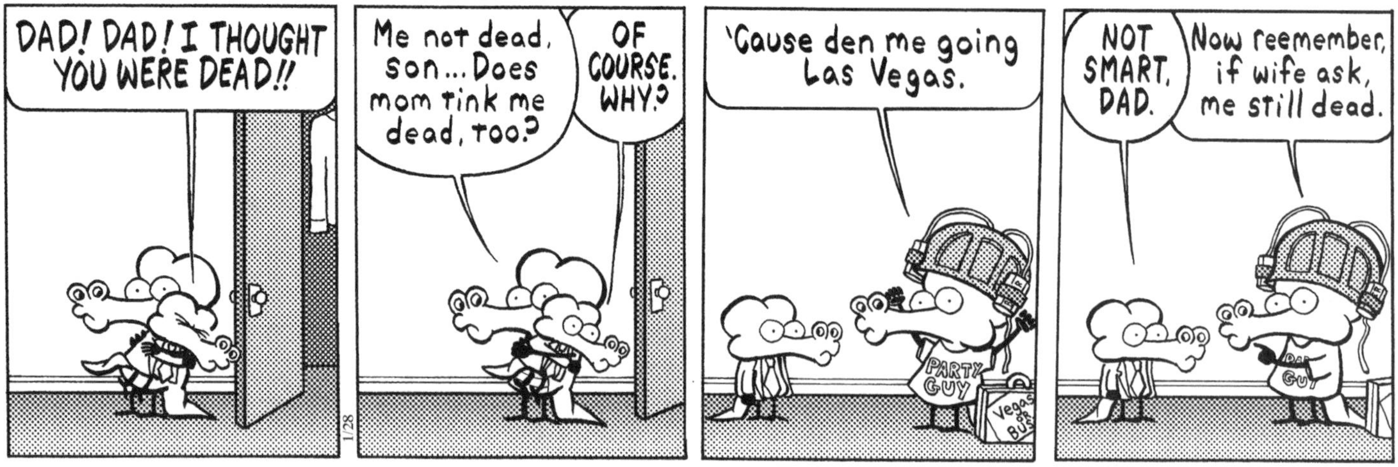
DAD! DAD! I THOUGHT YOU WERE DEAD!!
Me not dead, son... Does mom tink me dead, too?
OF COURSE. WHY?
'Cause den me going Las Vegas.
PARTY GUY
NOT SMART, DAD.
Now reemember, if wife ask, me still dead.
1/28

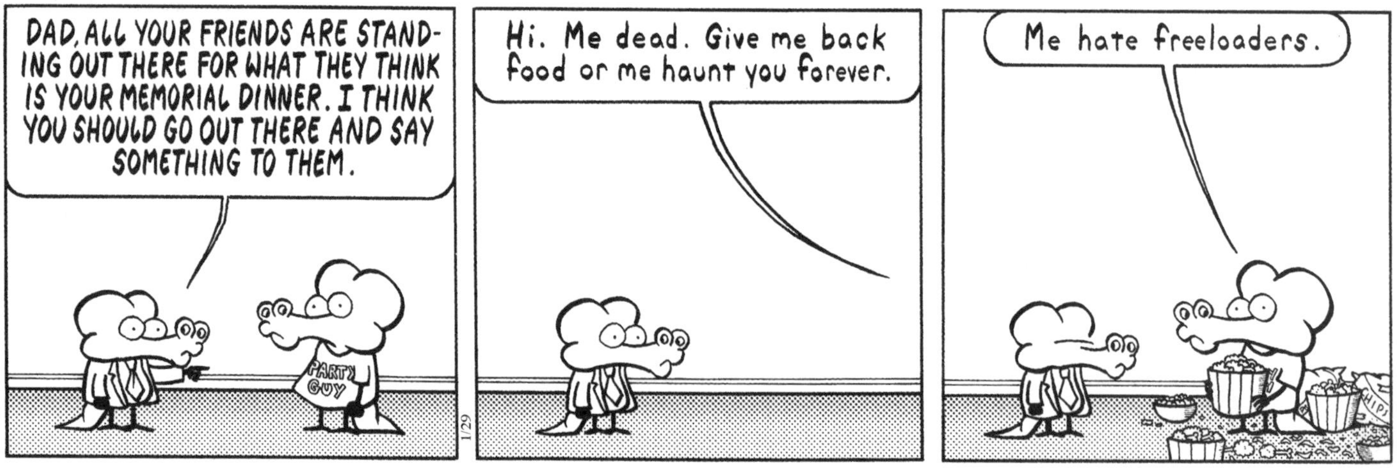
DAD, ALL YOUR FRIENDS ARE STANDING OUT THERE FOR WHAT THEY THINK IS YOUR MEMORIAL DINNER. I THINK YOU SHOULD GO OUT THERE AND SAY SOMETHING TO THEM.
PARTY GUY
Hi. Me dead. Give me back food or me haunt you forever.
Me hate freeloaders.
1/29

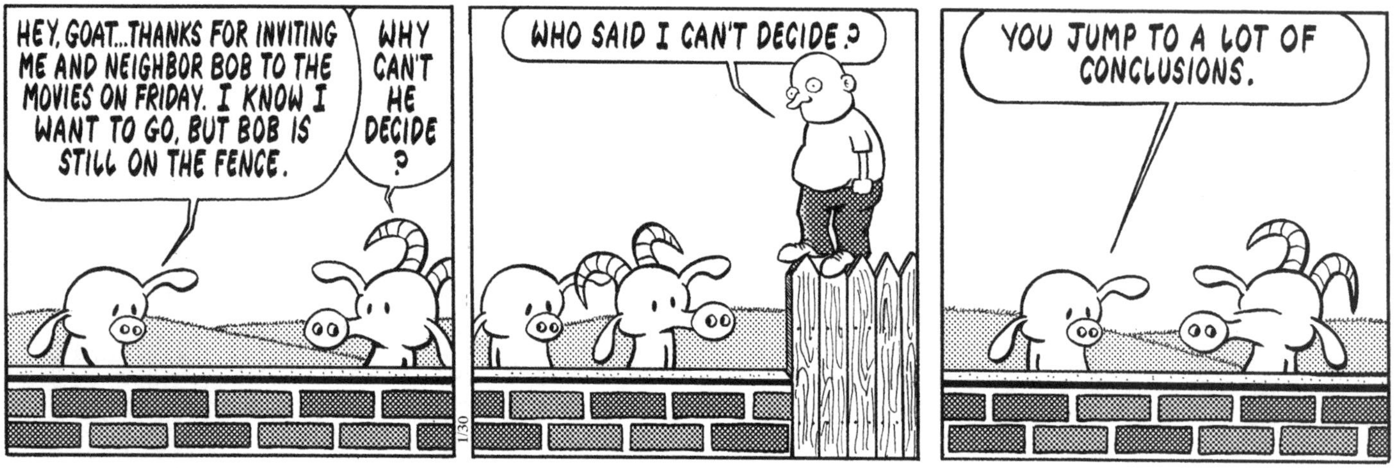
HEY, GOAT...THANKS FOR INVITING ME AND NEIGHBOR BOB TO THE MOVIES ON FRIDAY. I KNOW I WANT TO GO, BUT BOB IS STILL ON THE FENCE.
WHY CAN'T HE DECIDE?
WHO SAID I CAN'T DECIDE?
YOU JUMP TO A LOT OF CONCLUSIONS.
1/30

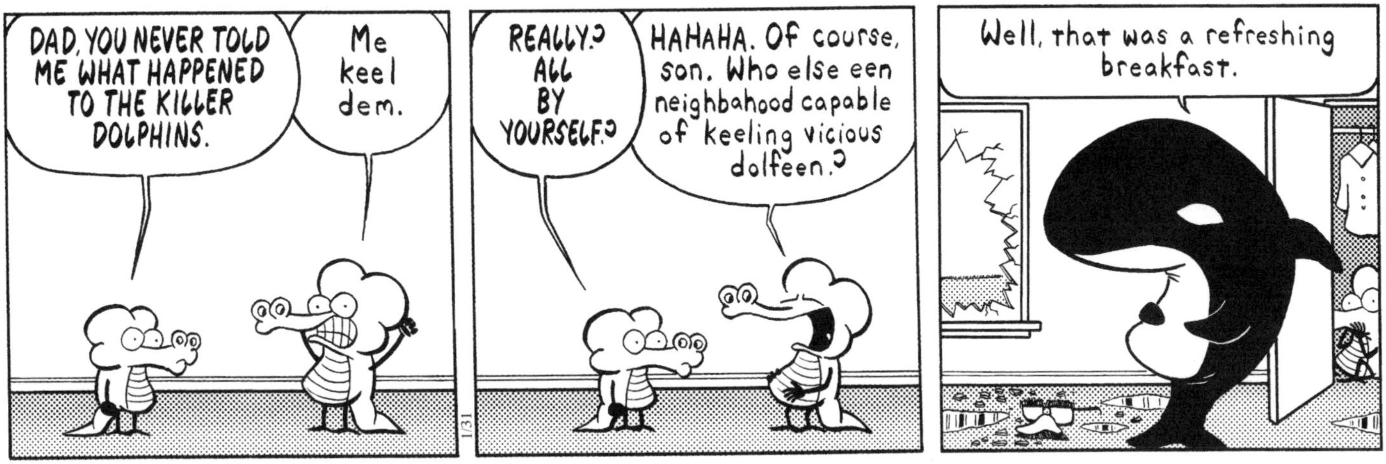
DAD, YOU NEVER TOLD ME WHAT HAPPENED TO THE KILLER DOLPHINS.
Me keel dem.
1/31
REALLY? ALL BY YOURSELF?
HAHAHA. Of course, son. Who else een neighbahood capable of keeling vicious dolfeen?
Well, that was a refreshing breakfast.

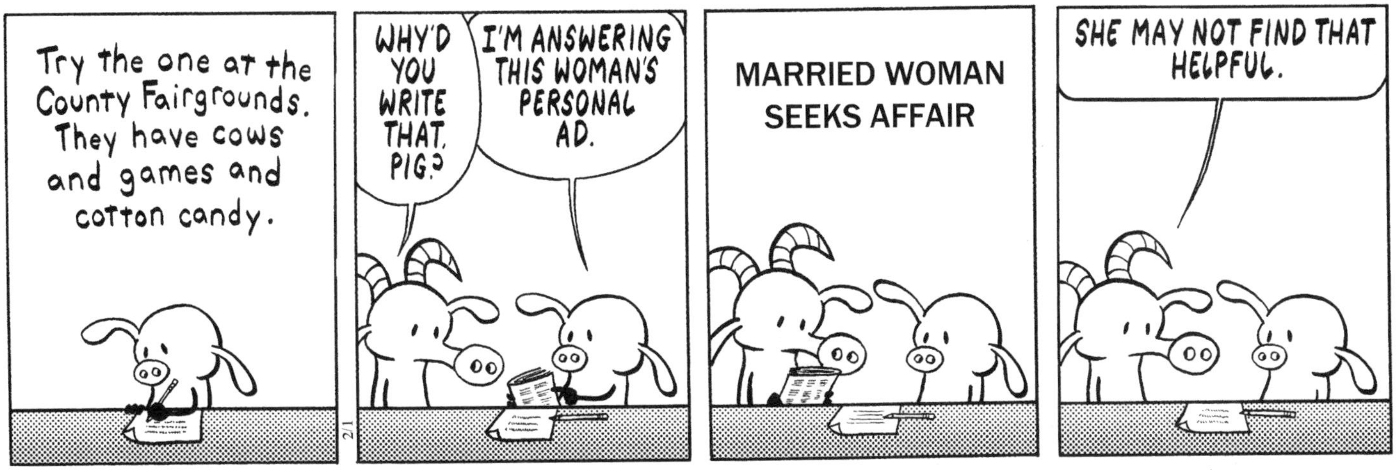
Try the one at the County Fairgrounds. They have cows and games and cotton candy.
2/1
WHY'D YOU WRITE THAT, PIG?
I'M ANSWERING THIS WOMAN'S PERSONAL AD.
MARRIED WOMAN SEEKS AFFAIR
SHE MAY NOT FIND THAT HELPFUL.

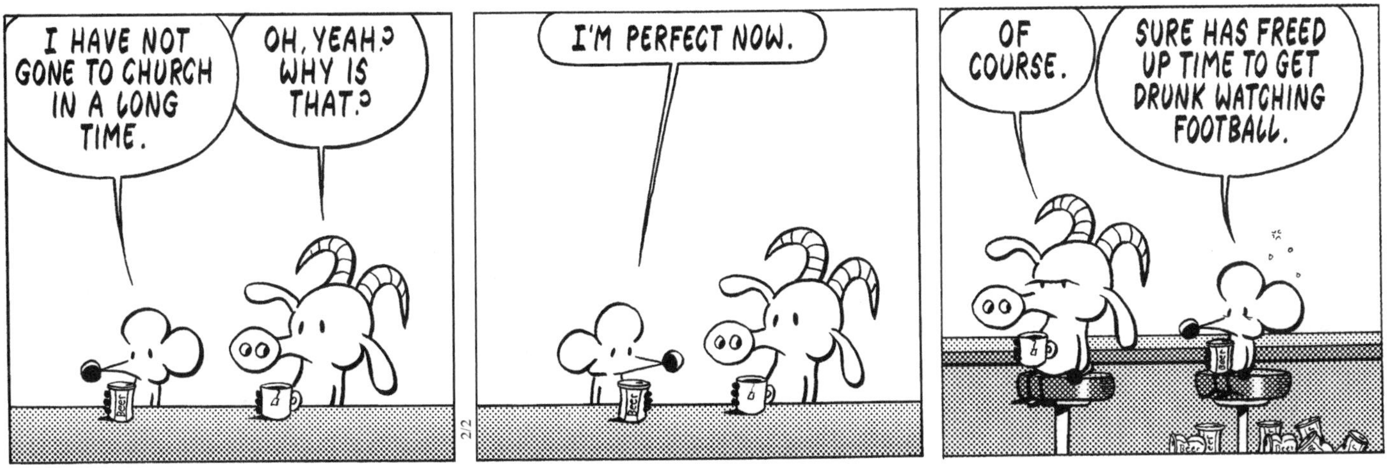
I HAVE NOT GONE TO CHURCH IN A LONG TIME.
OH, YEAH? WHY IS THAT?
2/2
I'M PERFECT NOW.
OF COURSE.
SURE HAS FREED UP TIME TO GET DRUNK WATCHING FOOTBALL.

STORY UPDATE:

Larry's family thought Larry was killed by ferocious dolphins. He was not. Larry is now exploiting the situation.

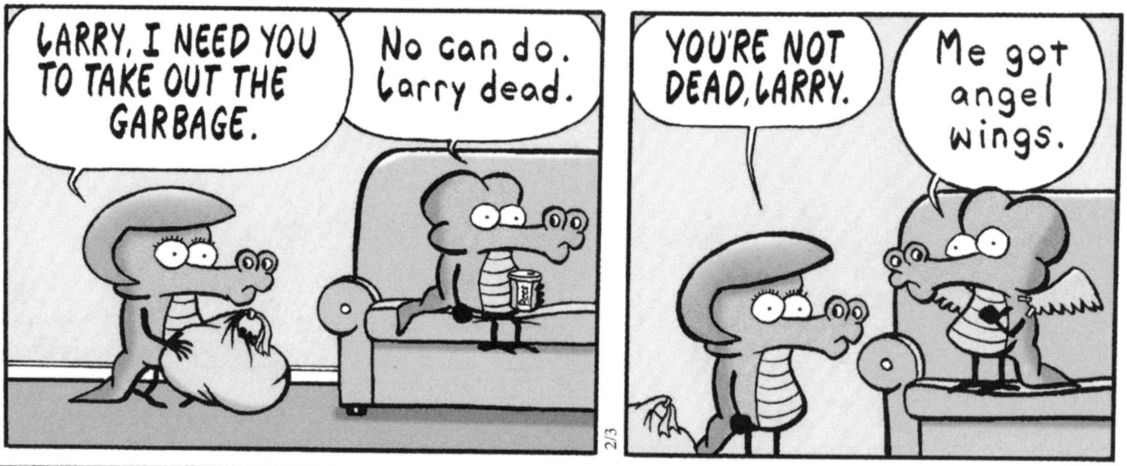
LARRY, I NEED YOU TO TAKE OUT THE GARBAGE.
No can do. Larry dead.
YOU'RE NOT DEAD, LARRY.
Me got angel wings.

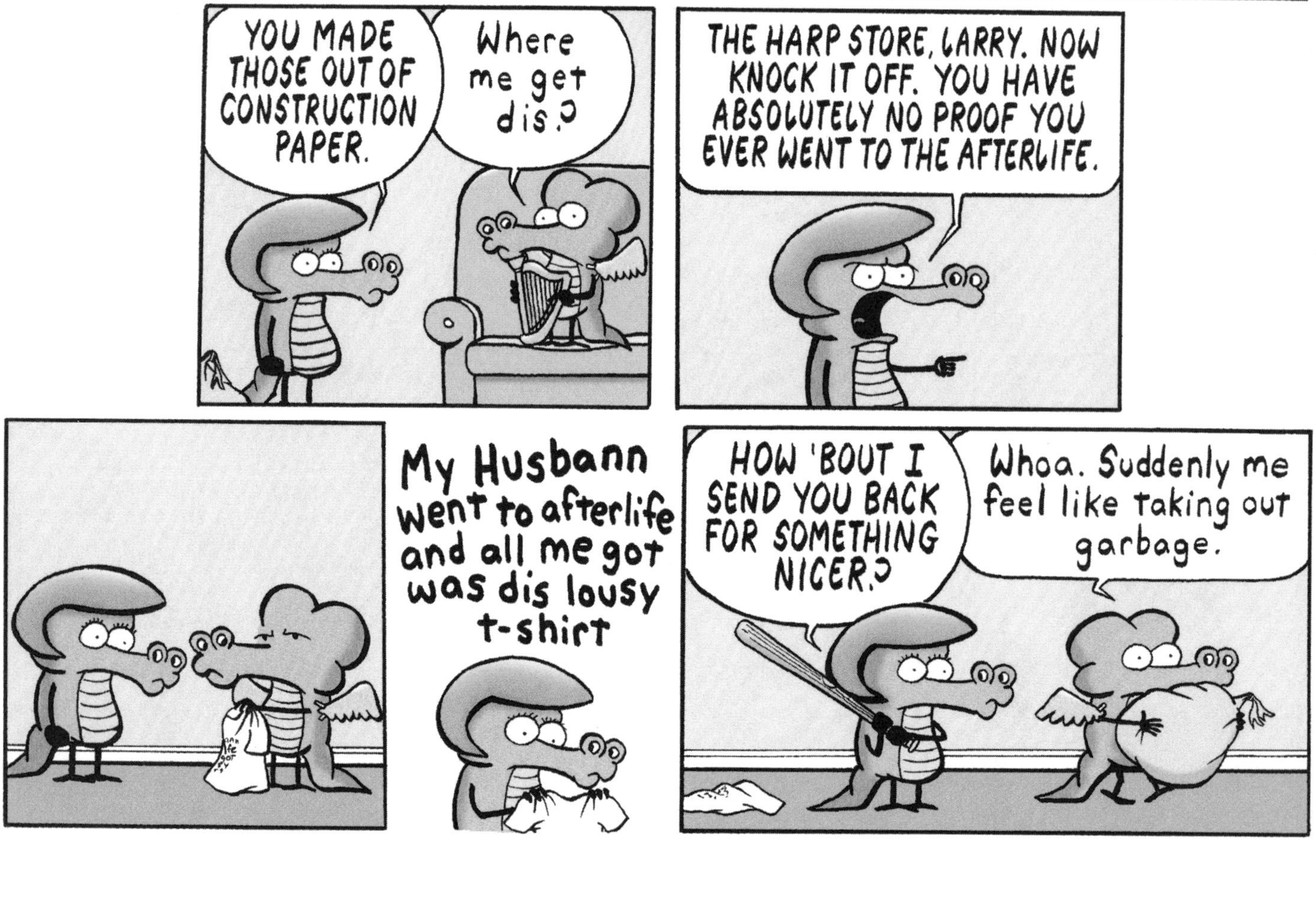
YOU MADE THOSE OUT OF CONSTRUCTION PAPER.
Where me get dis?
THE HARP STORE, LARRY. NOW KNOCK IT OFF. YOU HAVE ABSOLUTELY NO PROOF YOU EVER WENT TO THE AFTERLIFE.
My Husbann went to afterlife and all me got was dis lousy t-shirt
HOW 'BOUT I SEND YOU BACK FOR SOMETHING NICER?
Whoa. Suddenly me feel like taking out garbage.

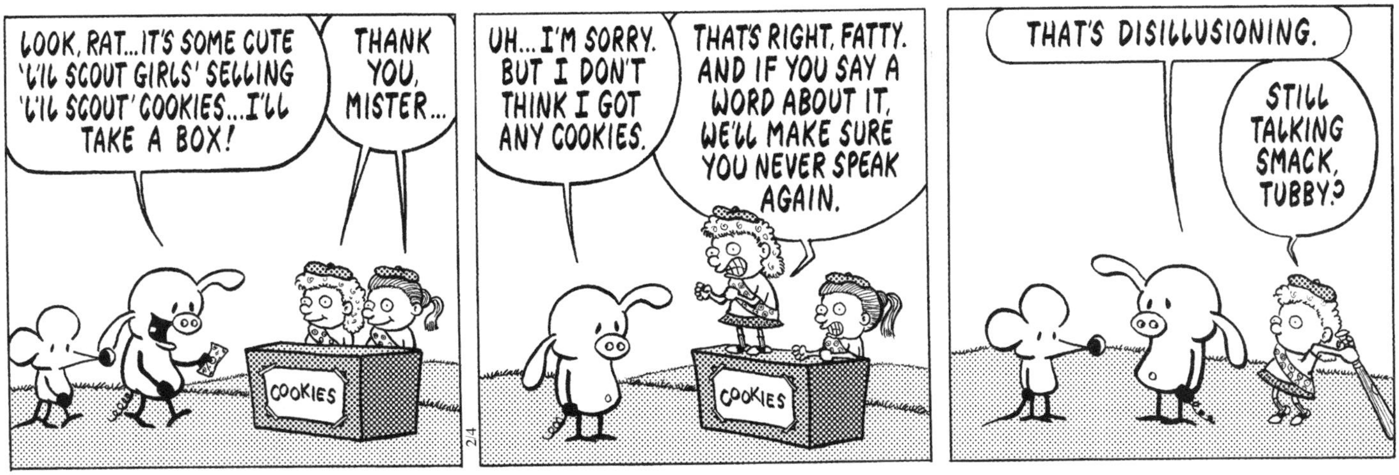
LOOK, RAT...IT'S SOME CUTE 'LIL SCOUT GIRLS' SELLING 'LIL SCOUT' COOKIES...I'LL TAKE A BOX!
THANK YOU, MISTER...
COOKIES
2/4
UH...I'M SORRY. BUT I DON'T THINK I GOT ANY COOKIES.
THAT'S RIGHT, FATTY. AND IF YOU SAY A WORD ABOUT IT, WE'LL MAKE SURE YOU NEVER SPEAK AGAIN.
COOKIES
THAT'S DISILLUSIONING.
STILL TALKING SMACK, TUBBY?

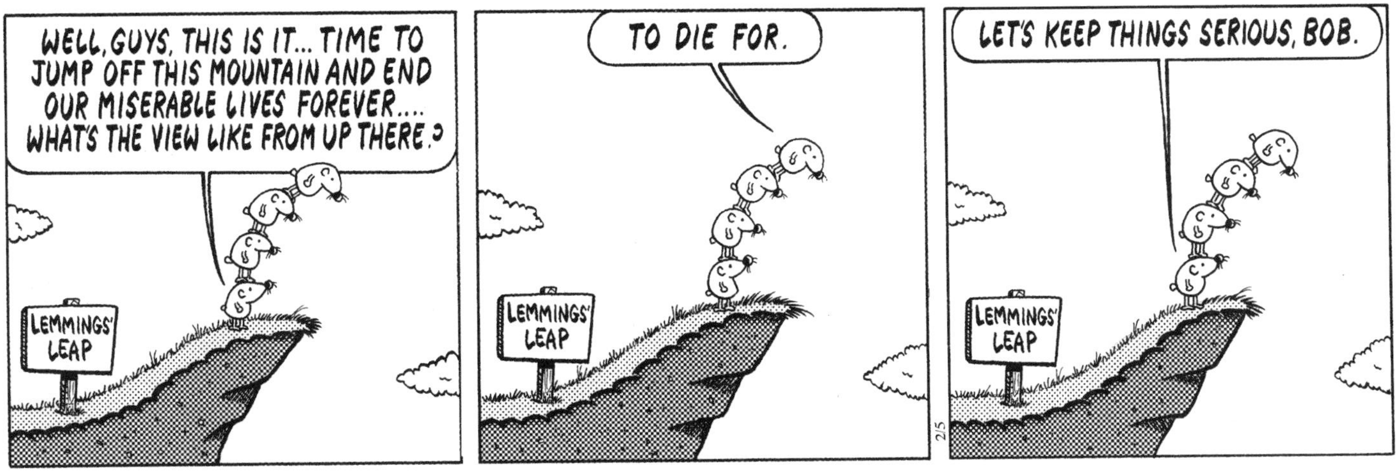
WELL, GUYS, THIS IS IT... TIME TO JUMP OFF THIS MOUNTAIN AND END OUR MISERABLE LIVES FOREVER.... WHAT'S THE VIEW LIKE FROM UP THERE?
LEMMINGS' LEAP
TO DIE FOR.
LEMMINGS' LEAP
2/5
LET'S KEEP THINGS SERIOUS, BOB.
LEMMINGS' LEAP

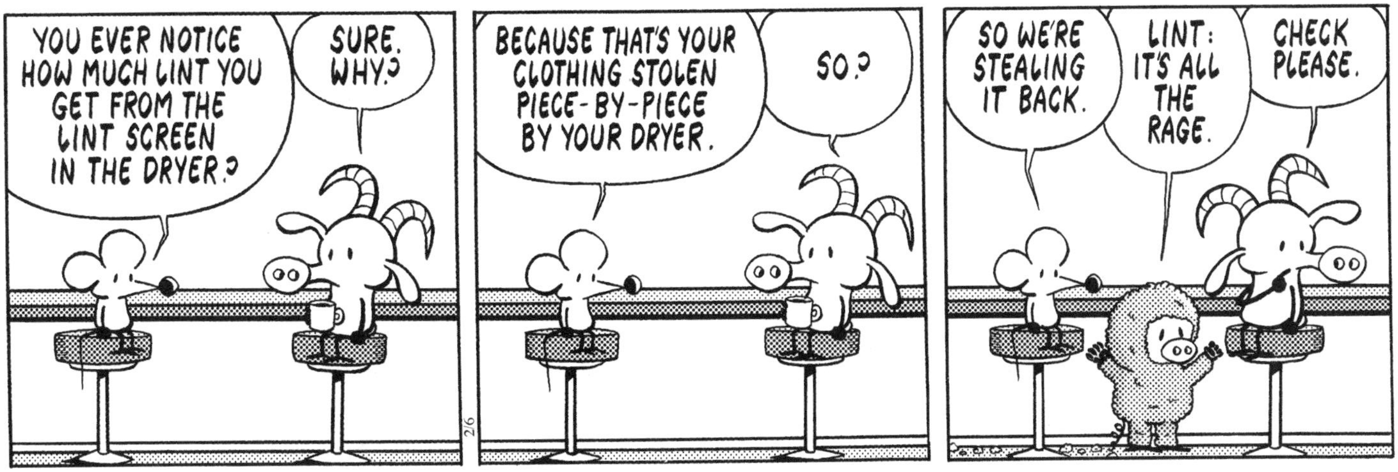
YOU EVER NOTICE HOW MUCH LINT YOU GET FROM THE LINT SCREEN IN THE DRYER?
SURE. WHY?
2/6
BECAUSE THAT'S YOUR CLOTHING STOLEN PIECE-BY-PIECE BY YOUR DRYER.
SO?
SO WE'RE STEALING IT BACK.
LINT: IT'S ALL THE RAGE.
CHECK PLEASE.

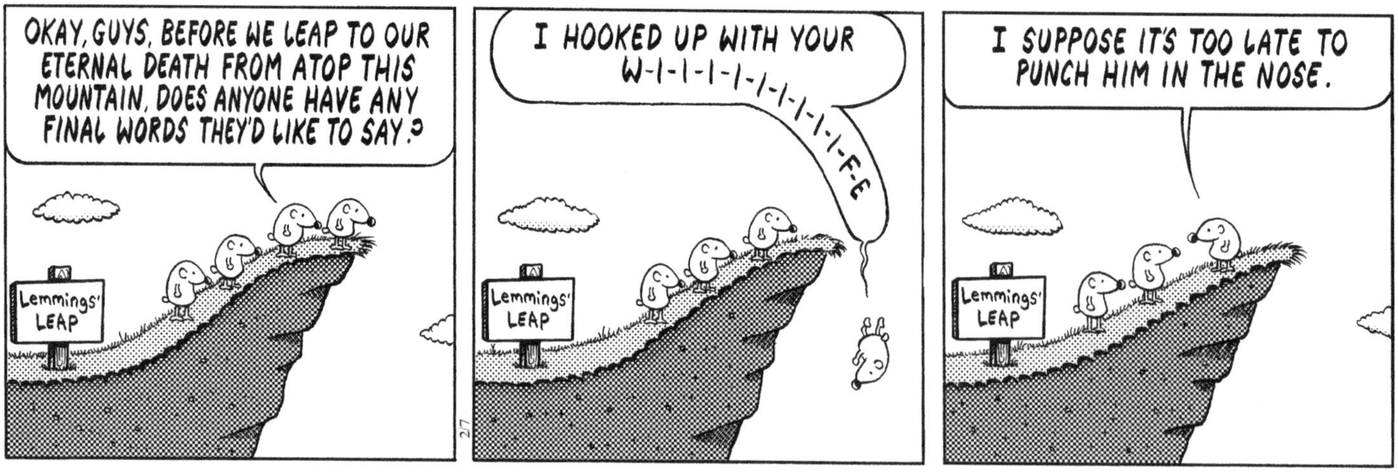
OKAY, GUYS, BEFORE WE LEAP TO OUR ETERNAL DEATH FROM ATOP THIS MOUNTAIN, DOES ANYONE HAVE ANY FINAL WORDS THEY'D LIKE TO SAY?
Lemmings' LEAP
2/7
I HOOKED UP WITH YOUR W-I-I-I-I-I-I-I-I-I-I-I-I-F-E
I SUPPOSE IT'S TOO LATE TO PUNCH HIM IN THE NOSE.

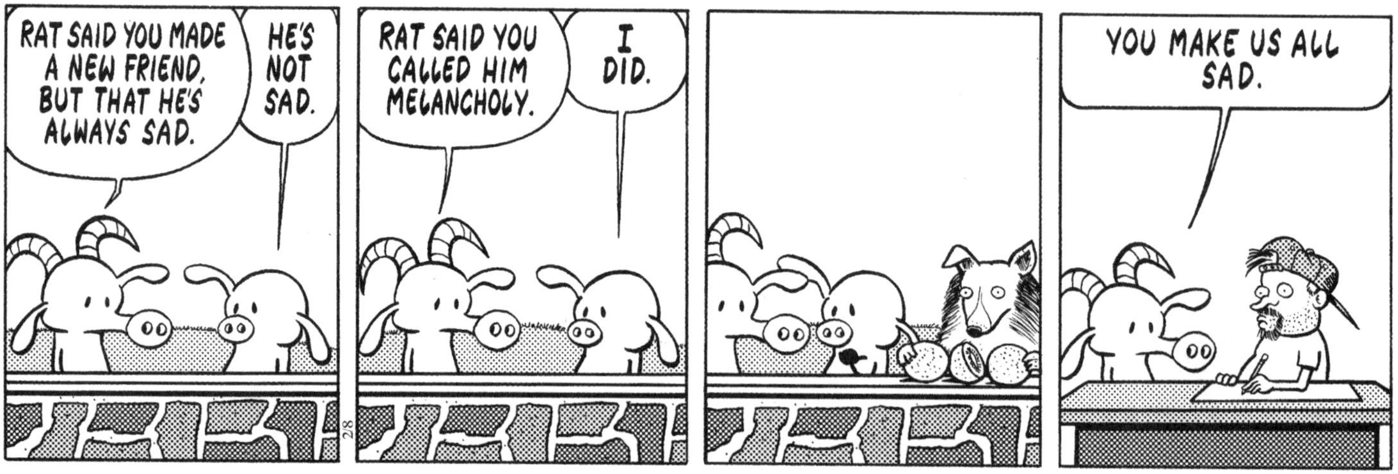
RAT SAID YOU MADE A NEW FRIEND, BUT THAT HE'S ALWAYS SAD.
HE'S NOT SAD.
2/8
RAT SAID YOU CALLED HIM MELANCHOLY.
I DID.
YOU MAKE US ALL SAD.

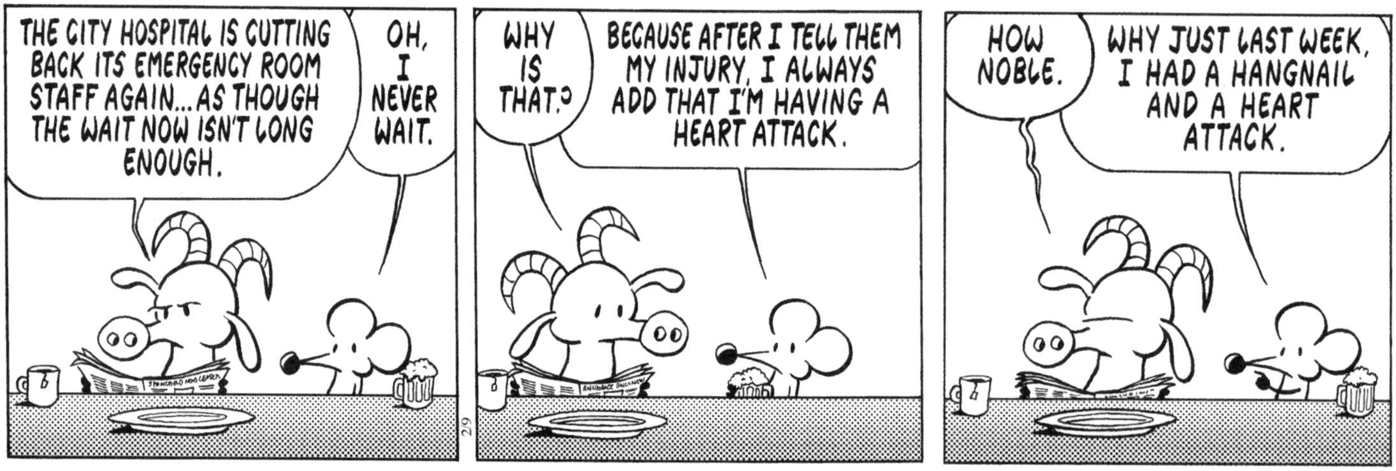
THE CITY HOSPITAL IS CUTTING BACK ITS EMERGENCY ROOM STAFF AGAIN...AS THOUGH THE WAIT NOW ISN'T LONG ENOUGH.
OH, I NEVER WAIT.
2/9
WHY IS THAT?
BECAUSE AFTER I TELL THEM MY INJURY, I ALWAYS ADD THAT I'M HAVING A HEART ATTACK.
HOW NOBLE.
WHY JUST LAST WEEK, I HAD A HANGNAIL AND A HEART ATTACK.

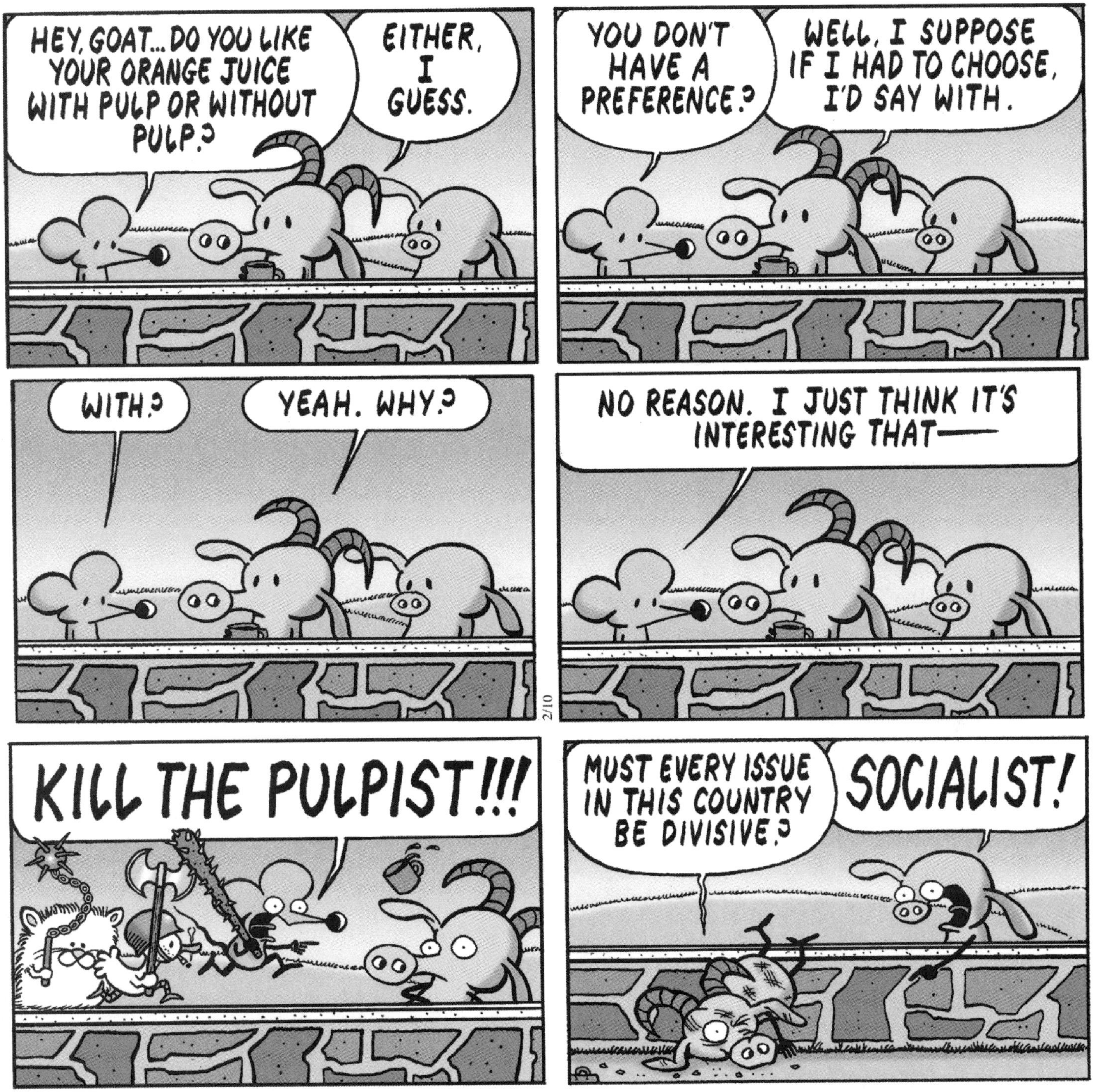
HEY, GOAT... DO YOU LIKE YOUR ORANGE JUICE WITH PULP OR WITHOUT PULP?
EITHER, I GUESS.
YOU DON'T HAVE A PREFERENCE?
WELL, I SUPPOSE IF I HAD TO CHOOSE, I'D SAY WITH.
WITH?
YEAH. WHY?
NO REASON. I JUST THINK IT'S INTERESTING THAT—
2/10
KILL THE PULPIST!!!
MUST EVERY ISSUE IN THIS COUNTRY BE DIVISIVE?
SOCIALIST!

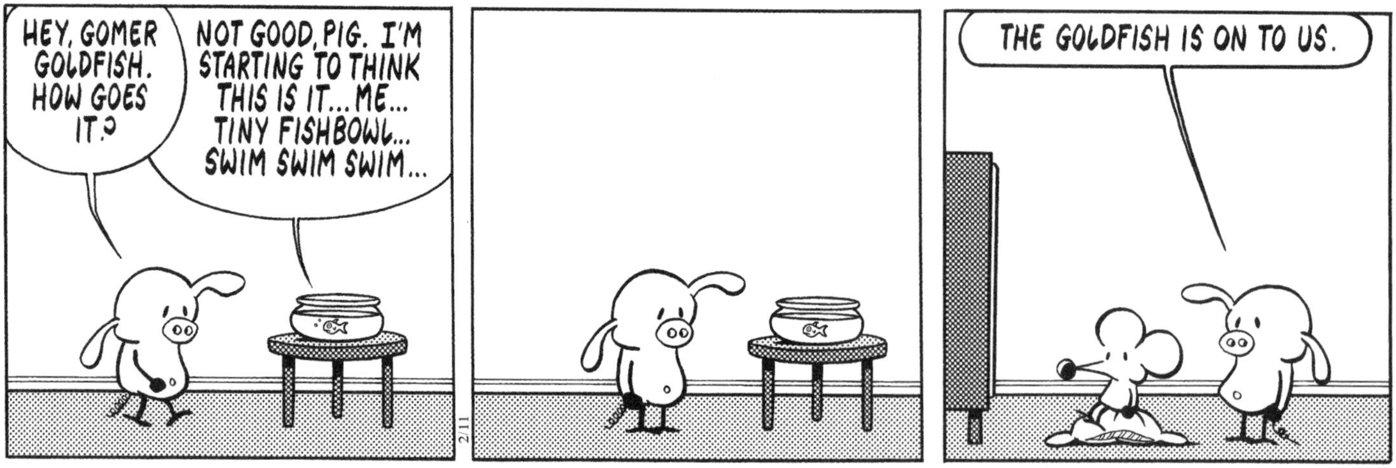
HEY, GOMER GOLDFISH. HOW GOES IT?
NOT GOOD, PIG. I'M STARTING TO THINK THIS IS IT... ME... TINY FISHBOWL... SWIM SWIM SWIM...
2/11
THE GOLDFISH IS ON TO US.

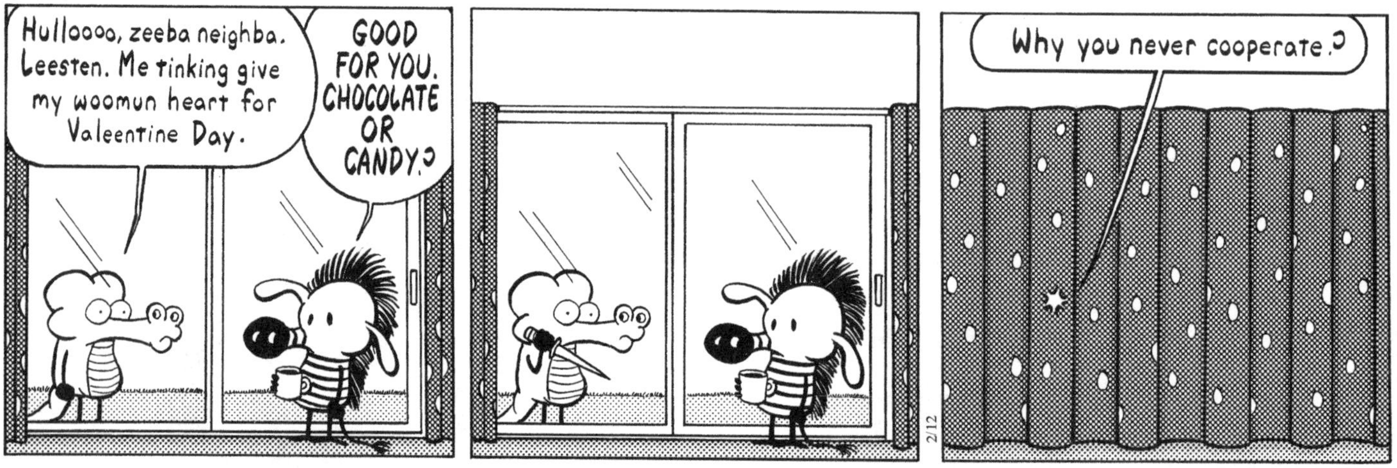
Hulloooo, zeeba neighba. Leesten. Me tinking give my woomun heart for Valeentine Day.
GOOD FOR YOU. CHOCOLATE OR CANDY?
2/12
Why you never cooperate?

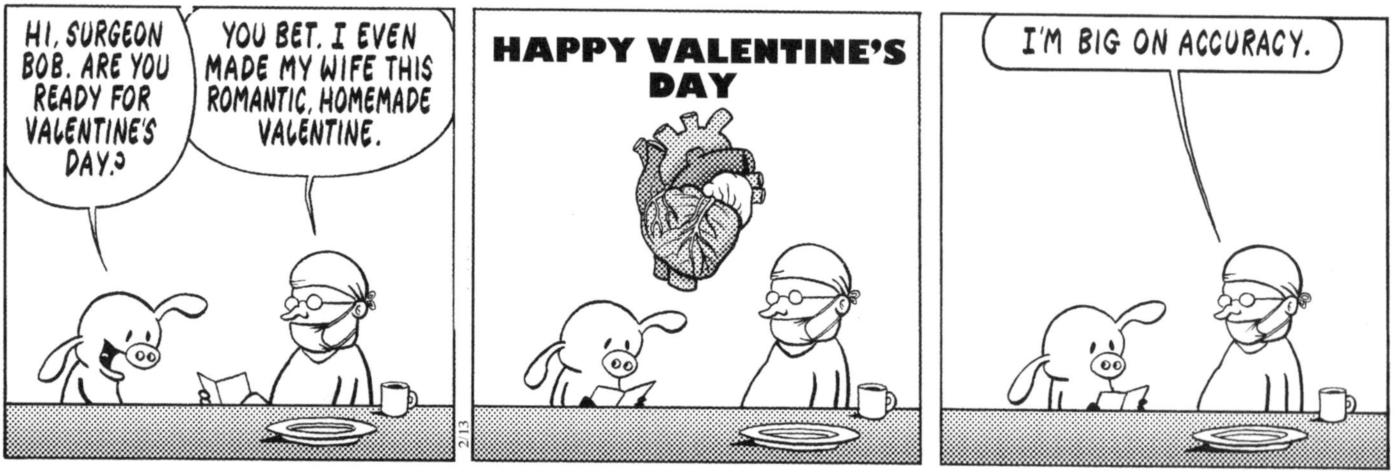
HI, SURGEON BOB. ARE YOU READY FOR VALENTINE'S DAY?
YOU BET. I EVEN MADE MY WIFE THIS ROMANTIC, HOMEMADE VALENTINE.
2/13
HAPPY VALENTINE'S DAY
I'M BIG ON ACCURACY.

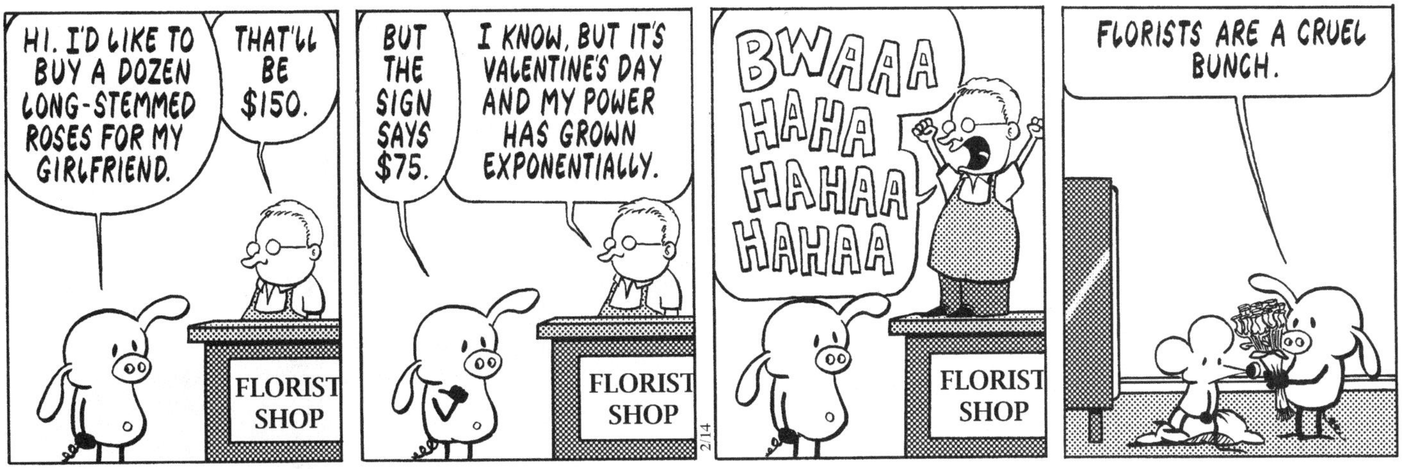
HI. I'D LIKE TO BUY A DOZEN LONG-STEMMED ROSES FOR MY GIRLFRIEND.
THAT'LL BE $150.
FLORIST SHOP
BUT THE SIGN SAYS $75.
I KNOW, BUT IT'S VALENTINE'S DAY AND MY POWER HAS GROWN EXPONENTIALLY.
2/14
BWAAA HAHA HAHAA HAHAA
FLORISTS ARE A CRUEL BUNCH.

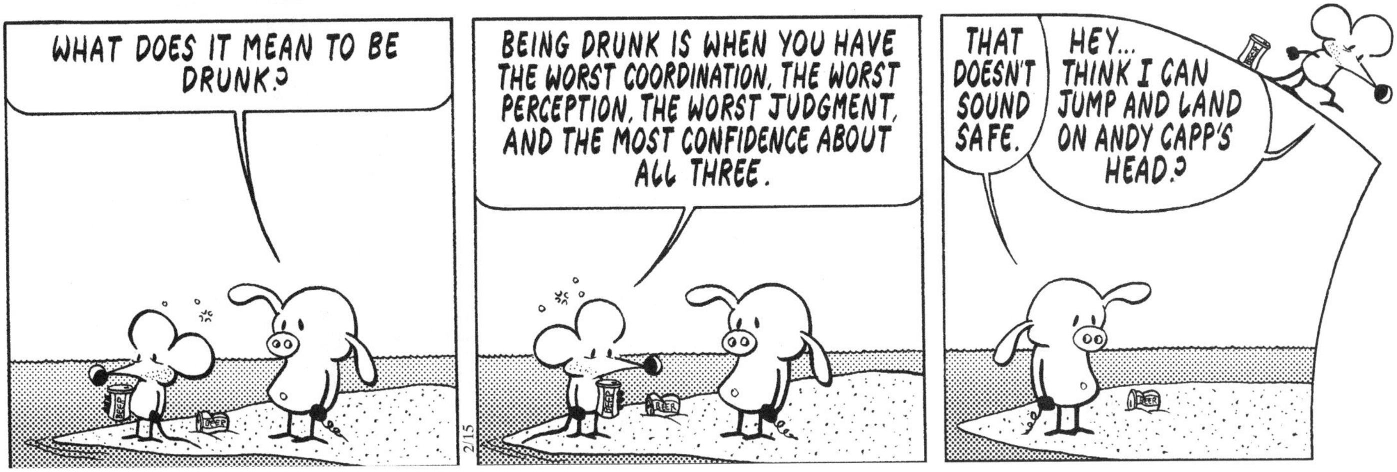
WHAT DOES IT MEAN TO BE DRUNK?
2/15
BEING DRUNK IS WHEN YOU HAVE THE WORST COORDINATION, THE WORST PERCEPTION, THE WORST JUDGMENT, AND THE MOST CONFIDENCE ABOUT ALL THREE.
THAT DOESN'T SOUND SAFE.
HEY... THINK I CAN JUMP AND LAND ON ANDY CAPP'S HEAD?

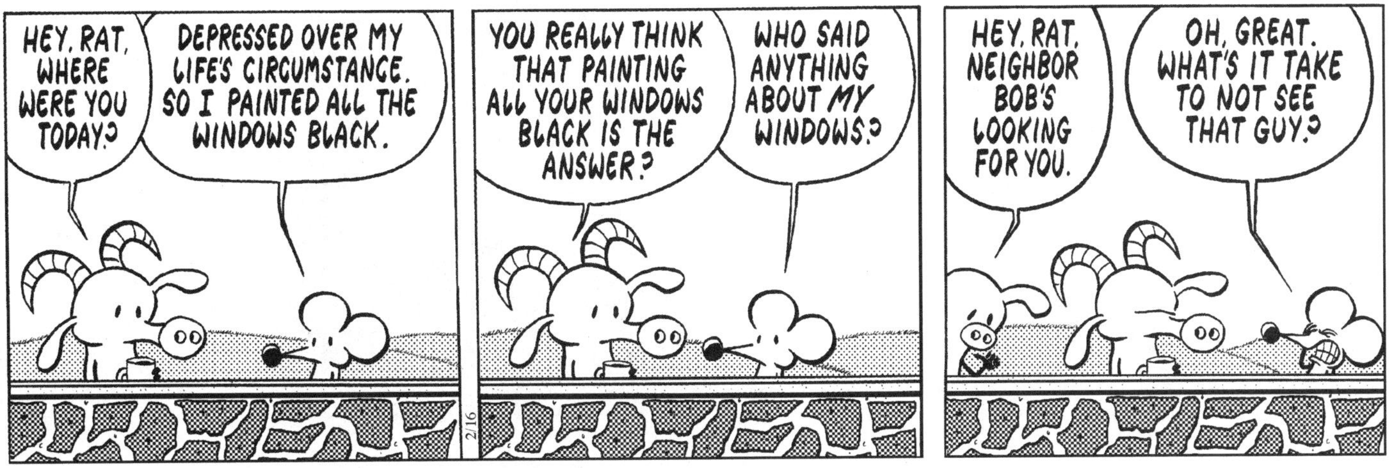
HEY, RAT, WHERE WERE YOU TODAY?
DEPRESSED OVER MY LIFE'S CIRCUMSTANCE. SO I PAINTED ALL THE WINDOWS BLACK.
2/16
YOU REALLY THINK THAT PAINTING ALL YOUR WINDOWS BLACK IS THE ANSWER?
WHO SAID ANYTHING ABOUT *MY* WINDOWS?
HEY, RAT, NEIGHBOR BOB'S LOOKING FOR YOU.
OH, GREAT. WHAT'S IT TAKE TO NOT SEE THAT GUY?

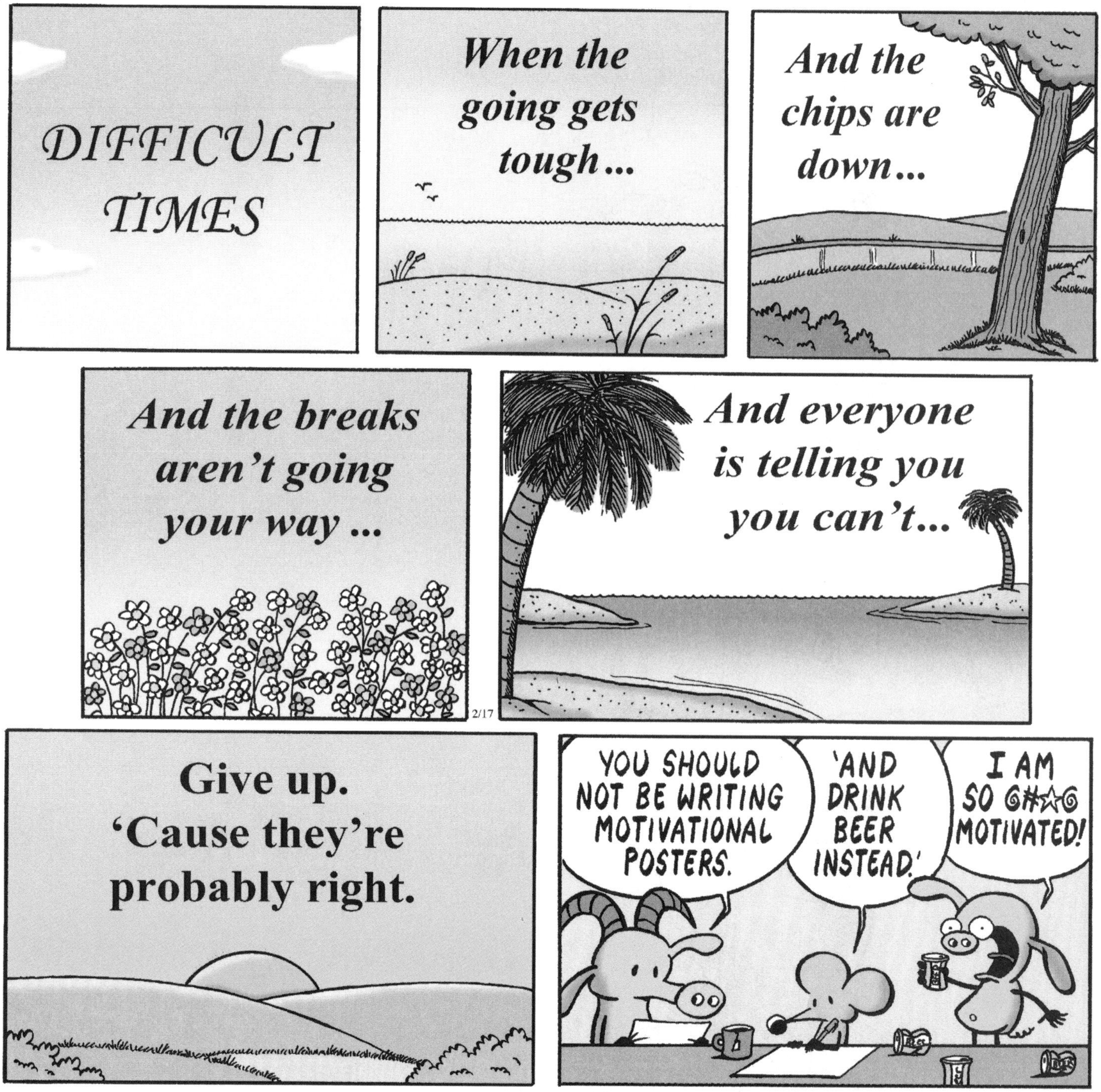
DIFFICULT TIMES
When the going gets tough...
And the chips are down...
And the breaks aren't going your way ...
2/17
And everyone is telling you you can't...
Give up. 'Cause they're probably right.
YOU SHOULD NOT BE WRITING MOTIVATIONAL POSTERS.
'AND DRINK BEER INSTEAD.'
I AM SO G#☆@ MOTIVATED!

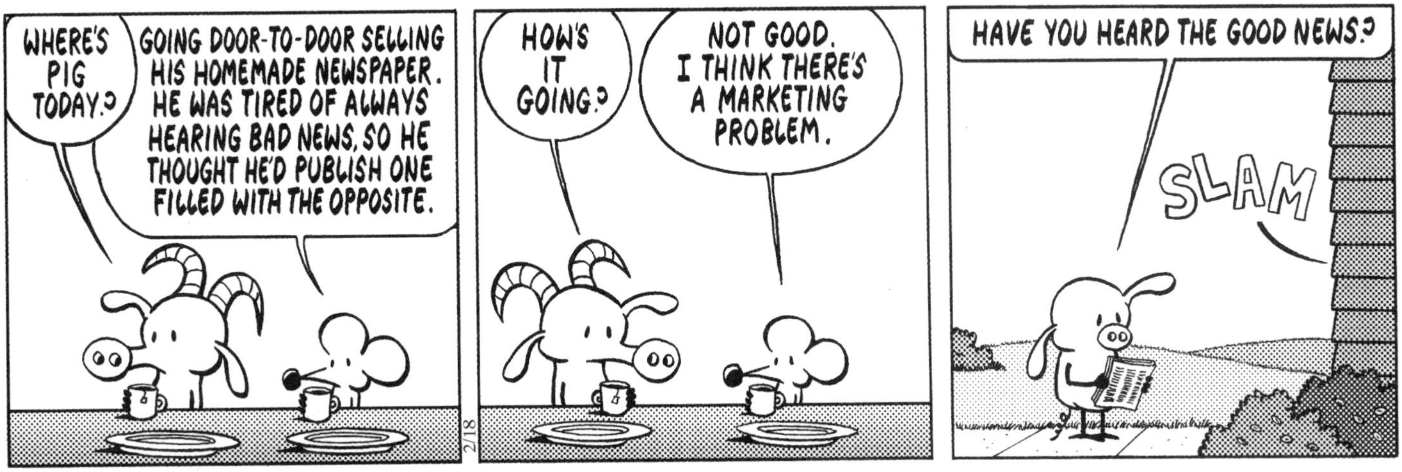
WHERE'S PIG TODAY?
GOING DOOR-TO-DOOR SELLING HIS HOMEMADE NEWSPAPER. HE WAS TIRED OF ALWAYS HEARING BAD NEWS, SO HE THOUGHT HE'D PUBLISH ONE FILLED WITH THE OPPOSITE.
2/18
HOW'S IT GOING?
NOT GOOD. I THINK THERE'S A MARKETING PROBLEM.
HAVE YOU HEARD THE GOOD NEWS?
SLAM

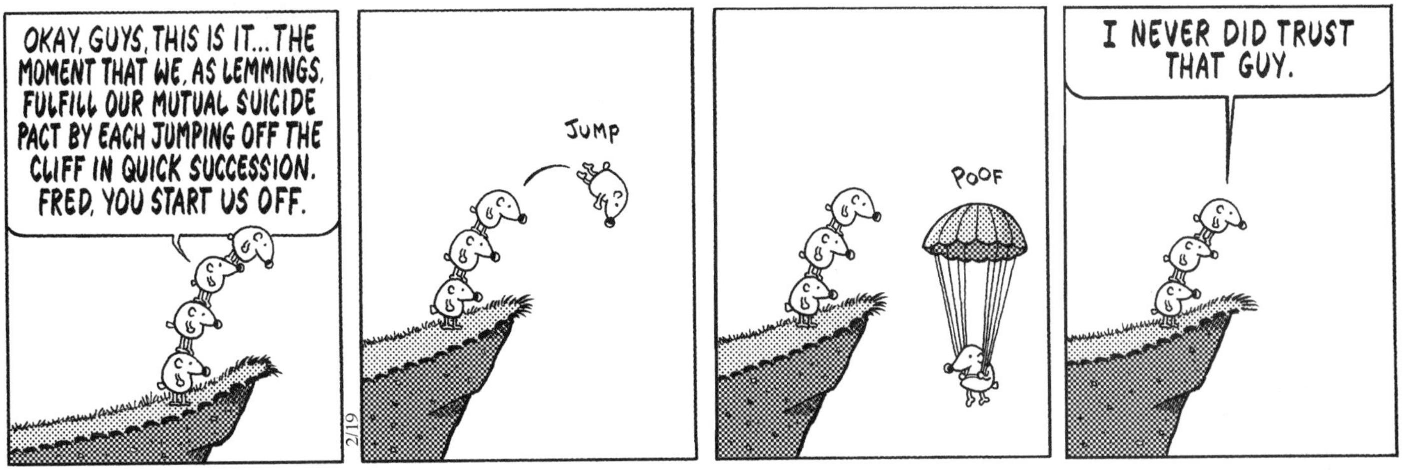
OKAY, GUYS, THIS IS IT... THE MOMENT THAT WE, AS LEMMINGS, FULFILL OUR MUTUAL SUICIDE PACT BY EACH JUMPING OFF THE CLIFF IN QUICK SUCCESSION. FRED, YOU START US OFF.
2/19
JUMP
POOF
I NEVER DID TRUST THAT GUY.

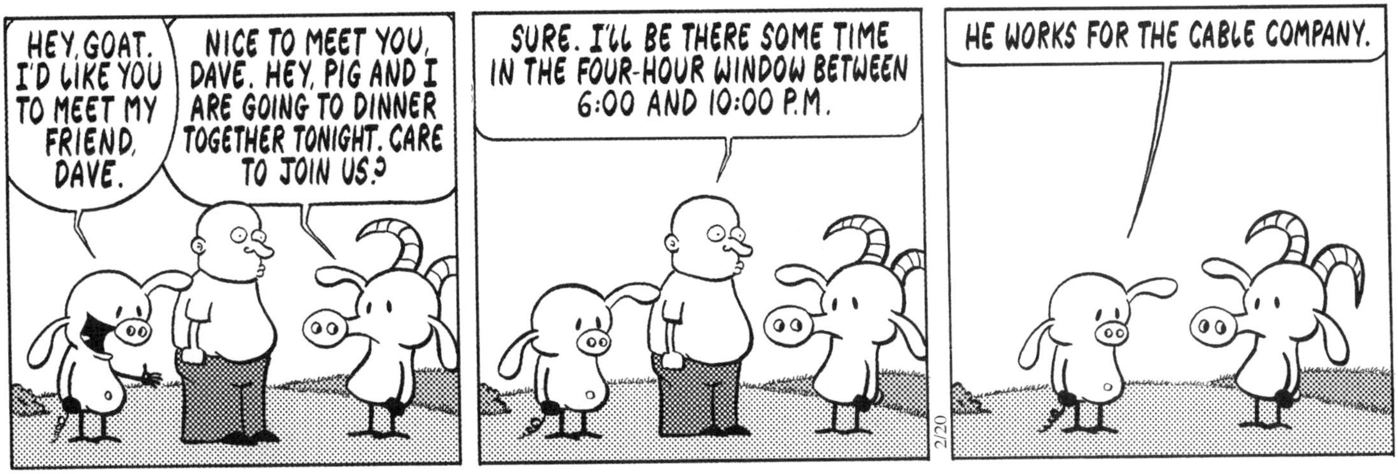
HEY, GOAT. I'D LIKE YOU TO MEET MY FRIEND, DAVE.
NICE TO MEET YOU, DAVE. HEY, PIG AND I ARE GOING TO DINNER TOGETHER TONIGHT. CARE TO JOIN US?
SURE. I'LL BE THERE SOME TIME IN THE FOUR-HOUR WINDOW BETWEEN 6:00 AND 10:00 P.M.
2/20
HE WORKS FOR THE CABLE COMPANY.

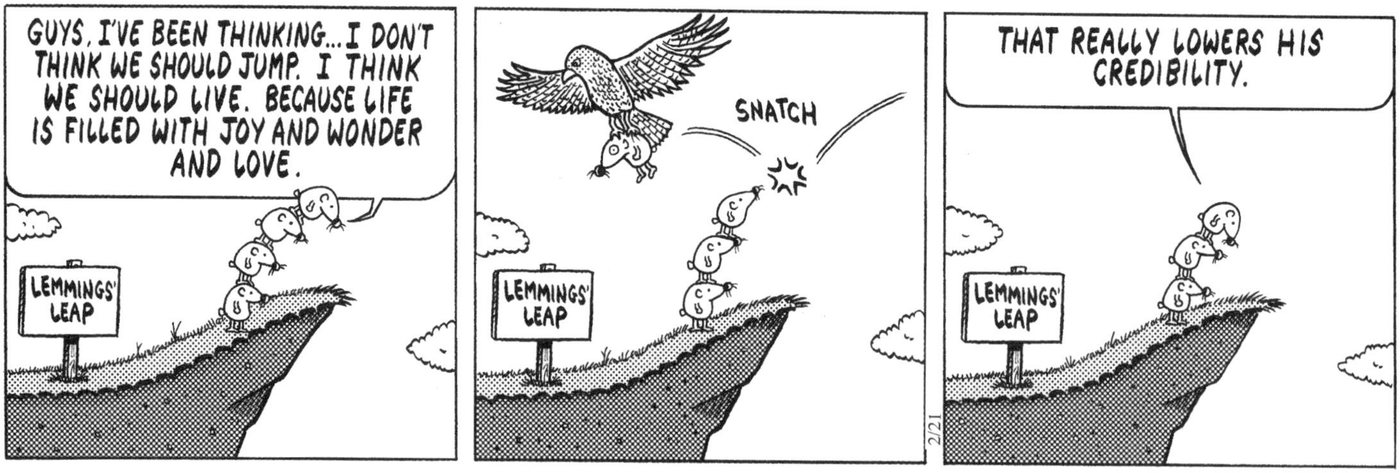
GUYS, I'VE BEEN THINKING... I DON'T THINK WE SHOULD JUMP. I THINK WE SHOULD LIVE. BECAUSE LIFE IS FILLED WITH JOY AND WONDER AND LOVE.
LEMMINGS' LEAP
LEMMINGS' LEAP
SNATCH
2/21
LEMMINGS' LEAP
THAT REALLY LOWERS HIS CREDIBILITY.

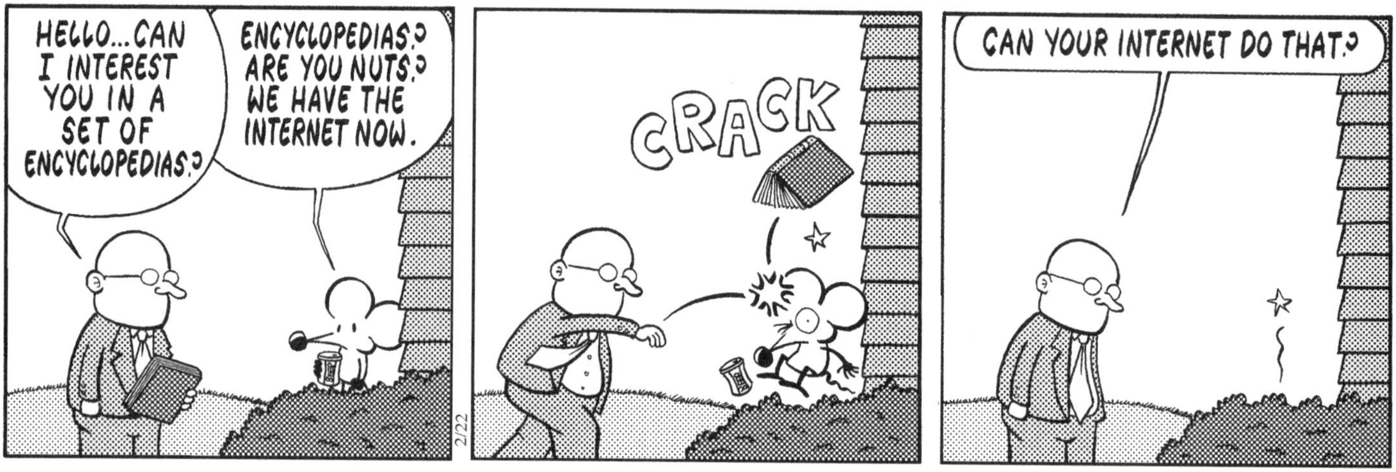
HELLO... CAN I INTEREST YOU IN A SET OF ENCYCLOPEDIAS?
ENCYCLOPEDIAS? ARE YOU NUTS? WE HAVE THE INTERNET NOW.
2/22
CRACK
CAN YOUR INTERNET DO THAT?

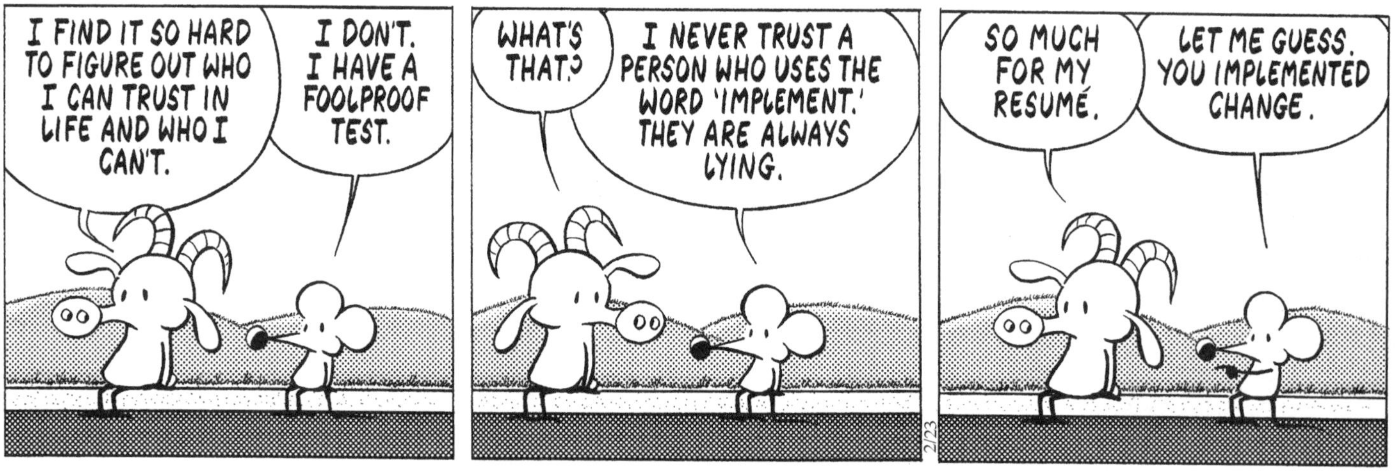
I FIND IT SO HARD TO FIGURE OUT WHO I CAN TRUST IN LIFE AND WHO I CAN'T.
I DON'T. I HAVE A FOOLPROOF TEST.
WHAT'S THAT?
I NEVER TRUST A PERSON WHO USES THE WORD 'IMPLEMENT.' THEY ARE ALWAYS LYING.
2/23
SO MUCH FOR MY RESUMÉ.
LET ME GUESS. YOU IMPLEMENTED CHANGE.

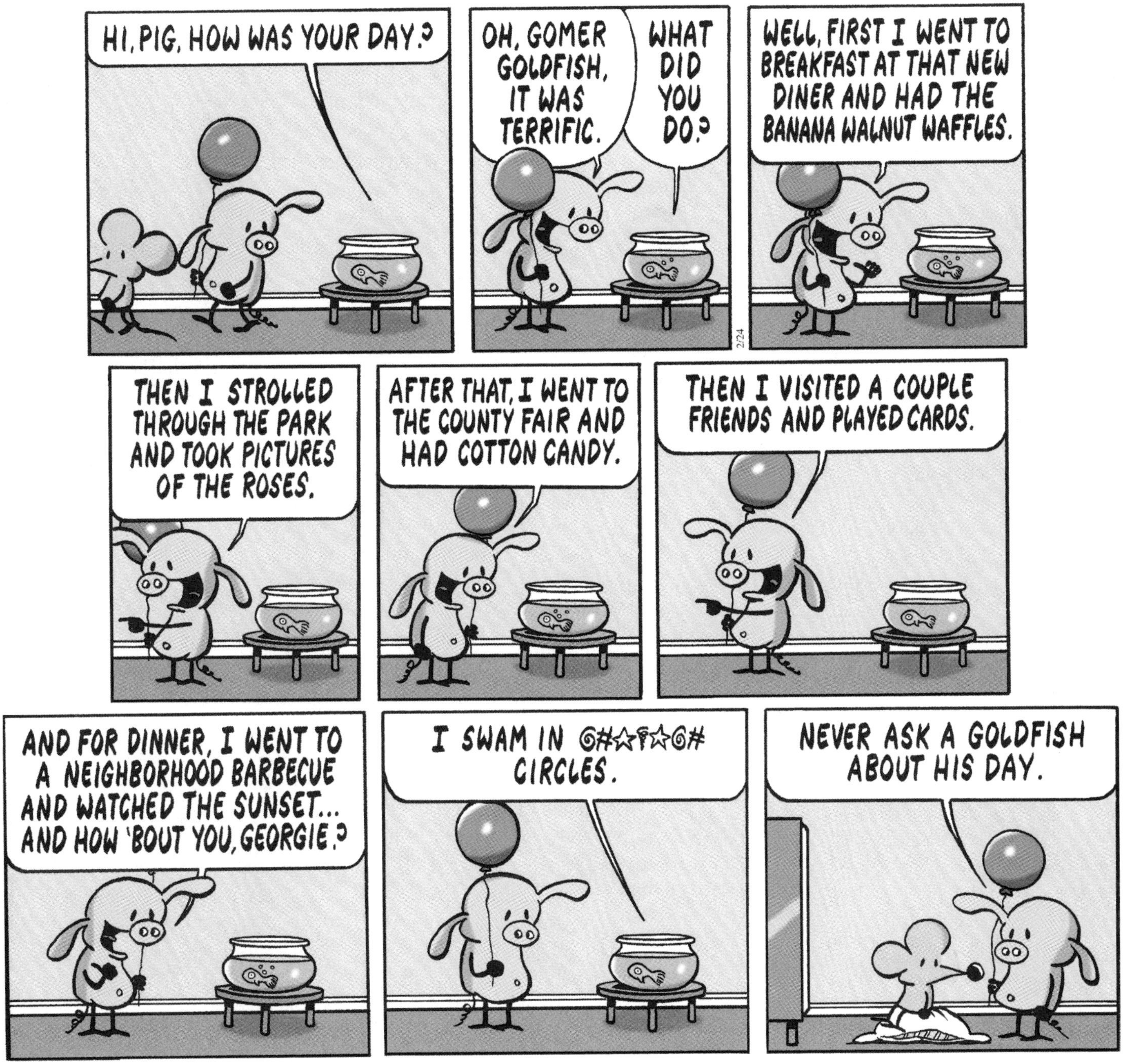

HI, PIG. HOW WAS YOUR DAY?
OH, GOMER GOLDFISH, IT WAS TERRIFIC.
WHAT DID YOU DO?
2/24
WELL, FIRST I WENT TO BREAKFAST AT THAT NEW DINER AND HAD THE BANANA WALNUT WAFFLES.
THEN I STROLLED THROUGH THE PARK AND TOOK PICTURES OF THE ROSES.
AFTER THAT, I WENT TO THE COUNTY FAIR AND HAD COTTON CANDY.
THEN I VISITED A COUPLE FRIENDS AND PLAYED CARDS.
AND FOR DINNER, I WENT TO A NEIGHBORHOOD BARBECUE AND WATCHED THE SUNSET... AND HOW 'BOUT YOU, GEORGIE?
I SWAM IN @#☆!☆@# CIRCLES.
NEVER ASK A GOLDFISH ABOUT HIS DAY.

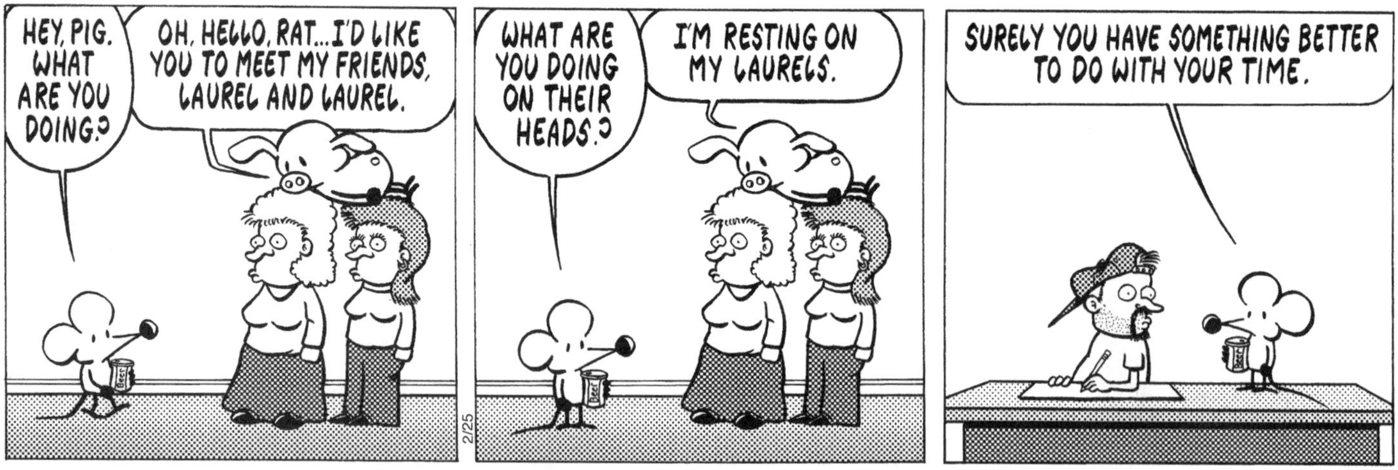
HEY, PIG. WHAT ARE YOU DOING?
OH, HELLO, RAT...I'D LIKE YOU TO MEET MY FRIENDS, LAUREL AND LAUREL.
WHAT ARE YOU DOING ON THEIR HEADS?
I'M RESTING ON MY LAURELS.
SURELY YOU HAVE SOMETHING BETTER TO DO WITH YOUR TIME.
2/25

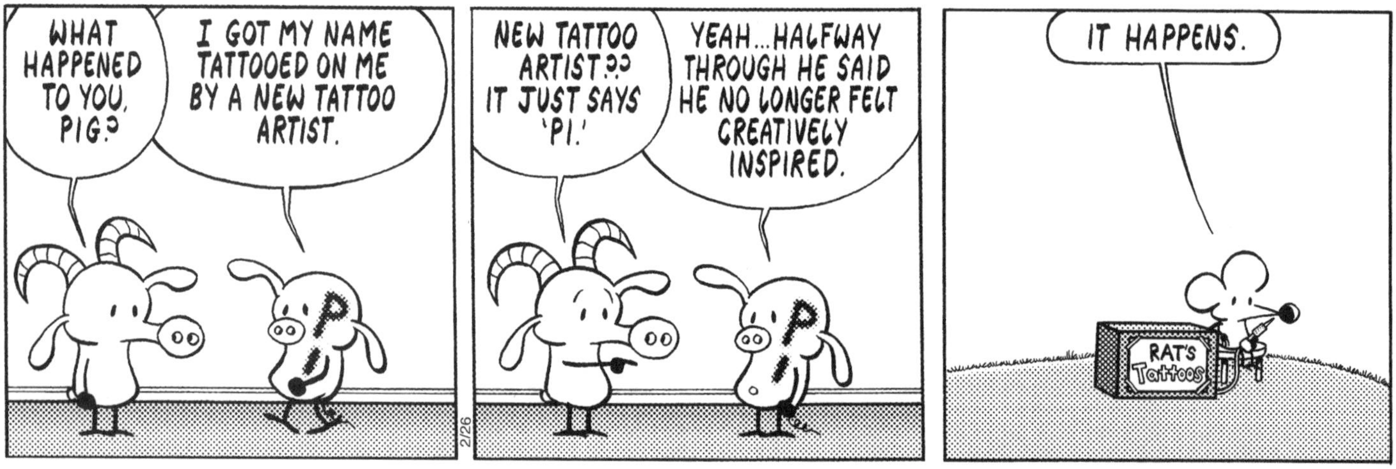
WHAT HAPPENED TO YOU, PIG?
I GOT MY NAME TATTOOED ON ME BY A NEW TATTOO ARTIST.
NEW TATTOO ARTIST?? IT JUST SAYS 'PI.'
YEAH...HALFWAY THROUGH HE SAID HE NO LONGER FELT CREATIVELY INSPIRED.
IT HAPPENS.
RAT'S Tattoos
2/26

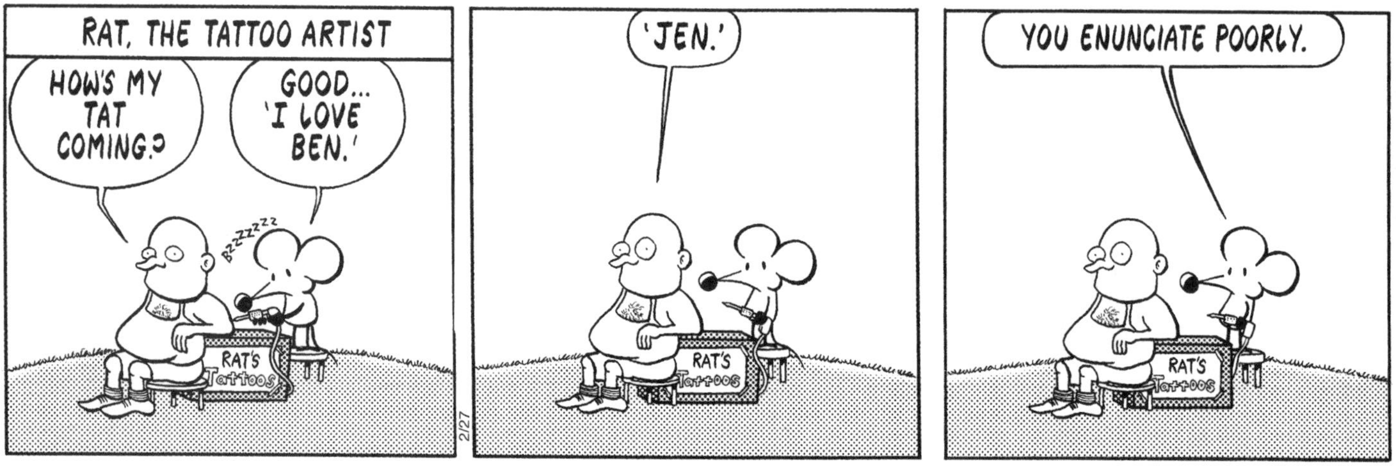
RAT, THE TATTOO ARTIST
HOW'S MY TAT COMING?
GOOD... 'I LOVE BEN.'
'JEN.'
YOU ENUNCIATE POORLY.
RAT'S Tattoos
2/27

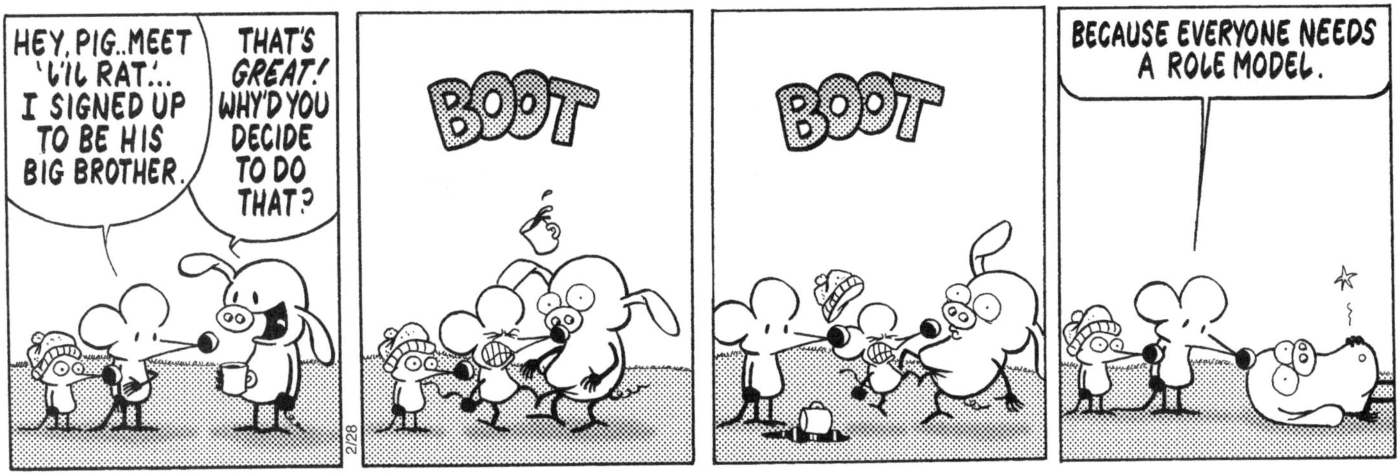
HEY, PIG..MEET 'LIL RAT!... I SIGNED UP TO BE HIS BIG BROTHER.
THAT'S *GREAT!* WHY'D YOU DECIDE TO DO THAT?
2/28
BOOT
BOOT
BECAUSE EVERYONE NEEDS A ROLE MODEL.

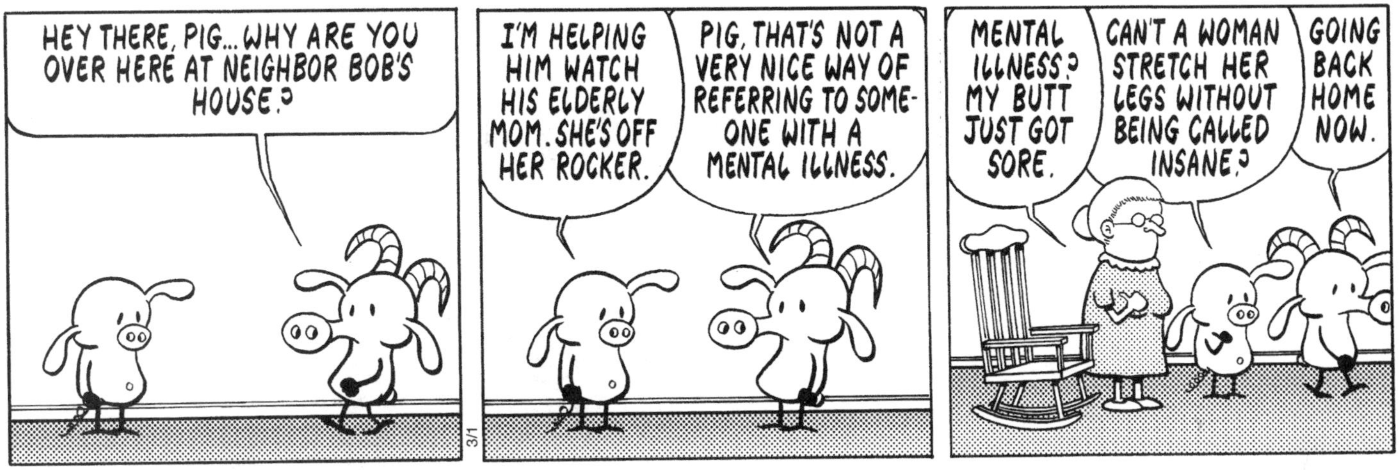
HEY THERE, PIG... WHY ARE YOU OVER HERE AT NEIGHBOR BOB'S HOUSE?
3/1
I'M HELPING HIM WATCH HIS ELDERLY MOM. SHE'S OFF HER ROCKER.
PIG, THAT'S NOT A VERY NICE WAY OF REFERRING TO SOME-ONE WITH A MENTAL ILLNESS.
MENTAL ILLNESS? MY BUTT JUST GOT SORE.
CAN'T A WOMAN STRETCH HER LEGS WITHOUT BEING CALLED INSANE?
GOING BACK HOME NOW.

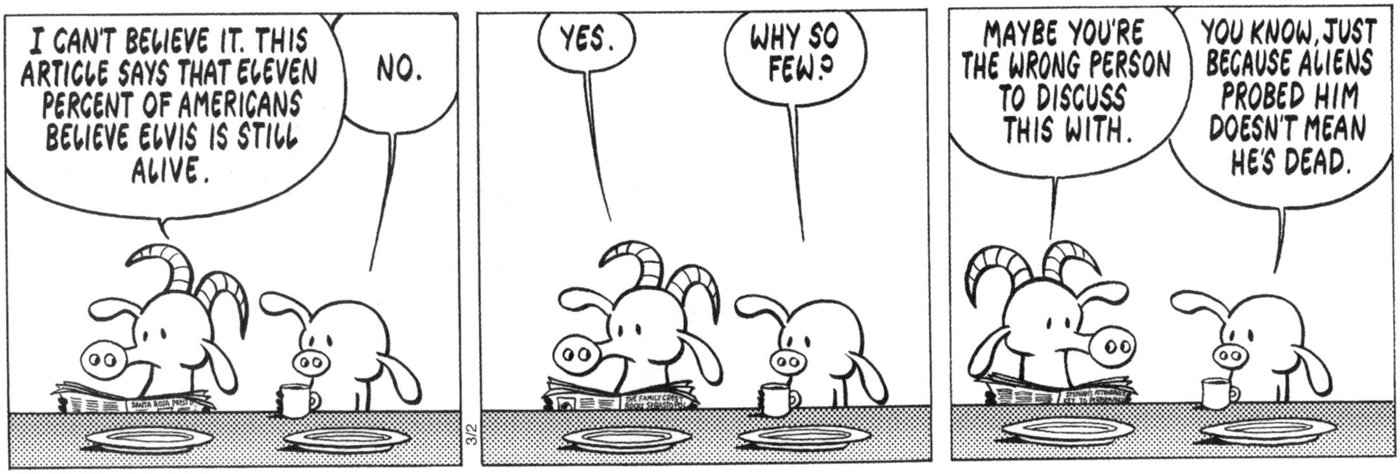
I CAN'T BELIEVE IT. THIS ARTICLE SAYS THAT ELEVEN PERCENT OF AMERICANS BELIEVE ELVIS IS STILL ALIVE.
NO.
3/2
YES.
WHY SO FEW?
MAYBE YOU'RE THE WRONG PERSON TO DISCUSS THIS WITH.
YOU KNOW, JUST BECAUSE ALIENS PROBED HIM DOESN'T MEAN HE'S DEAD.

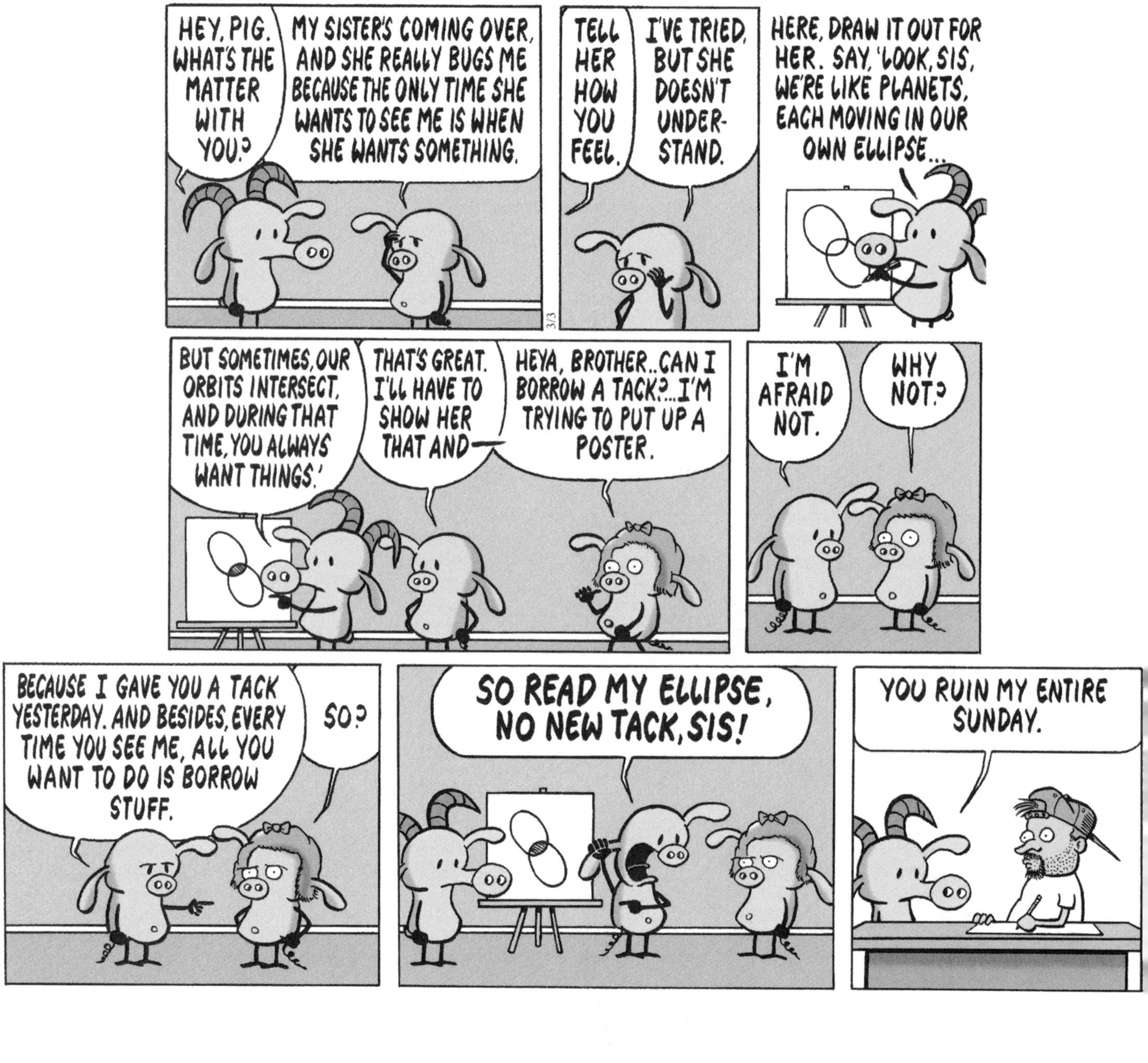
HEY, PIG. WHAT'S THE MATTER WITH YOU?
MY SISTER'S COMING OVER, AND SHE REALLY BUGS ME BECAUSE THE ONLY TIME SHE WANTS TO SEE ME IS WHEN SHE WANTS SOMETHING.
3/3
TELL HER HOW YOU FEEL.
I'VE TRIED, BUT SHE DOESN'T UNDERSTAND.
HERE, DRAW IT OUT FOR HER. SAY, 'LOOK, SIS, WE'RE LIKE PLANETS, EACH MOVING IN OUR OWN ELLIPSE...
BUT SOMETIMES, OUR ORBITS INTERSECT, AND DURING THAT TIME, YOU ALWAYS WANT THINGS.'
THAT'S GREAT. I'LL HAVE TO SHOW HER THAT AND—
HEYA, BROTHER..CAN I BORROW A TACK?...I'M TRYING TO PUT UP A POSTER.
I'M AFRAID NOT.
WHY NOT?
BECAUSE I GAVE YOU A TACK YESTERDAY. AND BESIDES, EVERY TIME YOU SEE ME, ALL YOU WANT TO DO IS BORROW STUFF.
SO?
SO READ MY ELLIPSE, NO NEW TACK, SIS!
YOU RUIN MY ENTIRE SUNDAY.

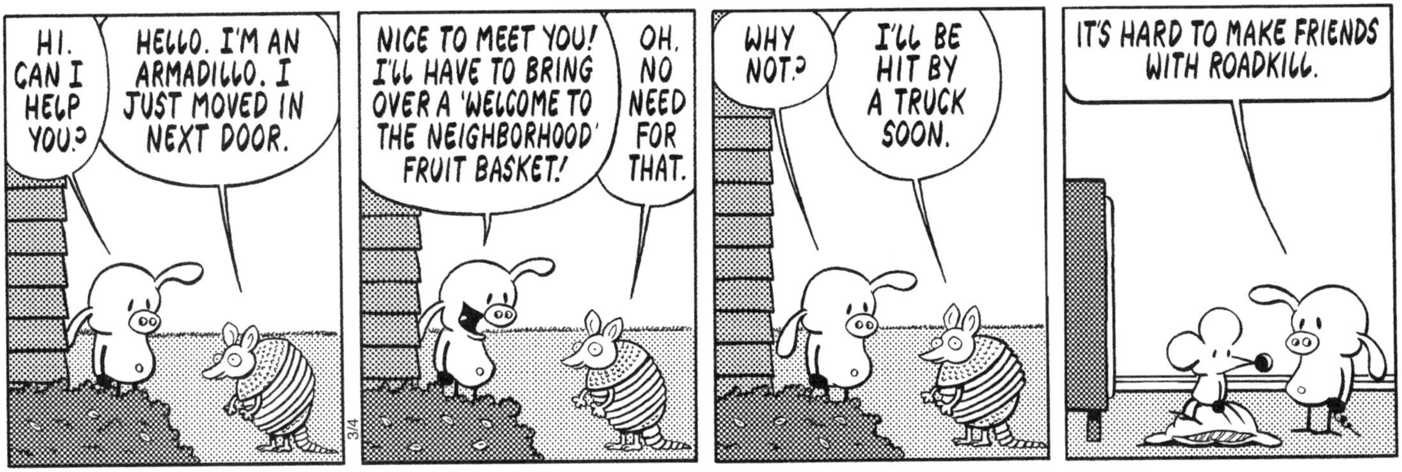
HI. CAN I HELP YOU?
HELLO. I'M AN ARMADILLO. I JUST MOVED IN NEXT DOOR.
NICE TO MEET YOU! I'LL HAVE TO BRING OVER A 'WELCOME TO THE NEIGHBORHOOD' FRUIT BASKET!
OH, NO NEED FOR THAT.
WHY NOT?
I'LL BE HIT BY A TRUCK SOON.
IT'S HARD TO MAKE FRIENDS WITH ROADKILL.
3/4

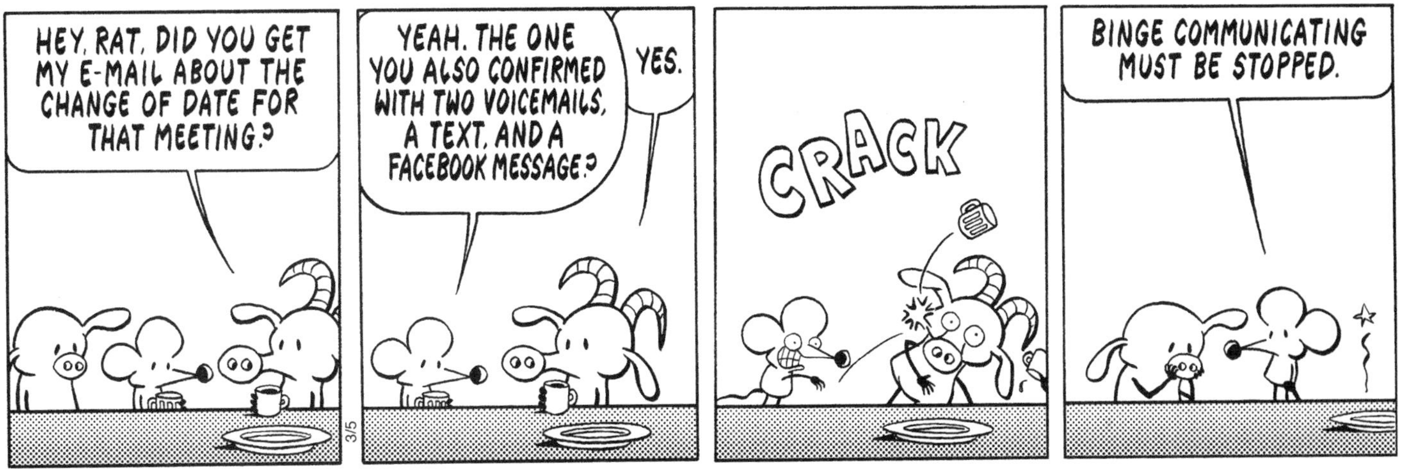
HEY, RAT, DID YOU GET MY E-MAIL ABOUT THE CHANGE OF DATE FOR THAT MEETING?
YEAH. THE ONE YOU ALSO CONFIRMED WITH TWO VOICEMAILS, A TEXT, AND A FACEBOOK MESSAGE?
YES.
CRACK
BINGE COMMUNICATING MUST BE STOPPED.
3/5

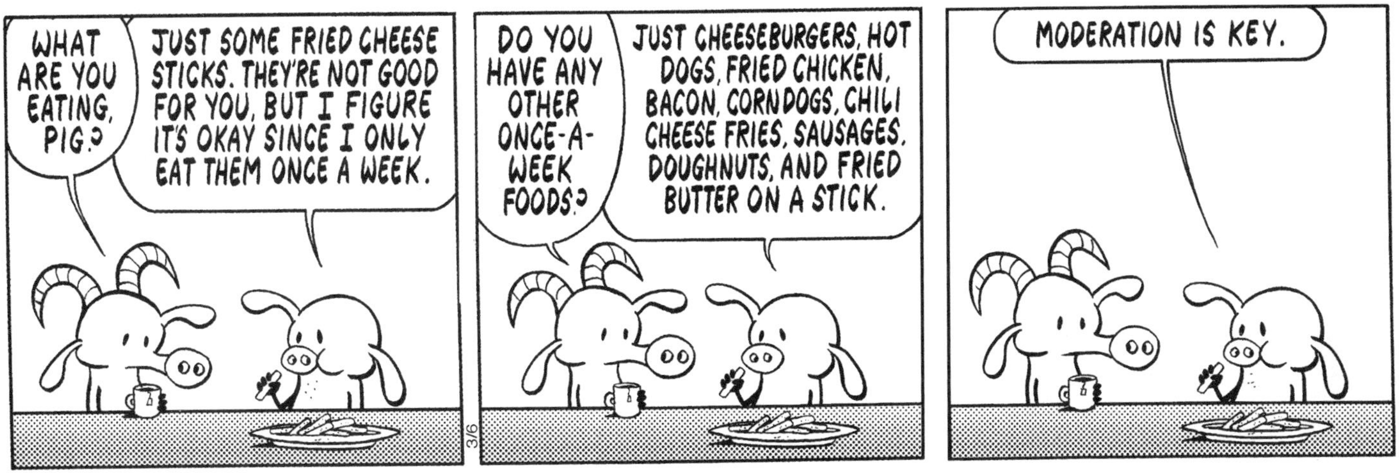
WHAT ARE YOU EATING, PIG?
JUST SOME FRIED CHEESE STICKS. THEY'RE NOT GOOD FOR YOU, BUT I FIGURE IT'S OKAY SINCE I ONLY EAT THEM ONCE A WEEK.
DO YOU HAVE ANY OTHER ONCE-A-WEEK FOODS?
JUST CHEESEBURGERS, HOT DOGS, FRIED CHICKEN, BACON, CORNDOGS, CHILI CHEESE FRIES, SAUSAGES, DOUGHNUTS, AND FRIED BUTTER ON A STICK.
MODERATION IS KEY.
3/6

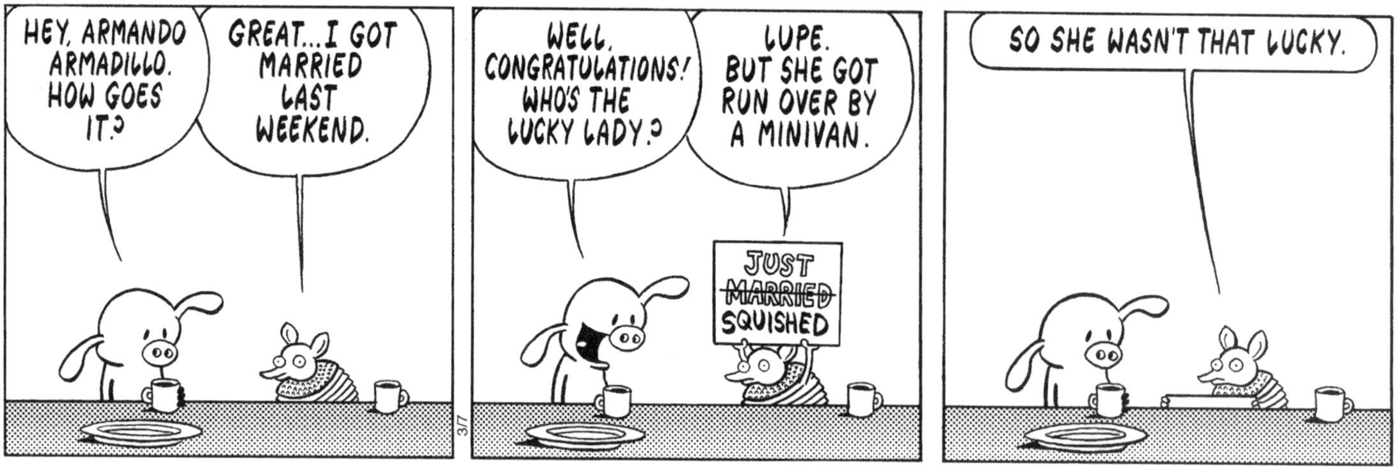
HEY, ARMANDO ARMADILLO. HOW GOES IT?
GREAT...I GOT MARRIED LAST WEEKEND.
WELL, CONGRATULATIONS! WHO'S THE LUCKY LADY?
LUPE. BUT SHE GOT RUN OVER BY A MINIVAN.
JUST ~~MARRIED~~ SQUISHED
SO SHE WASN'T THAT LUCKY.
3/7

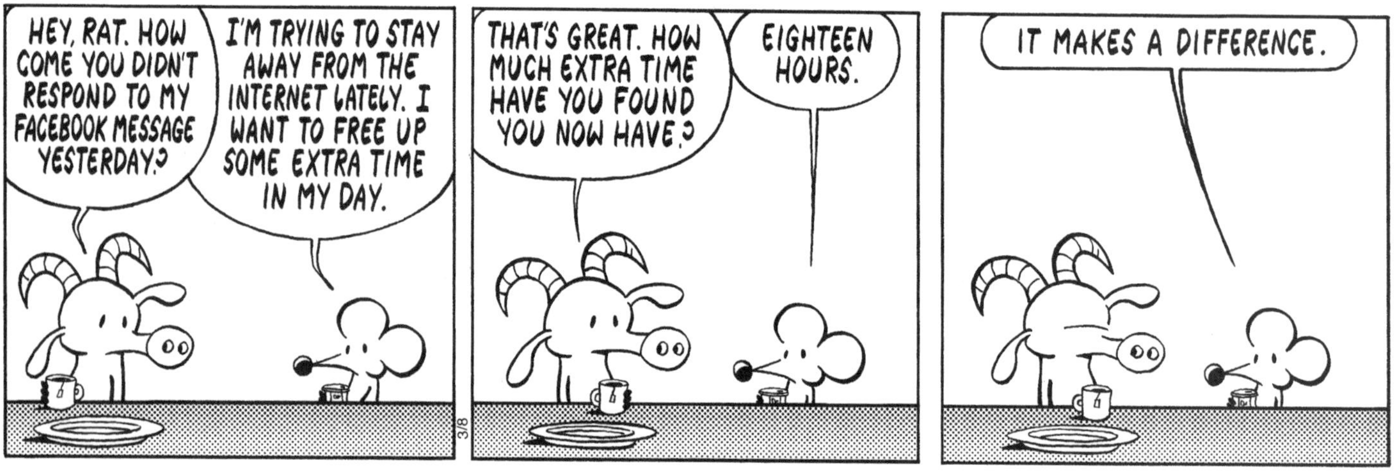
HEY, RAT. HOW COME YOU DIDN'T RESPOND TO MY FACEBOOK MESSAGE YESTERDAY?
I'M TRYING TO STAY AWAY FROM THE INTERNET LATELY. I WANT TO FREE UP SOME EXTRA TIME IN MY DAY.
THAT'S GREAT. HOW MUCH EXTRA TIME HAVE YOU FOUND YOU NOW HAVE?
EIGHTEEN HOURS.
IT MAKES A DIFFERENCE.
3/8

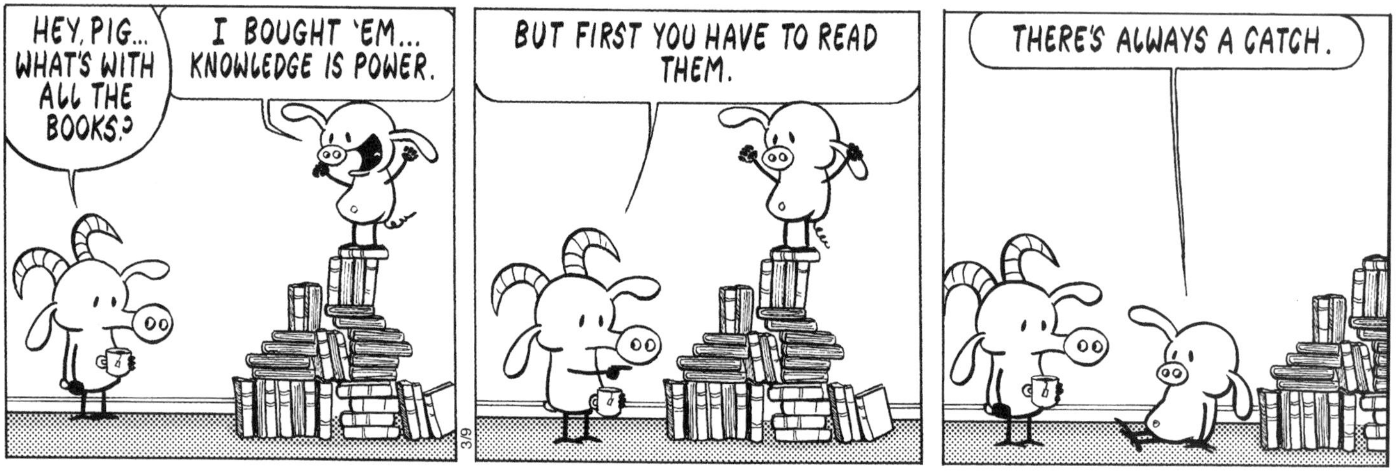
HEY, PIG... WHAT'S WITH ALL THE BOOKS?
I BOUGHT 'EM... KNOWLEDGE IS POWER.
BUT FIRST YOU HAVE TO READ THEM.
THERE'S ALWAYS A CATCH.
3/9

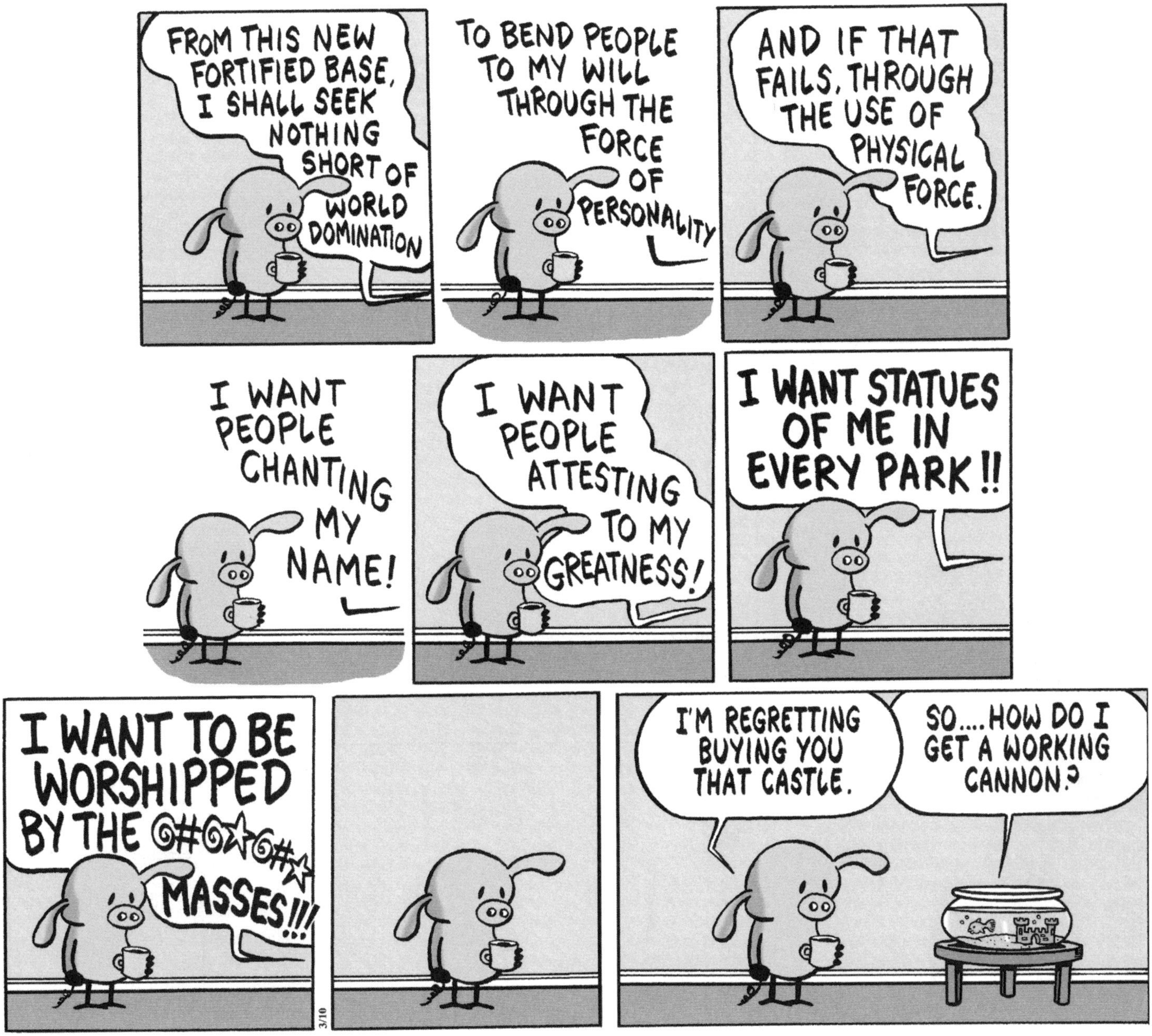
FROM THIS NEW FORTIFIED BASE, I SHALL SEEK NOTHING SHORT OF WORLD DOMINATION
TO BEND PEOPLE TO MY WILL THROUGH THE FORCE OF PERSONALITY
AND IF THAT FAILS, THROUGH THE USE OF PHYSICAL FORCE.
I WANT PEOPLE CHANTING MY NAME!
I WANT PEOPLE ATTESTING TO MY GREATNESS!
I WANT STATUES OF ME IN EVERY PARK!!
I WANT TO BE WORSHIPPED BY THE @#@☆@#☆ MASSES!!!
3/10
I'M REGRETTING BUYING YOU THAT CASTLE.
SO.... HOW DO I GET A WORKING CANNON?

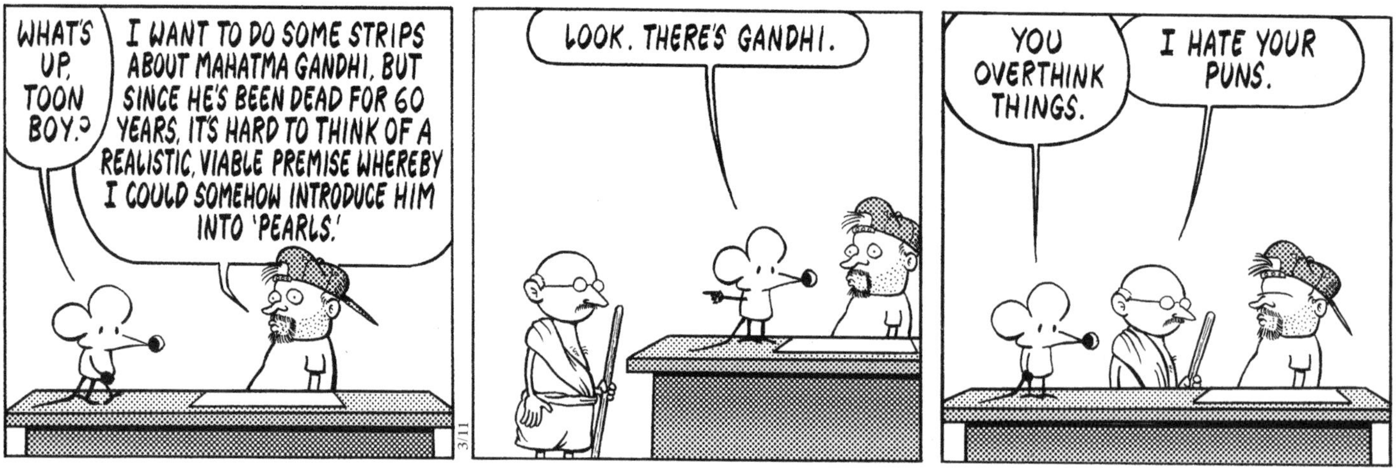
WHAT'S UP, TOON BOY?
I WANT TO DO SOME STRIPS ABOUT MAHATMA GANDHI, BUT SINCE HE'S BEEN DEAD FOR 60 YEARS, IT'S HARD TO THINK OF A REALISTIC, VIABLE PREMISE WHEREBY I COULD SOMEHOW INTRODUCE HIM INTO 'PEARLS.'
3/11
LOOK. THERE'S GANDHI.
YOU OVERTHINK THINGS.
I HATE YOUR PUNS.

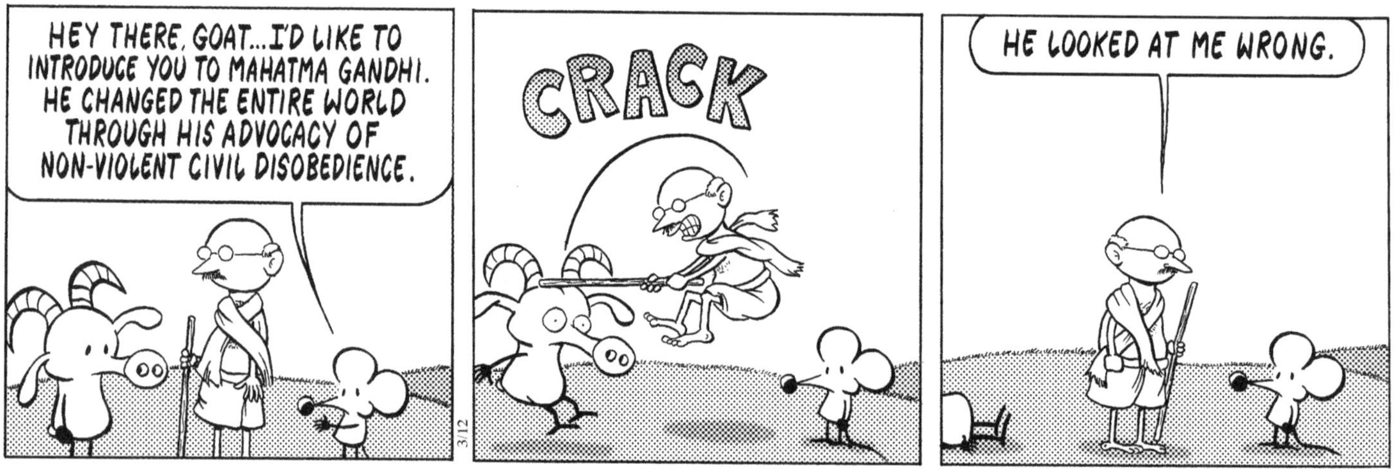
HEY THERE, GOAT...I'D LIKE TO INTRODUCE YOU TO MAHATMA GANDHI. HE CHANGED THE ENTIRE WORLD THROUGH HIS ADVOCACY OF NON-VIOLENT CIVIL DISOBEDIENCE.
3/12
CRACK
HE LOOKED AT ME WRONG.

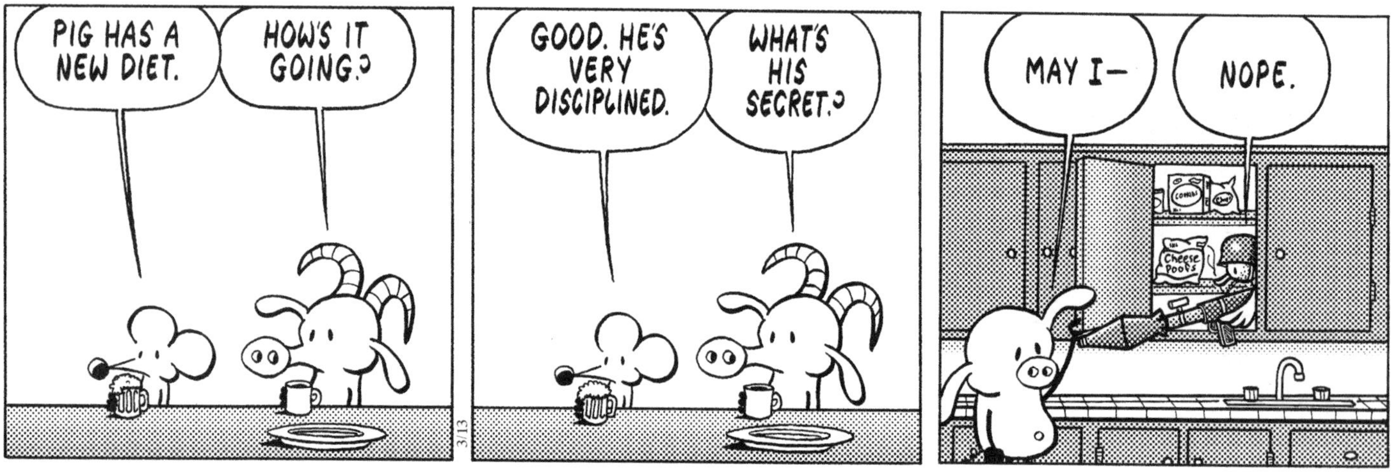
PIG HAS A NEW DIET.
HOW'S IT GOING?
3/13
GOOD. HE'S VERY DISCIPLINED.
WHAT'S HIS SECRET?
MAY I—
NOPE.

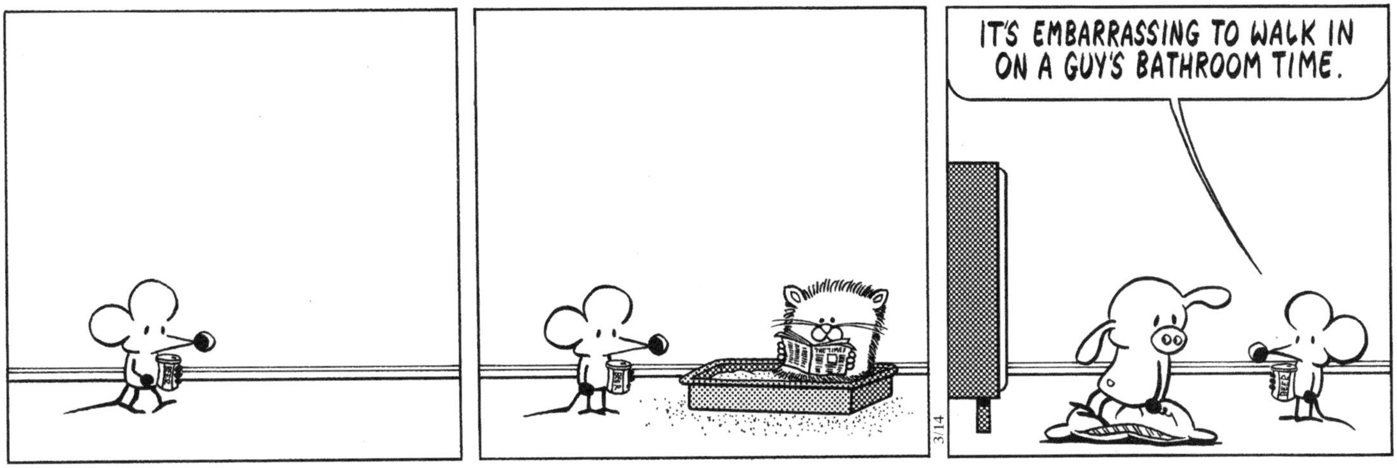
IT'S EMBARRASSING TO WALK IN ON A GUY'S BATHROOM TIME.
3/14

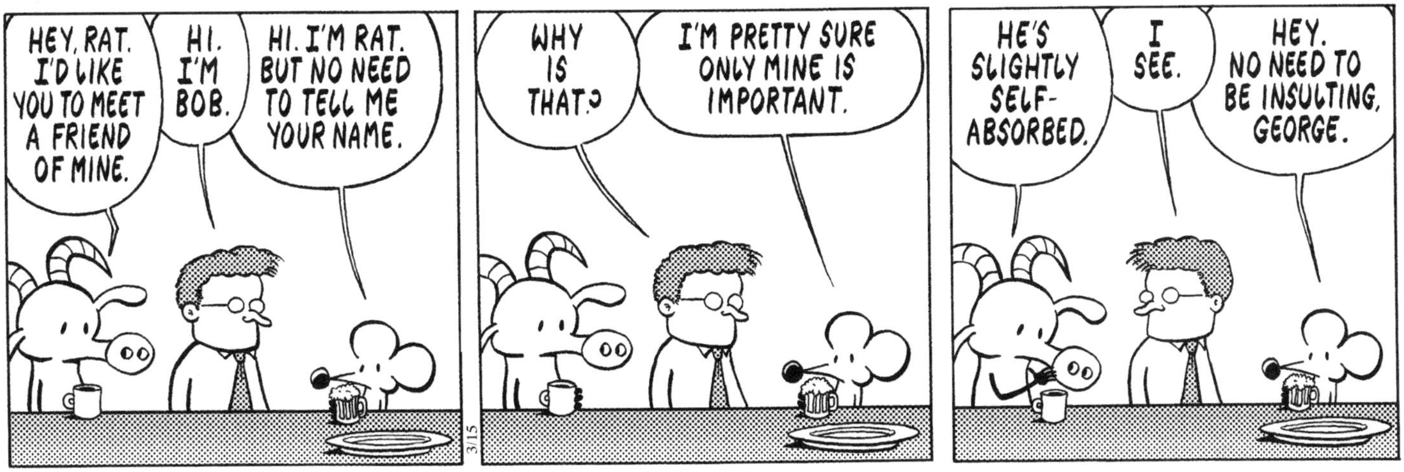
HEY, RAT. I'D LIKE YOU TO MEET A FRIEND OF MINE.
HI. I'M BOB.
HI. I'M RAT. BUT NO NEED TO TELL ME YOUR NAME.
WHY IS THAT?
I'M PRETTY SURE ONLY MINE IS IMPORTANT.
HE'S SLIGHTLY SELF-ABSORBED.
I SEE.
HEY. NO NEED TO BE INSULTING, GEORGE.
3/15

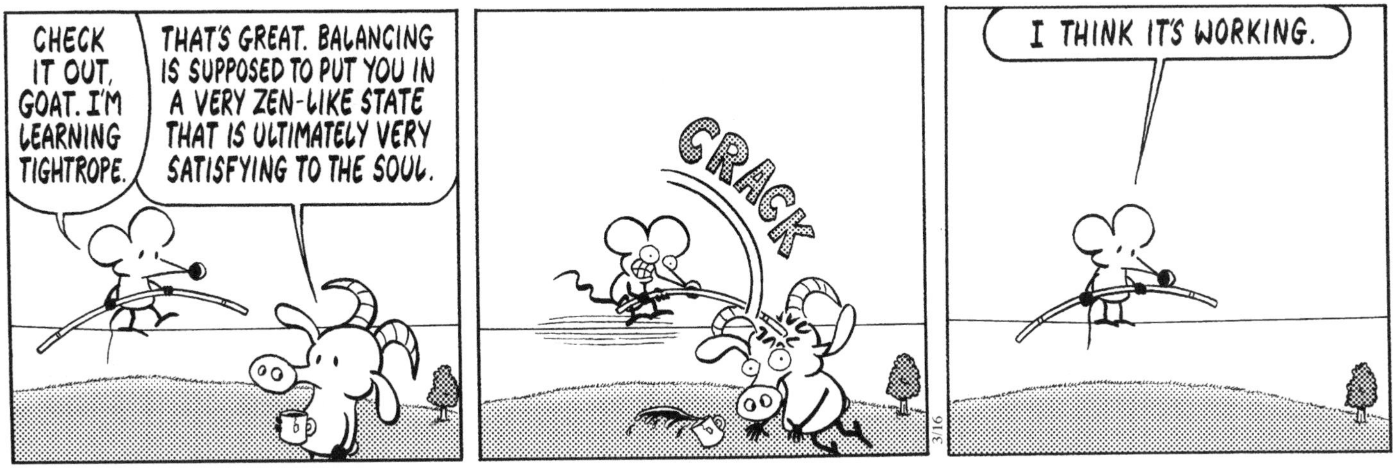
CHECK IT OUT, GOAT. I'M LEARNING TIGHTROPE.
THAT'S GREAT. BALANCING IS SUPPOSED TO PUT YOU IN A VERY ZEN-LIKE STATE THAT IS ULTIMATELY VERY SATISFYING TO THE SOUL.
CRACK
I THINK IT'S WORKING.
3/16

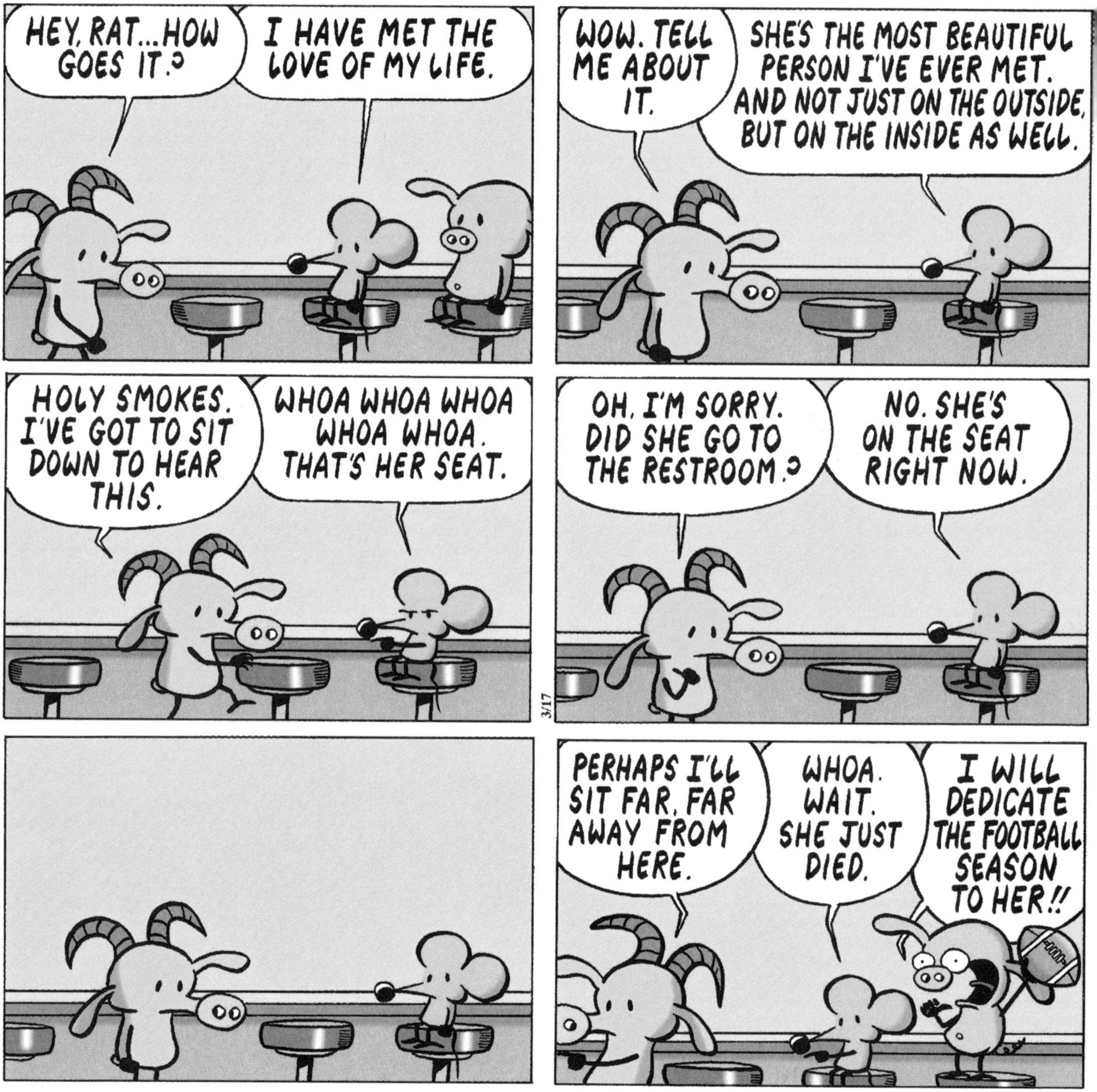
HEY, RAT...HOW GOES IT?
I HAVE MET THE LOVE OF MY LIFE.
WOW. TELL ME ABOUT IT.
SHE'S THE MOST BEAUTIFUL PERSON I'VE EVER MET. AND NOT JUST ON THE OUTSIDE, BUT ON THE INSIDE AS WELL.
HOLY SMOKES. I'VE GOT TO SIT DOWN TO HEAR THIS.
WHOA WHOA WHOA WHOA WHOA. THAT'S HER SEAT.
OH, I'M SORRY. DID SHE GO TO THE RESTROOM?
NO. SHE'S ON THE SEAT RIGHT NOW.
3/17
PERHAPS I'LL SIT FAR, FAR AWAY FROM HERE.
WHOA. WAIT. SHE JUST DIED.
I WILL DEDICATE THE FOOTBALL SEASON TO HER!!

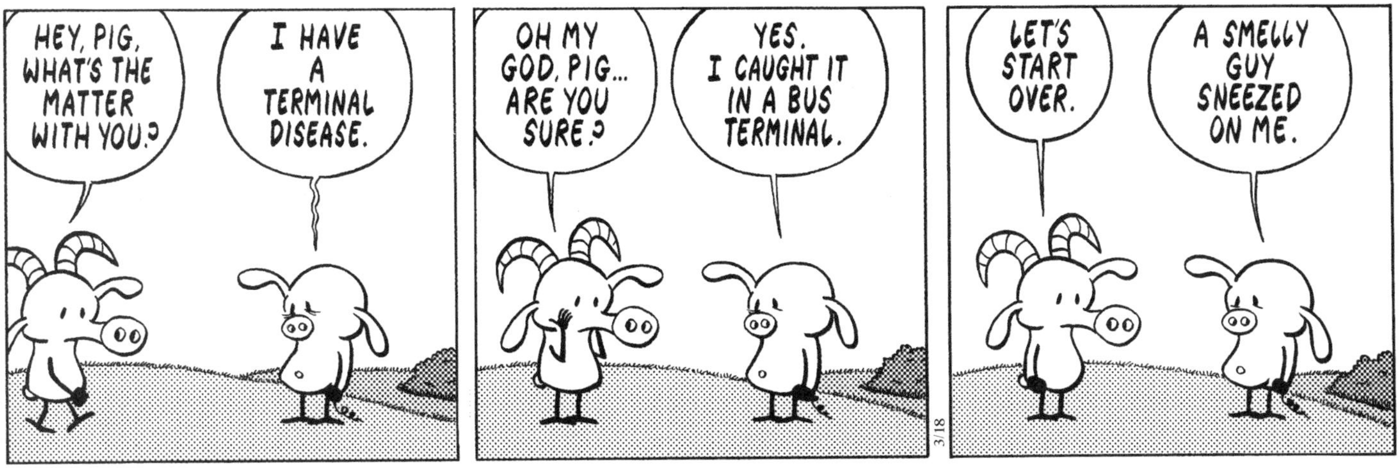
HEY, PIG, WHAT'S THE MATTER WITH YOU?
I HAVE A TERMINAL DISEASE.
OH MY GOD, PIG... ARE YOU SURE?
YES. I CAUGHT IT IN A BUS TERMINAL.
3/18
LET'S START OVER.
A SMELLY GUY SNEEZED ON ME.

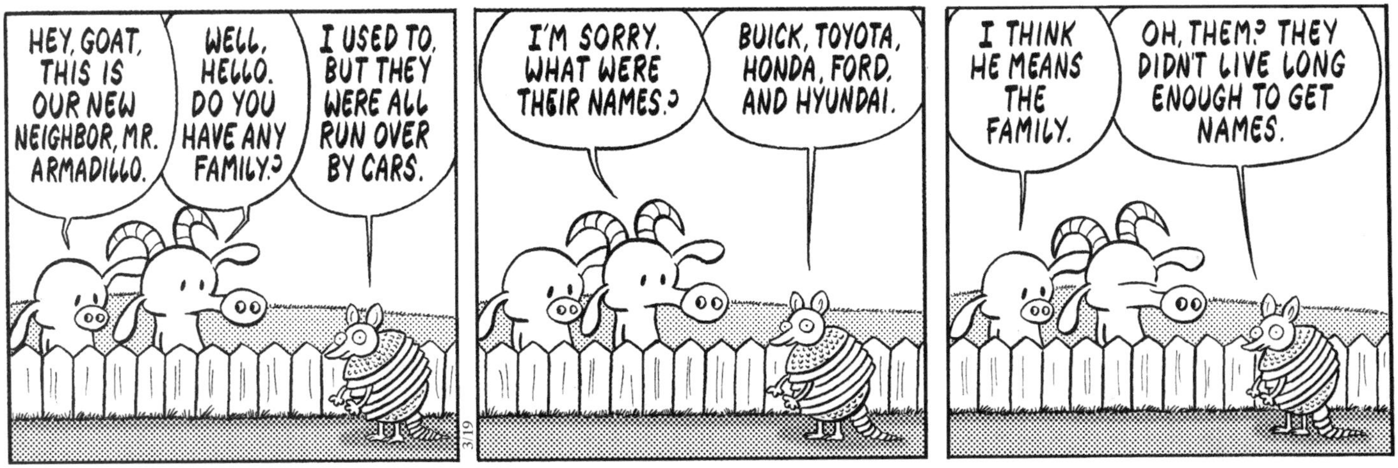
HEY, GOAT, THIS IS OUR NEW NEIGHBOR, MR. ARMADILLO.
WELL, HELLO. DO YOU HAVE ANY FAMILY?
I USED TO, BUT THEY WERE ALL RUN OVER BY CARS.
3/19
I'M SORRY. WHAT WERE THEIR NAMES?
BUICK, TOYOTA, HONDA, FORD, AND HYUNDAI.
I THINK HE MEANS THE FAMILY.
OH, THEM? THEY DIDN'T LIVE LONG ENOUGH TO GET NAMES.

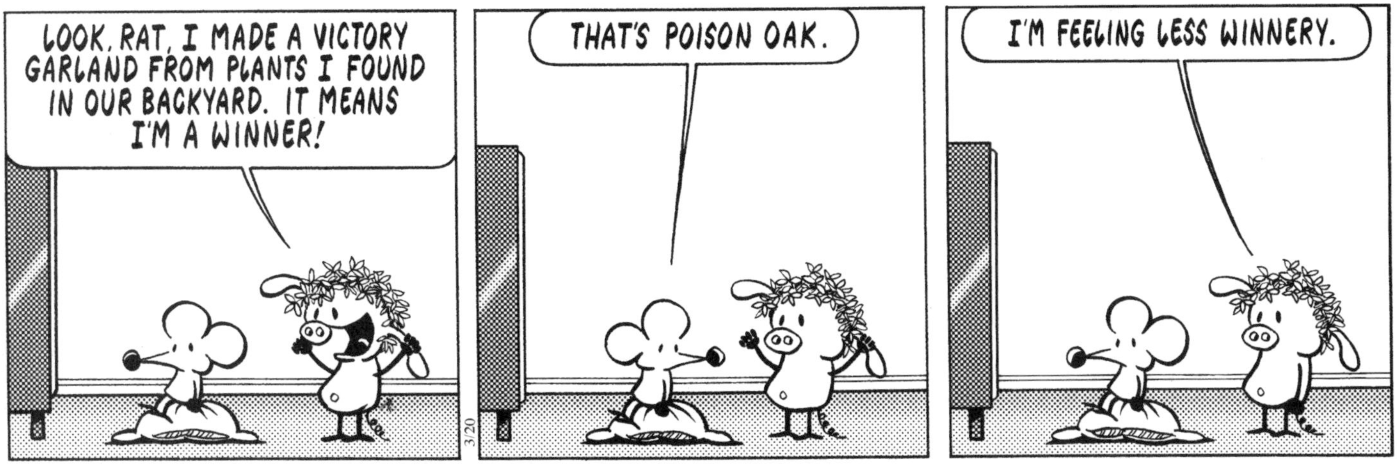
LOOK, RAT, I MADE A VICTORY GARLAND FROM PLANTS I FOUND IN OUR BACKYARD. IT MEANS I'M A WINNER!
3/20
THAT'S POISON OAK.
I'M FEELING LESS WINNERY.

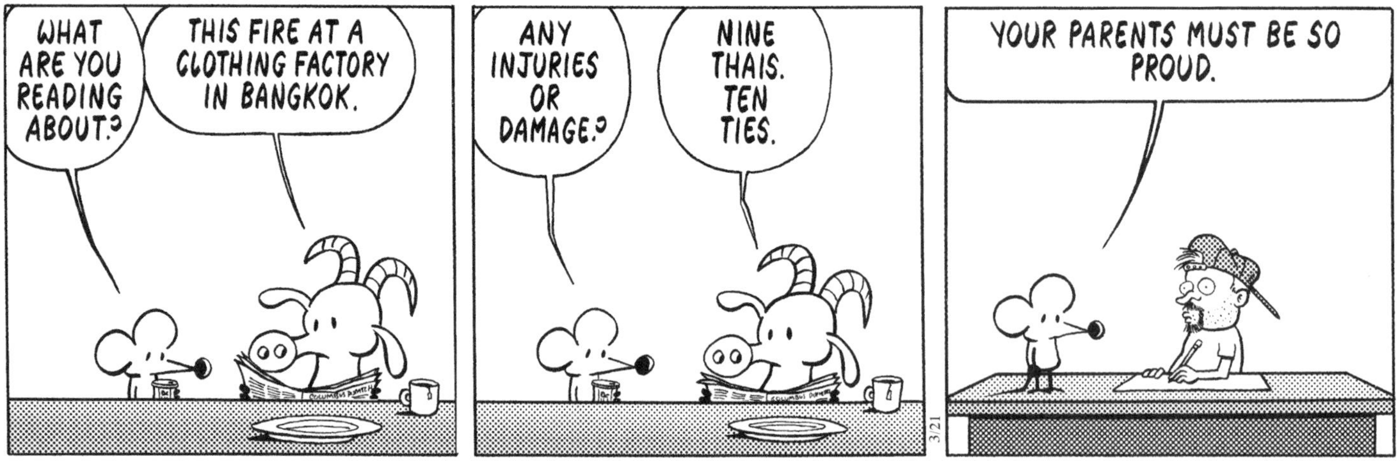
WHAT ARE YOU READING ABOUT?
THIS FIRE AT A CLOTHING FACTORY IN BANGKOK.
ANY INJURIES OR DAMAGE?
NINE THAIS. TEN TIES.
YOUR PARENTS MUST BE SO PROUD.
3/21

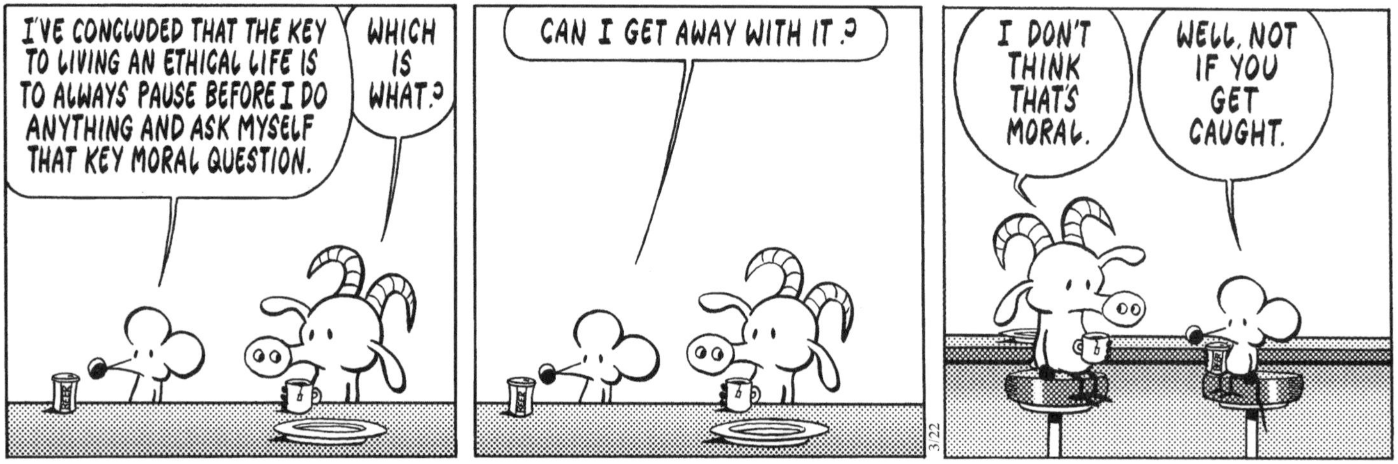
I'VE CONCLUDED THAT THE KEY TO LIVING AN ETHICAL LIFE IS TO ALWAYS PAUSE BEFORE I DO ANYTHING AND ASK MYSELF THAT KEY MORAL QUESTION.
WHICH IS WHAT?
CAN I GET AWAY WITH IT?
I DON'T THINK THAT'S MORAL.
WELL, NOT IF YOU GET CAUGHT.
3/22

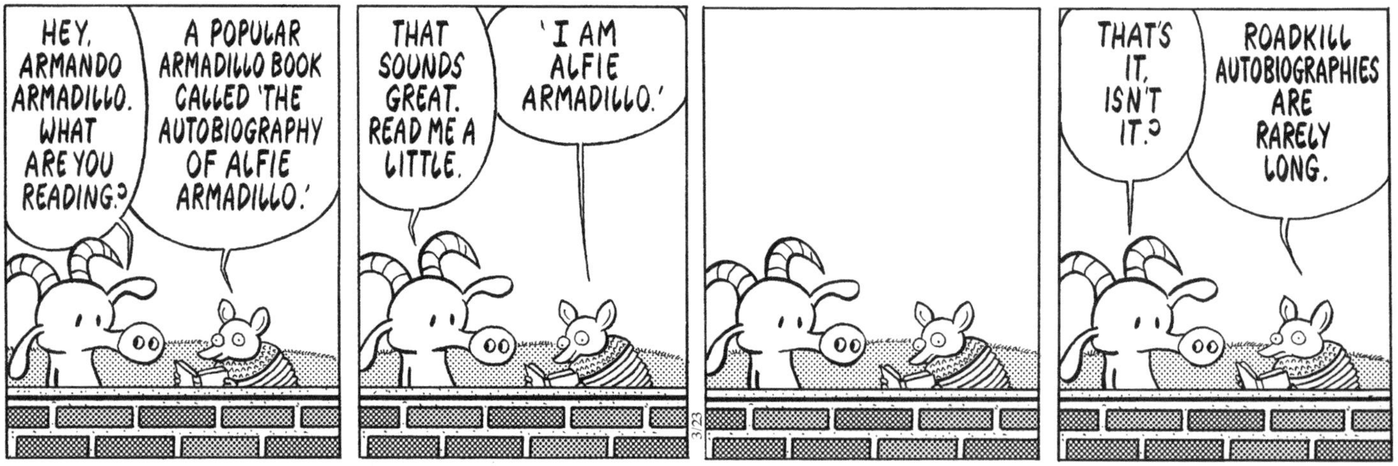
HEY, ARMANDO ARMADILLO. WHAT ARE YOU READING?
A POPULAR ARMADILLO BOOK CALLED 'THE AUTOBIOGRAPHY OF ALFIE ARMADILLO.'
THAT SOUNDS GREAT. READ ME A LITTLE.
'I AM ALFIE ARMADILLO.'
THAT'S IT, ISN'T IT?
ROADKILL AUTOBIOGRAPHIES ARE RARELY LONG.
3/23

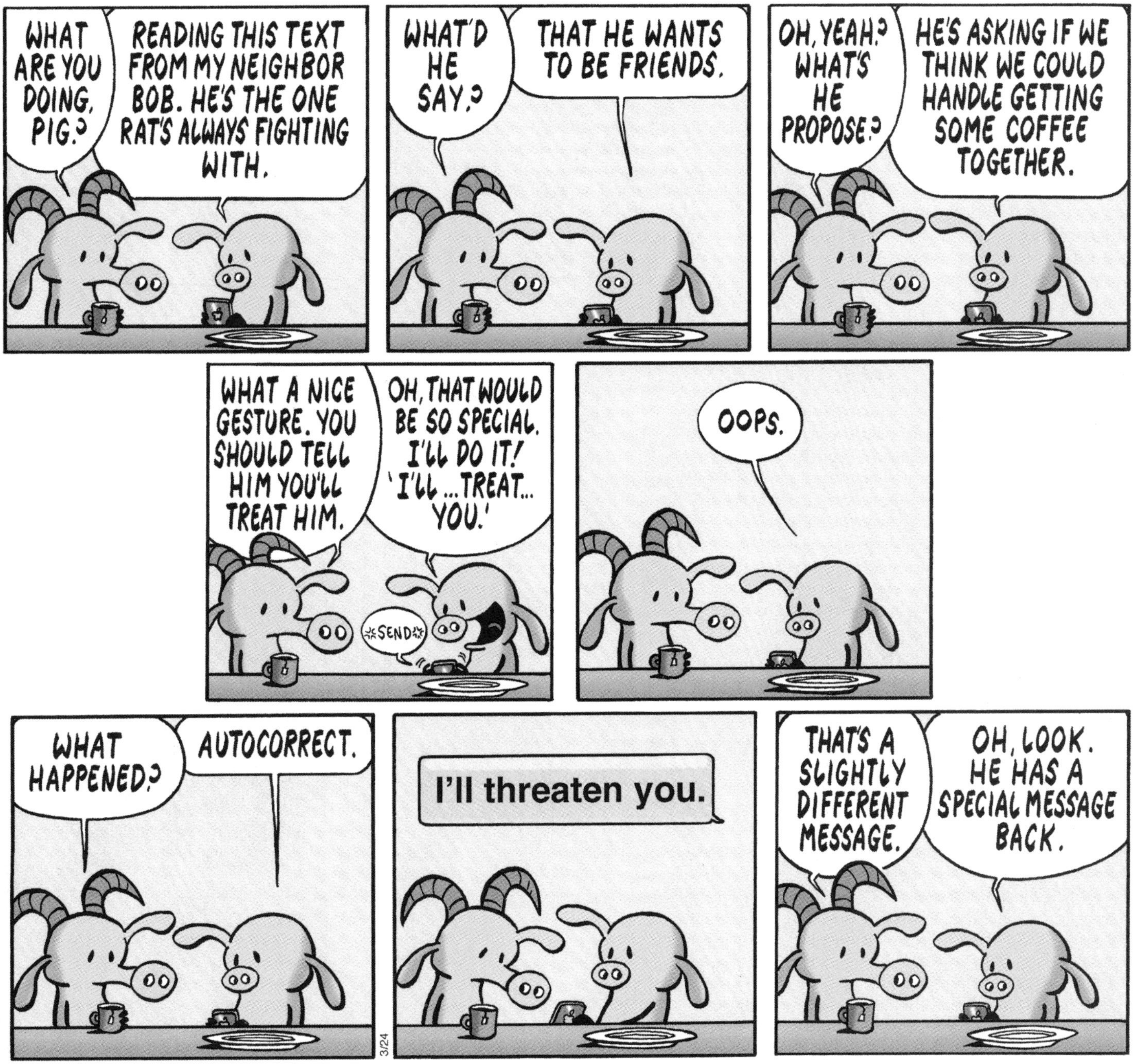
WHAT ARE YOU DOING, PIG?
READING THIS TEXT FROM MY NEIGHBOR BOB. HE'S THE ONE RAT'S ALWAYS FIGHTING WITH.
WHAT'D HE SAY?
THAT HE WANTS TO BE FRIENDS.
OH, YEAH? WHAT'S HE PROPOSE?
HE'S ASKING IF WE THINK WE COULD HANDLE GETTING SOME COFFEE TOGETHER.
WHAT A NICE GESTURE. YOU SHOULD TELL HIM YOU'LL TREAT HIM.
OH, THAT WOULD BE SO SPECIAL. I'LL DO IT! 'I'LL ...TREAT... YOU.'
SEND
OOPS.
WHAT HAPPENED?
AUTOCORRECT.
3/24
I'll threaten you.
THAT'S A SLIGHTLY DIFFERENT MESSAGE.
OH, LOOK. HE HAS A SPECIAL MESSAGE BACK.

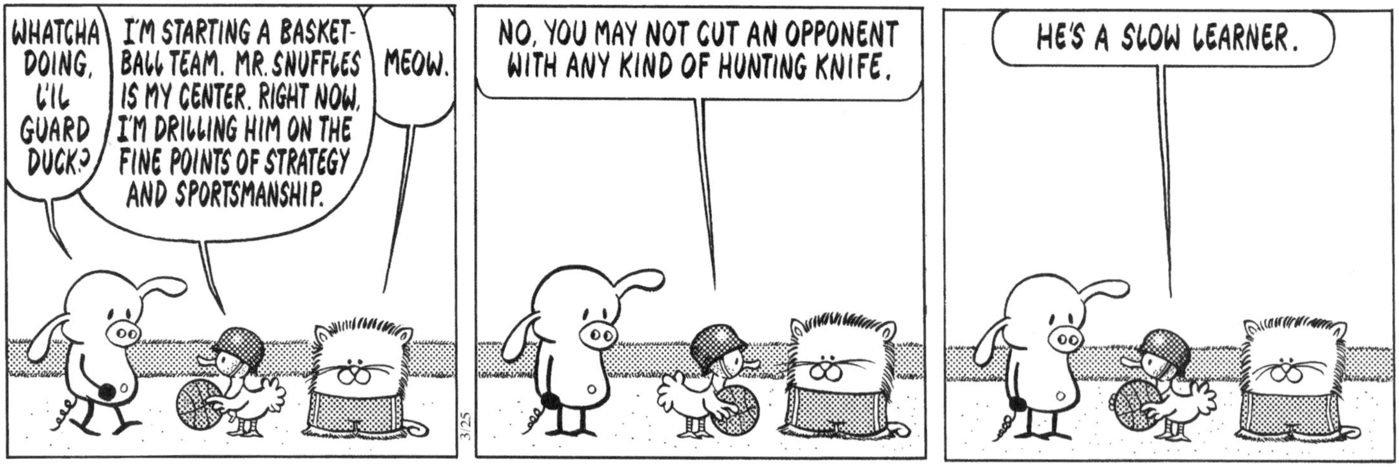
WHATCHA DOING, L'IL GUARD DUCK?
I'M STARTING A BASKETBALL TEAM. MR. SNUFFLES IS MY CENTER. RIGHT NOW, I'M DRILLING HIM ON THE FINE POINTS OF STRATEGY AND SPORTSMANSHIP.
MEOW.
3/25
NO, YOU MAY NOT CUT AN OPPONENT WITH ANY KIND OF HUNTING KNIFE.
HE'S A SLOW LEARNER.

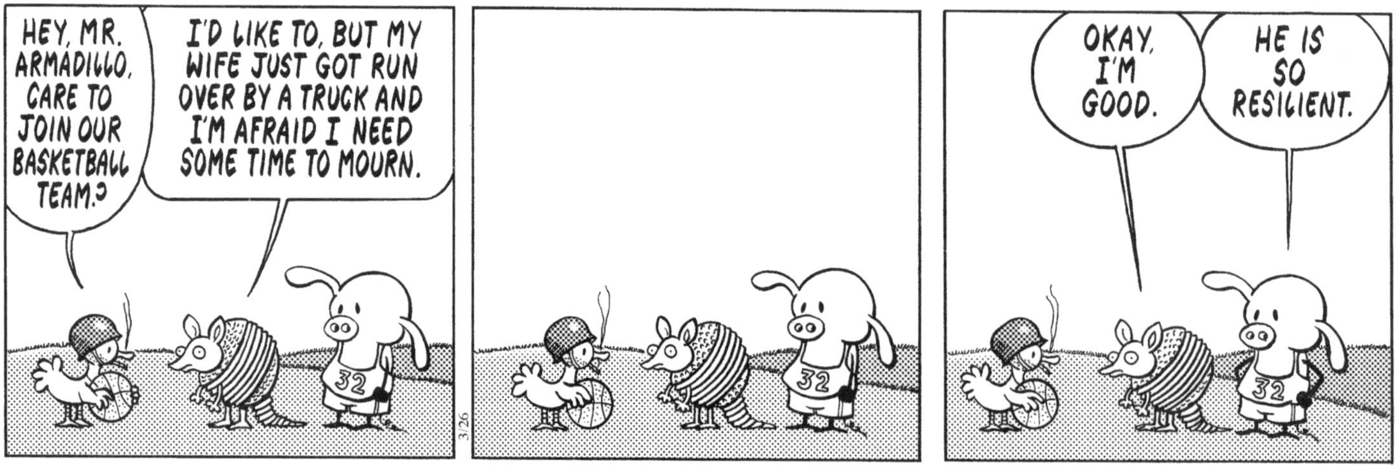
HEY, MR. ARMADILLO, CARE TO JOIN OUR BASKETBALL TEAM?
I'D LIKE TO, BUT MY WIFE JUST GOT RUN OVER BY A TRUCK AND I'M AFRAID I NEED SOME TIME TO MOURN.
3/26
32
OKAY, I'M GOOD.
HE IS SO RESILIENT.

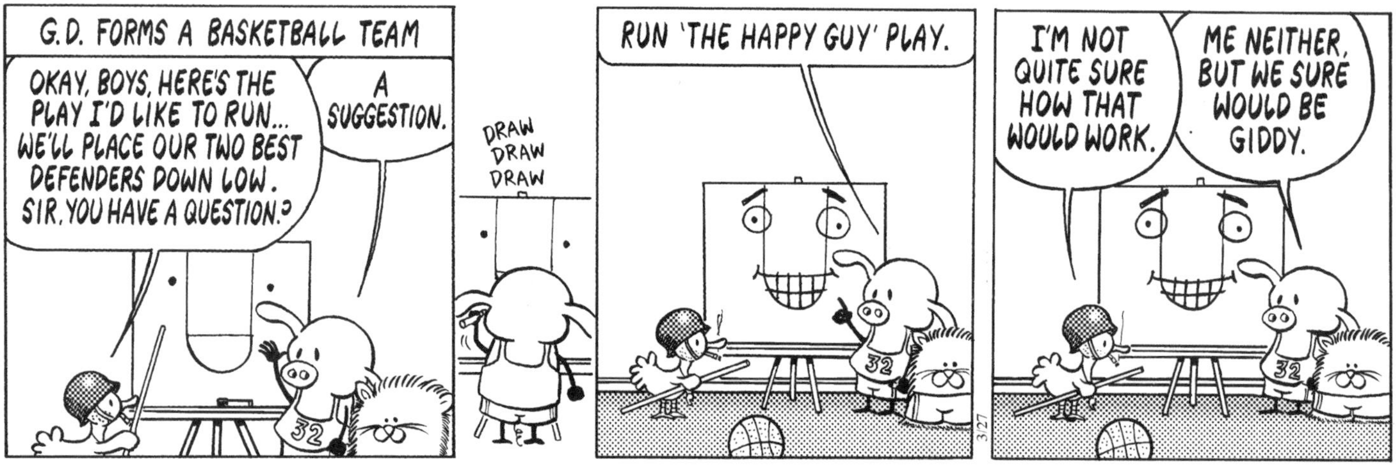
G.D. FORMS A BASKETBALL TEAM
OKAY, BOYS, HERE'S THE PLAY I'D LIKE TO RUN... WE'LL PLACE OUR TWO BEST DEFENDERS DOWN LOW. SIR, YOU HAVE A QUESTION?
A SUGGESTION.
DRAW DRAW DRAW
RUN 'THE HAPPY GUY' PLAY.
3/27
I'M NOT QUITE SURE HOW THAT WOULD WORK.
ME NEITHER, BUT WE SURE WOULD BE GIDDY.

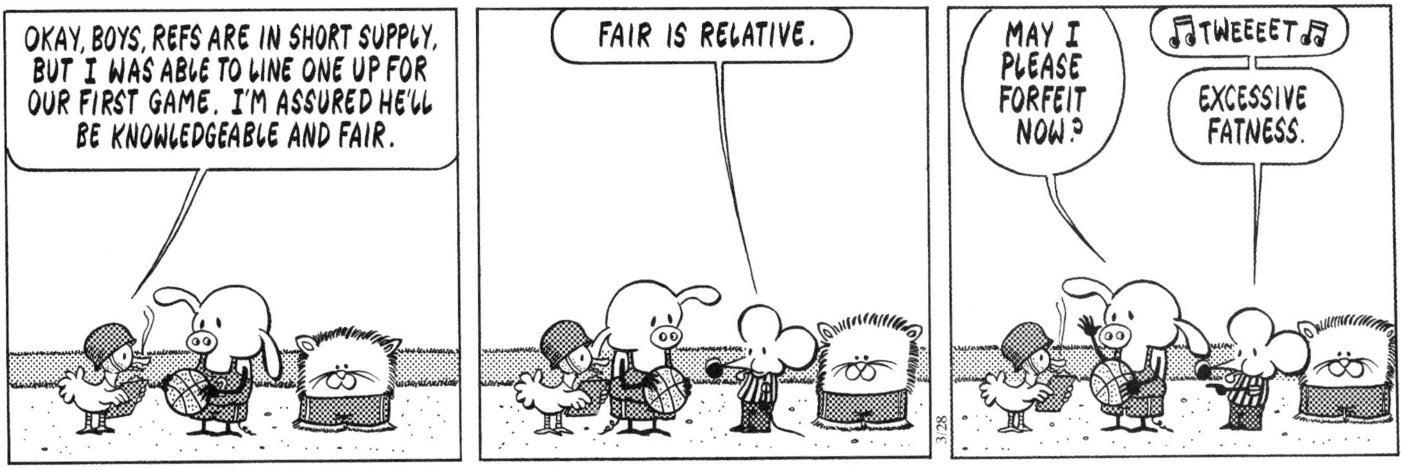
OKAY, BOYS, REFS ARE IN SHORT SUPPLY, BUT I WAS ABLE TO LINE ONE UP FOR OUR FIRST GAME. I'M ASSURED HE'LL BE KNOWLEDGEABLE AND FAIR.
FAIR IS RELATIVE.
MAY I PLEASE FORFEIT NOW?
♫TWEEEET♫
EXCESSIVE FATNESS.
3/28

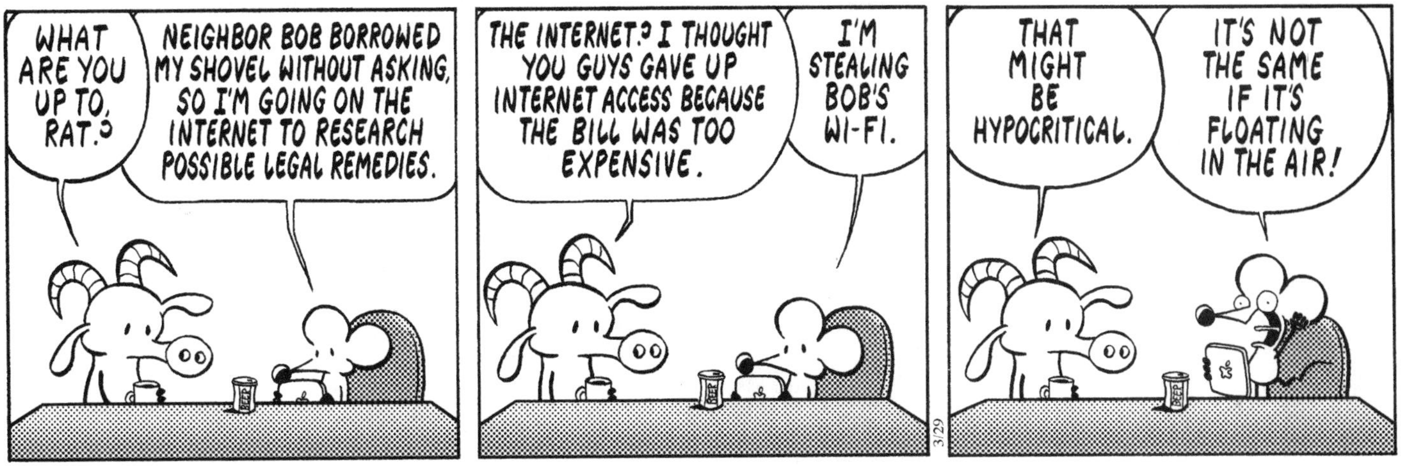
WHAT ARE YOU UP TO, RAT?
NEIGHBOR BOB BORROWED MY SHOVEL WITHOUT ASKING, SO I'M GOING ON THE INTERNET TO RESEARCH POSSIBLE LEGAL REMEDIES.
THE INTERNET? I THOUGHT YOU GUYS GAVE UP INTERNET ACCESS BECAUSE THE BILL WAS TOO EXPENSIVE.
I'M STEALING BOB'S WI-FI.
THAT MIGHT BE HYPOCRITICAL.
IT'S NOT THE SAME IF IT'S FLOATING IN THE AIR!
3/29

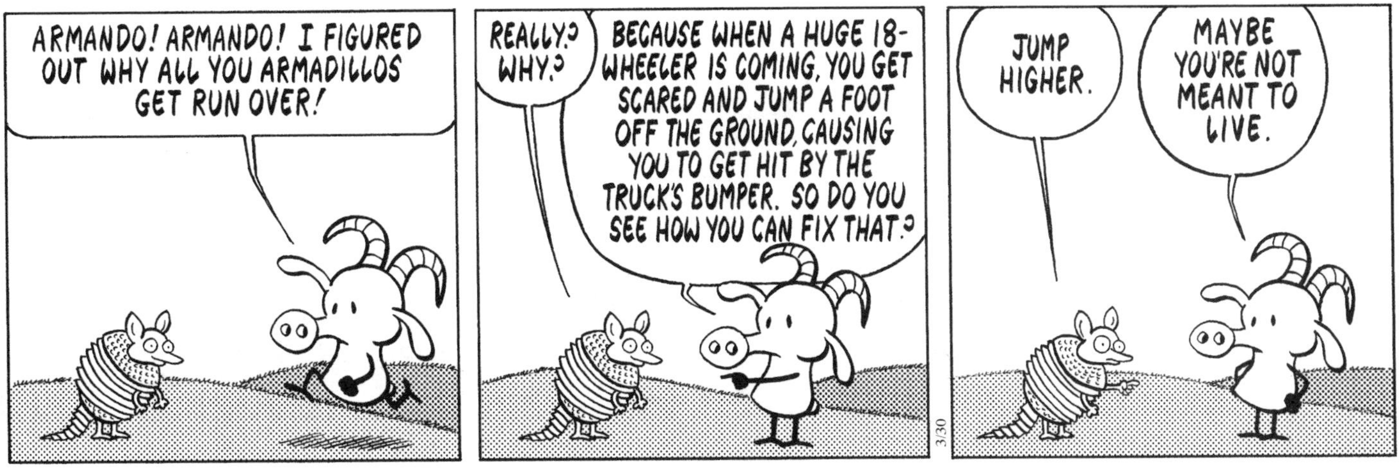
ARMANDO! ARMANDO! I FIGURED OUT WHY ALL YOU ARMADILLOS GET RUN OVER!
REALLY? WHY?
BECAUSE WHEN A HUGE 18-WHEELER IS COMING, YOU GET SCARED AND JUMP A FOOT OFF THE GROUND, CAUSING YOU TO GET HIT BY THE TRUCK'S BUMPER. SO DO YOU SEE HOW YOU CAN FIX THAT?
JUMP HIGHER.
MAYBE YOU'RE NOT MEANT TO LIVE.
3/30

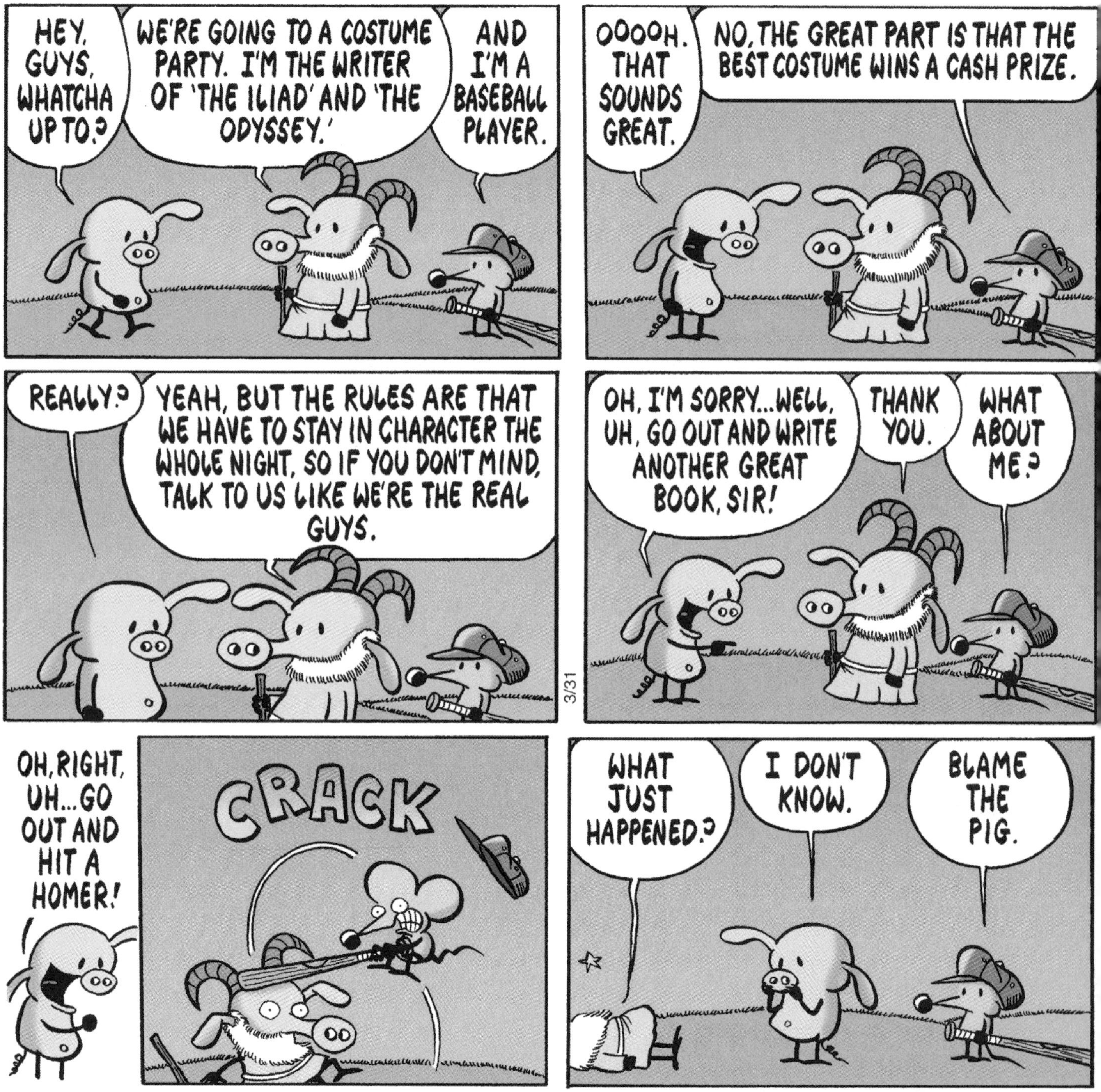
HEY, GUYS, WHATCHA UP TO?
WE'RE GOING TO A COSTUME PARTY. I'M THE WRITER OF 'THE ILIAD' AND 'THE ODYSSEY.'
AND I'M A BASEBALL PLAYER.
OOOOH. THAT SOUNDS GREAT.
NO, THE GREAT PART IS THAT THE BEST COSTUME WINS A CASH PRIZE.
REALLY?
YEAH, BUT THE RULES ARE THAT WE HAVE TO STAY IN CHARACTER THE WHOLE NIGHT, SO IF YOU DON'T MIND, TALK TO US LIKE WE'RE THE REAL GUYS.
3/31
OH, I'M SORRY...WELL, UH, GO OUT AND WRITE ANOTHER GREAT BOOK, SIR!
THANK YOU.
WHAT ABOUT ME?
OH, RIGHT, UH...GO OUT AND HIT A HOMER!
CRACK
WHAT JUST HAPPENED?
I DON'T KNOW.
BLAME THE PIG.

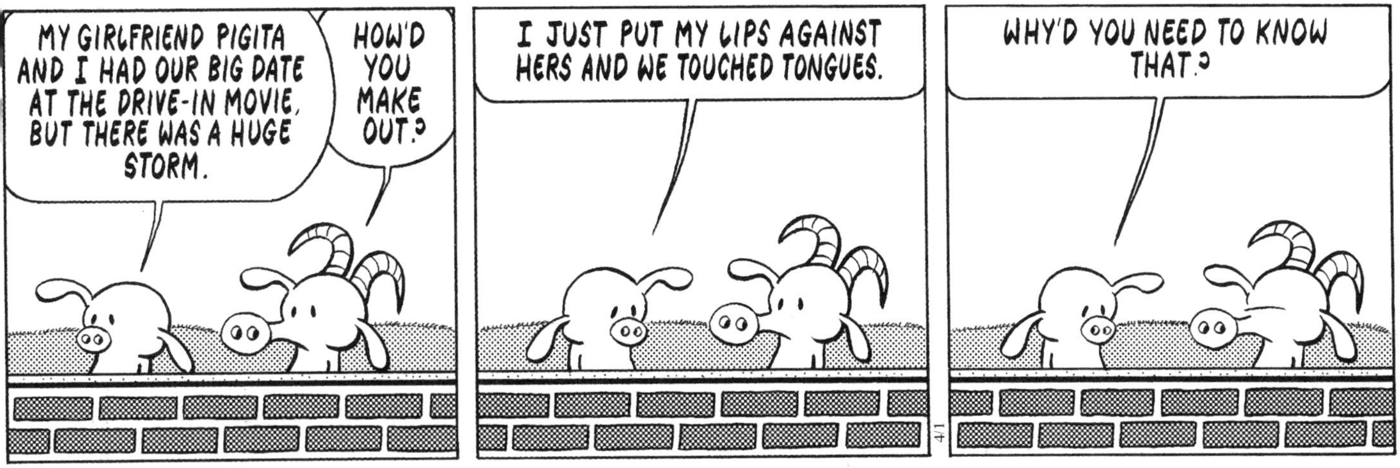
MY GIRLFRIEND PIGITA AND I HAD OUR BIG DATE AT THE DRIVE-IN MOVIE, BUT THERE WAS A HUGE STORM.
HOW'D YOU MAKE OUT?
I JUST PUT MY LIPS AGAINST HERS AND WE TOUCHED TONGUES.
WHY'D YOU NEED TO KNOW THAT?
4/1

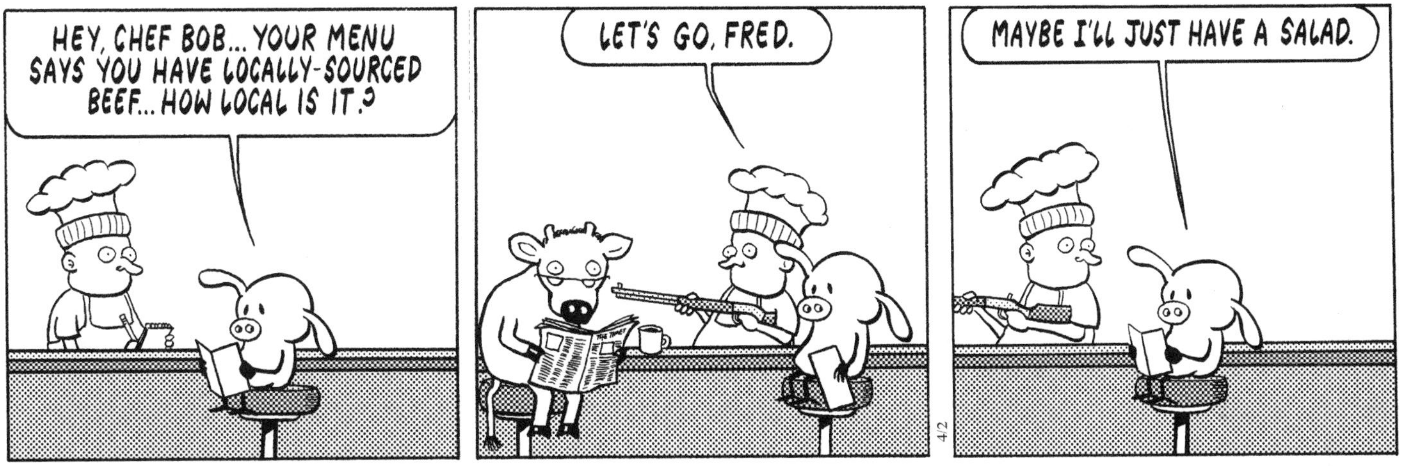
HEY, CHEF BOB... YOUR MENU SAYS YOU HAVE LOCALLY-SOURCED BEEF... HOW LOCAL IS IT?
LET'S GO, FRED.
MAYBE I'LL JUST HAVE A SALAD.
4/2

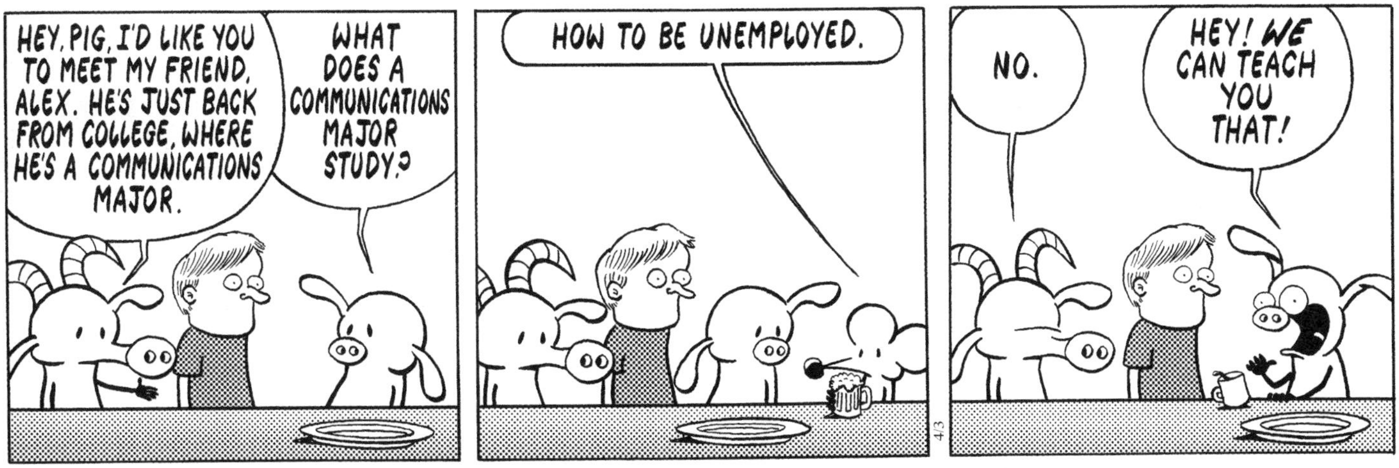
HEY, PIG, I'D LIKE YOU TO MEET MY FRIEND, ALEX. HE'S JUST BACK FROM COLLEGE, WHERE HE'S A COMMUNICATIONS MAJOR.
WHAT DOES A COMMUNICATIONS MAJOR STUDY?
HOW TO BE UNEMPLOYED.
NO.
HEY! WE CAN TEACH YOU THAT!
4/3

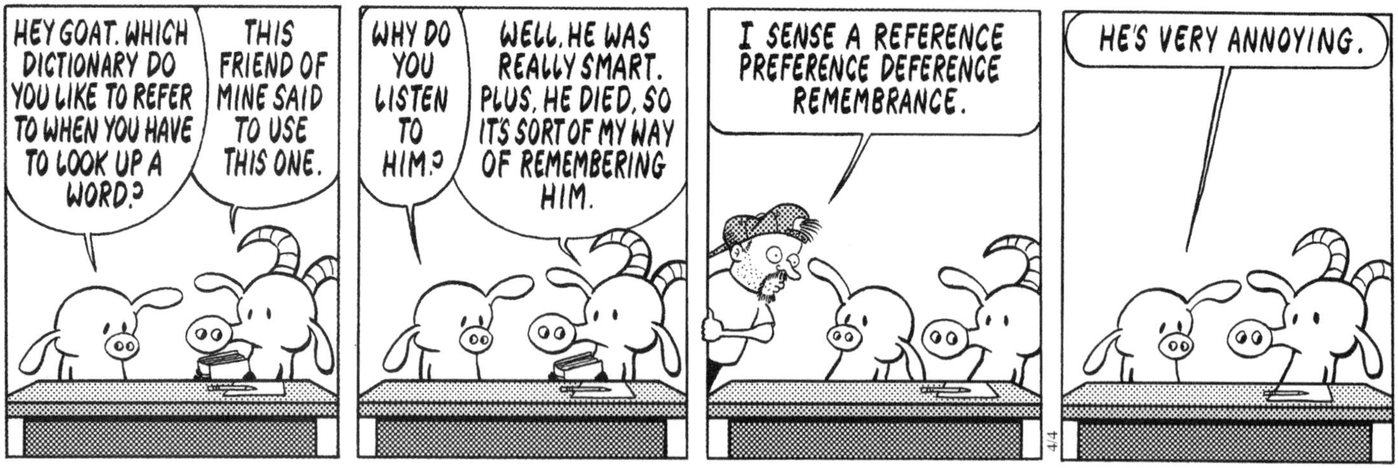
HEY GOAT. WHICH DICTIONARY DO YOU LIKE TO REFER TO WHEN YOU HAVE TO LOOK UP A WORD?
THIS FRIEND OF MINE SAID TO USE THIS ONE.
WHY DO YOU LISTEN TO HIM?
WELL, HE WAS REALLY SMART. PLUS, HE DIED, SO IT'S SORT OF MY WAY OF REMEMBERING HIM.
I SENSE A REFERENCE PREFERENCE DEFERENCE REMEMBRANCE.
HE'S VERY ANNOYING.
4/4

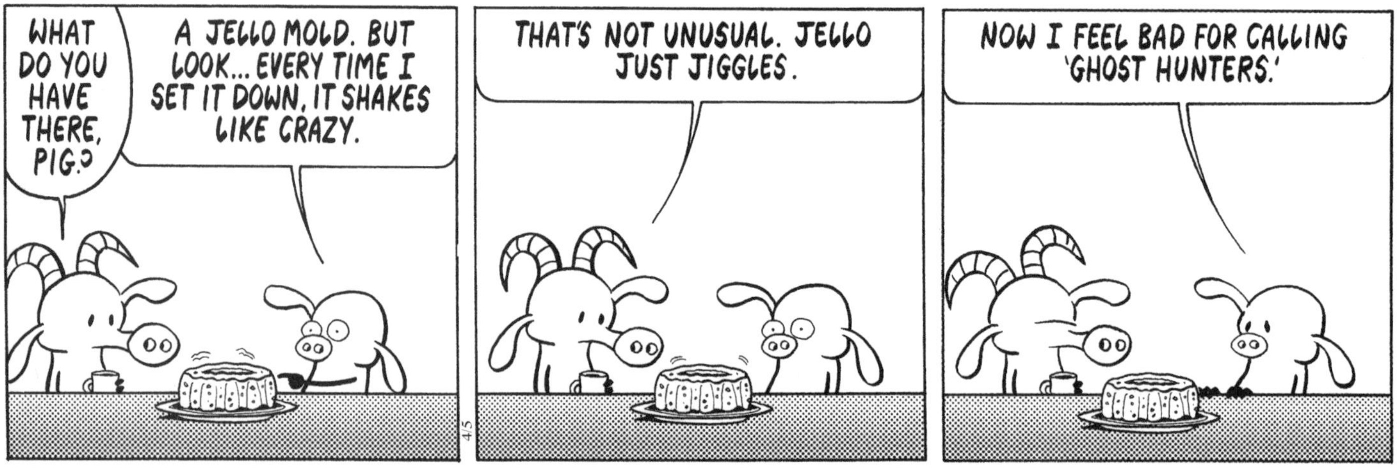
WHAT DO YOU HAVE THERE, PIG?
A JELLO MOLD. BUT LOOK... EVERY TIME I SET IT DOWN, IT SHAKES LIKE CRAZY.
4/5
THAT'S NOT UNUSUAL. JELLO JUST JIGGLES.
NOW I FEEL BAD FOR CALLING 'GHOST HUNTERS.'

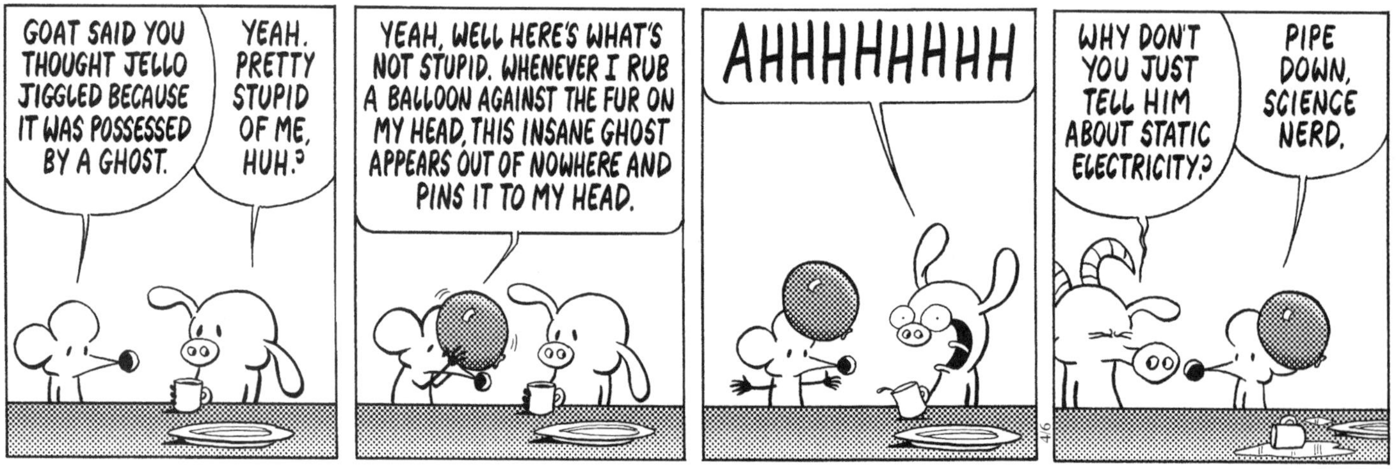
GOAT SAID YOU THOUGHT JELLO JIGGLED BECAUSE IT WAS POSSESSED BY A GHOST.
YEAH. PRETTY STUPID OF ME, HUH?
YEAH, WELL HERE'S WHAT'S NOT STUPID. WHENEVER I RUB A BALLOON AGAINST THE FUR ON MY HEAD, THIS INSANE GHOST APPEARS OUT OF NOWHERE AND PINS IT TO MY HEAD.
AHHHHHHHH
4/6
WHY DON'T YOU JUST TELL HIM ABOUT STATIC ELECTRICITY?
PIPE DOWN, SCIENCE NERD.

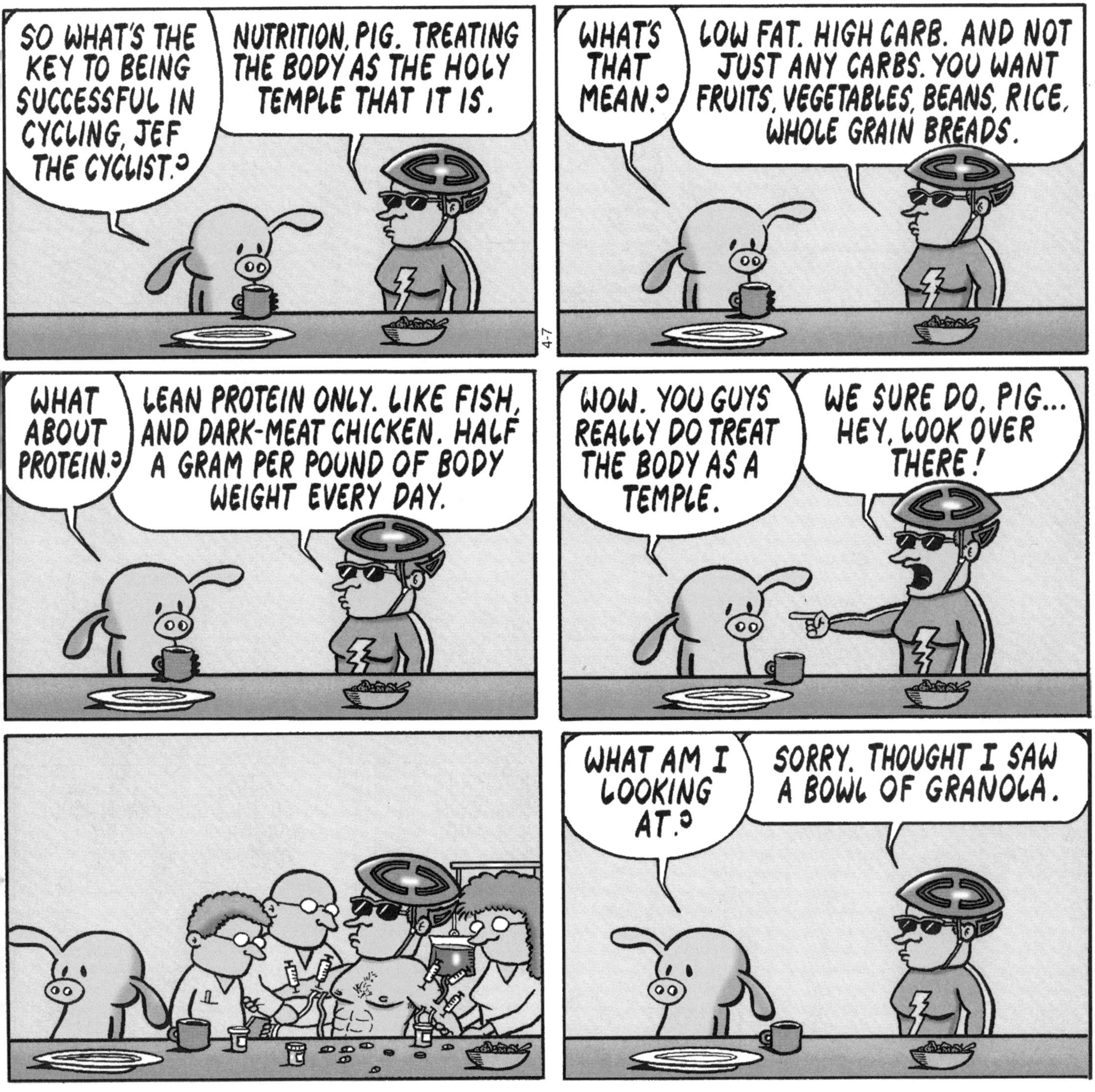
SO WHAT'S THE KEY TO BEING SUCCESSFUL IN CYCLING, JEF THE CYCLIST?
NUTRITION, PIG. TREATING THE BODY AS THE HOLY TEMPLE THAT IT IS.
4-7
WHAT'S THAT MEAN?
LOW FAT. HIGH CARB. AND NOT JUST ANY CARBS. YOU WANT FRUITS, VEGETABLES, BEANS, RICE, WHOLE GRAIN BREADS.
WHAT ABOUT PROTEIN?
LEAN PROTEIN ONLY. LIKE FISH, AND DARK-MEAT CHICKEN. HALF A GRAM PER POUND OF BODY WEIGHT EVERY DAY.
WOW. YOU GUYS REALLY DO TREAT THE BODY AS A TEMPLE.
WE SURE DO, PIG... HEY, LOOK OVER THERE!
WHAT AM I LOOKING AT?
SORRY. THOUGHT I SAW A BOWL OF GRANOLA.

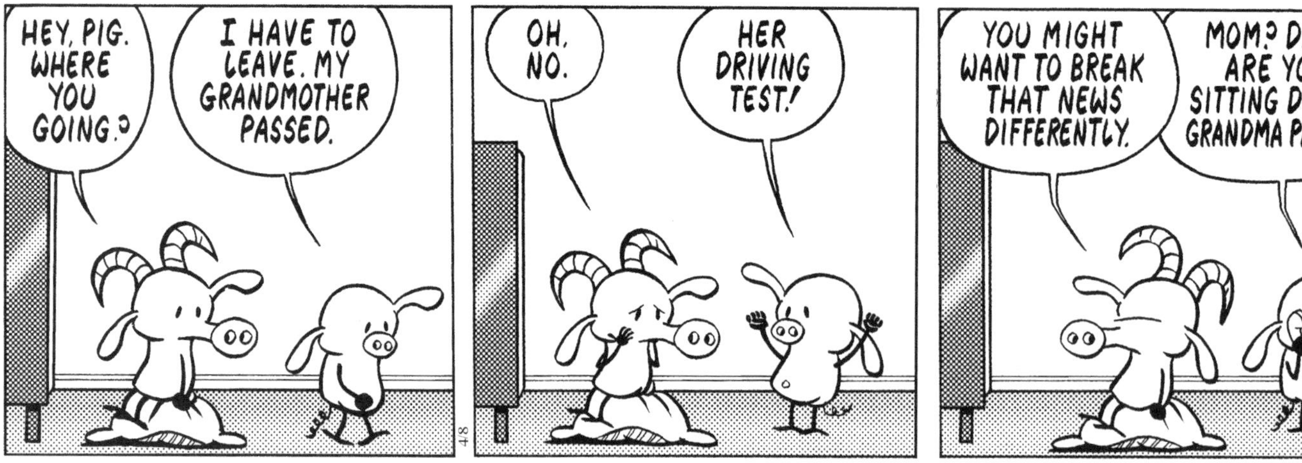
HEY, PIG. WHERE YOU GOING?
I HAVE TO LEAVE. MY GRANDMOTHER PASSED.
OH, NO.
HER DRIVING TEST!
YOU MIGHT WANT TO BREAK THAT NEWS DIFFERENTLY.
MOM? DAD? ARE YOU SITTING DOWN? GRANDMA PASSED.

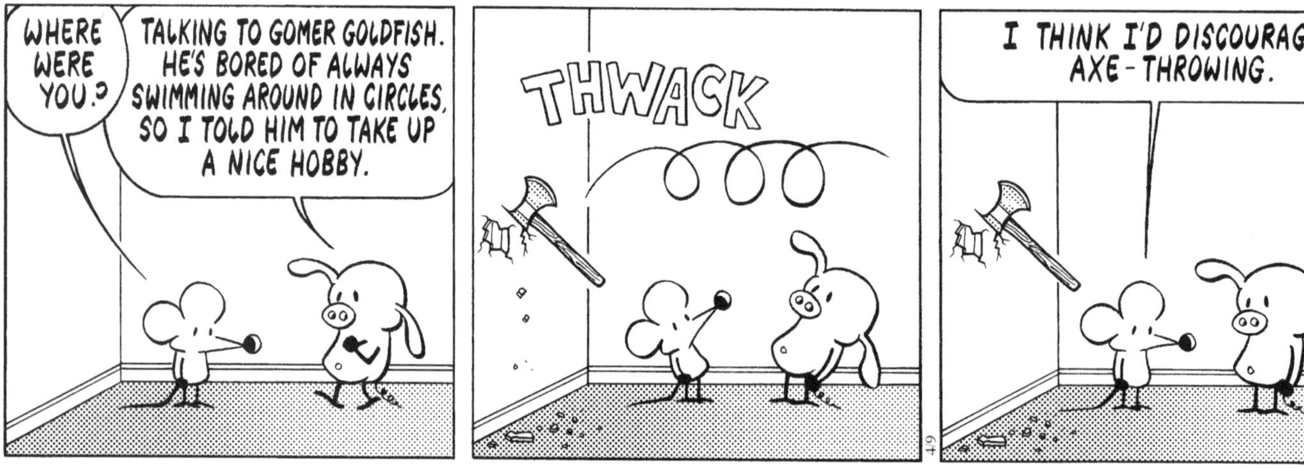
WHERE WERE YOU?
TALKING TO GOMER GOLDFISH. HE'S BORED OF ALWAYS SWIMMING AROUND IN CIRCLES, SO I TOLD HIM TO TAKE UP A NICE HOBBY.
THWACK
I THINK I'D DISCOURAGE AXE-THROWING.

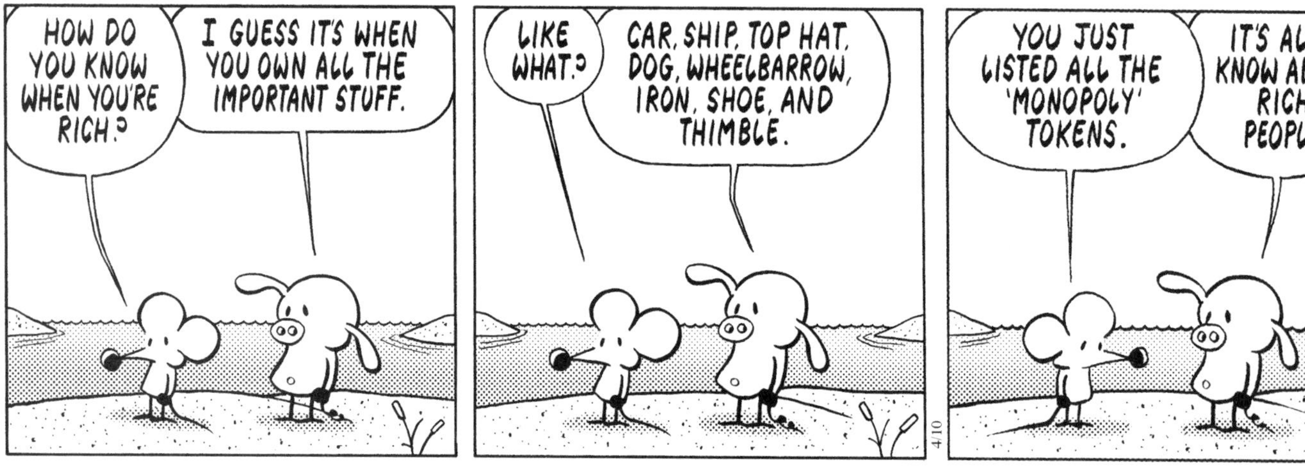
HOW DO YOU KNOW WHEN YOU'RE RICH?
I GUESS IT'S WHEN YOU OWN ALL THE IMPORTANT STUFF.
LIKE WHAT?
CAR, SHIP, TOP HAT, DOG, WHEELBARROW, IRON, SHOE, AND THIMBLE.
YOU JUST LISTED ALL THE 'MONOPOLY' TOKENS.
IT'S ALL I KNOW ABOUT RICH PEOPLE.

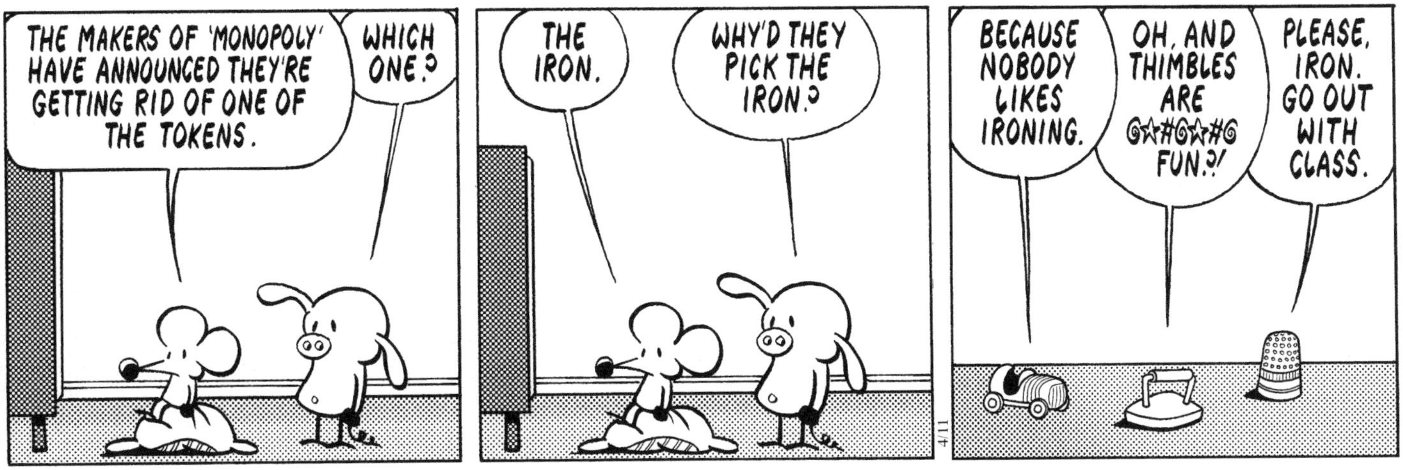
THE MAKERS OF 'MONOPOLY' HAVE ANNOUNCED THEY'RE GETTING RID OF ONE OF THE TOKENS.
WHICH ONE?
THE IRON.
WHY'D THEY PICK THE IRON?
BECAUSE NOBODY LIKES IRONING.
OH, AND THIMBLES ARE @☆#@☆#@ FUN?!
PLEASE, IRON. GO OUT WITH CLASS.
4/11

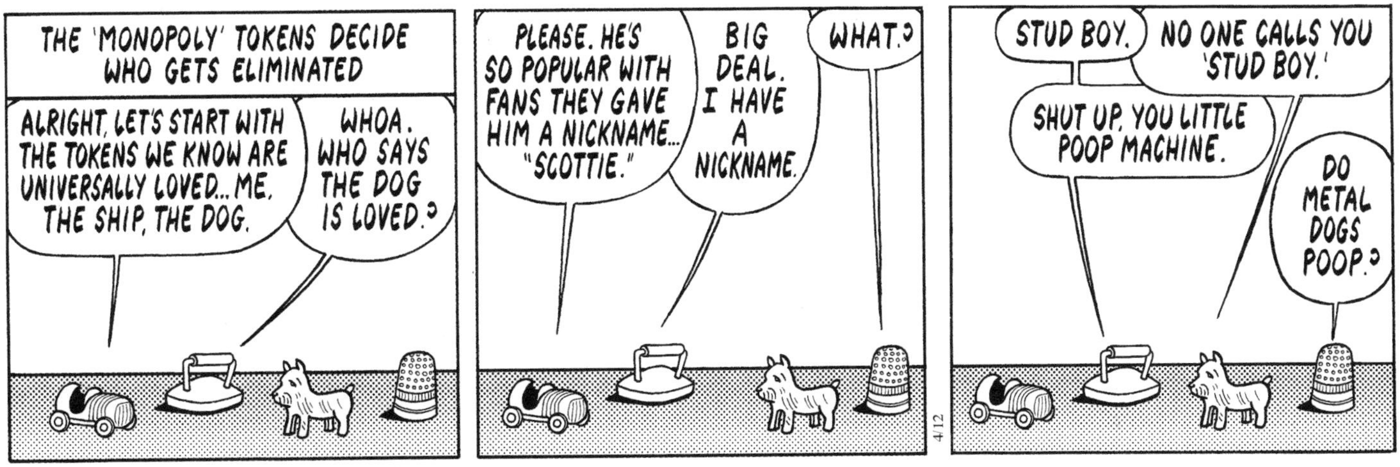
THE 'MONOPOLY' TOKENS DECIDE WHO GETS ELIMINATED
ALRIGHT, LET'S START WITH THE TOKENS WE KNOW ARE UNIVERSALLY LOVED... ME, THE SHIP, THE DOG.
WHOA. WHO SAYS THE DOG IS LOVED?
PLEASE. HE'S SO POPULAR WITH FANS THEY GAVE HIM A NICKNAME... "SCOTTIE."
BIG DEAL. I HAVE A NICKNAME.
WHAT?
STUD BOY.
NO ONE CALLS YOU 'STUD BOY.'
SHUT UP, YOU LITTLE POOP MACHINE.
DO METAL DOGS POOP?
4/12

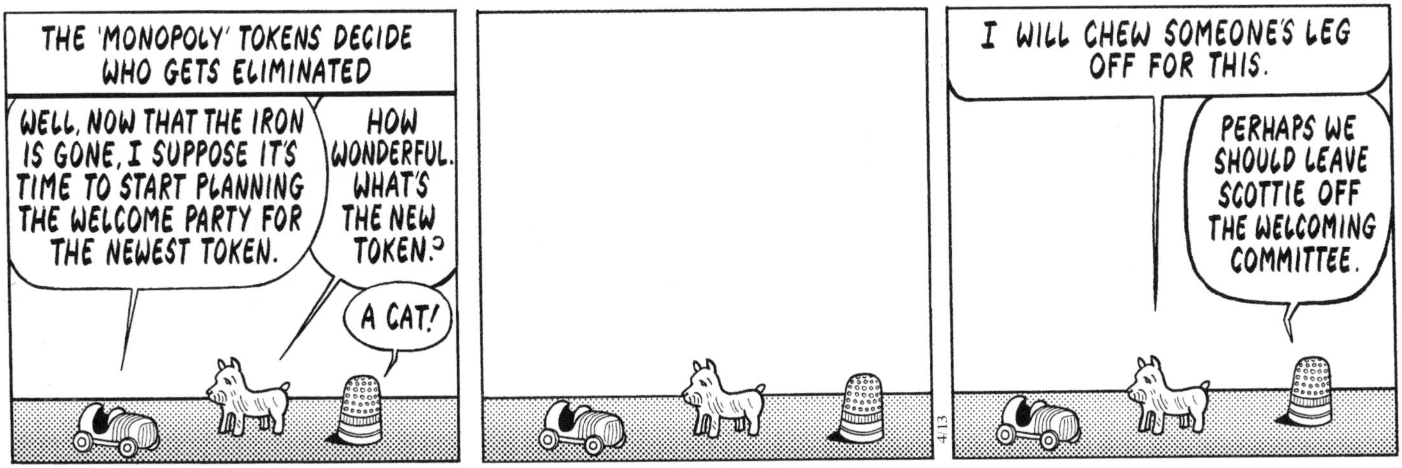
THE 'MONOPOLY' TOKENS DECIDE WHO GETS ELIMINATED
WELL, NOW THAT THE IRON IS GONE, I SUPPOSE IT'S TIME TO START PLANNING THE WELCOME PARTY FOR THE NEWEST TOKEN.
HOW WONDERFUL. WHAT'S THE NEW TOKEN?
A CAT!
I WILL CHEW SOMEONE'S LEG OFF FOR THIS.
PERHAPS WE SHOULD LEAVE SCOTTIE OFF THE WELCOMING COMMITTEE.
4/13

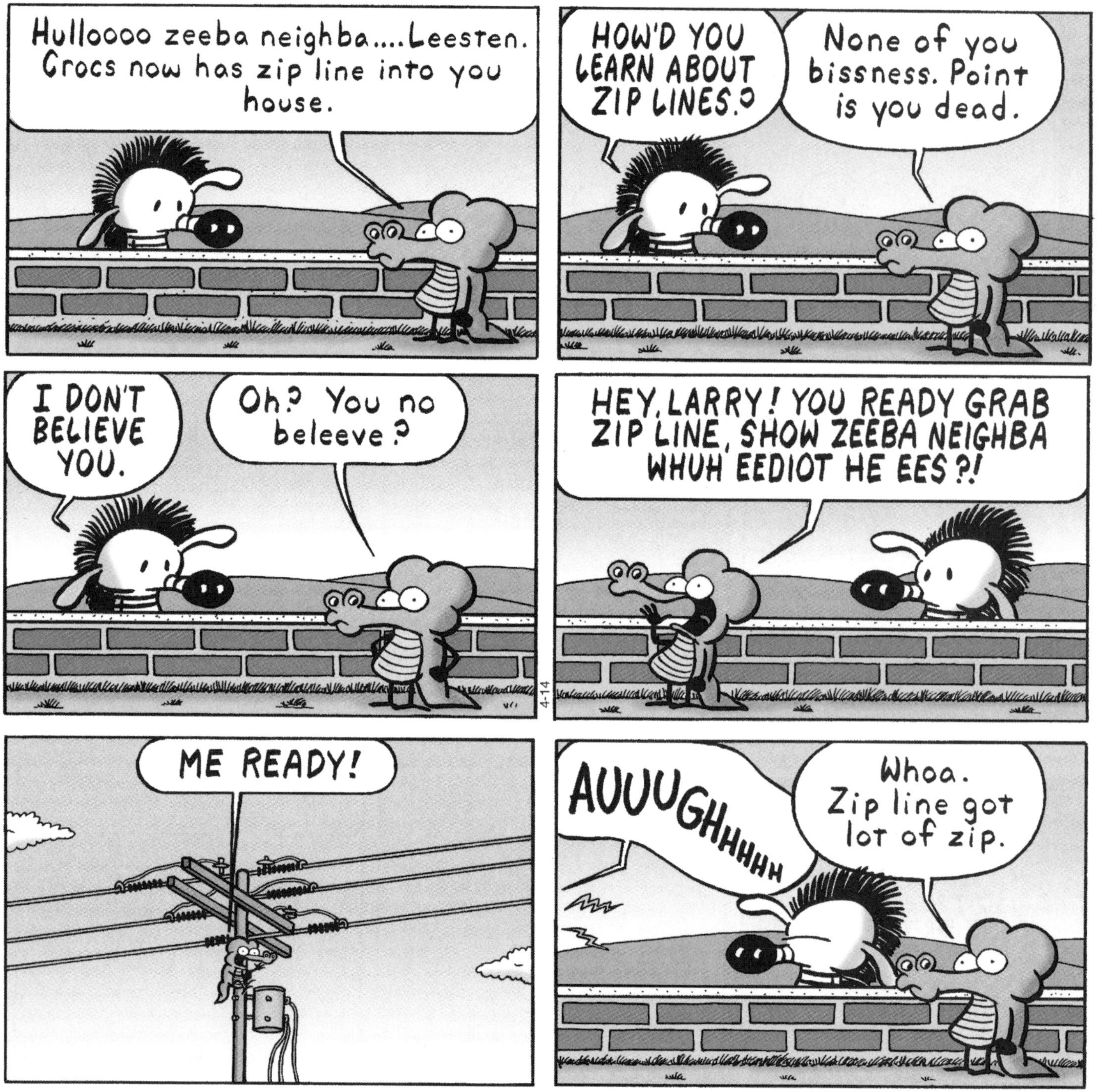
Hulloooo zeeba neighba....Leesten. Crocs now has zip line into you house.
HOW'D YOU LEARN ABOUT ZIP LINES?
None of you bissness. Point is you dead.
I DON'T BELIEVE YOU.
Oh? You no beleeve?
4-14
HEY, LARRY! YOU READY GRAB ZIP LINE, SHOW ZEEBA NEIGHBA WHUH EEDIOT HE EES?!
ME READY!
AUUUGHHHHH
Whoa. Zip line got lot of zip.

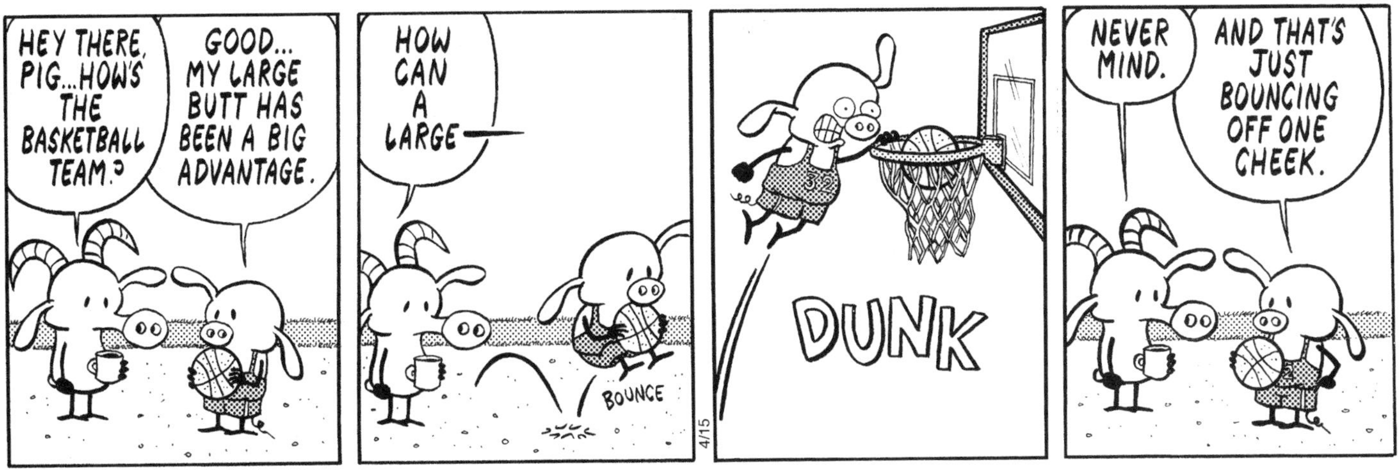
HEY THERE, PIG...HOW'S THE BASKETBALL TEAM?
GOOD... MY LARGE BUTT HAS BEEN A BIG ADVANTAGE.
HOW CAN A LARGE—
BOUNCE
DUNK
4/15
NEVER MIND.
AND THAT'S JUST BOUNCING OFF ONE CHEEK.

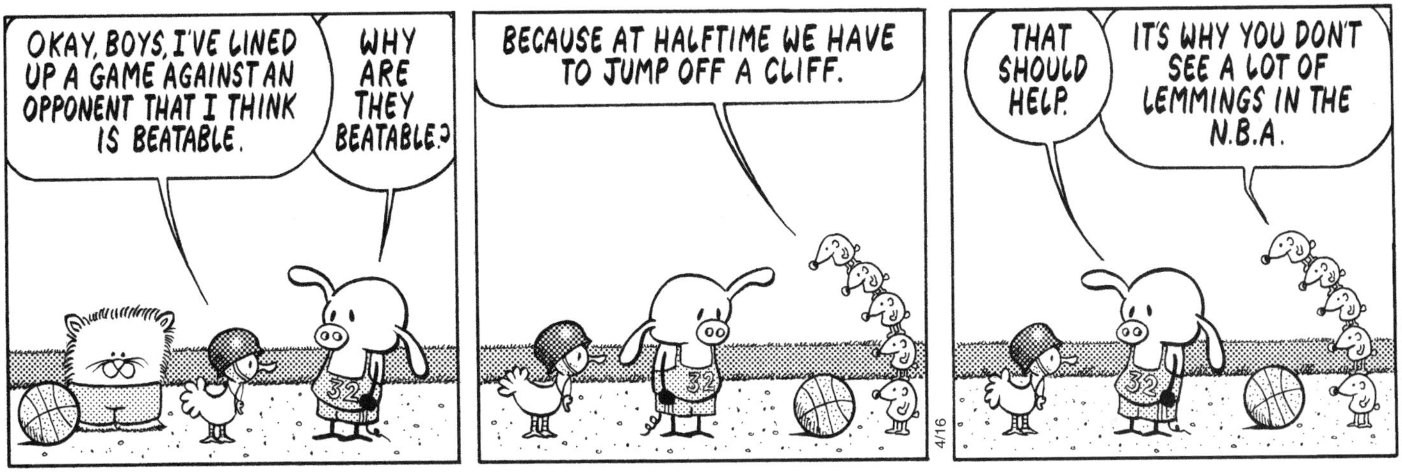
OKAY, BOYS, I'VE LINED UP A GAME AGAINST AN OPPONENT THAT I THINK IS BEATABLE.
WHY ARE THEY BEATABLE?
BECAUSE AT HALFTIME WE HAVE TO JUMP OFF A CLIFF.
4/16
THAT SHOULD HELP.
IT'S WHY YOU DON'T SEE A LOT OF LEMMINGS IN THE N.B.A.

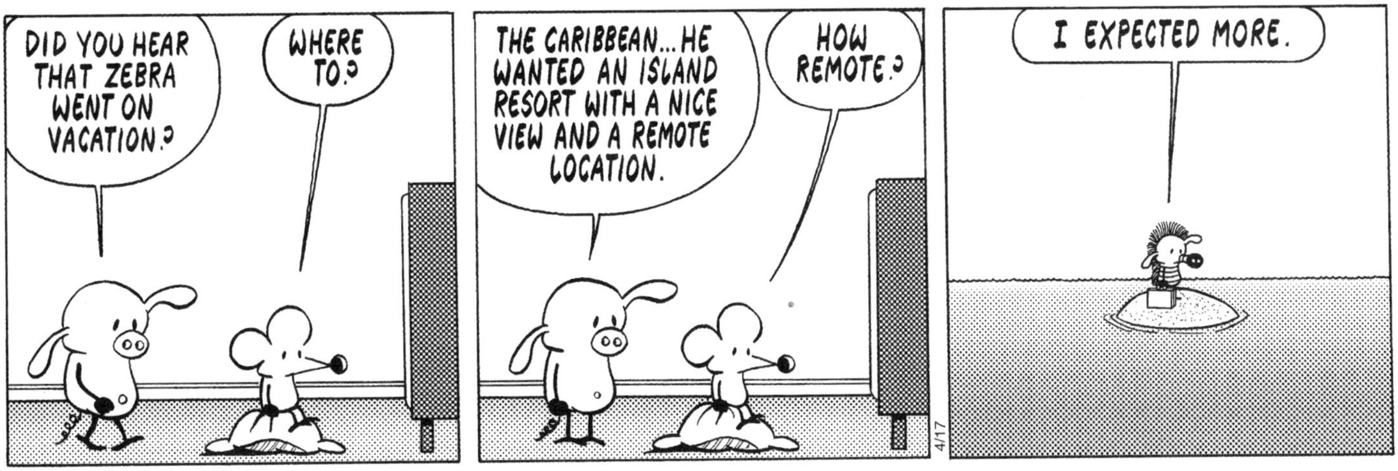
DID YOU HEAR THAT ZEBRA WENT ON VACATION?
WHERE TO?
THE CARIBBEAN... HE WANTED AN ISLAND RESORT WITH A NICE VIEW AND A REMOTE LOCATION.
HOW REMOTE?
4/17
I EXPECTED MORE.

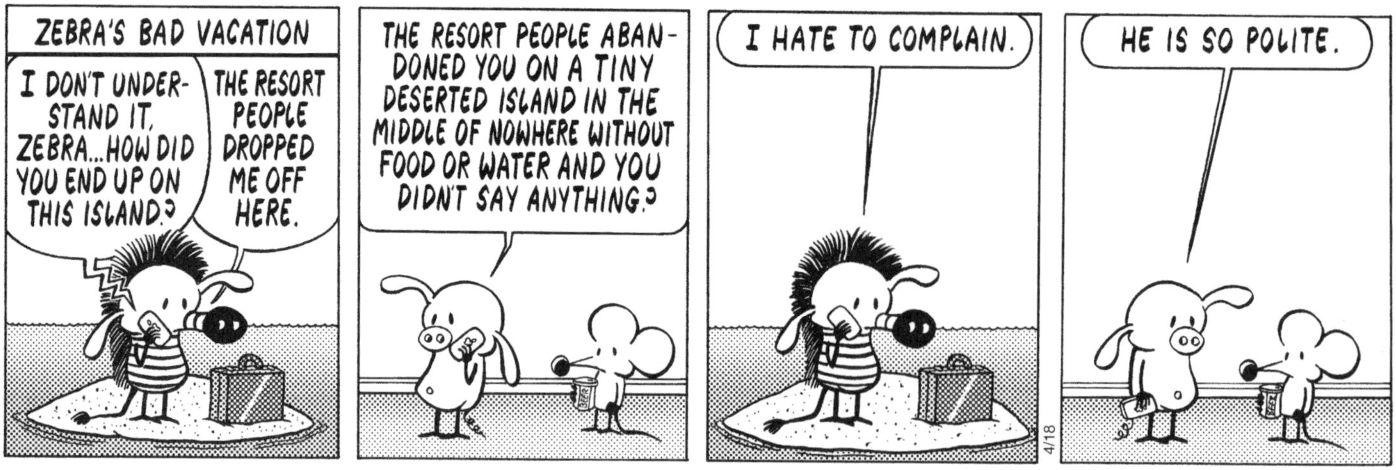
ZEBRA'S BAD VACATION
I DON'T UNDERSTAND IT, ZEBRA...HOW DID YOU END UP ON THIS ISLAND?
THE RESORT PEOPLE DROPPED ME OFF HERE.
THE RESORT PEOPLE ABANDONED YOU ON A TINY DESERTED ISLAND IN THE MIDDLE OF NOWHERE WITHOUT FOOD OR WATER AND YOU DIDN'T SAY ANYTHING?
I HATE TO COMPLAIN.
HE IS SO POLITE.
4/18

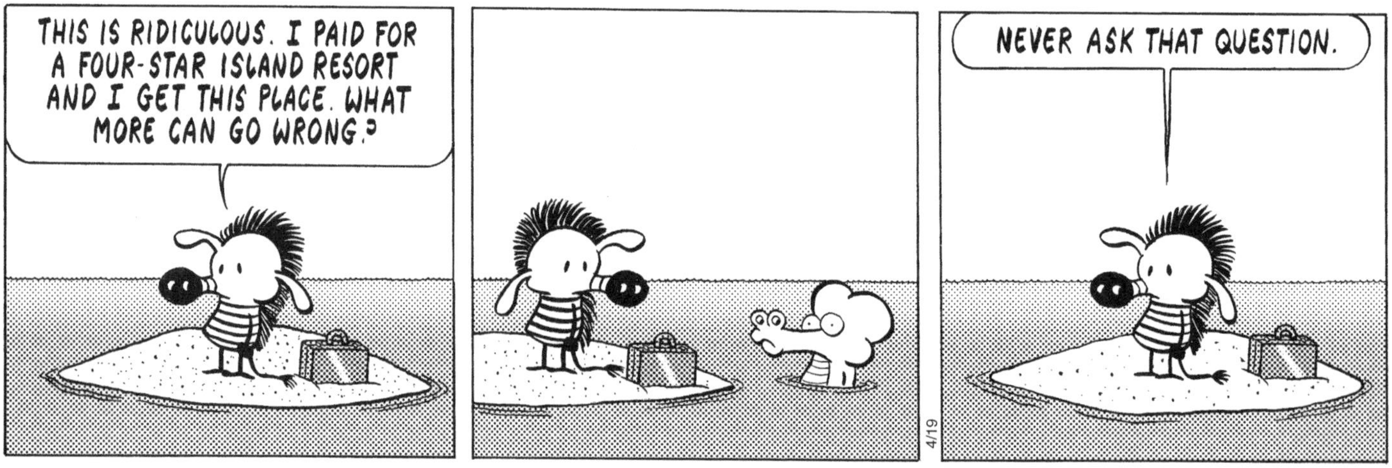
THIS IS RIDICULOUS. I PAID FOR A FOUR-STAR ISLAND RESORT AND I GET THIS PLACE. WHAT MORE CAN GO WRONG?
NEVER ASK THAT QUESTION.
4/19

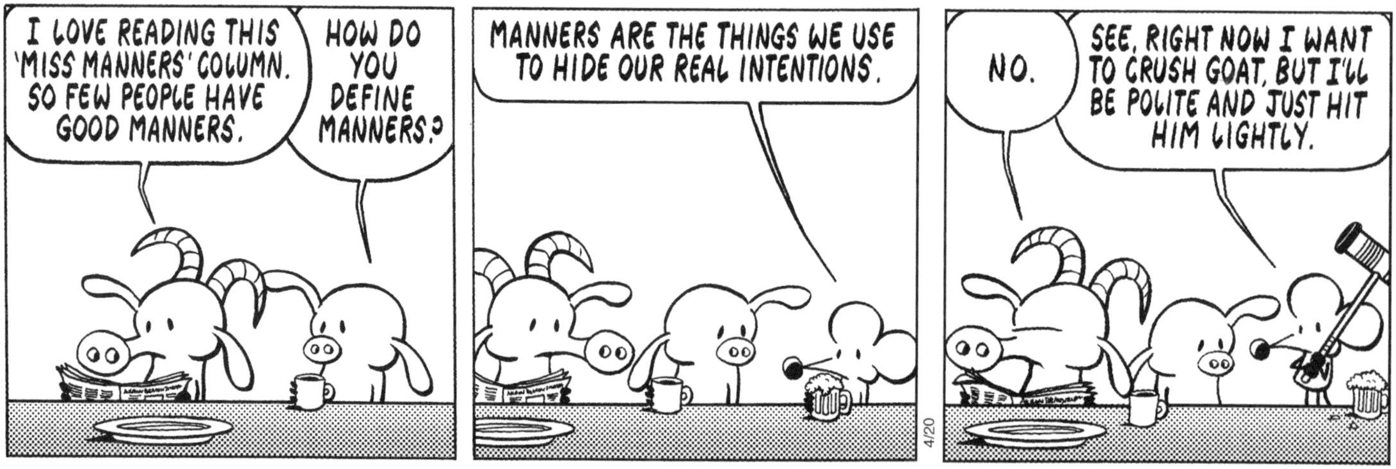
I LOVE READING THIS 'MISS MANNERS' COLUMN. SO FEW PEOPLE HAVE GOOD MANNERS.
HOW DO YOU DEFINE MANNERS?
MANNERS ARE THE THINGS WE USE TO HIDE OUR REAL INTENTIONS.
NO.
SEE, RIGHT NOW I WANT TO CRUSH GOAT, BUT I'LL BE POLITE AND JUST HIT HIM LIGHTLY.
4/20

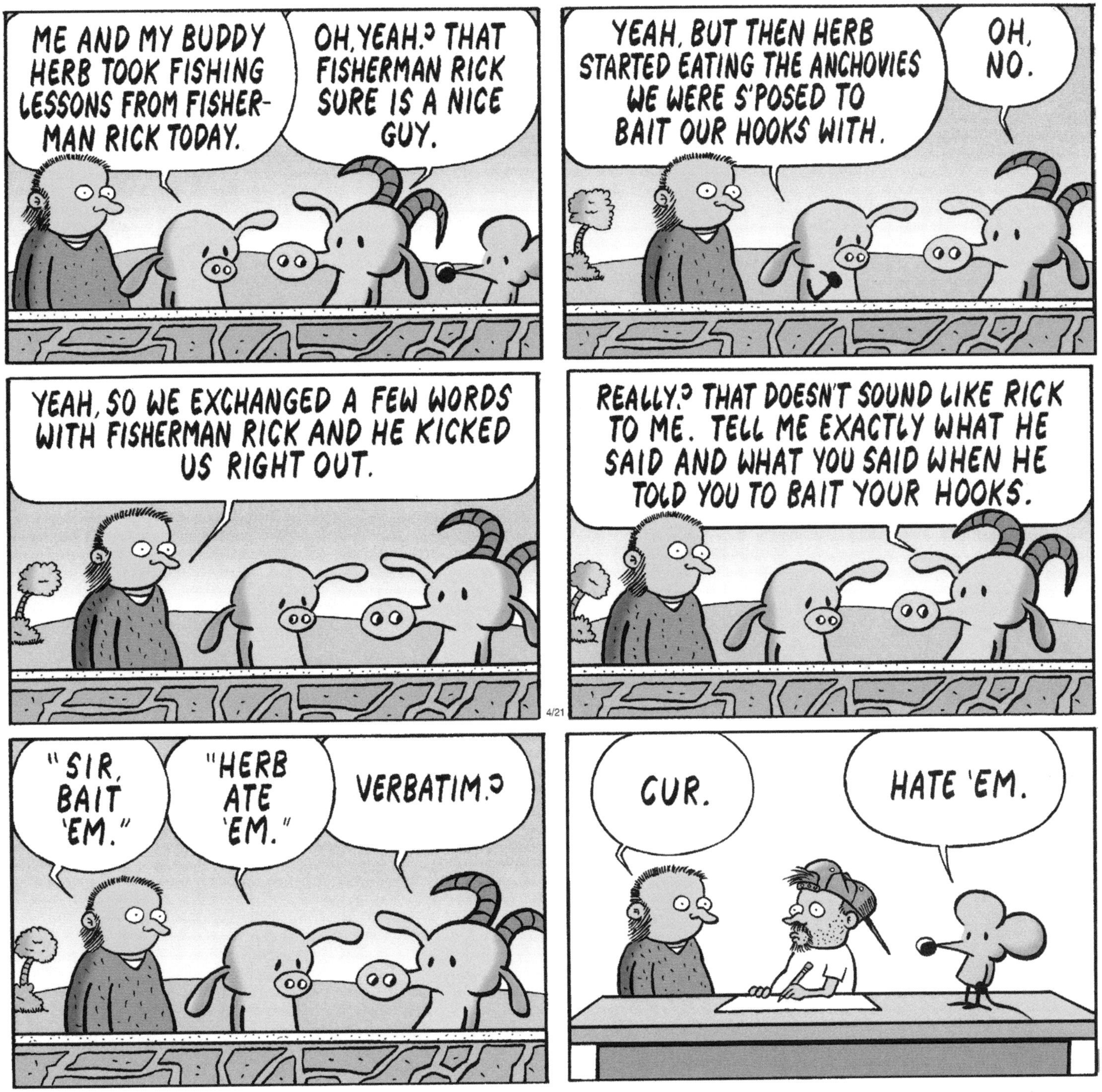

ME AND MY BUDDY HERB TOOK FISHING LESSONS FROM FISHERMAN RICK TODAY.
OH, YEAH? THAT FISHERMAN RICK SURE IS A NICE GUY.
YEAH, BUT THEN HERB STARTED EATING THE ANCHOVIES WE WERE S'POSED TO BAIT OUR HOOKS WITH.
OH, NO.
YEAH, SO WE EXCHANGED A FEW WORDS WITH FISHERMAN RICK AND HE KICKED US RIGHT OUT.
REALLY? THAT DOESN'T SOUND LIKE RICK TO ME. TELL ME EXACTLY WHAT HE SAID AND WHAT YOU SAID WHEN HE TOLD YOU TO BAIT YOUR HOOKS.
4/21
"SIR, BAIT 'EM."
"HERB ATE 'EM."
VERBATIM?
CUR.
HATE 'EM.

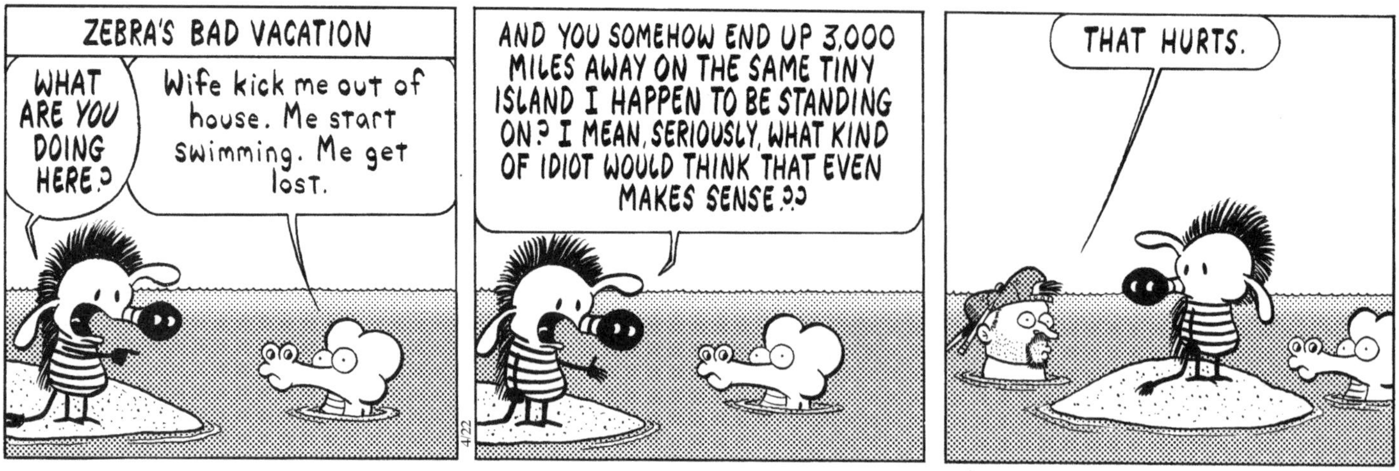
ZEBRA'S BAD VACATION
WHAT ARE YOU DOING HERE?
Wife kick me out of house. Me start swimming. Me get lost.
AND YOU SOMEHOW END UP 3,000 MILES AWAY ON THE SAME TINY ISLAND I HAPPEN TO BE STANDING ON? I MEAN, SERIOUSLY, WHAT KIND OF IDIOT WOULD THINK THAT EVEN MAKES SENSE??
THAT HURTS.
4/22

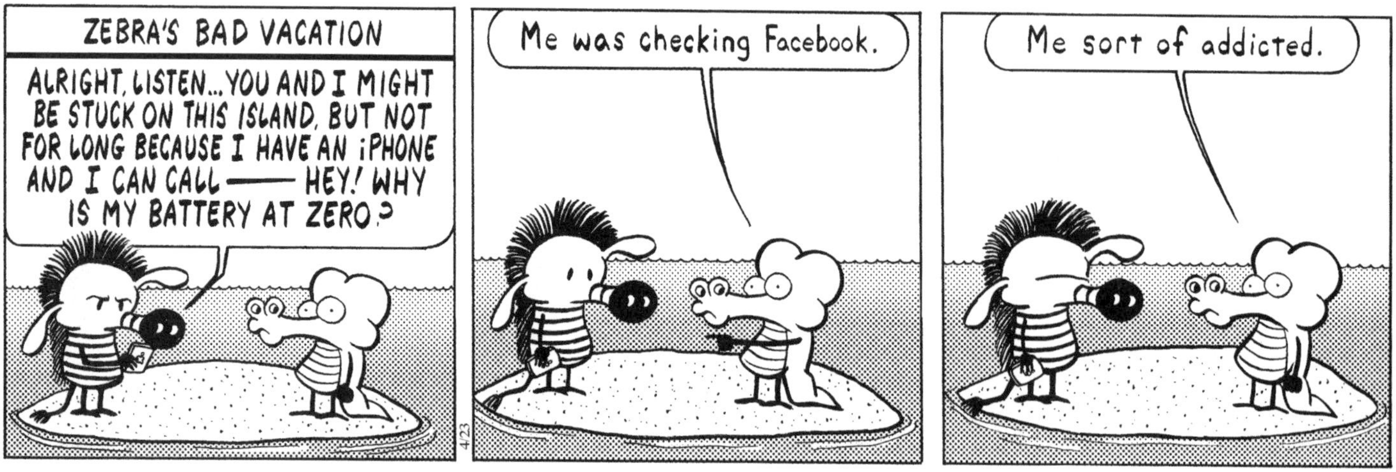
ZEBRA'S BAD VACATION
ALRIGHT, LISTEN... YOU AND I MIGHT BE STUCK ON THIS ISLAND, BUT NOT FOR LONG BECAUSE I HAVE AN iPHONE AND I CAN CALL —— HEY! WHY IS MY BATTERY AT ZERO?
Me was checking Facebook.
Me sort of addicted.
4/23

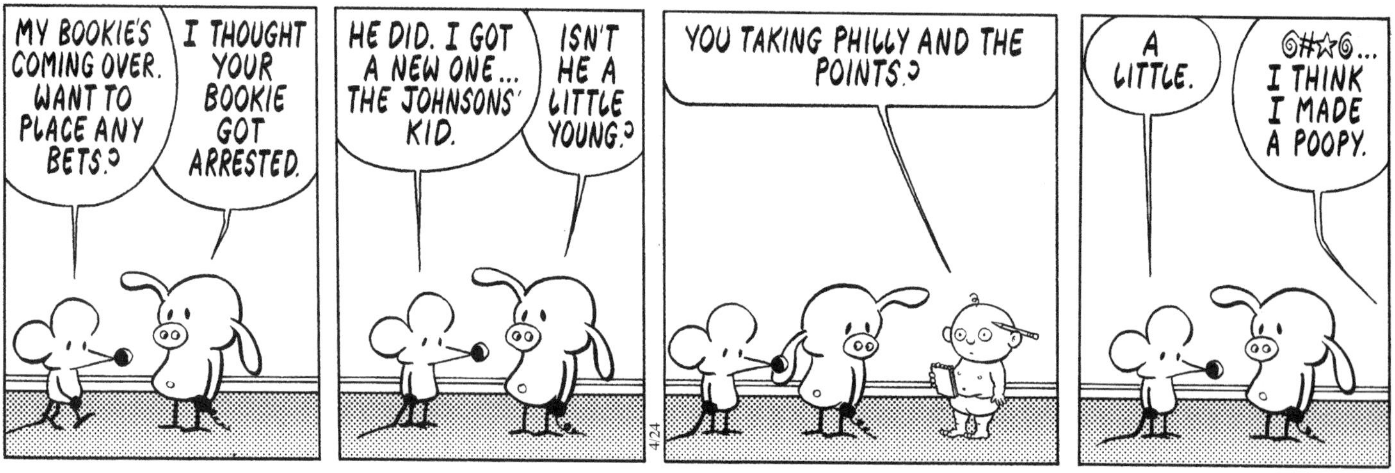
MY BOOKIE'S COMING OVER. WANT TO PLACE ANY BETS?
I THOUGHT YOUR BOOKIE GOT ARRESTED.
HE DID. I GOT A NEW ONE... THE JOHNSONS' KID.
ISN'T HE A LITTLE YOUNG?
YOU TAKING PHILLY AND THE POINTS?
A LITTLE.
@#☆@... I THINK I MADE A POOPY.
4/24

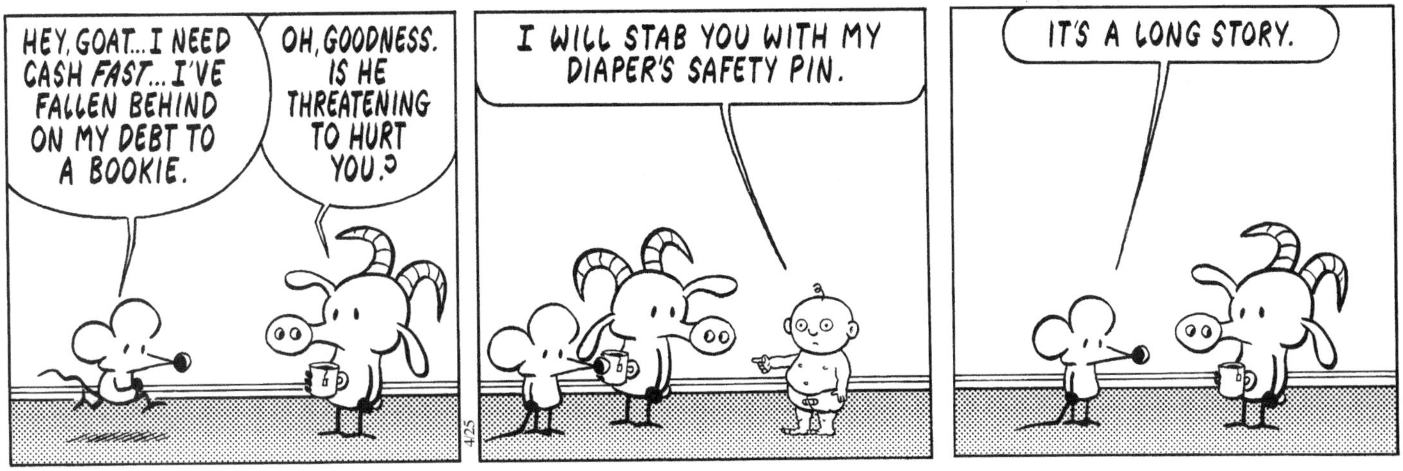
HEY, GOAT... I NEED CASH FAST... I'VE FALLEN BEHIND ON MY DEBT TO A BOOKIE.
OH, GOODNESS. IS HE THREATENING TO HURT YOU?
4/25
I WILL STAB YOU WITH MY DIAPER'S SAFETY PIN.
IT'S A LONG STORY.

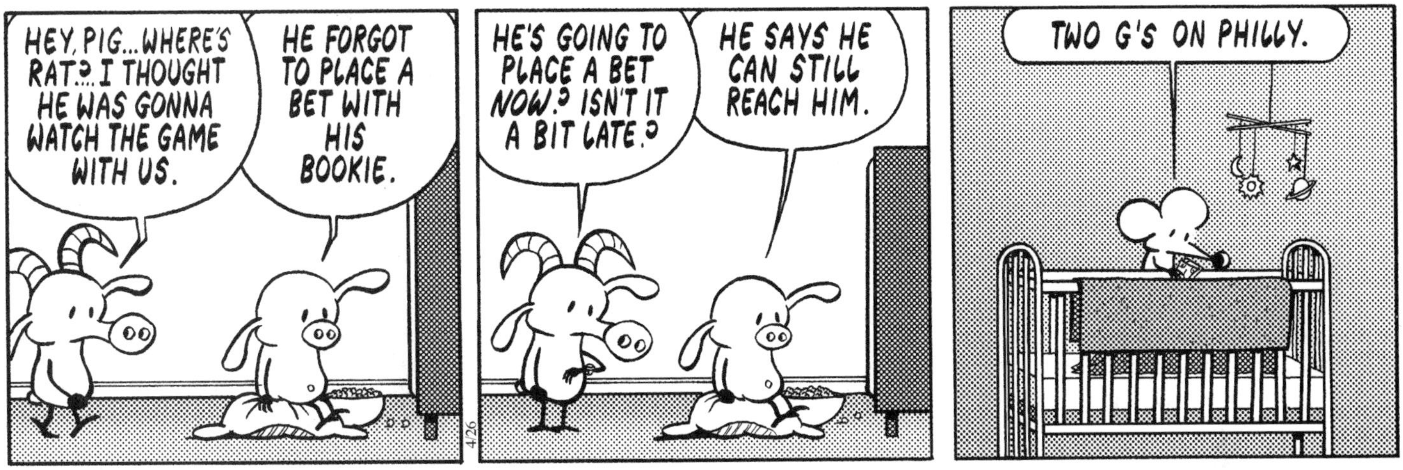
HEY, PIG... WHERE'S RAT?... I THOUGHT HE WAS GONNA WATCH THE GAME WITH US.
HE FORGOT TO PLACE A BET WITH HIS BOOKIE.
4/26
HE'S GOING TO PLACE A BET NOW? ISN'T IT A BIT LATE?
HE SAYS HE CAN STILL REACH HIM.
TWO G'S ON PHILLY.

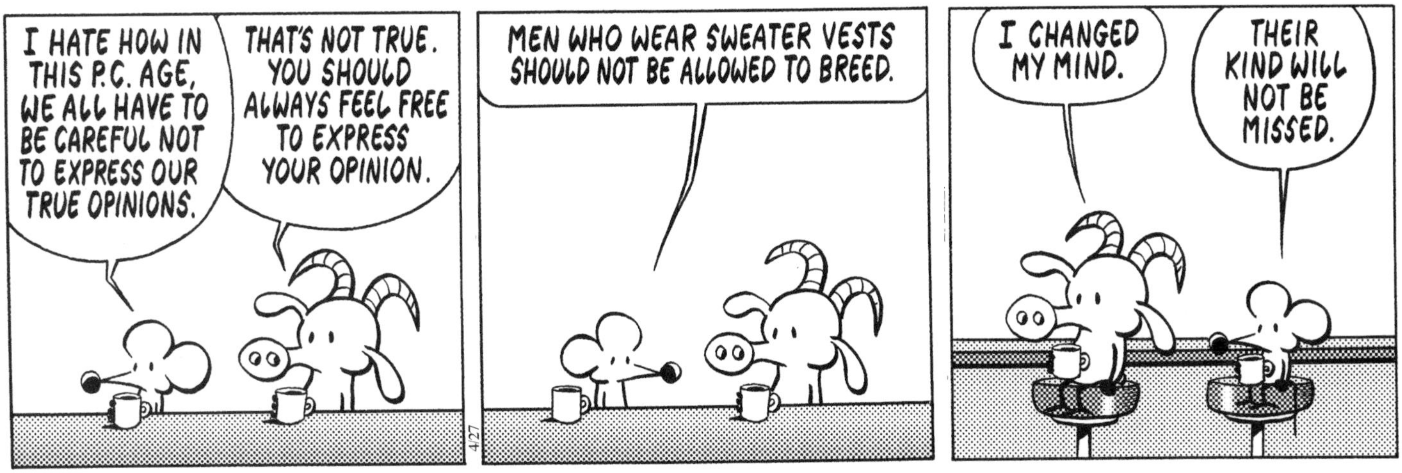
I HATE HOW IN THIS P.C. AGE, WE ALL HAVE TO BE CAREFUL NOT TO EXPRESS OUR TRUE OPINIONS.
THAT'S NOT TRUE. YOU SHOULD ALWAYS FEEL FREE TO EXPRESS YOUR OPINION.
4/27
MEN WHO WEAR SWEATER VESTS SHOULD NOT BE ALLOWED TO BREED.
I CHANGED MY MIND.
THEIR KIND WILL NOT BE MISSED.

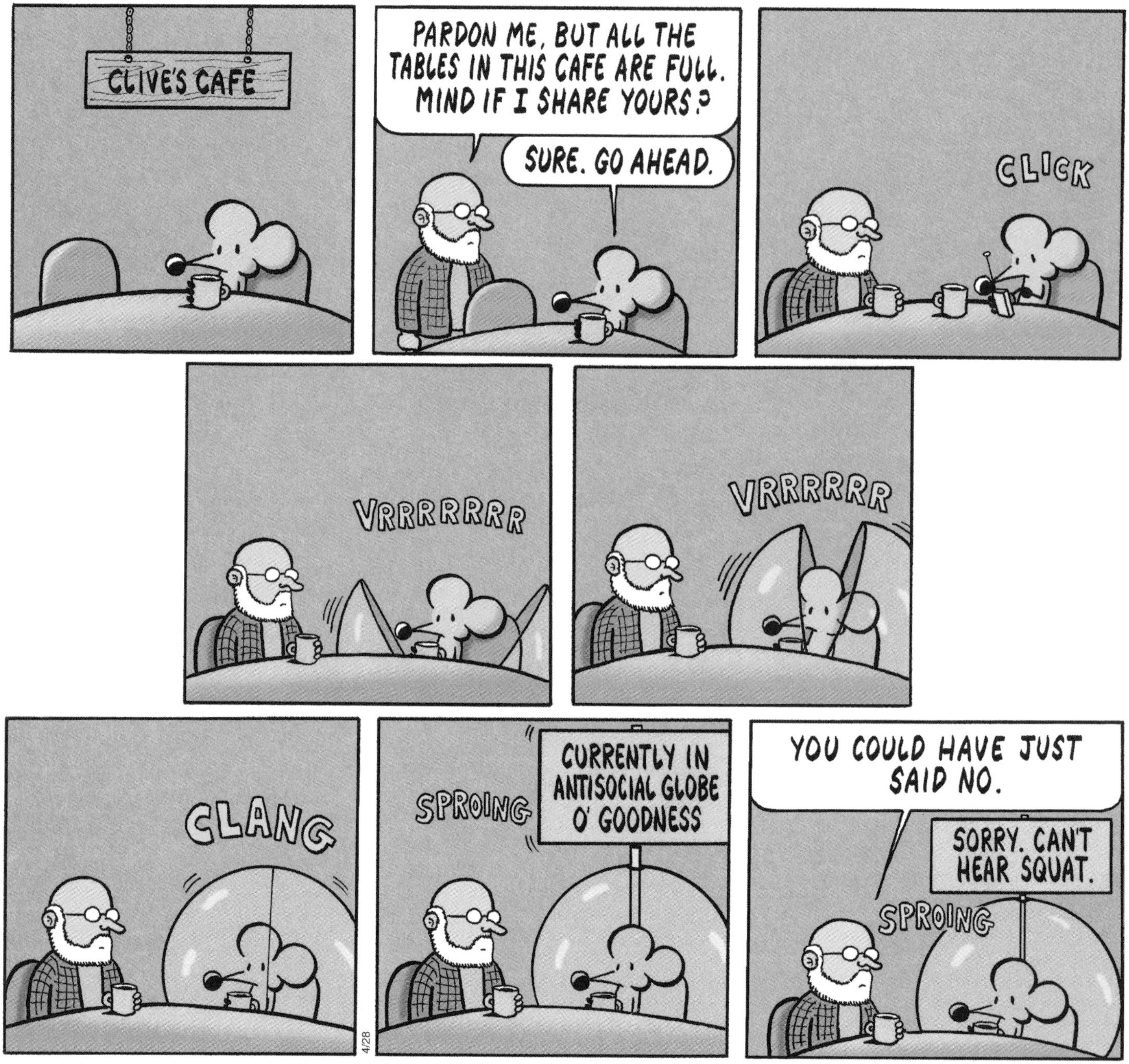
CLIVE'S CAFE
PARDON ME, BUT ALL THE TABLES IN THIS CAFE ARE FULL. MIND IF I SHARE YOURS?
SURE. GO AHEAD.
CLICK
VRRRRRRR
VRRRRRRR
CLANG
4/28
SPROING
CURRENTLY IN ANTISOCIAL GLOBE O' GOODNESS
YOU COULD HAVE JUST SAID NO.
SORRY. CAN'T HEAR SQUAT.
SPROING

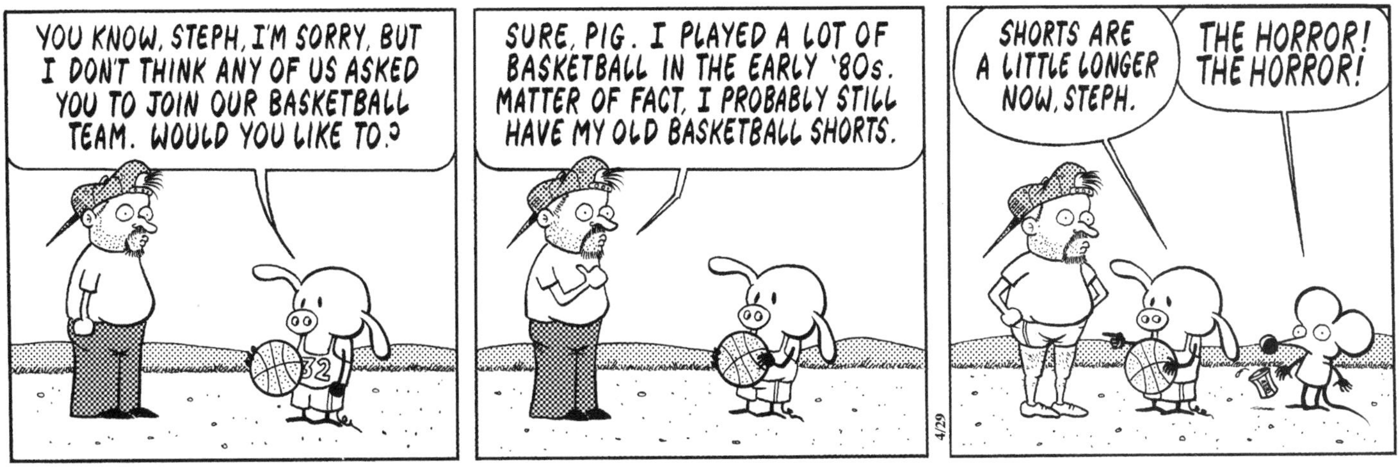
YOU KNOW, STEPH, I'M SORRY, BUT I DON'T THINK ANY OF US ASKED YOU TO JOIN OUR BASKETBALL TEAM. WOULD YOU LIKE TO?
SURE, PIG. I PLAYED A LOT OF BASKETBALL IN THE EARLY '80s. MATTER OF FACT, I PROBABLY STILL HAVE MY OLD BASKETBALL SHORTS.
SHORTS ARE A LITTLE LONGER NOW, STEPH.
THE HORROR! THE HORROR!
4/29

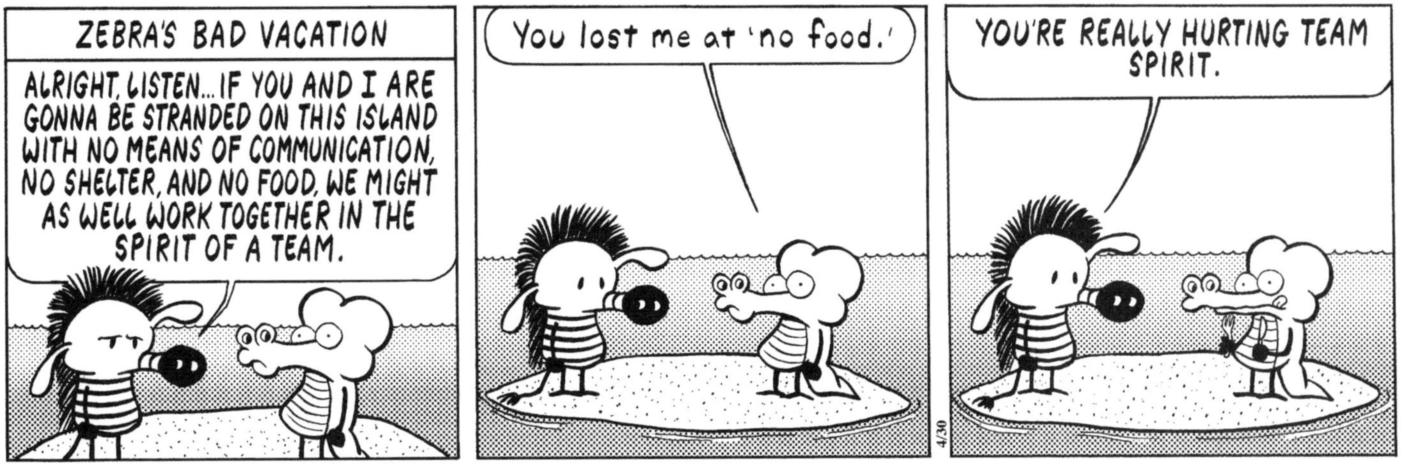
ZEBRA'S BAD VACATION
ALRIGHT, LISTEN... IF YOU AND I ARE GONNA BE STRANDED ON THIS ISLAND WITH NO MEANS OF COMMUNICATION, NO SHELTER, AND NO FOOD, WE MIGHT AS WELL WORK TOGETHER IN THE SPIRIT OF A TEAM.
You lost me at 'no food.'
YOU'RE REALLY HURTING TEAM SPIRIT.
4/30

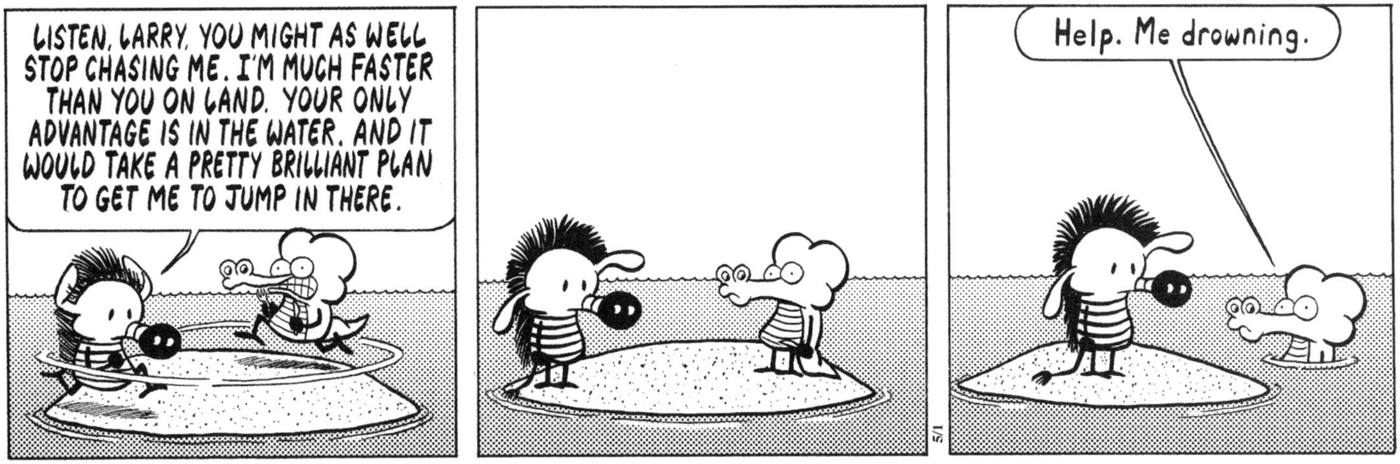
LISTEN, LARRY, YOU MIGHT AS WELL STOP CHASING ME. I'M MUCH FASTER THAN YOU ON LAND. YOUR ONLY ADVANTAGE IS IN THE WATER. AND IT WOULD TAKE A PRETTY BRILLIANT PLAN TO GET ME TO JUMP IN THERE.
Help. Me drowning.
5/1

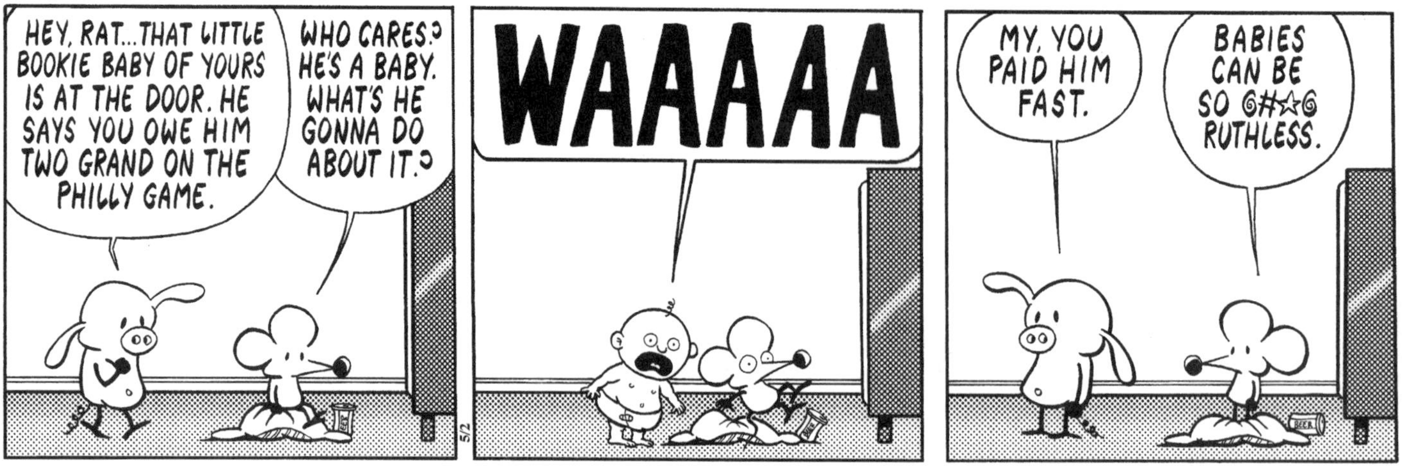
HEY, RAT...THAT LITTLE BOOKIE BABY OF YOURS IS AT THE DOOR. HE SAYS YOU OWE HIM TWO GRAND ON THE PHILLY GAME.
WHO CARES? HE'S A BABY. WHAT'S HE GONNA DO ABOUT IT?
5/2
WAAAAA
MY, YOU PAID HIM FAST.
BABIES CAN BE SO @#☆@ RUTHLESS.

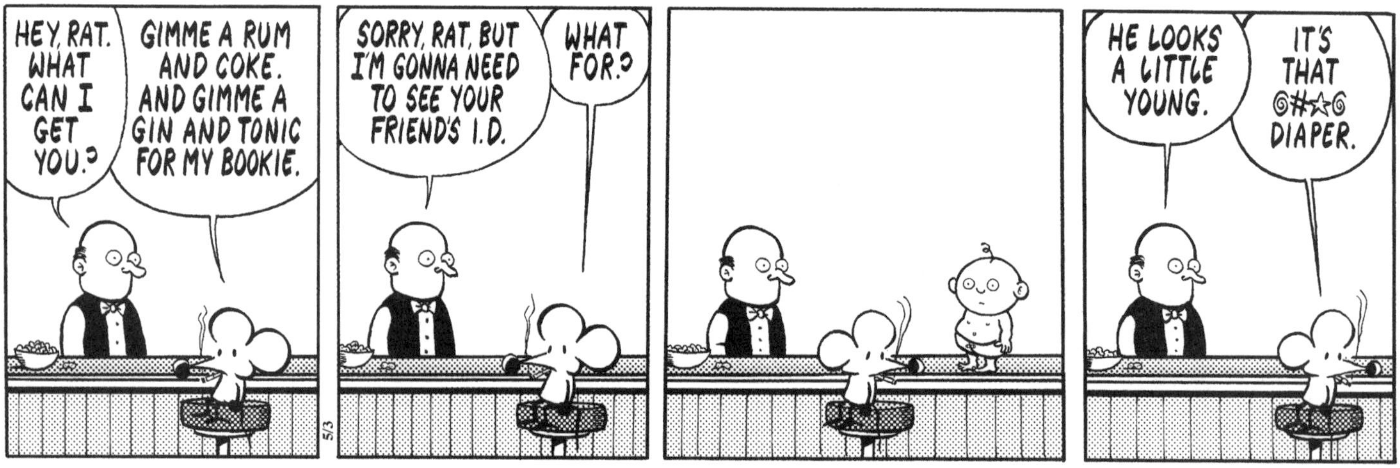
HEY, RAT. WHAT CAN I GET YOU?
GIMME A RUM AND COKE. AND GIMME A GIN AND TONIC FOR MY BOOKIE.
5/3
SORRY, RAT, BUT I'M GONNA NEED TO SEE YOUR FRIEND'S I.D.
WHAT FOR?
HE LOOKS A LITTLE YOUNG.
IT'S THAT @#☆@ DIAPER.

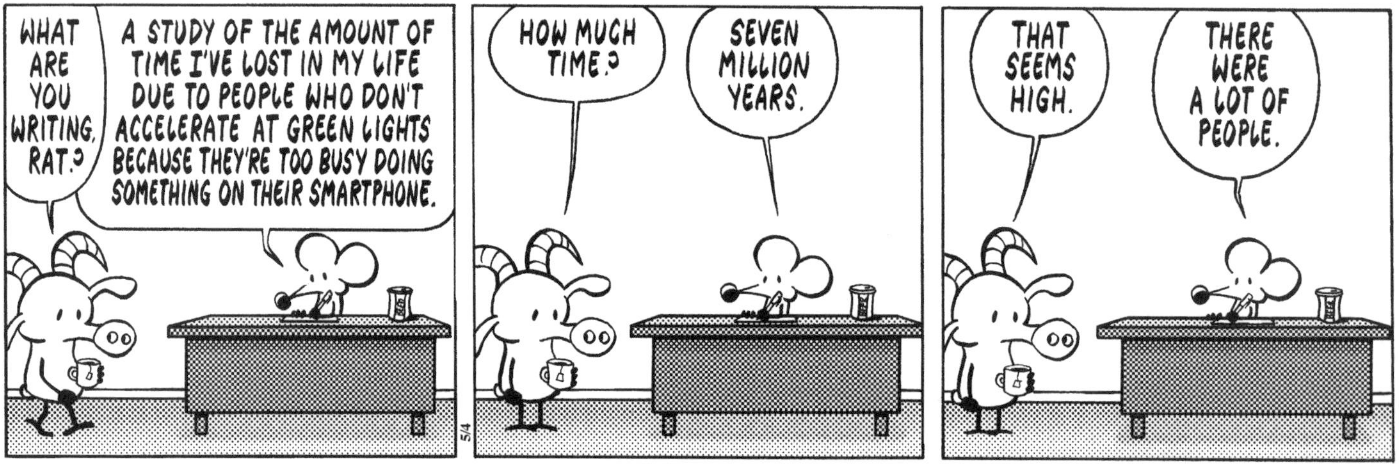
WHAT ARE YOU WRITING, RAT?
A STUDY OF THE AMOUNT OF TIME I'VE LOST IN MY LIFE DUE TO PEOPLE WHO DON'T ACCELERATE AT GREEN LIGHTS BECAUSE THEY'RE TOO BUSY DOING SOMETHING ON THEIR SMARTPHONE.
5/4
HOW MUCH TIME?
SEVEN MILLION YEARS.
THAT SEEMS HIGH.
THERE WERE A LOT OF PEOPLE.

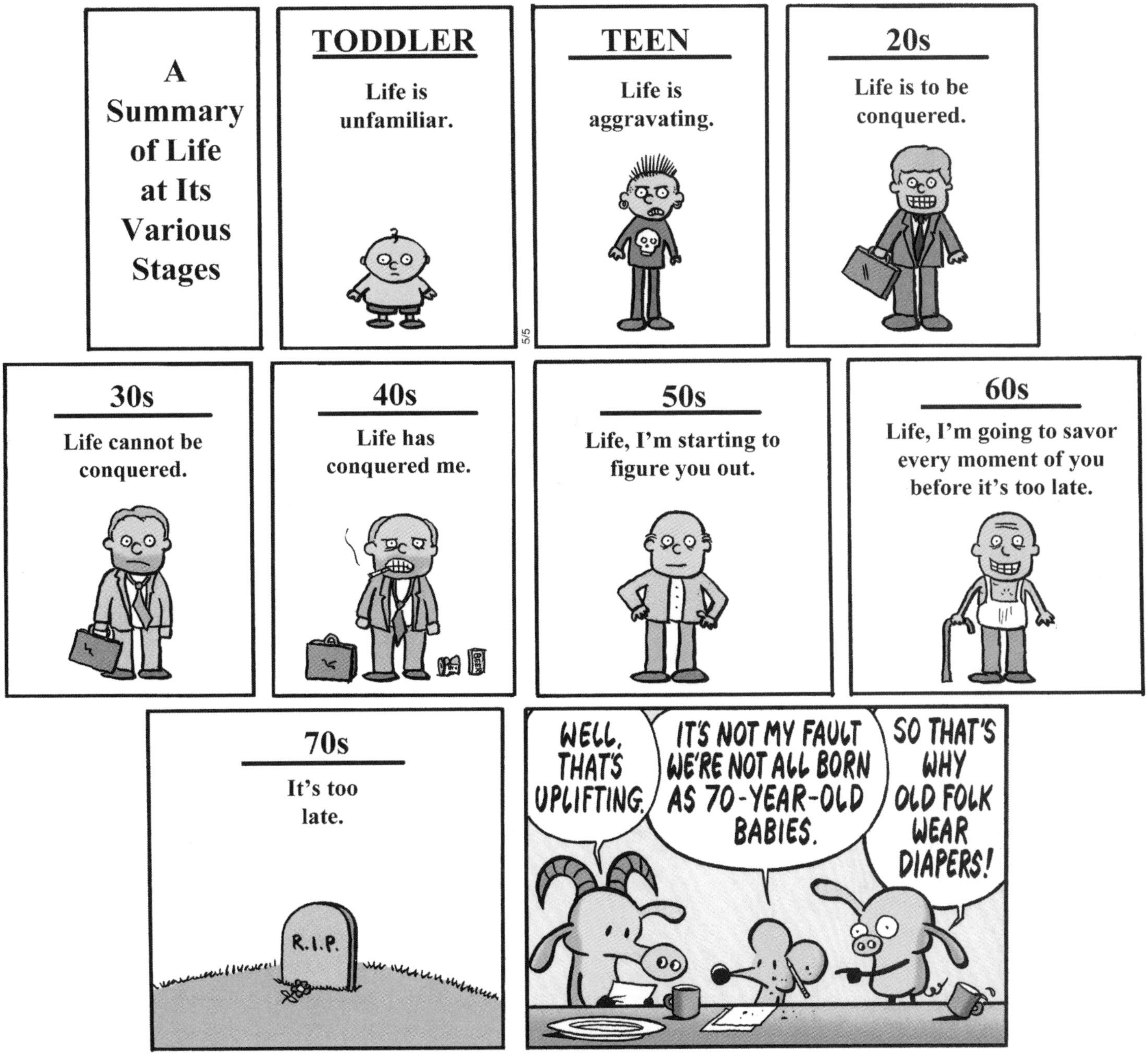
A Summary of Life at Its Various Stages
TODDLER
Life is unfamiliar.
TEEN
Life is aggravating.
20s
Life is to be conquered.
30s
Life cannot be conquered.
40s
Life has conquered me.
BEER
50s
Life, I'm starting to figure you out.
60s
Life, I'm going to savor every moment of you before it's too late.
70s
It's too late.
R.I.P.
WELL, THAT'S UPLIFTING.
IT'S NOT MY FAULT WE'RE NOT ALL BORN AS 70-YEAR-OLD BABIES.
SO THAT'S WHY OLD FOLK WEAR DIAPERS!

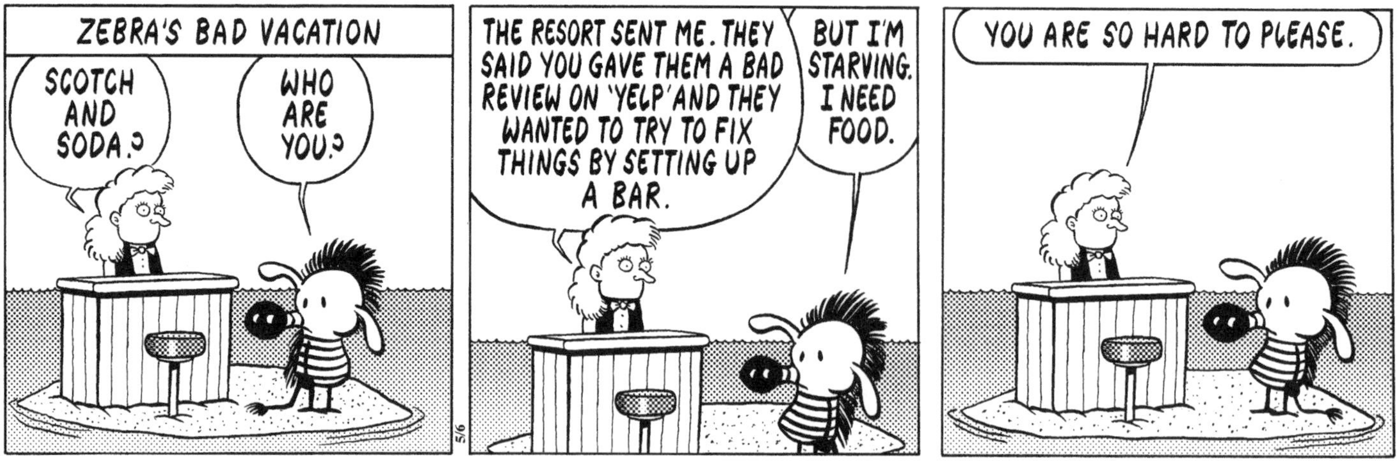
ZEBRA'S BAD VACATION
SCOTCH AND SODA?
WHO ARE YOU?
5/6
THE RESORT SENT ME. THEY SAID YOU GAVE THEM A BAD REVIEW ON 'YELP' AND THEY WANTED TO TRY TO FIX THINGS BY SETTING UP A BAR.
BUT I'M STARVING. I NEED FOOD.
YOU ARE SO HARD TO PLEASE.

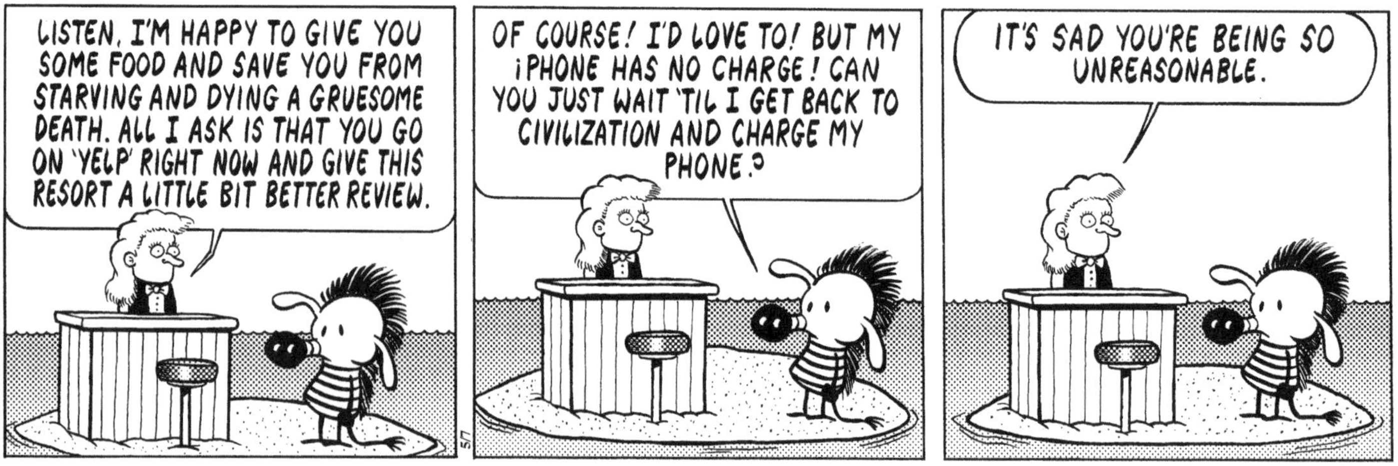
LISTEN, I'M HAPPY TO GIVE YOU SOME FOOD AND SAVE YOU FROM STARVING AND DYING A GRUESOME DEATH. ALL I ASK IS THAT YOU GO ON 'YELP' RIGHT NOW AND GIVE THIS RESORT A LITTLE BIT BETTER REVIEW.
5/7
OF COURSE! I'D LOVE TO! BUT MY iPHONE HAS NO CHARGE! CAN YOU JUST WAIT 'TIL I GET BACK TO CIVILIZATION AND CHARGE MY PHONE?
IT'S SAD YOU'RE BEING SO UNREASONABLE.

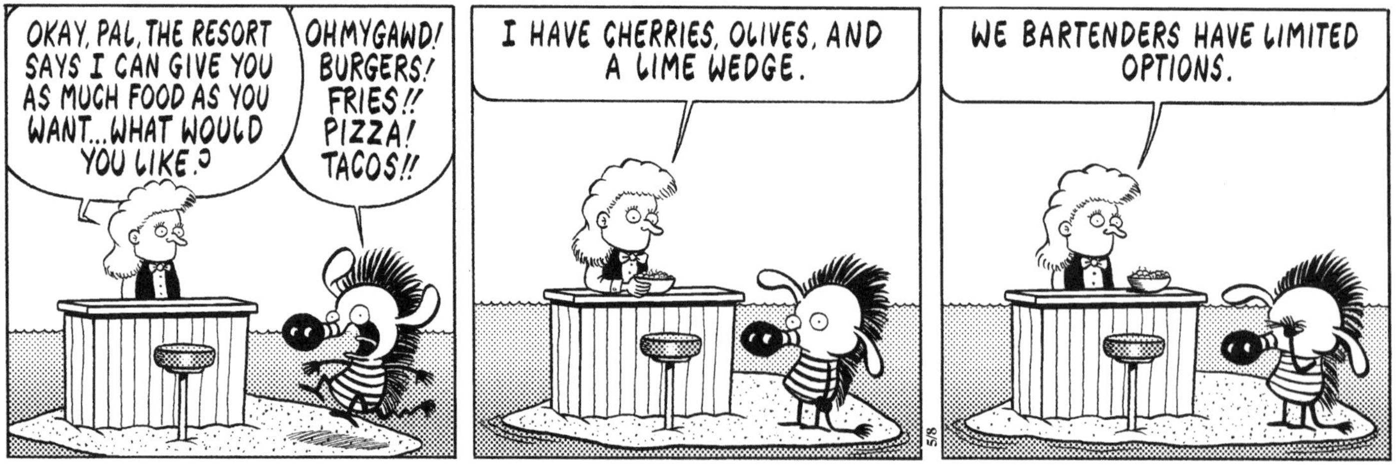
OKAY, PAL, THE RESORT SAYS I CAN GIVE YOU AS MUCH FOOD AS YOU WANT...WHAT WOULD YOU LIKE?
OHMYGAWD! BURGERS! FRIES!! PIZZA! TACOS!!
I HAVE CHERRIES, OLIVES, AND A LIME WEDGE.
5/8
WE BARTENDERS HAVE LIMITED OPTIONS.

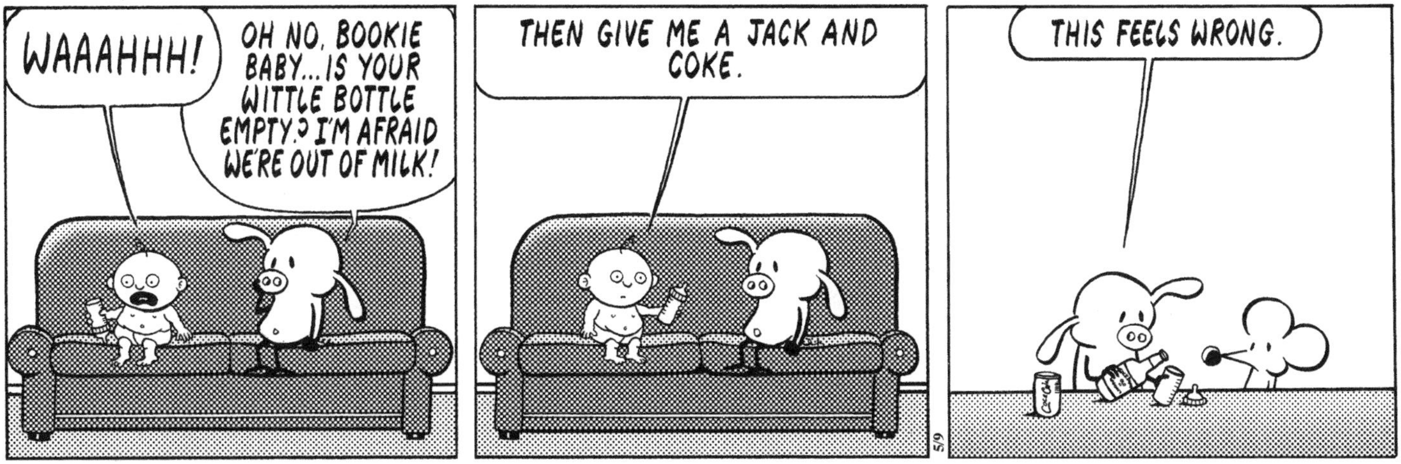
WAAAHHH!
OH NO, BOOKIE BABY... IS YOUR WITTLE BOTTLE EMPTY? I'M AFRAID WE'RE OUT OF MILK!
THEN GIVE ME A JACK AND COKE.
THIS FEELS WRONG.
5/9

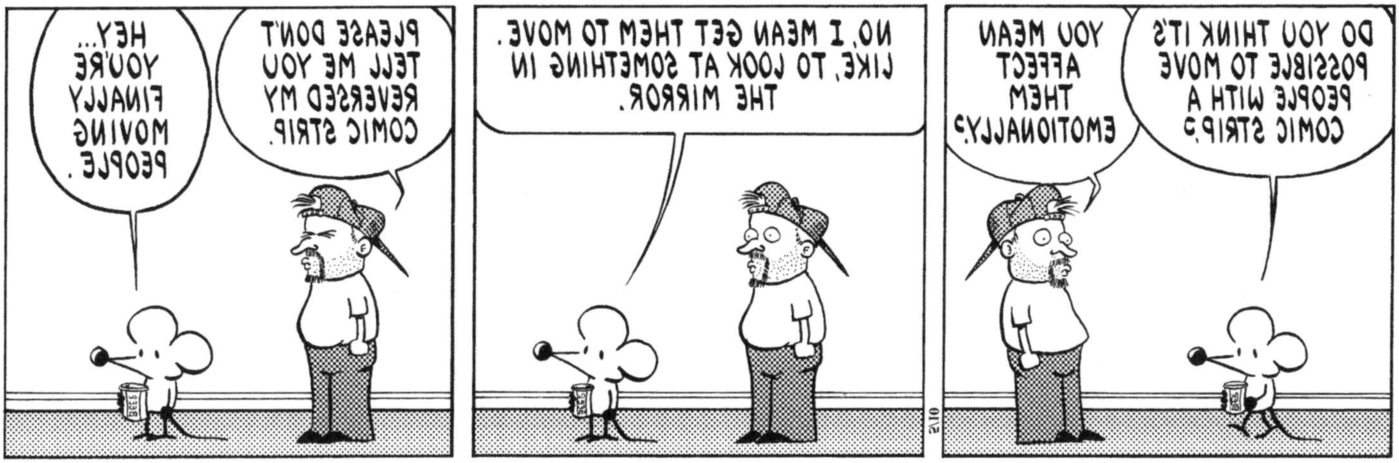
DO YOU THINK IT'S POSSIBLE TO MOVE PEOPLE WITH A COMIC STRIP?
YOU MEAN AFFECT THEM EMOTIONALLY?
NO, I MEAN GET THEM TO MOVE. LIKE, TO LOOK AT SOMETHING IN THE MIRROR.
PLEASE DON'T TELL ME YOU REVERSED MY COMIC STRIP.
HEY... YOU'RE FINALLY MOVING PEOPLE.
5/10

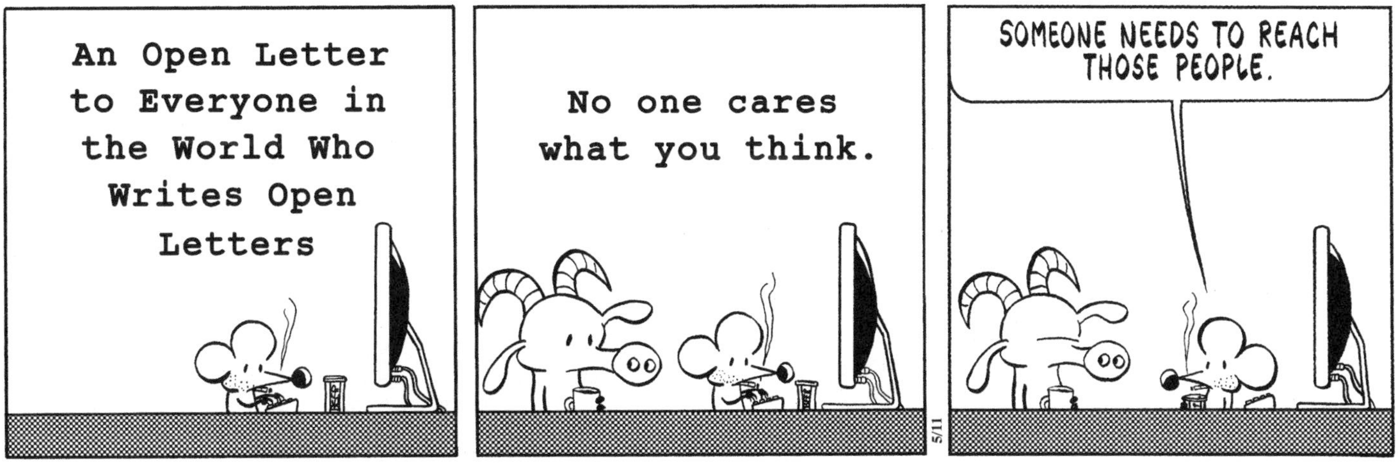
An Open Letter to Everyone in the World Who Writes Open Letters
No one cares what you think.
SOMEONE NEEDS TO REACH THOSE PEOPLE.
5/11

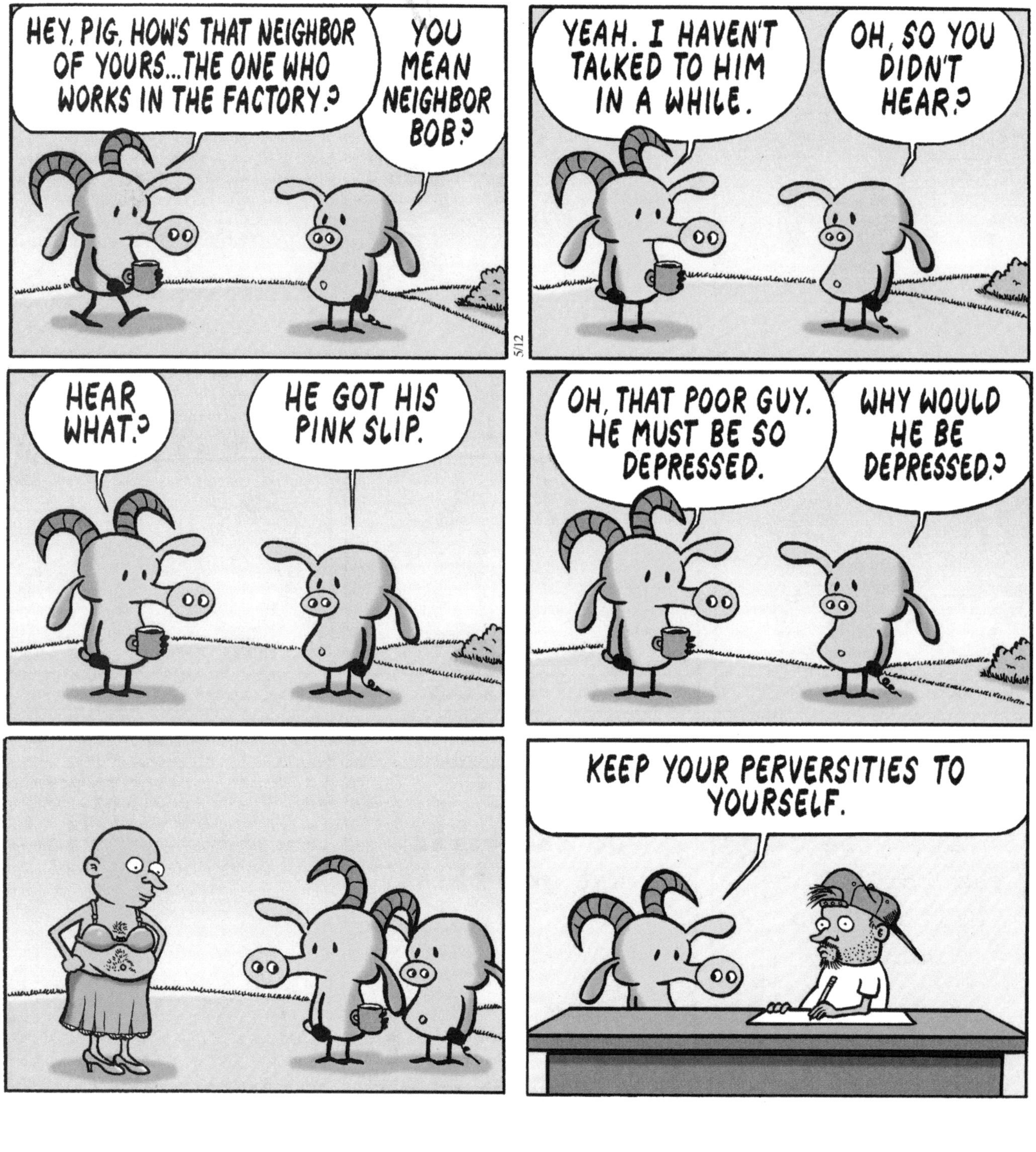
HEY, PIG, HOW'S THAT NEIGHBOR OF YOURS...THE ONE WHO WORKS IN THE FACTORY?
YOU MEAN NEIGHBOR BOB?
YEAH. I HAVEN'T TALKED TO HIM IN A WHILE.
OH, SO YOU DIDN'T HEAR?
HEAR WHAT?
HE GOT HIS PINK SLIP.
OH, THAT POOR GUY. HE MUST BE SO DEPRESSED.
WHY WOULD HE BE DEPRESSED?
KEEP YOUR PERVERSITIES TO YOURSELF.
5/12

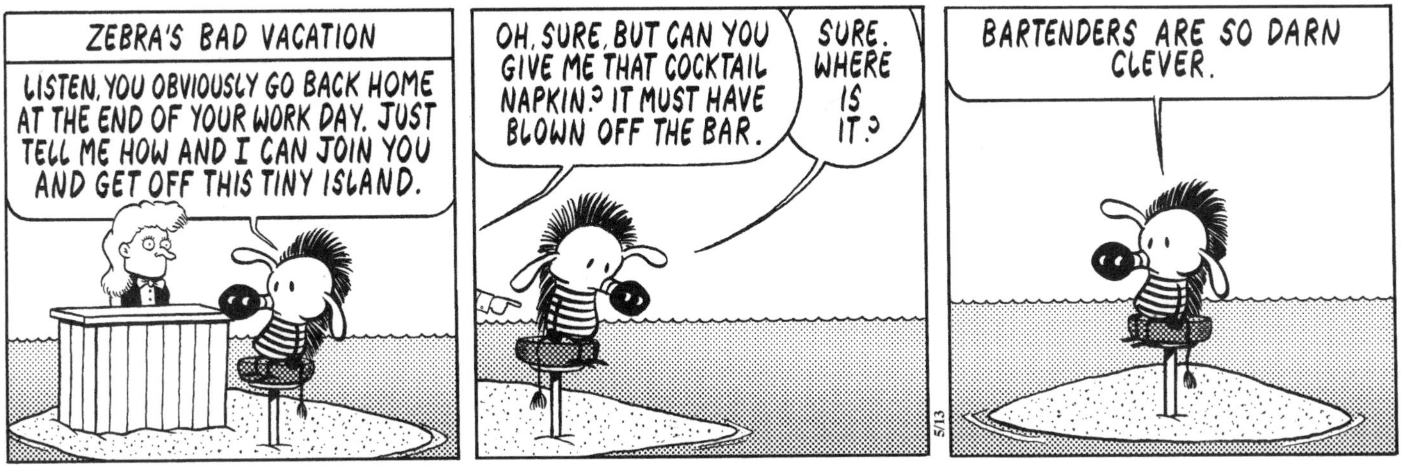
ZEBRA'S BAD VACATION
LISTEN, YOU OBVIOUSLY GO BACK HOME AT THE END OF YOUR WORK DAY. JUST TELL ME HOW AND I CAN JOIN YOU AND GET OFF THIS TINY ISLAND.
OH, SURE, BUT CAN YOU GIVE ME THAT COCKTAIL NAPKIN? IT MUST HAVE BLOWN OFF THE BAR.
SURE. WHERE IS IT?
BARTENDERS ARE SO DARN CLEVER.
5/13

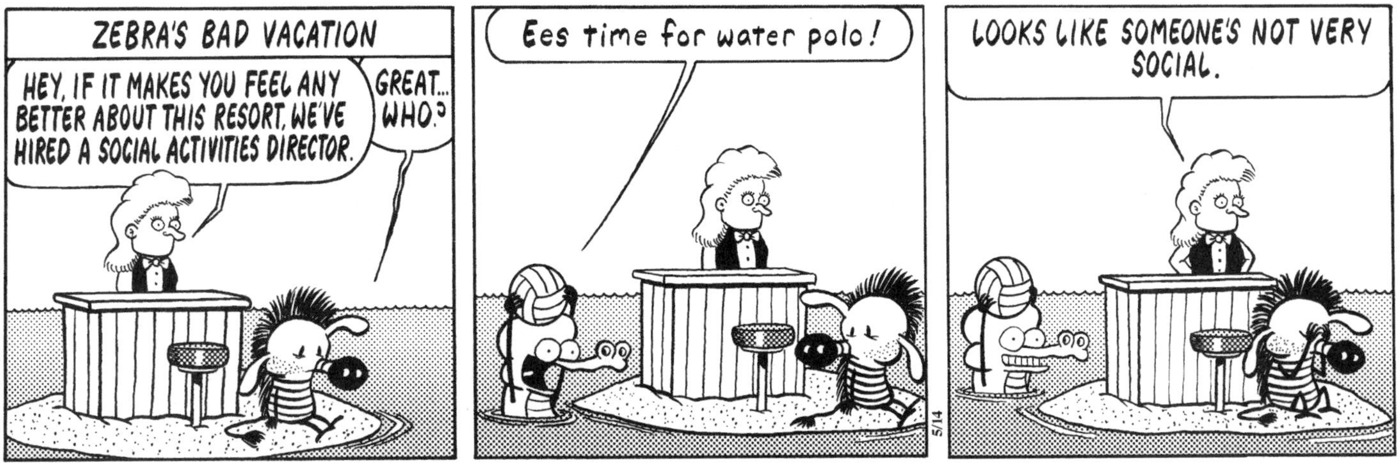
ZEBRA'S BAD VACATION
HEY, IF IT MAKES YOU FEEL ANY BETTER ABOUT THIS RESORT, WE'VE HIRED A SOCIAL ACTIVITIES DIRECTOR.
GREAT... WHO?
Ees time for water polo!
LOOKS LIKE SOMEONE'S NOT VERY SOCIAL.
5/14

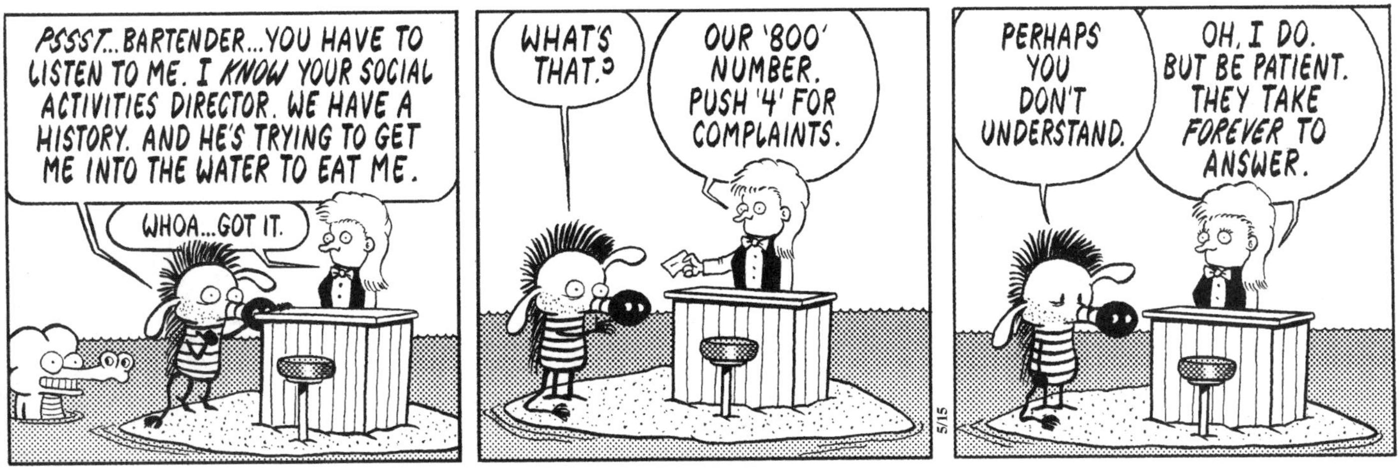
PSSST... BARTENDER... YOU HAVE TO LISTEN TO ME. I KNOW YOUR SOCIAL ACTIVITIES DIRECTOR. WE HAVE A HISTORY. AND HE'S TRYING TO GET ME INTO THE WATER TO EAT ME.
WHOA... GOT IT.
WHAT'S THAT?
OUR '800' NUMBER. PUSH '4' FOR COMPLAINTS.
PERHAPS YOU DON'T UNDERSTAND.
OH, I DO. BUT BE PATIENT. THEY TAKE FOREVER TO ANSWER.
5/15

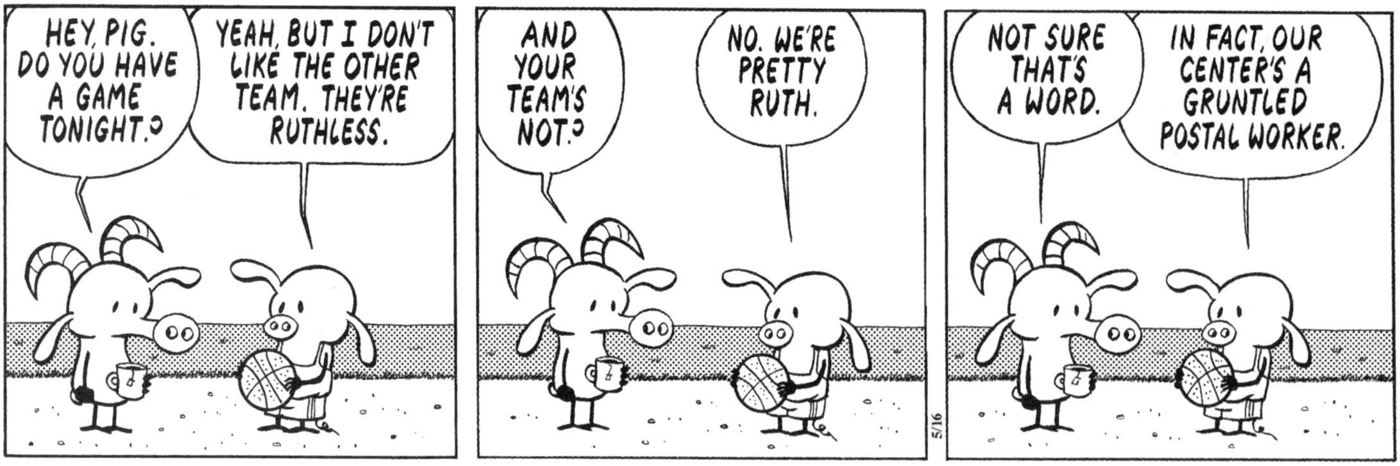
HEY, PIG. DO YOU HAVE A GAME TONIGHT?
YEAH, BUT I DON'T LIKE THE OTHER TEAM. THEY'RE RUTHLESS.
AND YOUR TEAM'S NOT?
NO. WE'RE PRETTY RUTH.
5/16
NOT SURE THAT'S A WORD.
IN FACT, OUR CENTER'S A GRUNTLED POSTAL WORKER.

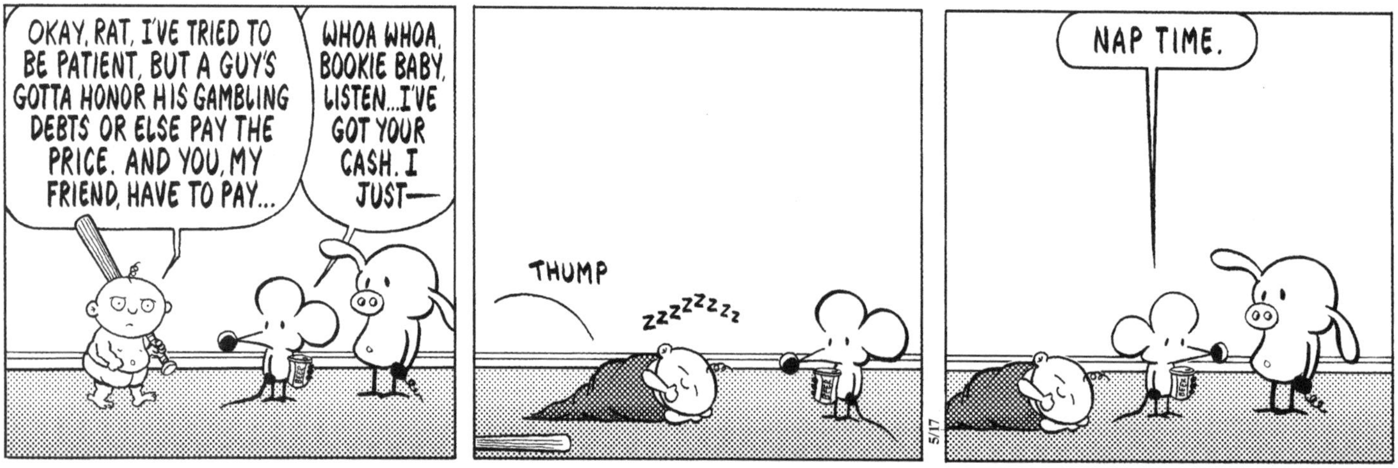
OKAY, RAT, I'VE TRIED TO BE PATIENT, BUT A GUY'S GOTTA HONOR HIS GAMBLING DEBTS OR ELSE PAY THE PRICE. AND YOU, MY FRIEND, HAVE TO PAY...
WHOA WHOA, BOOKIE BABY, LISTEN...I'VE GOT YOUR CASH. I JUST—
THUMP
ZZZZZZZZ
5/17
NAP TIME.

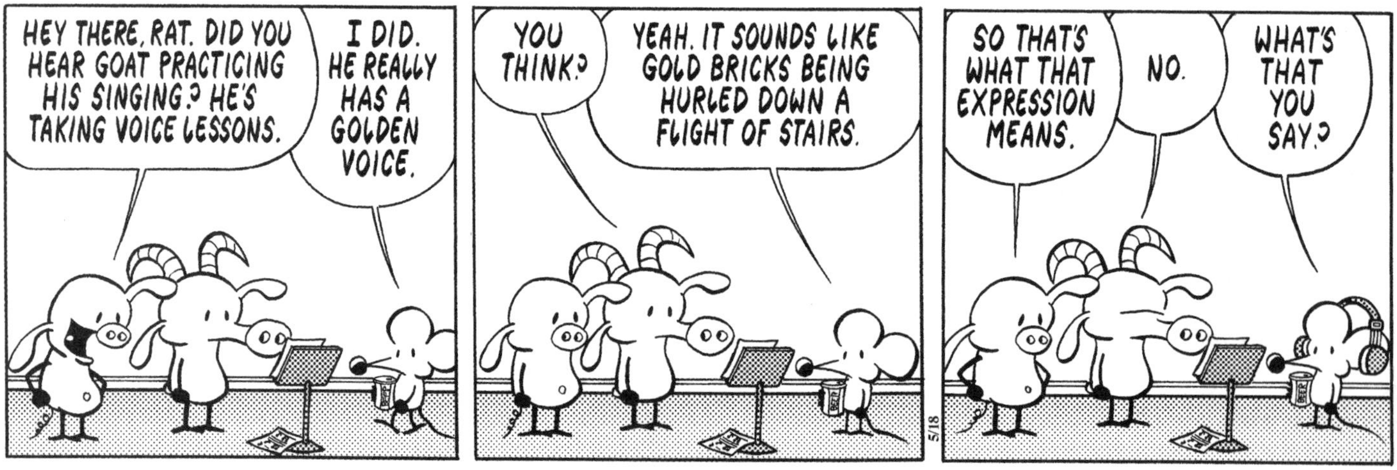
HEY THERE, RAT. DID YOU HEAR GOAT PRACTICING HIS SINGING? HE'S TAKING VOICE LESSONS.
I DID. HE REALLY HAS A GOLDEN VOICE.
YOU THINK?
YEAH. IT SOUNDS LIKE GOLD BRICKS BEING HURLED DOWN A FLIGHT OF STAIRS.
5/18
SO THAT'S WHAT THAT EXPRESSION MEANS.
NO.
WHAT'S THAT YOU SAY?

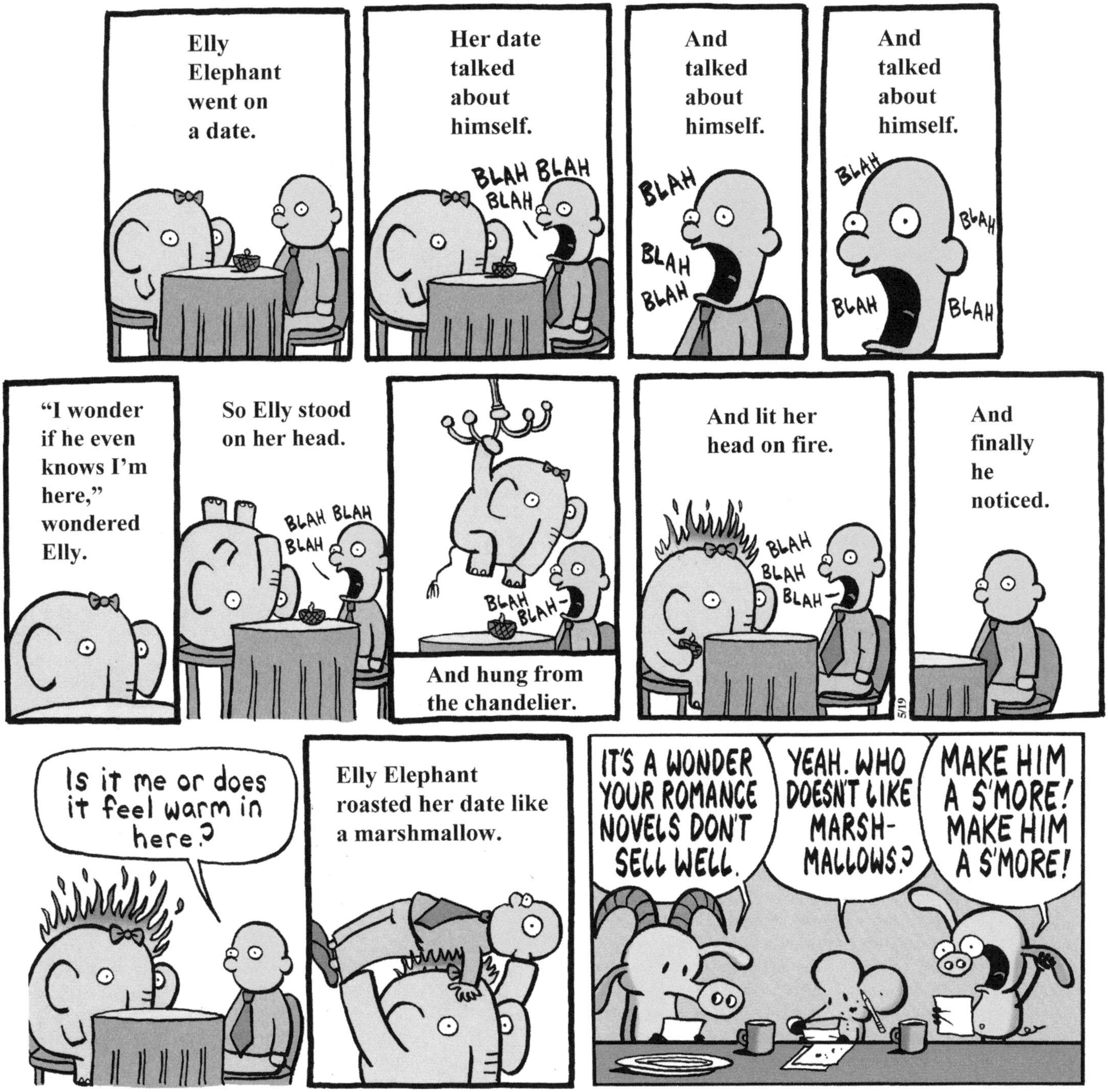
Elly Elephant went on a date.
Her date talked about himself.
BLAH BLAH BLAH
And talked about himself.
BLAH BLAH BLAH
And talked about himself.
BLAH BLAH BLAH BLAH
"I wonder if he even knows I'm here," wondered Elly.
So Elly stood on her head.
BLAH BLAH BLAH
BLAH BLAH
And hung from the chandelier.
And lit her head on fire.
BLAH BLAH BLAH
And finally he noticed.
5/19
Is it me or does it feel warm in here?
Elly Elephant roasted her date like a marshmallow.
IT'S A WONDER YOUR ROMANCE NOVELS DON'T SELL WELL.
YEAH. WHO DOESN'T LIKE MARSH-MALLOWS?
MAKE HIM A S'MORE! MAKE HIM A S'MORE!

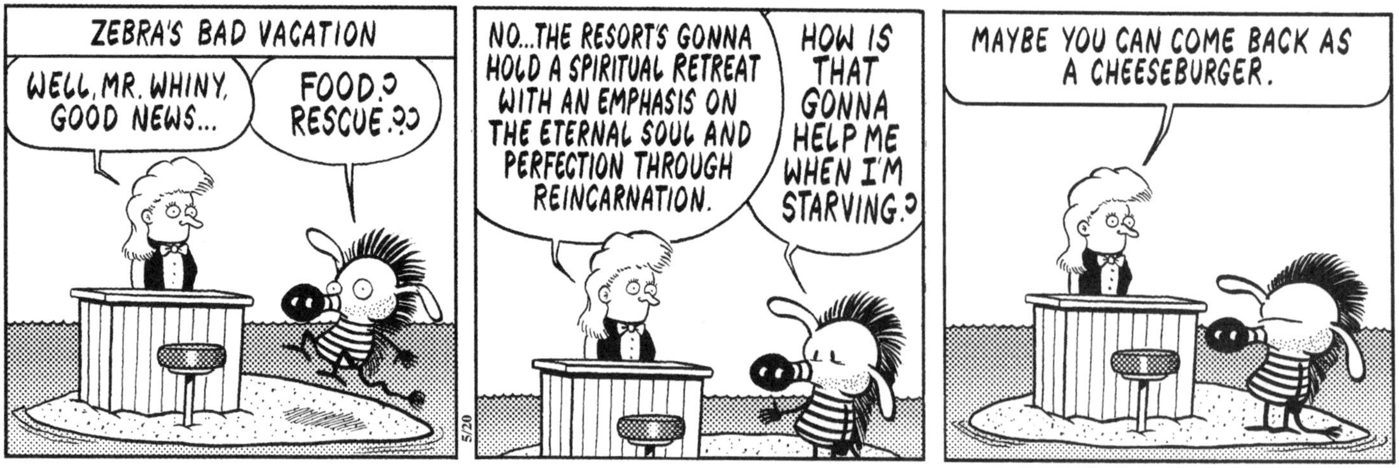
ZEBRA'S BAD VACATION
WELL, MR. WHINY, GOOD NEWS...
FOOD?? RESCUE?!?
NO...THE RESORT'S GONNA HOLD A SPIRITUAL RETREAT WITH AN EMPHASIS ON THE ETERNAL SOUL AND PERFECTION THROUGH REINCARNATION.
HOW IS THAT GONNA HELP ME WHEN I'M STARVING?
MAYBE YOU CAN COME BACK AS A CHEESEBURGER.
5/20

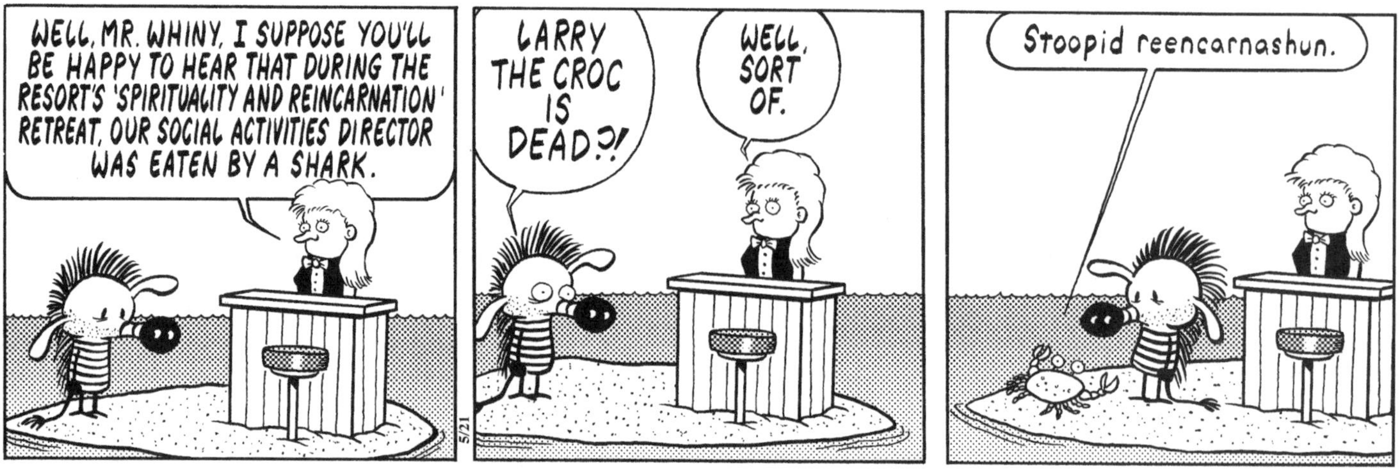
WELL, MR. WHINY, I SUPPOSE YOU'LL BE HAPPY TO HEAR THAT DURING THE RESORT'S 'SPIRITUALITY AND REINCARNATION' RETREAT, OUR SOCIAL ACTIVITIES DIRECTOR WAS EATEN BY A SHARK.
LARRY THE CROC IS DEAD?!
WELL, SORT OF.
Stoopid reencarnashun.
5/21

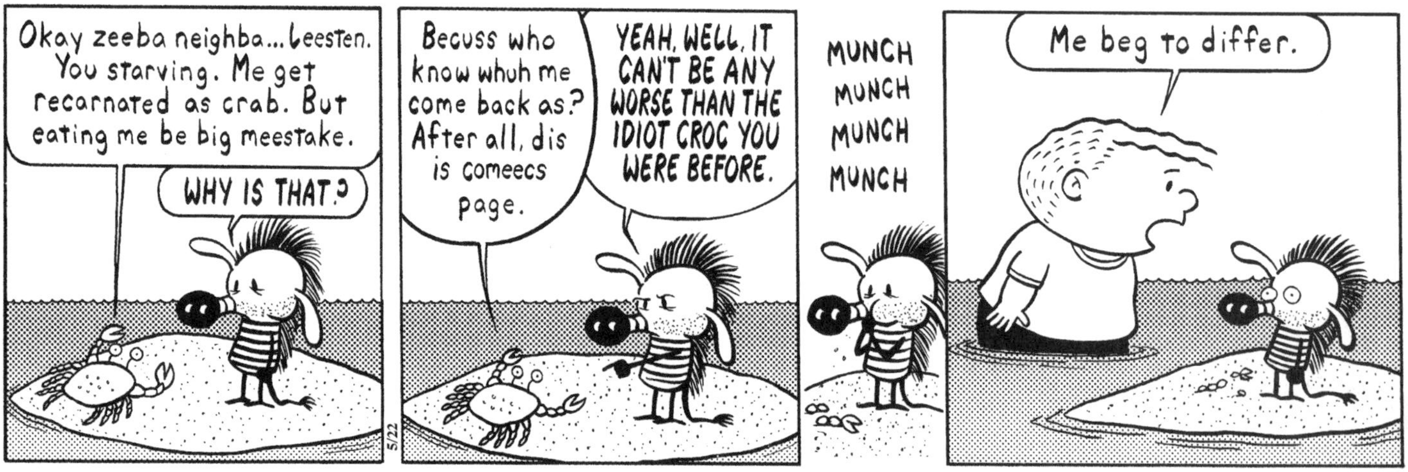
Okay zeeba neighba...leesten. You starving. Me get recarnated as crab. But eating me be big meestake.
WHY IS THAT?
Becuss who know whuh me come back as? After all, dis is comeecs page.
YEAH, WELL, IT CAN'T BE ANY WORSE THAN THE IDIOT CROC YOU WERE BEFORE.
MUNCH MUNCH MUNCH MUNCH
Me beg to differ.
5/22

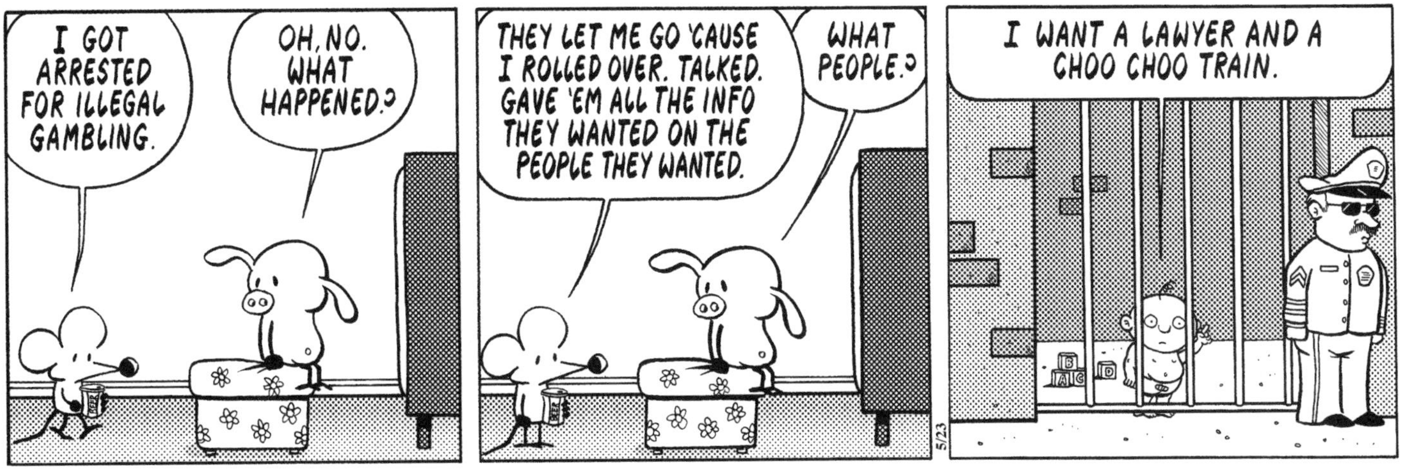
I GOT ARRESTED FOR ILLEGAL GAMBLING.
OH, NO. WHAT HAPPENED?
THEY LET ME GO 'CAUSE I ROLLED OVER. TALKED. GAVE 'EM ALL THE INFO THEY WANTED ON THE PEOPLE THEY WANTED.
WHAT PEOPLE?
5/23
I WANT A LAWYER AND A CHOO CHOO TRAIN.

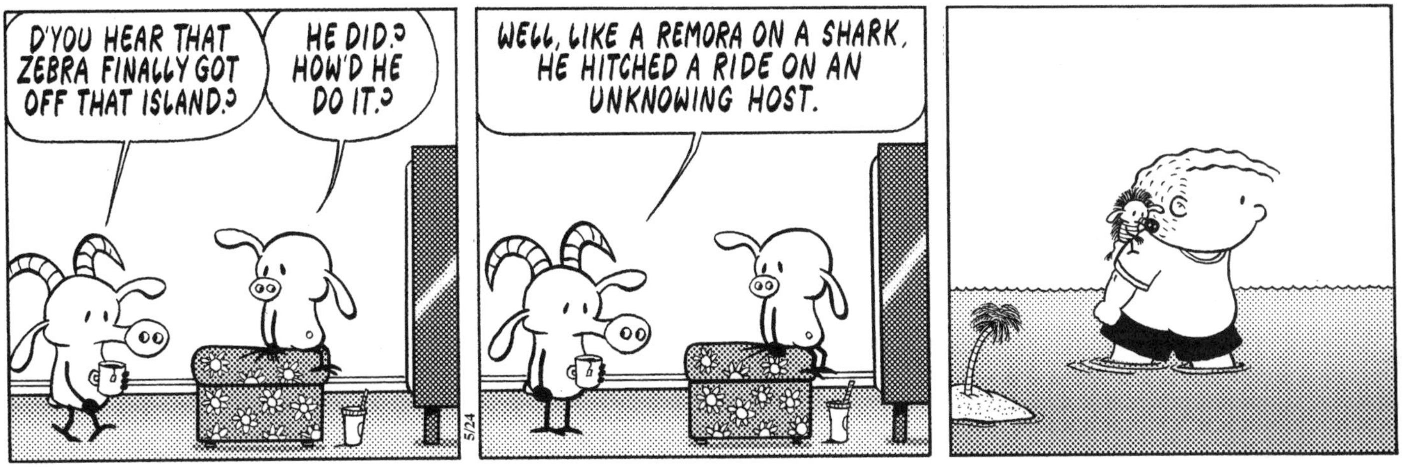
D'YOU HEAR THAT ZEBRA FINALLY GOT OFF THAT ISLAND?
HE DID? HOW'D HE DO IT?
5/24
WELL, LIKE A REMORA ON A SHARK, HE HITCHED A RIDE ON AN UNKNOWING HOST.

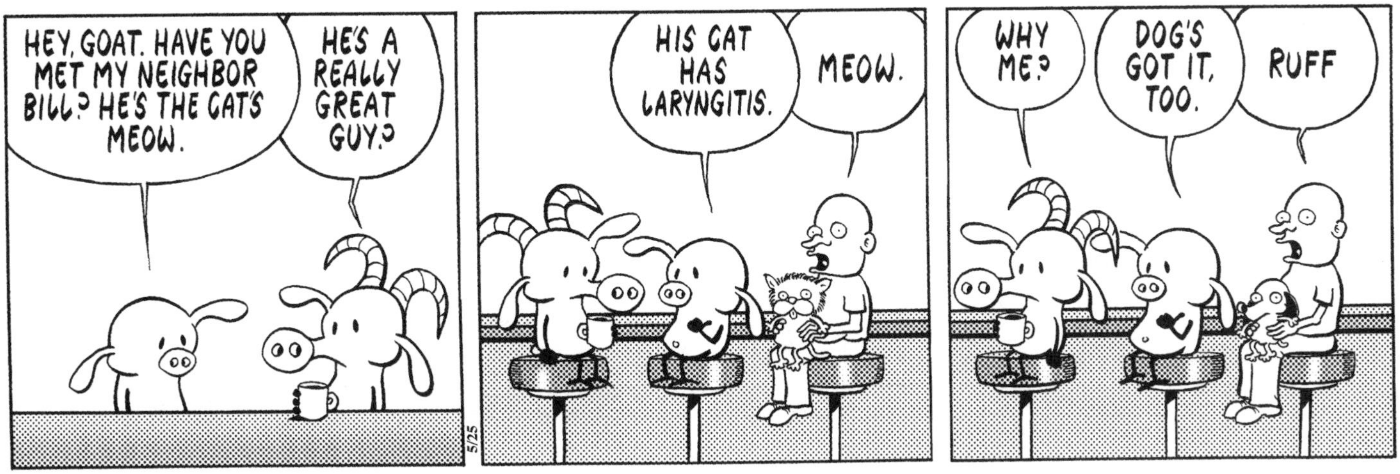
HEY, GOAT. HAVE YOU MET MY NEIGHBOR BILL? HE'S THE CAT'S MEOW.
HE'S A REALLY GREAT GUY?
5/25
HIS CAT HAS LARYNGITIS.
MEOW.
WHY ME?
DOG'S GOT IT, TOO.
RUFF

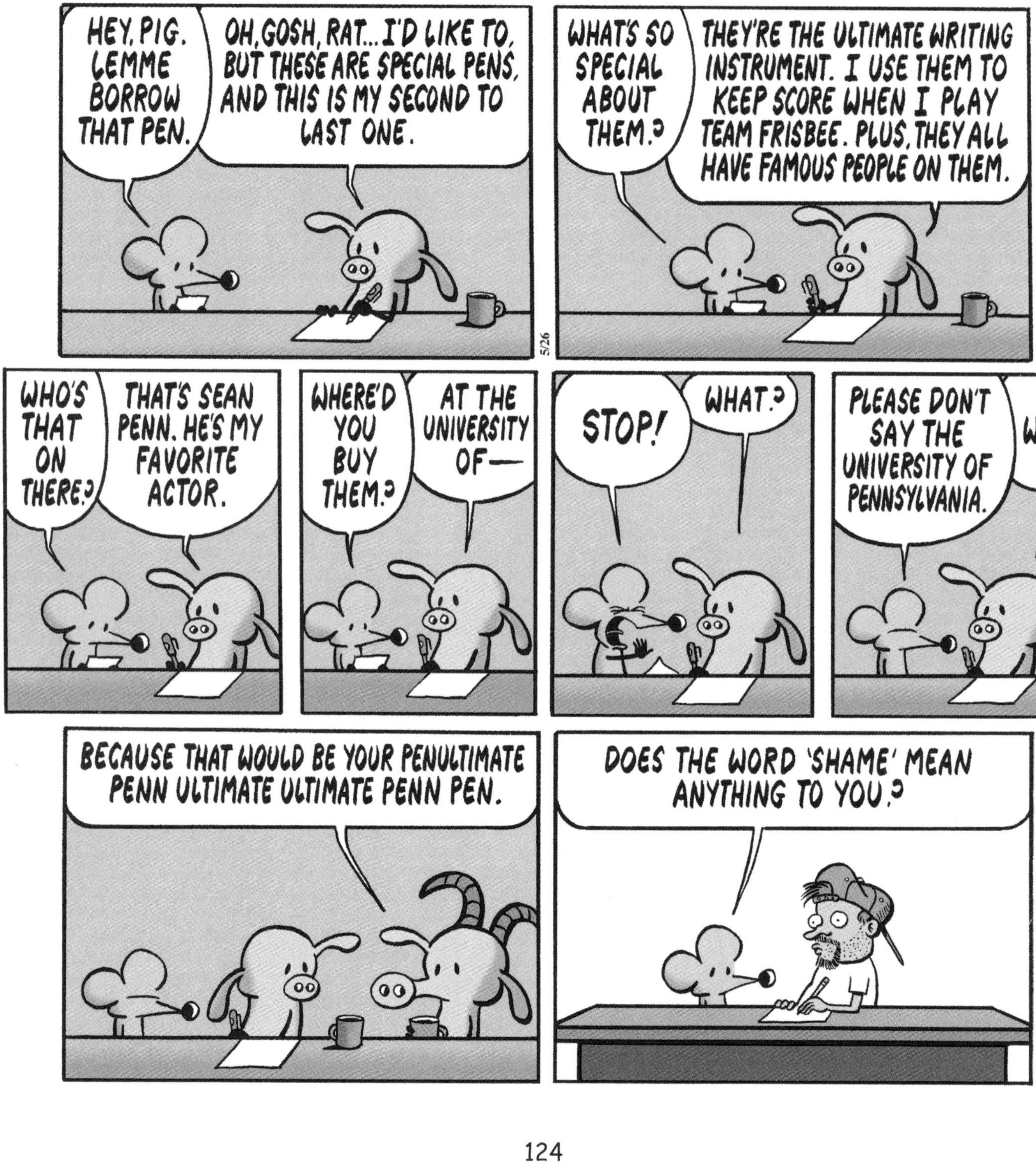
HEY, PIG. LEMME BORROW THAT PEN.
OH, GOSH, RAT... I'D LIKE TO, BUT THESE ARE SPECIAL PENS, AND THIS IS MY SECOND TO LAST ONE.
5/26
WHAT'S SO SPECIAL ABOUT THEM?
THEY'RE THE ULTIMATE WRITING INSTRUMENT. I USE THEM TO KEEP SCORE WHEN I PLAY TEAM FRISBEE. PLUS, THEY ALL HAVE FAMOUS PEOPLE ON THEM.
WHO'S THAT ON THERE?
THAT'S SEAN PENN. HE'S MY FAVORITE ACTOR.
WHERE'D YOU BUY THEM?
AT THE UNIVERSITY OF—
STOP!
WHAT?
PLEASE DON'T SAY THE UNIVERSITY OF PENNSYLVANIA.
WHY?
BECAUSE THAT WOULD BE YOUR PENULTIMATE PENN ULTIMATE ULTIMATE PENN PEN.
DOES THE WORD 'SHAME' MEAN ANYTHING TO YOU?

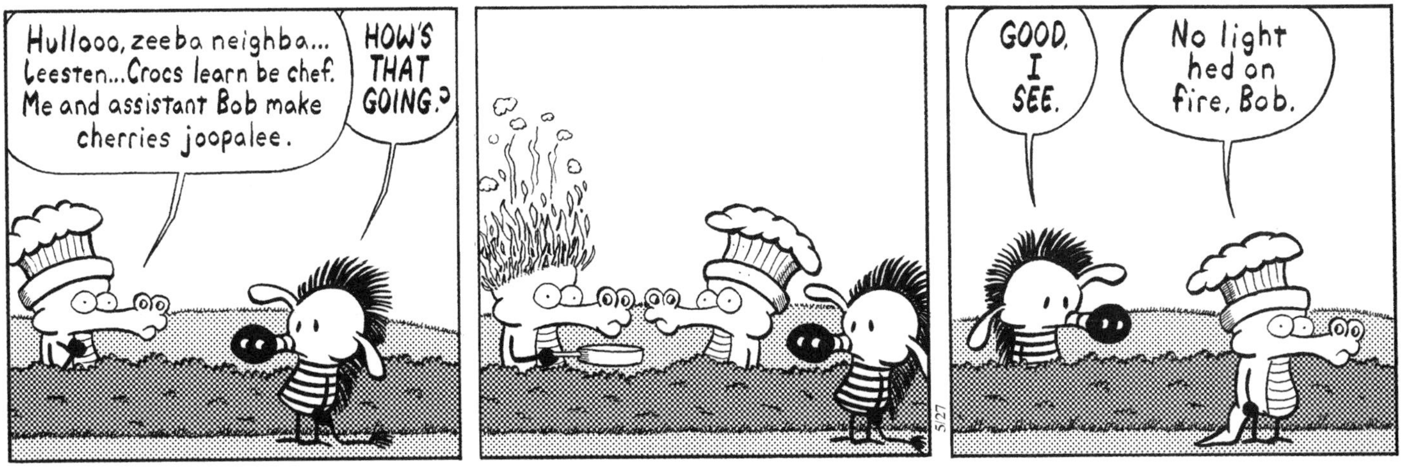
Hullooo, zeeba neighba... Leesten...Crocs learn be chef. Me and assistant Bob make cherries joopalee.
HOW'S THAT GOING?
5/27
GOOD, I SEE.
No light hed on fire, Bob.

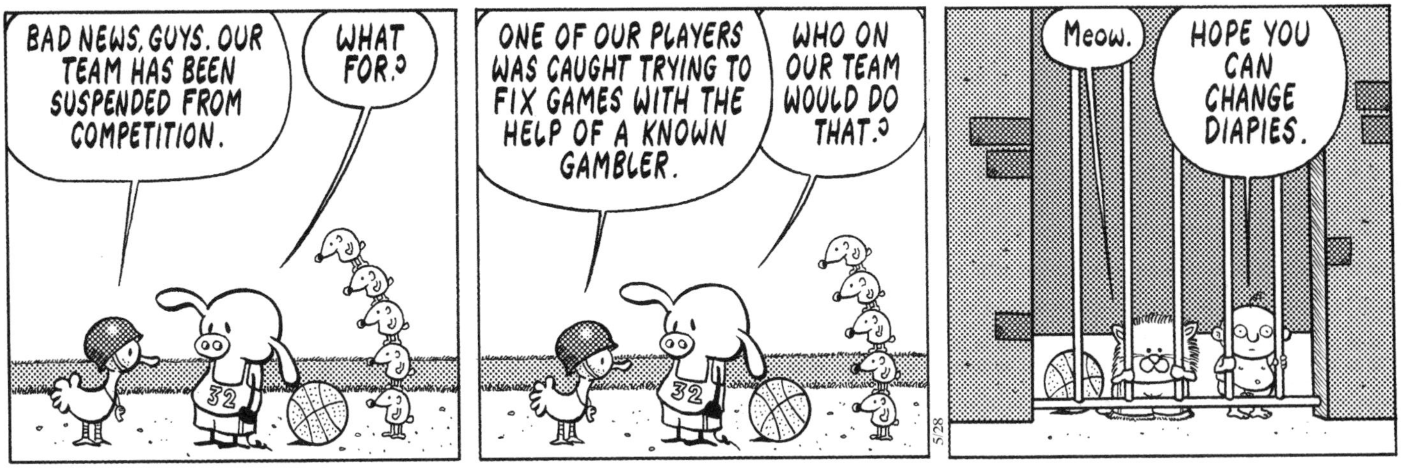
BAD NEWS, GUYS. OUR TEAM HAS BEEN SUSPENDED FROM COMPETITION.
WHAT FOR?
ONE OF OUR PLAYERS WAS CAUGHT TRYING TO FIX GAMES WITH THE HELP OF A KNOWN GAMBLER.
WHO ON OUR TEAM WOULD DO THAT?
5/28
Meow.
HOPE YOU CAN CHANGE DIAPIES.

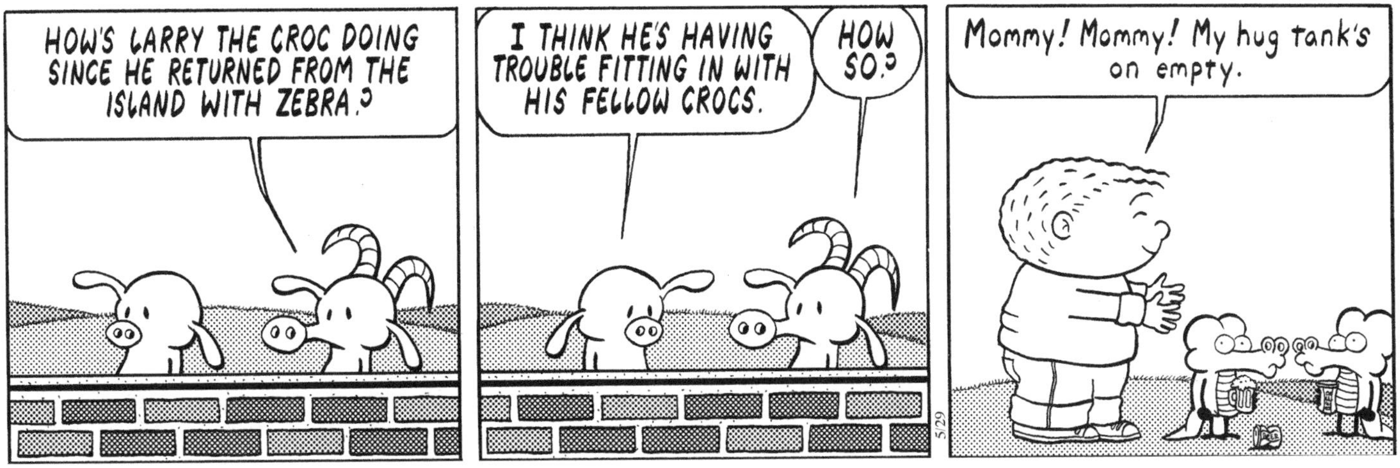
HOW'S LARRY THE CROC DOING SINCE HE RETURNED FROM THE ISLAND WITH ZEBRA?
I THINK HE'S HAVING TROUBLE FITTING IN WITH HIS FELLOW CROCS.
HOW SO?
5/29
Mommy! Mommy! My hug tank's on empty.

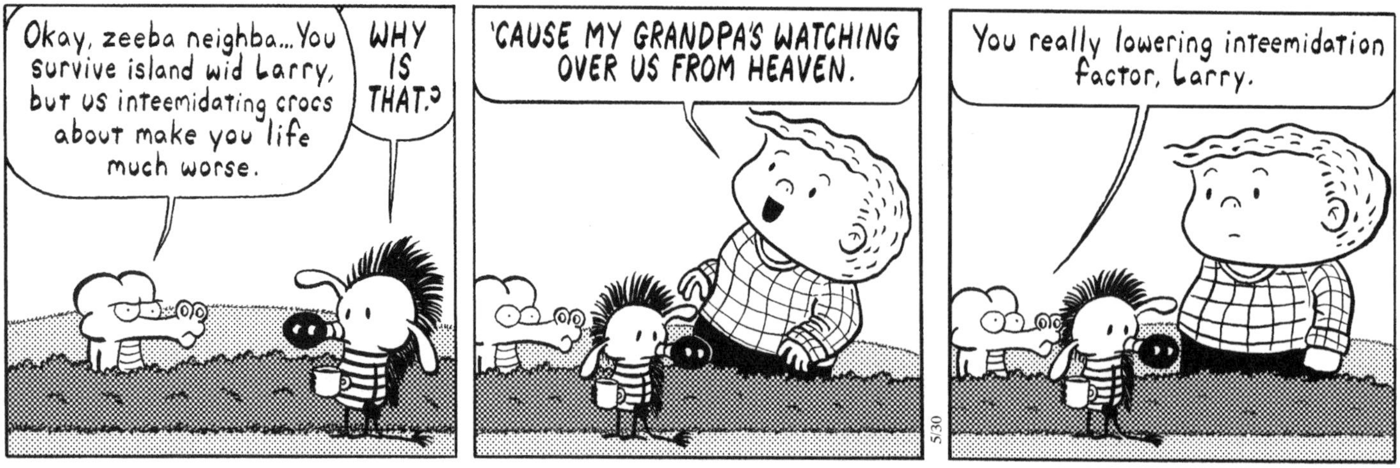
Okay, zeeba neighba... You survive island wid Larry, but us inteemidating crocs about make you life much worse.
WHY IS THAT?
'CAUSE MY GRANDPA'S WATCHING OVER US FROM HEAVEN.
You really lowering inteemidation factor, Larry.
5/30

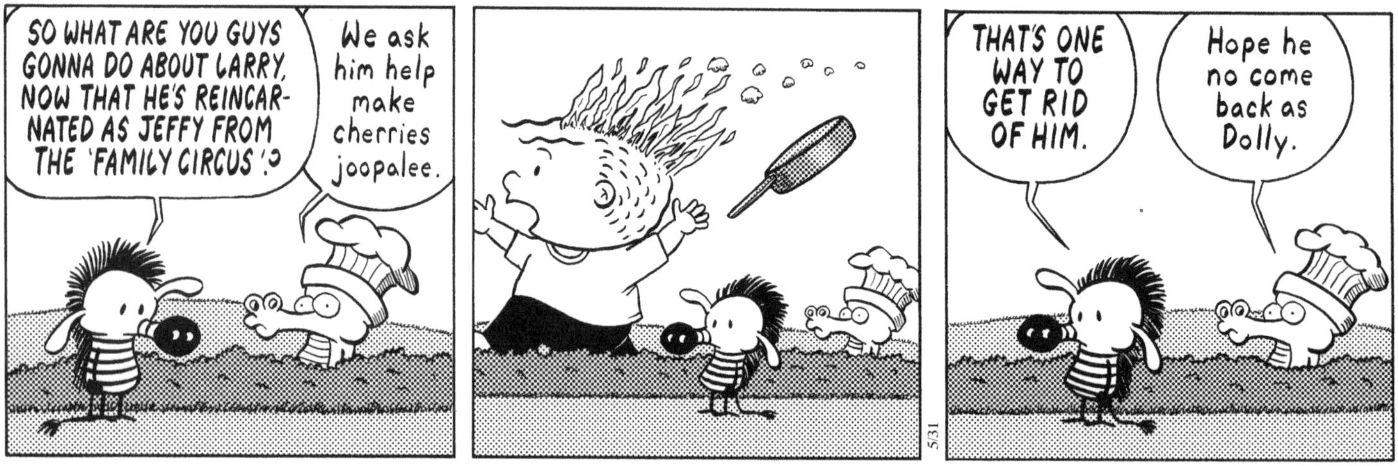
SO WHAT ARE YOU GUYS GONNA DO ABOUT LARRY, NOW THAT HE'S REINCARNATED AS JEFFY FROM THE 'FAMILY CIRCUS'?
We ask him help make cherries joopalee.
THAT'S ONE WAY TO GET RID OF HIM.
Hope he no come back as Dolly.
5/31

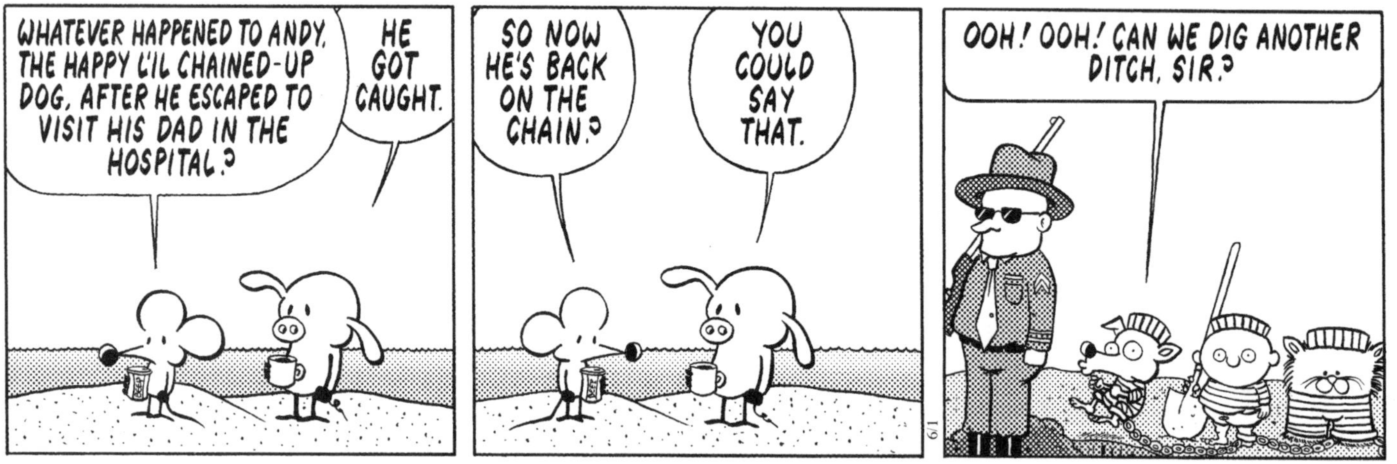
WHATEVER HAPPENED TO ANDY, THE HAPPY L'IL CHAINED-UP DOG, AFTER HE ESCAPED TO VISIT HIS DAD IN THE HOSPITAL?
HE GOT CAUGHT.
SO NOW HE'S BACK ON THE CHAIN?
YOU COULD SAY THAT.
OOH! OOH! CAN WE DIG ANOTHER DITCH, SIR?
6/1

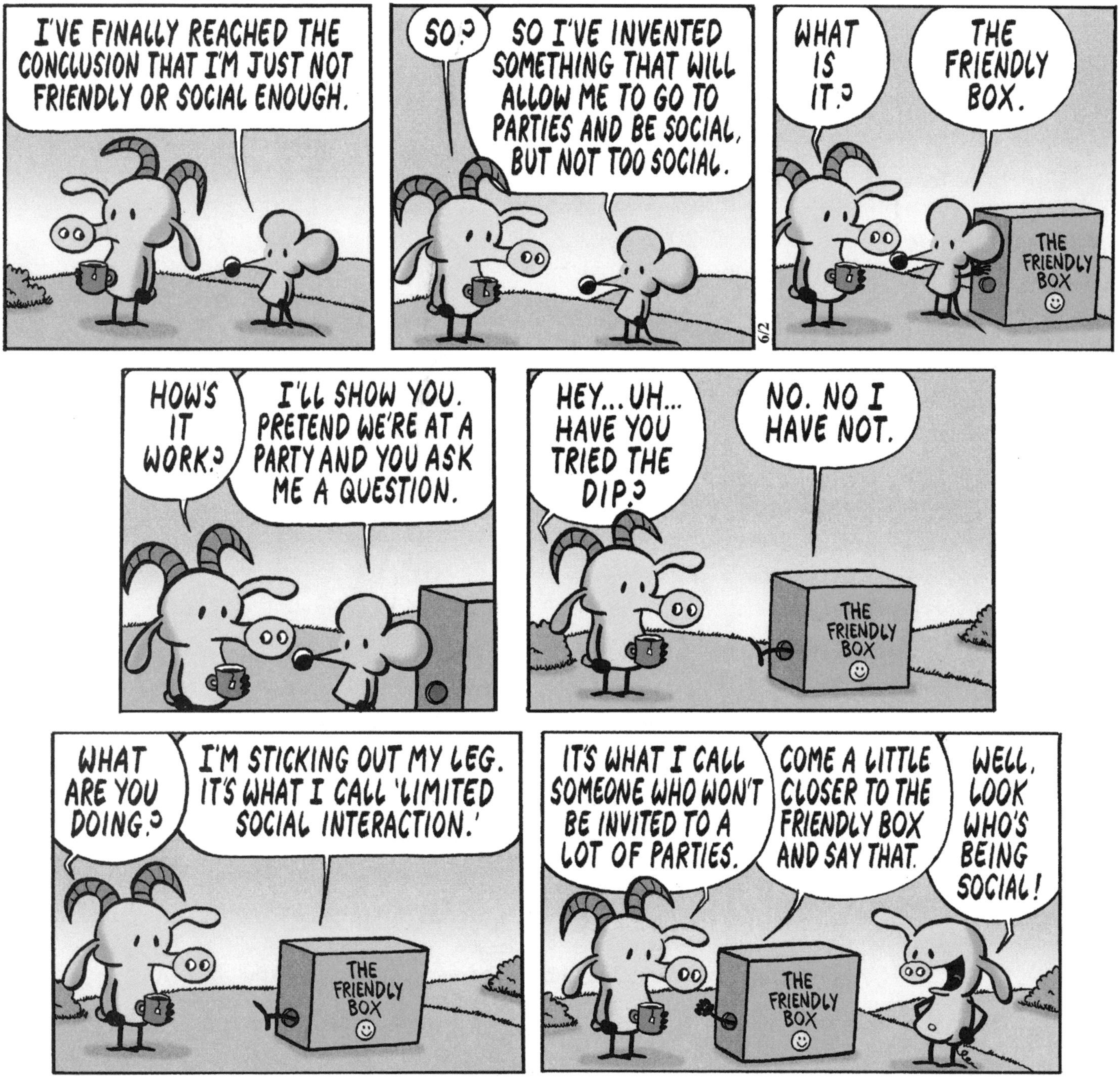
I'VE FINALLY REACHED THE CONCLUSION THAT I'M JUST NOT FRIENDLY OR SOCIAL ENOUGH.
SO?
SO I'VE INVENTED SOMETHING THAT WILL ALLOW ME TO GO TO PARTIES AND BE SOCIAL, BUT NOT TOO SOCIAL.
6/2
WHAT IS IT?
THE FRIENDLY BOX.
THE FRIENDLY BOX
HOW'S IT WORK?
I'LL SHOW YOU. PRETEND WE'RE AT A PARTY AND YOU ASK ME A QUESTION.
HEY... UH... HAVE YOU TRIED THE DIP?
NO. NO I HAVE NOT.
THE FRIENDLY BOX
WHAT ARE YOU DOING?
I'M STICKING OUT MY LEG. IT'S WHAT I CALL 'LIMITED SOCIAL INTERACTION.'
THE FRIENDLY BOX
IT'S WHAT I CALL SOMEONE WHO WON'T BE INVITED TO A LOT OF PARTIES.
COME A LITTLE CLOSER TO THE FRIENDLY BOX AND SAY THAT.
WELL, LOOK WHO'S BEING SOCIAL!
THE FRIENDLY BOX

Pearls Before Swine is distributed internationally by Universal Uclick.

Breaking Stephan copyright © 2014 by Stephan Pastis. All rights reserved. Printed in the United States of America. No part of this book may be used or reproduced in any manner whatsoever without written permission except in the case of reprints in the context of reviews.

Andrews McMeel Publishing, LLC
an Andrews McMeel Universal company
1130 Walnut Street, Kansas City, Missouri 64106

www.andrewsmcmeel.com

15 16 17 18 19 RR2 11 10 9 8 7 6 5 4 3 2

ISBN: 978-1-4494-5830-0

Library of Congress Control Number: 2014935610

Pearls Before Swine can be viewed on the Internet at
www.pearlscomic.com

These strips appeared in newspapers from September 3, 2012 to June 2, 2013.

———— **ATTENTION: SCHOOLS AND BUSINESSES** ————

Andrews McMeel books are available at quantity discounts with bulk purchase for educational, business, or sales promotional use. For information, please e-mail the Andrews McMeel Publishing Special Sales Department:
specialsales@amuniversal.com.